America's Jewish Women

ALSO BY PAMELA S. NADELL

Women Who Would Be Rabbis:
A History of Women's Ordination, 1889–1985

Conservative Judaism in America:
A Biographical Dictionary and Sourcebook

Three Hundred and Fifty Years: An Album of Jewish Memory,
co-authored with Michael Feldman, Karla Goldman,
Scott Martin Kosofsky, Jonathan D. Sarna, and Gary P. Zola

EDITED BY PAMELA S. NADELL

Making Women's Histories: Beyond National Perspectives,
co-edited with Kate Haulman

New Essays in American Jewish History,
co-edited with Jonathan D. Sarna and Lance Sussman

American Jewish Women's History: A Reader

Women and American Judaism: Historical Perspectives,
co-edited with Jonathan D. Sarna

America's
Jewish
Women

A HISTORY FROM
COLONIAL TIMES TO TODAY

Pamela S. Nadell

W. W. Norton & Company

INDEPENDENT PUBLISHERS SINCE 1923

NEW YORK | LONDON

For information about permission to reproduce selections from this book,
write to Permissions, W. W. Norton & Company, Inc.,
500 Fifth Avenue, New York, NY 10110

For information about special discounts for bulk purchases, please contact
W. W. Norton Special Sales at specialsales@wwnorton.com or 800-233-4830

Manufacturing by Lake Book
Book design by Brooke Koven
Production manager: Anna Oler

Library of Congress Cataloging-in-Publication Data

Names: Nadell, Pamela Susan, author.
Title: America's Jewish women : a history from colonial times to today /
Pamela S. Nadell.
Description: First Edition. | New York : W. W. Norton & Company, [2019] |
Includes bibliographical references and index.
Identifiers: LCCN 2018050106 | ISBN 9780393651232 (hardcover)
Subjects: LCSH: Jewish women—United States—History. | Jewish women—
Political activity—United States. | Feminism—Religious aspects—Judaism.
Classification: LCC HQ1172 .N33 2019 | DDC 305.48/8924073—dc23
LC record available at https://lccn.loc.gov/2018050106

W. W. Norton & Company, Inc., 500 Fifth Avenue, New York, N.Y. 10110
www.wwnorton.com

W. W. Norton & Company Ltd., 15 Carlisle Street, London W1D 3BS

1 2 3 4 5 6 7 8 9 0

For Ed, again

CONTENTS

INTRODUCTION   xi

Prologue   3

1: "Many are the blessings I partake of":
   America's Early Jewish Women   9

2: "Mothers in Israel":
   The American Jewesses   55

3: "A new kind of Jewess": *Eastern European
   Jewish Women in America*   109

4: "Woman is looking around and ahead":
   Wider Worlds   157

5: "Down from the pedestal . . . up from
   the laundry room": *Into the Future*   217

ACKNOWLEDGMENTS   263
NOTES   267
INDEX   303

INTRODUCTION

I N FAMILY PHOTOS, I see America's Jewish women changing over the years. One of my great-grandmother shows her wearing a *sheitel*, a wig some observant married Jewish women wear, and a black brocaded dress with a high lace collar. She was, even by the standards of the early 1900s, old-fashioned. Other photos, lining the walls of my home and cluttering my shelves, find her daughter, my grandmother, about fourteen, stylish in a white lace and cotton dress, wearing pumps with tiny bows. Another image shows my mother, in a park on a warm spring afternoon, wearing a black pencil skirt and white blouse. The baby in a bonnet she cradles is me. In more recent photos, I wear my workingwoman's wardrobe—a black pantsuit. Digital images of my daughter sliding across my computer screen reveal a student wearing skinny jeans and tall boots.

As our clothing differed, so too did the fabric of our lives. My great-grandmother was one of the more than two million Jewish immigrants who came to America at the turn of the twentieth century. Her daughter, my grandmother, raised children in the Great Depression. My grandmother's youngest, my mother, worked as a secretary, stopped to raise a family, and later, after the children were grown, became a realtor. I, the first in my family to graduate college, rode the coattails of a revolution raising expectations for what

America's women could do and achieve. As for my daughter, what opportunities the years ahead will bring, I can only imagine.

If the past serves as prologue, then it suggests that enormous changes will define her generation as they did those of the women in my family. The homes made, the families raised, the work pursued, the politics embraced, even the games played are molded by our moment in time. The great crises of wars and economic busts, the technological marvels of each era—whether washing machines or smartphones—the everyday occupations of feeding families and visiting relatives are woven into women's lives across the years.

Yet a singular bright thread distinguishes the women in my photos from other American women. We are not only American women. We are America's Jewish women. For much of my life I have been mulling over these images, envisioning the stories behind them as well as the tales of the Jewish women who came before us. *America's Jewish Women: A History from Colonial Times to Today* is the result.

At dinners over the years, acquaintances have bristled when I said I was writing this history. "Impossible," they responded, pointing to themselves and to the other Jewish women around the table to show just how different each one was. Then they would sit back, convinced that they had proven their point, that I should walk away from this book.

But as a historian, I beg to differ. In the wake of the new wave of feminism of the 1960s, scholars began writing women into history, their contribution to advancing the status of women in American life. Few then had any inkling that America's Jewish women had a history of their own. But three graduate students—Paula Hyman, Charlotte Baum, and Sonya Michel—pointed the way, in 1976, with *The Jewish Woman in America*.

Now, in the twenty-first century, *America's Jewish Women*, resting on decades of scholarship, narrates the unique story of the Jewish women who, for more than three and a half centuries, have called America home. At its heart lies the assertion that Jewish women were a part of America's women and yet, throughout history, have remained distinctly apart from them.

That these women were Jews mattered. But *America's Jewish Women* recognizes that what it meant to be a Jew has varied enormously. Some Jewish women have placed Judaism at the center of their lives. Their days and years have rotated around Sabbaths and holidays and a world of Jewish rituals, organizations, and causes. Others have cared less about religion yet carried within them a powerful sense of Jewishness, the everyday experience of being a Jew. That identity shaped some of their choices about education, marriage, work, and community. For others, being Jewish was an occasional distraction. Still others denied that being Jewish had any relevance for their lives at all. They were just Americans or just women, or perhaps they called themselves by some other name. Yet across the years, some of those Jewish women too discovered that, no matter how they labeled themselves, others still called them Jews.

This history of America's Jewish women casts its net over all these women—the religiously observant and the fiercely secular, the needy immigrants and the savvy businesswomen, the feisty matrons and the spirited women who became rabbis. In the chapters ahead, we will hear stories of Jewish women who made homes in colonial seaports, frontier towns, urban ghettoes, and suburban streets, whose lives were most closely bound up with family, neighborhood, work, and community. We will read of weddings, marriages, and babies, of foods cooked and served, of communities built, of life in times of war and crisis and in times of peace and prosperity.

We will also discover the many whose lives, spreading over larger canvasses, left deep footprints in the history of the nation they called home. *America's Jewish Women* brings to life some of those who, making their marks in different fields—education, politics, industry, labor, journalism, health care, charity work, popular culture—left a legacy that reverberated across American history.

America's freedoms, which permitted my great-grandmother to keep her wig when others discarded theirs, opened up an array of new avenues for each generation. We will meet the colonial mother heartbroken over her daughter's intermarriage, the Confederate spy facing down a general, the poet of the "huddled masses" heralding Zionism, the factory worker taunting scabs, the Communist sending her daughter to school on Jewish holidays, the Holocaust survivor feted on national TV, the lawyer striding into Congress.

That air of freedom, its opportunities and challenges, emboldened America's Jewish women and inspired their activism and deep commitments to changes they thought would make this world a better place. Their history became one of remarkable political engagement. In their neighborhoods, they rioted against the high price of kosher meat. Picketing outside factories, they demanded safe working conditions and a living wage. Their Jewish women's organizations campaigned against the perils of white slavery and championed Zionism. Jewish housewives combatted antisemitism. Jewish lesbians decried homophobia.

Years ago a Jewish woman asked: "What is the difference between a bookkeeper and a Supreme Court justice?" "One generation," quipped Supreme Court justice Ruth Bader Ginsburg. This book is for the curious who want to know how that happened and who wonder about the generations of America's Jewish women, like those in my photographs, who came before.

America's Jewish Women

Prologue

TWO OF THE nation's early Jewish women stand at opposite poles of this story. The first, Grace Mendes Seixas Nathan (1752–1831), lived her life bound by the commonplace roles of wife and mother. The second, her great-granddaughter, the writer Emma Lazarus (1849–87), won acclaim for her poetry and prose. Her poem "The New Colossus," inscribed on a plaque in the pedestal of the Statue of Liberty, has welcomed millions to America with the words, "Give me your tired, your poor / Your huddled masses yearning to breathe free." A woman of purposeful action, she left her mark in her day and far beyond.[1]

Grace Nathan lived out her days as a woman, an American, and a Jew. So did Emma Lazarus. As women, they were defined and constrained by the conventions of their times that fixed standards of appropriate behavior for women of their social class. As Americans, they reveled in their nation's freedoms, religious liberties, and opportunities. As Jews, their faith pivoted around an ancient tradition, historic memory, and practices that set them apart.

In the century between their births, the world changed. Sailing ships had carried America's first Jewish women, like Grace Nathan's mother, across the Atlantic. In coastal seaports they cooked over open hearths, braved a revolution, and witnessed the birth of a new nation. The women of Lazarus's era saw their nation rent asunder by war, commemorated the centennial of its birth, and met the first of the millions of immigrants traveling aboard steamships bound for America. Despite the passage of time, constants remained as each generation invented and reinvented myriad combinations of how to live as women, Americans, and Jews. The lives of Nathan and Lazarus illustrate just two of the innumerable permutations devised.

Lazarus's poem "The Exodus (August 3, 1492)" recollects a time when Jews were forced into exile. In it, the narrator remembers her ancestors—their hearts broken—driven from Spain, forsaking their vines, fields, and forebears' graves. She wishes that a bird could have consoled the desolate exiles, whispering, even as they took to their dusty road, that Columbus's ships were about to "bequeath a Continent to Freedom!"[2]

Great-grandmother Nathan was descended from Portugal through her father Isaac Mendes Seixas. More than two centuries before his birth, that nation had also expelled its Jews. Her father's side dwelled there in the days when it was impossible to live openly as one. Her mother, Rachel Levy, was born in London, the eldest of the seven children of the German-born Moses Levy and his second wife, Grace Mears Levy, of London and Jamaica. The product of multiple heritages, Nathan was born on the American continent. She was so ardent a patriot that, during the War of 1812, she boasted confidently that her brave new nation, which had prevailed over Great Britain once, would triumph again. The remarkable events of her day—wars and revolution—intruded into her life as they would into the lives of America's Jewish women across the ages. Yet most of Grace Nathan's life was taken up neither with world affairs nor with thoughts about the nation aborning but rather with the quotidian. First as daughters and sisters, then as wives and mothers, later as widows and grandmothers, women, Jewish and gentile, centered their lives on home and family.[3]

Marriage, of course, was a chief concern. Grace Mendes Seixas wed the British-born merchant, American patriot, militiaman, and synagogue leader Simon Nathan. Later she gossiped disapprovingly about a neighbor's "*hum-drum* wedding," one befitting a poor man, not worthy of one who was her neighbor. Surely hers was a more splendid affair. Lazarus never wed, but she wrote about weddings. Musing "In the Jewish Synagogue at Newport"—built in Rhode Island in 1763, it was no longer used in her day—she wrote: "The funeral and the marriage, now, alas! / We know not which is sadder to recall; / For youth and happiness have followed age, / And green grass lieth gently over all."[4]

Between "the funeral and the marriage" often came children. In an era when childbirth too often brought death to mother and babe, Nathan eagerly awaited happy news from relatives far away about what she euphemistically called a "*Certain Event*." In verses, Lazarus marveled at the lovely mother at whose side "breathed the Prince, her child."[5]

Caring for family meant seeing them through sickness. Nathan worried about her niece, who, for three weeks, had been spitting up blood, the result, according to the doctors, of her tight corset. As Simon Nathan aged and became infirm in body and mind, she wrote of how she had to dress and undress her husband as if he were a child. Her great-granddaughter also took care of relatives and conjured up another nurse, "God's angel" Florence Nightingale, the British reformer who made nursing a respectable occupation for women, weeping "in the room / Of agony and gloom."[6]

Writing of weddings, births, and nursing unites Nathan and Lazarus to women across the ages. Yet when these two contemplated religion and their people, they stood apart from the vast majority of American women who were, of course, Christians, pious or not. Lazarus imagined hearing the prayers of the weary in the Newport synagogue. The devout Nathan, praying to God Almighty, regarded the trials of her life as lessons in submission to the Divine will. On her deathbed, she affirmed: "I *die* in the *full faith* of my *religion*."[7]

In the days when mostly men wrote history, historians assumed that mostly men made history. One early authority on American Jewish history asserted that Nathan, and women like her, had little chance of entering into history other than as appendages to famous men. He mentions Nathan only because her husband was an important merchant and her brother New York's Jewish religious leader. For this scholar, the affairs at the core of her life—marriage, children, homemaking—seemed timeless, outside the bounds of history. The few women then making history in their own right were those of public accomplishment, like Emma Lazarus. But after feminism surged in the 1960s, a new generation of scholars, writing into history the domesticity at the heart of many women's lives, paved the way for Grace Nathan and wives and mothers across the American Jewish generations to claim their places in this book.[8]

Of course, women like Emma Lazarus, who discovered new opportunities and obligations and left legacies extending beyond their families and their moment in time, find places here too. Lazarus celebrated that this great land had granted her people the freedom to follow Moses's law, to sing David's songs, "and to think / The thoughts Gabirol to Spinoza taught," referring to two of Iberian Jewry's greatest minds, the eleventh-century poet Solomon ibn Gabirol and the Dutch philosopher of Portuguese origins, condemned for heresy, Baruch (Benedict de) Spinoza (1631–77).[9]

This nation's exultation of liberty inspired these women to aspire to "the utmost good." Making their mark in the worlds of work, politics, religion, education, social service, and culture, the latter where Lazarus left her imprint, figures, well known in their day and sometimes beyond, constructed new ways of being women, Americans, and Jews and carved out their own avenues to achieve "the utmost good."[10]

In a testament outlining her ethics for her only child, Nathan too displayed the same bold testing of boundaries that her great-granddaughter evidenced when she claimed the thoughts of the heretic Spinoza. Nathan commanded her son to mourn only for seven days at her death, despite Jewish custom requiring men not to shave for at least thirty days after the death of a parent. But Nathan, a woman inspired by the liberties of the nation whose birth she had witnessed, made her own law.[11]

Grace Nathan and Emma Lazarus have set the stage for this narrative of ordinary and extraordinary American Jewish women.

They have introduced America's Jewish women into a world where they are simultaneously a part of American women and yet stand apart from them. They have announced that Jewish women, living in the shadow of this nation's liberties, have earned their place in history. Now the lights dim, and the curtains open into the homes of America's earliest Jewish women.

I

"Many are the blessings I partake of"

AMERICA'S EARLY JEWISH WOMEN

IN THE AUTUMN of 1654, shortly before the Jewish New Year, twenty-three men, women, and children fled the long arm of the Holy Inquisition that had just reached into the New World colony of Recife in Brazil. Leaving Recife, they sailed to the Dutch colonial seaport of New Amsterdam, soon to be renamed New York. By one account, there were four couples and two widows; the rest were children and unmarried young people. Of the women, we know the names only of two, most likely because they were widowed heads of households. In this manner Ricke Nunes and Judith Mercado became America's first Jewish women. Unlike Grace Nathan and Emma Lazarus, neither left a legacy of her life in her own words. To peer into their world, we must use our imaginations.[1]

"What a rare find is a capable wife!"

THE EARLY American Jewish community was tiny, at most 2,500 souls by the time of the American Revolution. The community was exceedingly diverse. American Jews came from England, France, Germany, Holland, Poland, the West Indies, and the British colonies. They settled in the bustling seaports of Newport, New York, Philadelphia, Charleston, and Savannah. Sephardic Judaism, the religious rites practiced by the descendants of the men and women Lazarus had envisioned trudging out of Spain, dominated synagogue life. But in terms of sheer numbers, Ashkenazic Jews, who hailed from German lands as had Nathan's grandfather, quickly surpassed the original Sephardic settlers.

At a time when Jews elsewhere were so often locked behind ghetto walls, colonial Jews found a remarkable degree of toleration and diversity. On city byways, they saw native women, dressed in skins and moccasins; Europeans and Africans, free, indentured, and enslaved. Their neighbors were a variety of Protestants—Calvinists, Lutherans, Huguenots, Presbyterians, Quakers, Baptists—Catholics, and even some Muslims. They mingled, did business, and socialized with their neighbors.

On the surface, the lives of early America's Jewish women mirrored those of their neighbors. They spun wool and fetched water, cooked for boarders, and unpacked shipping crates. They wed and became wives. In bringing life into the world, they became mothers and faced death. In the colonies, one in five women died in childbirth. Those who lived raised their children and, with tears, buried too many.

In dozens of portraits, well-to-do Jewish women are gowned and posed, just like Christian women. For hers, Nathan, who celebrated the "many blessings" she partook of across her life, wore a bonnet ruffled and tied with a bow; her lace collar, high, starched, and frilled; her tippet, a filmy shawl, tucked into her bodice. But in an era when religion permeated every thought, marked time, and gave meaning to crises public and private, that these women were Jews mattered deeply.[2]

Inventories of goods done after a person's death permit a peek into a colonial Jewish woman's home. In 1702 New York's Judah Samuel died, leaving an account of his worldly goods testifying to the modest life of his wife, Rachel Hendricks Samuel. Likely she died first since his catalog lists her possessions. Perhaps both fell victim to a smallpox epidemic that claimed five hundred souls that spring. Rachel had owned but a few clothes: a gown, a petticoat, an apron, a handkerchief, and a woman's stays. Her kitchen held a tankard, a saltcellar, a pot for cooking soups and stews, a kettle, and a frying pan. So far, nothing differentiates the Samuels' home from that of their neighbors. But a Hebrew Bible and five prayer books did. Could Rachel read them? That is doubtful. But perhaps in her short life—she was probably forty-two when she died—she had prayed over candles kindled in her two brass candlesticks, as commanded of Jewish women on Sabbaths and holiday eves.[3]

Other Jewish women lived in more well-appointed homes. When Joseph Bueno died, he bequeathed to Rachell, his wife of sixty-seven years, all his household goods, furniture, and jewels. Had he not done so, the common law of coverture, which governed married women's status and prohibited them from owning property in their own right, would have limited her widow's share of his estate. Now the clock, the looking glass, the pewter dishes, and the oak dining table—all belonged to her. There were also Delftware dishes, glasses, and twenty-five china cups and saucers displayed in a case. Were these for special meals for Sabbaths and holidays? Was their silver cup for blessing the Sabbath wine? Did the brass candlesticks hold her Sabbath candles?

Did their neighbors ever look with curiosity at their Torah scroll, with its traditional wrapping and ornaments? During worship, on Sabbath mornings and also on Mondays and Thursdays, men read aloud from that sacred scroll containing the first five books of the Hebrew Bible. Over the course of a year, they would complete a cycle from the first verse of Genesis to the last of Deuteronomy. Handwritten on parchment sheets sewn together, mounted on two rollers, a Torah, when not in use, is enclosed in a case and crowned with ornaments. That Joseph bequeathed one suggests that New York Jews worshipped in the Bueno home, as Jews may do so in any place where ten men, the quorum—*minyan*—needed for prayer, gather. A synagogue is not required, and New York Jews would not build one until 1730, more than two decades after he died.[4]

Other household objects, besides a Hebrew Bible, a Torah scroll,

and prayer books, marked out homes as Jewish. When six generations of the New York Gomez family put an *etrog*, the citron used
during the fall holiday of Sukkot, into a silver mustard pot, a con-
diment holder became a religious object. Colonial ladies of fine
breeding, practicing their needlework, embroidered biblical passages onto their samplers. But only a Jewish young lady would have
chosen Psalm 78. Its verses about God appointing "a law in Israel"
that fathers must teach to their children (Ps. 78:5) spoke of the biblical laws that bound Jews, commandments Christians replaced with
salvation in Jesus.[5]

In their homes, an array of activities kept women, Jewish and
gentile, and their daughters busy from dawn to dark. They filled
their days with spinning, weaving, dyeing, knitting, sewing, and
washing; roasting, frying, boiling, and baking; pickling and preserving. They tended the hearth, fetched water, made soap and candles, churned butter and made cheese, hoed the garden, and fed
the chickens. Some colonial Jewish women did these things themselves. Nathan's older sister Abigail Judah cared for her home and
her eleven children. The sisters' more prosperous sister-in-law,
Jochebed Seixas, who lived in Newport, had six slaves and one free
servant to help with her household of eleven.[6]

GRACE SEIXAS left no record of her wedding to Simon Nathan,
in August 1780 in Philadelphia, as the American Revolution raged.
Her well-to-do parents could have made an elegant affair, serving
Indian rum, French brandy, coffee, and cocoa, all of which were
then for sale in the city, despite the war.[7]

Although on the average, early American women, whether New
York Jews or New England Puritans, wed at age twenty-three, some
married younger. New York's Abigaill Levy wed Jacob Franks
when she was barely sixteen. She would bring her first child, Naphtali, into the world before her father's second wife bore her first
child, Rachel, who would become Grace Nathan's mother.

That Jacob Franks was eight years older than Abigaill was the norm. A man had to have the means to support a family before embarking on marriage. During the eighteenth century, the average age of Jewish grooms in New York was almost thirty-one.[8]

Decisions to marry were too important to leave to the young. Marriages cemented and extended family and commercial networks, binding the Jews of the Atlantic world. Sent to London when he came of age, Naphtali Franks traded with his father in New York and his brother in Philadelphia. When he wed his paternal cousin Phila, he bonded ever more tightly the various branches of the Levy-Franks family. After the sons of Esther and Luis (Louis) Gomez, the family of the mustard pot, wed wives from the Caribbean, family ties led to greater business enterprises.

Given marriage's economic significance, seeking parental approval was traditional. After Grace's brother Benjamin told his parents of his affection for Zipporah Levy, their father wrote her parents seeking consent for them to wed. Abigaill wrote her son Naphtali, across the ocean and the years, leaving a treasure trove of letters for us to read. She jested in one that she did not expect his sisters to be "Nuns." Yet they had better marry men who could keep them in style, who could afford a proper coach and six horses. Still, despite New York's tiny Jewish community of perhaps 250, she had no intention of consenting "to Any worthless body." As for the suit of David Gomez for her daughter Richa, Abigaill considered him "such a Stupid wretch" that not only would she refuse her consent, she was positive that Richa would spurn him too.[9]

If David Gomez proposed, Richa never wed him nor apparently anyone else then. Instead, as a maiden daughter, she cared for her father for more than a decade after her mother's death. When he died in 1769, he named her and a son-in-law of Phila and Oliver Delancey administrators of his estate. A few months later, Richa set sail for London, never to return to America. When she was in her sixties, she reportedly wed a much younger Jewish widower and became stepmother to his son.[10]

Weddings were scripted by time-honored Jewish tradition. A revolutionary-era illustrated *ketubah*, a marriage contract, handwritten in ancient Aramaic and signed by two witnesses, proved that the groom Haym Salomon promised his bride Rachel, the daughter of Moses Franks, of Abigaill's extended family, sustenance should he die or divorce her. In Philadelphia, the Presbyterian Dr. Benjamin Rush, a signer of the Declaration of Independence, was invited to the wedding of Rachel Phillips and Michael Levy in the bride's family home. The bride, likely dressed in satin and lace, silk stockings, and gloves, joined her groom under the *chuppah*, a brightly colored silk canopy, symbolizing their future home. There the doctor witnessed a wedding custom he had never seen before. Someone put a dish at the groom's feet and placed a glass in it. The groom shattered it, and the guests shouted congratulations.[11]

Marriages then as later could be happy, troubled, or utterly miserable. Perhaps thinking of her own long marriage, Abigaill Franks hoped that "HertSey," as she affectionately called Naphtali, using the Yiddish for "dear heart," would find friendship with his own wife. As far as we know, she neither met this daughter-in-law nor ever saw her son again after he left the New World for the Old.[12]

When marriages are miserable or unfruitful, Jewish law permits divorce. A Savannah couple, after just sixteen months of marriage, parted ways in 1799, the husband giving his wife a *get*, the Jewish divorce decree. One Jewish observer was thunderstruck; Jewish law may have permitted divorce, but it was so rare that he had never seen anything like this before among his people.[13]

Of course, married couples were expected to have children. Family size generally depended on the age of the bride; the younger the bride, the more children. The average eighteenth-century Jewish family had five or six, but Grace had only one. Rebecca Machado Phillips, wed at age sixteen and mother of the bride Rachel, fainted amid the crush at her daughter's wedding. Perhaps it was the heat, but she may also then have been pregnant with one of her twenty-one children. When in 1805 Grace's sister-in-law Zipporah—her parents had indeed consented to her marriage to Benjamin—gave birth to Leah, the last of her twenty-one children, a wit quipped that they had gone through almost all the names in the Bible.[14]

These Jewish mothers raised and educated their children; nursed them when they were sick; and in grief, buried some, a fate not uncommon in an age when yellow fever and smallpox wreaked havoc. About 40 percent of all children in colonial America died in infancy. Rebecca Phillips lost four of her children; Abigaill Franks buried two of her nine.

Abigaill was eighteen when Naphtali was born. Her next three arrived at regular two-year intervals; the birthdate of another is unknown. Then after a gap (were there miscarriages? unrecorded stillbirths?), she bore four more children in four years, the last when she was thirty-seven or thirty-eight. Her childbearing pattern speaks to the realities of colonial women so often "brot to bed." Women spent a good portion of their fertile adult lives either pregnant or nursing. Rebecca Phillips was forty-six when she gave birth to her last child.[15]

Nursing can suppress ovulation, offering women, as some eighteenth-century writers surmised, a natural period of infertility, in effect birth control. Perhaps as a young mother, Abigaill Franks had nursed her babies as colonial women routinely did for twelve or eighteen months; hence the roughly two-year intervals of her first children. But if later, as a well-to-do matron, she hired wet nurses, it would explain her bearing four children in four years.

Whether she observed Jewish laws regulating marital relations is unknown. Jewish law deems sexual pleasure, properly controlled and channeled in marriage, a joyful part of life. Judaism, however, prohibits sexual relations during a wife's menstrual cycle and for seven days after its cessation. A woman must then immerse in a *mikveh* (ritual bath) before she and her husband resume relations. Although she may dunk in a river or in any body of naturally occurring water, since antiquity Jews have built *mikvaot* for ritual purification, and the remains of seventeenth- and eighteenth-century *mikvaot* have been found in almost all the major Caribbean Jewish communities from those eras.[16]

To what extent Jewish women in the North American colonies obeyed these laws is unknown. Even before New York's Jews built a synagogue, later known as Shearith Israel, on the no longer extant

Mill Street in 1730, they erected a bathing house over a run of natural water as required for a *mikveh*. But until it was built, what did New York's Jewish wives do? Perhaps they immersed themselves in the East River in areas screened off for women to bathe.[17]

Were Philadelphia's Jewish women especially lax about this law? In 1784 Manuel Josephson petitioned the Jewish community in the City of Brotherly Love to build a *mikveh*. He condemned husbands and wives for violating the commandment of ritual immersion and feared that, if Jews abroad knew how lax American Jews were in this regard, they would never allow their sons and daughters to marry them. He hoped that once the *mikveh* was built, God would look with favor upon His people and send the Redeemer.[18]

Two years later the Philadelphia *mikveh* opened, but it seems to have been little used. Josephson urged the congregation's husbands to command their wives to do the ritual. But if they did, their wives ignored them. By then generations of Philadelphia's Jewish women had become adept at flouting this commandment.

IF, IN THEIR HOMES and with their families, early American Jewish wives were much like their neighbors, the extent of colonial Jewish women's commercial affairs may have set them apart. The prototypical male colonist was an artisan or a farmer, but colonial Jewish men were overwhelmingly merchants engaged in commerce. With her husband away at sea or in the hinterlands trading, a wife with a head for business, who could shuttle between the crying baby and keeping the account books, could stand in as a "deputy husband."[19]

Jewish women turned homemaking skills into business ventures. They ran kosher boardinghouses and grog shops, sold their own jams and pickles, and took in washing and ironing. They also traded, sold dry goods, exported preserves, and imported rum. Whether they stepped in for their husbands or had their own businesses, the experience proved invaluable. Given the discrepancy in age between Jewish spouses, a wife, who survived frequent childbirths, epidemics, and the disasters wrought by nature and man, could outlive her husband and find herself heading the household. Fifty-six-year-old Abigail Minis, whose daughter Hannah was the one who had shocked the community with her divorce, was left widowed with eight children to support. By the time Mrs. Minis died in Savannah, aged ninety-three, she had run a tavern and owned land in Georgia and South Carolina, where she raised cattle and sheep and had enslaved people do the work.

Although Grace's grandmother Grace Mears Levy Hays was well provided for when her first husband died in 1728—he left her 300 British pounds, 150 ounces of sterling silver plate, and his best Negro slave—he also left her the head of a family of twelve. Her stepsons advised: *Open a shop.* Although one historian surmised that she did so to "fill her spare time," it is far more likely that she needed the money. When she remarried seven years later, no one expected her new husband to help with the children, but surely he would lend a hand in the shop.[20]

"Our Sabbeth is coming on so fast."

RELIGION PERMEATED the lives of America's early women no matter which one they observed. For observant Jews, the approach of the Sabbath meant that all manner of work, even writing letters, must cease. In 1780 Savannah's Frances Sheftall rushed to seal a letter to her husband, writing, "Our Sabbeth is coming on so fast."[21]

For many Jewish women then and later, the rhythms of religious life, its daily, weekly, and yearly cycles of sacred time, as enacted in home and synagogue, governed their days. The cadences of Sabbaths and festivals, the rituals marking life's passages, the laws regulating foods consumed and marital relations, all served to fix borders between Jews and their Christian neighbors. Despite the many different places where early American Jews were born, these rhythms bound them into a community.

The synagogue—there was only one in each community—was its center. The split into Reform, Conservative, and Orthodox

Judaism lay in the future. In the colonies' five synagogues, officers called *parnassim*—no ordained rabbis had yet settled in America—arranged for worship and made sure that there was kosher meat throughout the year and matzo on Passover. They saw that life-cycle events were properly marked, and children suitably educated.

The officers were also responsible to care for the poor. Kitty Abrahams appealed to the board of Shearith Israel after her husband had been ill for so long that they were destitute. Their son was blind, and her own eyesight was failing. The synagogue helped her until her death eight years later. Many of the indigent were widows. By the time Martha Moravia died in 1787, she had been reduced to taking charity for six years from the Newport, Rhode Island, synagogue, the one Lazarus visited nearly a century later.[22]

Traditionally, few Jewish women attended religious services. Having no role to play in public worship, they had no need to be present. But America was different. Here Christian housewives went to church. Jewish women followed their lead and went to synagogue.

As was customary in congregations then, Jewish women were separated from men in a balcony. In the one in New York City, its balustrade came up to their chins, but in Newport, its railing was so low that female worshippers could lean over to follow the service below. When the men below glanced up from their devotions, "vertical flirting" ensued.[23]

In the balcony, the ladies gossiped. Abigaill Franks enjoyed listening to them, but the judgmental Mrs. Franks avoided those same ladies, "a Stupid Set of people," outside the synagogue. Perhaps Abigaill could follow the Hebrew service. Phila and Richa learned to read Hebrew in Shearith Israel's school.[24]

Jewish women supported their synagogues with gifts. They donated ritual objects and money to buy Torah scrolls. They left bequests in their wills to have their names recited in the Yom Kippur *yizkor* (memorial) prayers. Grace Nathan and Rebecca Phillips raised funds to buy essential items for Philadelphia's first synagogue, dedicated in 1782. In New York, Rachel Pinto left the congregation such a substantial sum that its leaders promised to recite her name in their memorial prayers until the coming of Israel's messiah.²⁵

Outside the synagogue, the home towered as the other pillar for transmitting Jewish culture and tradition. There women had starring roles. Their hearths and their tables, following the dietary laws of *kashrut*, signified that theirs were Jewish homes. Judaism's food restrictions go back to the Bible, where the ancient Israelites were enjoined as to which animals were permissible to eat. Later rules evolved for properly slaughtering and preparing meat. Keeping kosher also demands that dairy and meat never be consumed at the same meal and that there are separate dishes, utensils, and pots to use with dairy and meat. The women would not have cooked on Sabbaths and holidays, as all work was forbidden. They would have had to prepare enough food by Friday sunset to feed their family until the Sabbath ended on Saturday an hour after sunset. A different set of rules regulates foods consumed during the spring Passover holiday. For some, but by no means all, of America's Jewish women, from the colonial era down until today, keeping these laws and preparing customary Jewish dishes—foods fried in oil at Hanukkah; dairy items at Shavuot—announced that they were Jews.

For some, *kashrut* was essential. Abigaill Franks warned Naphtali about her London brother's kitchen, telling him never to eat anything there except for bread and butter, nor anywhere else where there might be any doubt about the keeping of the strict Jewish dietary laws.²⁶

But things were different in the Jewish cultural wasteland of Petersburg, Virginia. From there Rebecca Samuel wrote her parents that their *shochet* (kosher butcher) went to market, bought *treyf* (unkosher) meat, and then sold it as kosher. In New York, boardinghouse landlady Hetty Hays suspected that some lamb that she had bought had not been properly cleansed by the synagogue's *shochet*, as required by Jewish law. She notified the congregation. The evidence was insufficient to condemn him, but it raised enough concern that the *parnassim* ordered her to re-kosher all her plates and utensils. Whatever method was required then—perhaps boiling the utensils, possibly soaking dishes in multiple changes of water over several days—it was surely arduous in an era when water came from a well.[27]

Yet the importance of a kosher home for some is misleading. The most striking feature of colonial Jewish religious life was that it ran the full gamut from piety to willful disregard. Rebecca Samuel considered not just the *shochet*, but also the dozen Jews in Petersburg, who kept their shops open on the Sabbath and who did not even have a Torah, unworthy of the name. Craving a synagogue, despairing that her children would become like Gentiles, she and her husband left a thriving business hoping to decamp to the larger and presumably more observant Jewish community of Charleston.

AS REBECCA SAMUEL'S concerns show, women's paramount investment in Jewish life lay in raising the next generation of American Jews. Children learned to read, write, and cipher at home from parents and tutors or in religious schools, like the one Shearith Israel maintained for two decades before the Revolutionary War. Girls from homes of privilege also studied music, dancing, and needlework. Abigaill Franks's daughters played the harpsichord and learned French and Spanish. At home and in the synagogue, they also surely absorbed Judaism's fundamental tenets, the duties incumbent on women of the Jewish nation, and even some Hebrew.

Given the tiny size of these early Jewish communities, Jewish lives were, despite the religious divide, inextricably intertwined with those of their Christian neighbors. In March 1734, after eight weeks at sea, a few dozen Salzburg Lutherans landed in Savannah. German-born Perla and Benjamin Sheftall, who had been in the colony less than a year, invited them to breakfast. Surely Perla cooked and supervised its "good rice-soup." Sharing German language and heritage with the Salzburgers, the Sheftalls continued to extend themselves, showing "so much love," wrote the pastors, "that no one could ask any more."[28]

Early American Jews felt comfortable enough to invite Christians to breakfast, to a wedding, and even to the synagogue service. Those Lutherans may never again have dined with the Sheftalls. Benjamin Rush may have attended only a single Jewish wedding. Yet they, and other early American Christians, counted Jews as friends and were often curious about Jewish rituals.

Rush also attended the circumcision of Rebecca Phillips's son Aaron in Philadelphia, at a time when circumcision among gentiles was not as prevalent as today. While the women, abuzz with sympathy for mother and babe, remained upstairs, the good doctor stood among the men to witness the operation that, for millennia, has initiated eight-day-old male infants into the biblical covenant that God made with Abraham. Circumcision was such an important ritual that Savannah's first Jews brought a circumcision knife to America. They quickly put it to good use, for less than two weeks after landing, one of the recent arrivals gave birth to a son.

THE PENNSYLVANIA State House's Liberty Bell, the one that cracked, bears the inscription "Proclaim Liberty throughout all the Land unto all the Inhabitants thereof" (Lev. 25:10). In America, a pioneering spirit of adventure and an aura of freedom gave birth to an independence of mind. Jewish women heard liberty's call. Sensing possibilities and opportunities, they could become, in America, as Grace Nathan was, agents of religious change and, because religious change breeds discord, agents of disruption.

Arguments among women upstairs in the cramped balcony of New York's Shearith Israel's synagogue sometimes spilled over to the men praying below. In 1760 a few of the women, frustrated with their places in the gallery—perhaps only the bench closest to the railing afforded a glimpse of the service downstairs—took matters into their own hands. On one Sabbath, two of Grace's relations fought over the same spot. As Josse Hays and her cousin argued, Josse's uncle stormed into the gallery and tossed his niece out.

Lengthening the bench so that Josse could sit next to her mother did not mollify her father. Aggravated over the affair, the *parnassim* eventually fined him for defying their authority.[29]

Five years later another dispute erupted in the women's gallery. On the eve of Yom Kippur, the most solemn day in the Jewish calendar, Gitlah Hays brought her neighbor, Margaret Still, a Christian, to synagogue. It was a warm September eve, and the *parnassim* had the balcony's windows taken off their sashes to let in as much air as possible. Then a sudden thunderstorm struck, soaking Gitlah and her unfortunate guest. Fuming and surely embarrassed, Gitlah went home and corralled her husband to defy the elders and rehang the window the next morning. By the time she arrived at services, the other seven women in the stifling gallery had opened it. Gitlah shut it; they opened it; she shut it again. Then the ladies complained to their men. One marched up to the gallery, took the window off its hinges, and headed for the yard. When Gitlah's husband saw what had been done, he stormed out, and a fracas ensued. The *parnassim* expelled him from the congregation, excommunicating him, a historic practice whereby the community's leaders ban anyone from having intercourse with those defying their authority. Hays filed a criminal suit, charging assault and battery, in New York Superior Court. He lost. It was several years before the Hays family returned to Shearith Israel.[30]

Abigaill Franks was observant and expected the same of her family. Her menfolk prayed at home if not at the synagogue, and she prepared special holiday meals. Yet she too imbibed liberty's spirit of innovation. Yearning for a modernized Judaism, long before others would start constructing one, she groused to Naphtali about her frustrations with its senseless ceremonies, absurd superstitions, and punctilious rituals that she felt exceeded what the law intended. If "a Calvin or Luther would rise amongst Us," she daringly advanced, "I would be the first of there [*sic*] followers."[31]

However, the costs of this open society and such impulses were high. When her daughter Phila married outside the faith, Abigaill's spirit was crushed: "Soe Depresst that it was a pain . . . to Speak or See Any one." Resolving never again to see her daughter—and no one knows if she ever relented—she retreated to her country house in Brooklyn.³²

Such tension over intermarriage prefigures its rise in later years. In early America, however, the intermarriage rate was low, perhaps 10 to 15 percent of all Jewish marriages, and the phenomenon was noticeably gendered. Colonial Jewish men intermarried more frequently than their more sheltered sisters. On rare occasions, a wife who had "not the happiness to be born a Jewess" might become one, but most surely did not. Yet if Jewish men did not utterly abandon Judaism when they intermarried, they could often retain their place in the congregation.³³

Jewish women could do no such thing. Instead, as Phila Franks Delancey learned, even as her father tried and failed to persuade her mother to reconcile with her, they were often shunned. Another who intermarried thought her sister had "a heart of stone"; if not, she would have managed to steal away to see her. Perhaps Abigaill intuited the gendered costs of intermarriage, how when a woman left her parents' home to marry a Christian, she left the Jewish community behind. Abigaill's son David continued to attend synagogue even as he let his wife raise their six children in her Christian faith. Presumably son Naphtali and his wife raised their children as Jews. Nevertheless, not one of Abigaill's grandchildren seems to have passed Judaism on to their next generation.³⁴

Yet the size of the community sharply curtailed Jewish women's marriage prospects. In Savannah, when Abigail Minis's five daughters came of age in the 1760s, there were only five potential Jewish mates in the entire city. Two were too young for the oldest Minis girls; one daughter refused one of the bachelors; another loved a Christian who died at sea, leaving her, although they never wed, his entire estate; and Hannah, as we saw, married and quickly divorced. Men could travel elsewhere to find a Jewish bride—the Gomez men married women from the Caribbean, Naphtali Franks wed in England—but colonial Jewish daughters had to wait at home for grooms to come to claim them. When Abigail Minis died, her four surviving daughters, the youngest of whom was forty-six, were all unmarried.

"The balls flew like haile during the cannonading": The American Revolution and the New Republic

MUCH HAS been written about Jewish men and their sacrifices for the patriotic cause: Perhaps as many as a hundred, including Grace Nathan's husband, fought for the American Revolution. But little is known about Jewish women's wartime experiences. Wars affect men and women in different ways. American women may not have shouldered muskets, but they helped found the new nation. As consumers and household managers, they boycotted goods, like tea, that the British taxed. They raised funds for their cause, supplied militias with food and clothing, and ran absent husbands' farms and businesses. Once fighting broke out, the war literally came home. The British occupied cities and quartered soldiers in private houses. Occasionally wives, with no other means of support, tagged along after soldier husbands, working in the army's hospitals, laundries, and kitchens.

About a fifth of all colonists remained loyal to the Crown; about two-fifths were patriots; and the rest tried, for as long as possible, to avoid taking sides. Whether or not American Jews split along similar lines, by war's end, most living in the new United States had embraced the patriot cause.

The paramount Jewish wartime experience was exile. Once more Jews scattered and dispersed, this time not from Zion but from their homes in the American colonies. With the British occupying cities with significant Jewish populations—New York (1776), Newport (1776), Philadelphia (1777), Savannah (1778), and Charleston (1780)—patriotic Jews sought refuge with friends and relatives elsewhere.

The Philadelphia merchant Barnard Gratz dispatched his only daughter, Rachel, to the safe haven of relatives in Lancaster. There she continued her schooling and begged her father to send a new fan and lining for a cloak, even as the prices of the goods that she wanted soared. But the war intruded more deeply into her life, when she attended the funeral of a colonel buried with military honors, and she saw for herself war's devastation.[35]

In Savannah, Abigail Minis, in her seventies when war broke out, supplied provisions and other useful items to American and French troops trying to recapture the city in 1779. When the expedition failed, she appealed to Georgia's Tory governor to let her leave with her family, under a flag of truce, for Charleston, and to have agents appointed to safeguard her plantation while she was away. That he granted her requests suggests the delicate balance of wartime relations among acquaintances.[36]

Loyalist sympathizers were often forced into exile. Isaac da Costa, from England, was among the first Jews to settle in Boston. He was in Europe when war broke out, and he returned to the city to check on his estates. Refusing to swear loyalty to the patriots' cause, he was arrested, deported, and his estates occupied, if not confiscated. Eventually, he ended up in a British debtors' prison. His wife had to sell everything of value to pay his debts. Then she became ill from going about in all sorts of bad weather to eke out the meagerest of livings. Newport's Jacob Hart went into exile in England where he died impoverished, but not before the British Commission of Enquiry granted him a pension for his loyalist suffering. When his widow Esther laid claim to the pension, the commission reduced the sum since, with fewer family members, they supposedly required less income.[37]

The story of another Jewish woman caught up in the tumultuous moment shows the difficulty of maintaining one's politics. When, in 1776, the British took New York, Rachel Pinto went into exile in Connecticut. Four years later, after the British sacked New Haven and as the war dragged on, she decided to return home. She swore allegiance to the Crown, hoping to reclaim her house, but troops were billeted there. After the war, she sought compensation for its "rental." Whether she received any is unknown.

War compelled women, patriot and loyalist, whether they stayed in their homes or went into exile, to fend for themselves and their families. When the British captured her husband and eldest son, Frances Sheftall—she had married Perla and Benjamin's American-born son—found herself head of the household. Even after the men were paroled and banished to Philadelphia, she and the rest of the children languished in Charleston where, she wrote, the "balls flew like haile during the cannonading." Managing to collect monies owed her husband and doing needlework, she and the children lived on the edge of poverty. Eventually, she was reduced to taking in washing and ironing until her eldest son managed to reach Charleston, in 1781, under a flag of truce and return to Philadelphia with his mother and siblings.[38]

War, of course, took more precious things than one's home. During the siege of Savannah, British cannonballs killed at least six Jewish children. The devastation and havoc the British wrought in Newport had made one woman "crazy," observed a patriot. Worst of all, he wrote, "the vertue of several of our reputable ladys has been attacked and sullied by our destructive enemys."[39]

Yet for eighteen-year-old loyalist Rebecca Franks, a granddaughter of Abigaill and Jacob by their son David, life under the British occupation in Philadelphia and New York was jolly. Baptized at the Anglican Christ Church by her gentile mother, yet still referred to as "the beautiful Jewess," she enjoyed the social whirl of gallant officers, fancy balls, and elegant dress. For Rebecca Franks, war led to marriage to a British officer and to a home in England.[40]

ALL MEN "are endowed by their Creator with certain unalienable Rights," the Declaration of Independence proclaimed, but women were not mentioned. Nevertheless, the brand-new nation needed its women to become educated mothers to raise the next generation of sensible republicans. Even if the Declaration's self-evident truth "that all men are created equal" did not axiomatically include women, mothers and daughters of the new republic absorbed its spirit.

Yet despite independence, the course of Jewish women's lives scarcely changed. Families, once scattered, returned from exile, some with losses. Jewish men once again turned to commerce; widows, like Abigail Minis, rebuilt their businesses. But most Jewish women remained circumscribed within the family circle, expected, as one brother advised his sister before her wedding, to make it her "constant duty . . . to please" her husband and ever be guided by "a due sence of relegion."[41]

Nevertheless, after the Revolution, complaints about seating in New York's synagogue gallery continued to roil. Three years after freedom was won, the inequity of a special bench reserved for the women of the wealthy Gomez clan rankled, and they lost their place of privilege.[42]

Then on the second day of the Jewish New Year, the Judah sisters—Amelia, Sarah, and Rebecca, who were all in their twenties and unmarried—refused to take their assigned seats. Perhaps they wanted to sit in the front row, so that they could see the service below. But that bench was reserved for married women and a few venerable elderly. Irritated by fractious women grumbling about their place, the synagogue trustees fined the young women and told them that if they did not pay up, they would take them to court. Defiantly, the sisters, stirred by the spirit of the rebellion, retorted that, when the men could "convince us that we are subject to any laws they chance to make which is to hinder us from attending Divine Worship, they may endeavor to exercise their authority." The men made good on their word and charged the young women with trespassing to keep them out of the synagogue. In court, Amelia was fined the nominal sum of sixpence and court costs. Later all was forgiven to preserve the peace. This appeal to the American law of the land in the matter of women's synagogue seats would, by no means, be the last.[43]

A few years later two women, Abigail Hays and Rachel Myers, who have left little else behind in the historical record, astonishingly tried to open a path to women's religious leadership when they applied for the post of Shearith Israel's *shammash*, its salaried sexton, the man—it was always a man—who cared for the synagogue. What made them think of doing this? Had they known that, in Massachusetts, during the Revolutionary War, the court appointed three women, among them Abigail Adams, who would later be the

United States' second First Lady, to examine women suspected of British loyalty? Abigail's husband John quipped that, elected to an important office, she had stepped into a man's role, becoming a politician, a "judgess of the Tory ladies." Or were they aware that some Protestant groups had deaconesses and eldresses? Or did they simply think that many of the sexton's tasks—making candles, cleaning the lamps and silver, heating the water for the *mikveh*, supervising the baking of matzo, banging on doors to awaken congregants for morning services—could just as easily be done by a woman? We will never know what moved them. They did not get the job.[44]

But in 1815, following the death of her husband, the synagogue's sexton, Jennet Isaacs, became its "shammastress." She held the post for the next six years, with her son handling duties, like reading services, that only a man could fulfill. Perhaps the congregation just wanted to help their late sexton's widow and her large family. But perhaps she and her husband had done much of the synagogue's caretaking together during his lifetime.[45]

~✢✢~

MOST OF America's Jewish women had no interest in crossing the gender line fixed in the synagogue. But a few new avenues were opening to women in America, and some Jewish women set out on these byways. In a Richmond school for young ladies, Rachel Mordecai learned reading, writing, ciphering, decorum, penmanship, music, drawing, and needlework. When, in 1809, her father decided to open a boarding school for girls, the Warrenton, North Carolina Female Seminary, Rachel, now a gifted teacher, found herself at its center, just as American women began entering the teaching profession. Even before she would have children of her own to teach, Rachel was instructing the future mothers of the republic.[46]

Rachel did not become a mother for quite some time. Although she had, at first, refused the proposal of Aaron Lazarus (no relation to the poet Emma Lazarus), a widower with seven children, she eventually accepted, and at the age of thirty-two, she married him, after he assured her that educating his children would not be part of her duties as wife. In due course, as what she called the "evil" consequence of the happiness she and her husband shared, Rachel Lazarus gave birth to the first of her four children.

Expanding women's education in the new republic was not intended to benefit women, but to enable them to converse intelligently with their husbands, instill patriotism in their children, and run enlightened homes. Unexpectedly, gaining education enlarged women's desires. Even as most Jewish women found fulfillment as wives and mothers, some embarked on other paths. Some of those educated at the new female academies, like the one the Mordecais ran, became teachers, social reformers, and writers.

HISTORIANS FIRST stumbled on Rachel Mordecai not as an educator but as a letter writer. Her private correspondence with the Anglo-Irish novelist Maria Edgeworth, like that of Grace Nathan with her relatives, prefigured Jewish women's entrée into the world of American letters. Mordecai had long admired Edgeworth. But when the author published a novel whose despicable villain, unfortunately named Mr. Mordicai, chases his debtors to their deathbeds, the fan accused the novelist of unjustly portraying the Jewish people, "this race of men," as mean, rapacious, and immoral. Edgeworth's response was to publish a new novel whose appealing Jewish characters she based on her new friend Miss Mordecai. A lifetime of letters between the two sailed across the Atlantic.[47]

Rachel Mordecai Lazarus sits among a coterie of nineteenth-century Jewish female writers. Surely she never expected, nor had Grace Nathan, that someday others would read their personal correspondence. But other Jewish women, seeing "the sons and daughters of our tribe" exhilarated by the "gas of inspiration," wrote for the public, speaking up for their sex, their country, and their people.[48]

In 1819, so inspired, twenty-two-year-old Penina Moïse published her first poem in a local Charleston newspaper. For the next sixty years, newspapers and magazines from Charleston to Boston—including *Godey's Lady's Book*, whose midcentury circulation of 150,000 made it the most widely read periodical of its day—printed her poems, stories, and essays.

Some of Moïse's poems meditated on national and world events—Napoleon's defeat, an American martyr hanged by the British for treason. Judaism infused other writings of this woman who was also a teacher and Hebrew Sunday school principal. Anthologized with Charleston's best writers, she celebrated the biblical Miriam. When Moïse called to the "Daughters of Israel, arise! / The Sabbath morn to greet," she spoke to some of the first Reform Jewish women in America.[49]

Immigrant Jews and rabbis from German-speaking lands, coming to the United States in the mid-nineteenth century, brought over ideas about reforming Judaism. Yet even before most of them landed, a call for religious reform rang out in Moïse's hometown. In 1824 forty-seven men, appalled by the neglect of Judaism they saw around them and worried about their children's Jewish futures, petitioned Kahal Kadosh Beth Elohim, Charleston's only synagogue, to institute reforms. Aware of religious changes already under way in Germany, claiming that they had no intention of destroying Judaism but rather of adapting it to their age, they called for a shorter service with prayers and a sermon in English. It made no sense, they argued, to pray in a language no one understood. When Beth Elohim rejected the petition, the young men established the Reformed Society of Israelites. Perhaps Penina joined them in their monthly meetings; her brother Abraham was one of its leaders.

In any event, the Reformed Society never erected its own building. Instead, about a decade later, its remaining members returned to Beth Elohim and turned it into a Reform congregation. Installing an organ, they broke with the Jewish tradition of not playing instruments on Sabbaths and holidays, a practice that avoided the possibility of transgressing the biblical prohibition against work on the days of rest. Organs became hallmarks of Reform congregations. Penina wrote four-fifths of the songs in Beth Elohim's 1842 hymnal.

She also cried out to unfortunates persecuted abroad, including her own "oppressed race," urging them to brave the journey and come to this land of liberty. She thus anticipated by more than half a century Emma Lazarus's call to the "huddled masses yearning to breathe free."⁵⁰

Long before Lazarus wrote that line in "The New Colossus," she had written reams of poetry and prose, essays and journalism, and a novel and stories. In her short life—she died at the age of thirty-eight—she conversed with a wide circle of Christians and Jews, at home and abroad. Yet somehow she was never fully comfortable among either. A social divide separated, observed one who met Lazarus, the "real unconverted Jew (who had no objection to calling herself one)" from the Gentile.⁵¹

Yet for much of her life, Lazarus also felt like an outsider among Jews. Her great-grandmother had been devout, but Lazarus was distant from Judaism's rites and rituals. Only later would she feel compelled, as Mordecai had been, to take up her pen to defend her people.

"How abundantly the good seed spreads when planted"

NINETEENTH-CENTURY American men and women trumpeted the notion that they inhabited separate spheres. His were the public spaces of work and politics; hers, the domestic private realm. Of course, the reality and diversity of women's lives belied this notion, no matter how many tracts, essays, and men insisted on it. After all, Moïse and Lazarus and many other American women lived in both private and public realms.

American women left their homes, crossing their thresholds to step into all sorts of public associations. They established churches, hospitals, and schools. They organized societies to eradicate the nation's many ills—poverty, alcoholism, prostitution, slavery, even dueling. Joining her Christian neighbors in this important work, Philadelphia's Rebecca Gratz proclaimed: "How abundantly the good seed spreads when planted." In time, those seeds sprouted into a vibrant Jewish women's culture, a small foundation stone of the nation's civil society.⁵²

As the nineteenth century dawned, Rebecca Gratz, Rebecca Phillips, and more than a dozen other Philadelphia women—fifteen Christians, eight Jews—emulating the biblical woman of valor who "gives generously to the poor" (Prov. 31:20), founded the Female Association for the Relief of Women and Children in Reduced Circumstances. Twenty years earlier, during the Revolutionary War, a Philadelphia Ladies' Association had stitched over two thousand shirts for Washington's troops, each embroidered with the name of the woman who had sewn it. No Jewish women's names are found in its records. But in a new century, in a new republic, women from the same economic and social class crossed religious lines to aid gentlewomen and their unfortunate children who had fallen on hard times.[53]

Gratz, the Female Association's first secretary, held the post for twenty-two years. Born as the nation was coalescing, growing up in an observant home among the city's social and literary elites, she became, as a single woman, the nurse to her parents and siblings. When her sister Rachel died in childbirth, Rebecca, who never wed—according to an unsubstantiated legend, she loved a Christian but refused to intermarry—took her six half-orphaned nieces and nephews into her own home. She raised these children, even as she helped found and sustain women's organizations.[54]

The Female Association typified her endeavors. It aided only what were called the worthy poor, women who had once known better days but who were reduced to poverty by the death of a husband or a catastrophe, like a fire. This idea of parsing the poor into the deserving because of circumstances and the undeserving because of laziness or nature was the norm then and continues to this day. Not only did its members scrutinize who should receive their funds, but they also carefully safeguarded their treasury. Their constitution required that the treasurer be unmarried. If she married, she had to immediately resign, because in the 1800s the law was that, when a woman wed, her husband was entitled to manage her property. Gratz rightly feared that a married treasurer's husband might seize their assets. In every organization she helped lead, she made certain that women controlled the money.[55]

By 1829, Philadelphia had thirty-three female societies. Gratz helped found another of these, the nonsectarian Orphan Society, and was its secretary for nearly four decades. But because charitable Protestants offered the needy material aid with one hand and salvation through their religion with the other, Quaker and Catholic women created their own societies to help their impoverished women and children. Philadelphia's Jewish women, led by Gratz, did the same.

The Female Hebrew Benevolent Society, which she and other Philadelphia women established in 1819, became a model for Jewish women around the nation. A year later, when Shearith Israel established its female benevolent society, Emma Lazarus's mother Esther—Grace Nathan's granddaughter—was a founding member.

Gratz proved prescient in anticipating a growing need for Jewish women's benevolence. There were perhaps 3,000 Jews in America in 1820, but by the time she died in 1869, the number was closer to 200,000, the result of increased Jewish immigration from German states and elsewhere in Central Europe. The number of needy Jewish women grew exponentially. In Philadelphia, the Ladies' Hebrew Relief Sewing Association dispensed, in its very first year, over a thousand items of clothing, shoes, and blankets to the Jewish poor.[56]

Philadelphia's Female Hebrew Benevolent Society helped those they deemed honest, industrious women of good character and their children, who suffered from sickness and misfortune. It assisted recent immigrants starving in this land, peddlers with baskets still filled at the end of the day, and women widowed or deserted or married to men who could not support them. At Shearith Israel, the women ventured into the city's poorest wards, traversing filthy alleys, to bring food, clothing, and fuel to the hovels of the destitute.[57]

Nearly two decades later, taking another lesson from Christian women, Gratz founded the first Hebrew Sunday school. Protestant Sunday schools had appeared in the early republic to teach a bit of reading and writing to poor working children on their only day of rest. By the 1820s, as free public schools emerged across the nation, those Sunday schools were replaced by evangelical ones bent on imparting Protestant values, like self-discipline and orderliness, and teaching the young the Bible and the word of God. Philadelphia's American Sunday School Union boasted, in 1832, that it reached more than a quarter of the city's children.[58]

Gratz wanted to make certain that poor Jewish children, unschooled in their own faith and drawn perhaps by a warm place to spend a Sunday, were not among them. The state of Jewish education in America was then deplorable. There were few schools for Jewish children. Inspired by the Protestant Sunday school, Gratz, supported by Isaac Leeser, the spiritual leader of Philadelphia's Mikveh Israel congregation, invented the Hebrew Sunday school in 1838.

Because there were no Jewish primers available or even a Jewish English Bible translation, the American Sunday School Union helped out. It gave Gratz copies of the King James Bible and a child's catechism; she and the other teachers cut out and pasted over passages referring to Jesus. The few hours spent on Sunday morning opened with an assembly, prayer, and a scriptural reading, likely from the week's Torah portion. Then the students broke into classes by age: the youngest learned to recite the *Sh'ma*, Judaism's central prayer, "Hear O Israel, the Lord our God, the Lord is One," while the oldest mastered selected biblical books. Students demonstrated what they had accomplished at annual public exams, where the best and brightest of the young female graduates were recruited to join the school's teaching staff.[59]

Gratz thus not only inaugurated a new American-style system of Jewish education, but also launched women into careers as Jewish educators and religious authorities for children. For the first time in America, women became teachers of Judaism outside the confines of their homes. The idea quickly spread to Baltimore and Charleston, where Penina Moïse would head that Hebrew Sunday school, and traveled all the way to Australia.

In her seventies, the indefatigable Gratz and a group of women, moved by poor Jewish children peddling matches on Philadelphia's streets, embarked on yet another venture, establishing, in 1855, the first orphanage for Jewish children in the United States. During the heyday of building foundling homes, orphanages, and reformatories to shelter the children of the immigrant poor and those orphaned during the Civil War, Jewish foster homes appeared in a dozen cities from Cleveland to New Orleans, New York to San Francisco. Many of their wards were fatherless children whose widowed or deserted mothers could not afford to keep them.[60]

Life in these harsh institutions was highly regimented. Children wore uniforms. Orphans, never to be pampered, took cold showers. Bells segmented the day, announcing when to march from dormitory to morning prayers to dining room to schoolroom. Older girls did housework. The food was kosher, but there was not always enough to eat. Rabbis came by to give religious instruction. Although corporal punishment was limited to serious offenses, an alumnus of one remembered the screams of two little girls beaten for wetting their beds. Evenings were spent doing homework; bedtime was at nine p.m.

The orphanages employed teachers—surely some of them were Jewish women—who taught girls embroidery, dressmaking, and how to operate a sewing machine, skills they would need for an expected brief stint in the workforce until they married. They taught boys to work in trades or commerce to be able to fend for themselves after they graduated at fourteen or fifteen.

For almost twenty years, Philadelphia's Jewish women ran their foster home, giving prosperous women another venue for activity at a time when such endeavors were deemed woman's work. Then, perhaps because of growing demands and the need for more secure financing, the orphanage's control was transferred to a male board of managers. For a time, a ladies' associate board handled internal affairs—admissions, hiring staff, curriculum, and religious instruction. Eventually, men took over those too, leaving to Jewish women to plan fundraisers and entertainments for the children.

GRATZ'S TOWERING legacy of communal and religious leadership makes her one of the exceptional women in this book, one of a cohort of unmarried women, Christian and Jew, of her day who put religion at the core of their lives. They went to church or synagogue, taught Sunday school, cared for the sick and the needy, and shouldered responsibilities for their households and extended family. Gratz saw her three married sisters through twenty-seven childbirths and became a second mother to her half-orphaned nieces and nephews. But her single life gave her the independence and the freedom needed for public endeavors.

If, in never marrying, she and the coterie of similarly self-reliant, single Jewish women, with whom she worked, were atypical of Jewish women then—and we can only presume that most married, as there are no statistics on it—they were not alone in Philadelphia. A significant proportion—in some places a quarter, perhaps more—of Quaker women never wed.[61]

Long before government agencies helped those set adrift in a nation unsettled by urbanization, industrialization, and immigration, women like Gratz and her Philadelphia group provided critical social services. Whatever their opinion of marriage—and Rebecca Gratz wondered why there were so few examples of joyful marriages and thought little was more "destructive to happiness" than a miserable one—single women exercised authority and influence in the institutions they ran. The nineteenth-century Jewish women who never wed—and Henrietta Szold, whom we will meet in the next chapter, stands with them—carved out lives of great purpose and service to their communities and country.[62]

"The emancipation of the Jewish woman was begun in Albany"

MEANWHILE synagogues and churches were also undergoing change. Churches that had once segregated men and women during prayer now sat them together in family pews. During the evangelical revival of the Second Great Awakening, Methodist and Baptist women had preached in public. Christian women were finding new callings, joining missions, organizing Sunday schools, and teaching the Bible.

In Europe, notions about liberalizing Judaism and modernizing worship were part of Jews' rush to leave the ghettoes behind. As new governments embraced Enlightenment ideals about the separation of church and state, they began accepting Jews as full citizens. But Jews knew that their part of the bargain for emancipation from the ghettoes required adapting Judaism to the modern world. The extent of adaptations deemed permissible—which Jewish laws and customs, if any, could be modified or even jettisoned—would fix the lines among the different expressions of Judaism in synagogues in Europe and the United States.

America had no ordained rabbi leading a congregation before 1840. American Jewish religious leaders, like Gershom Mendes Seixas, Grace Nathan's brother, and Isaac Leeser, who led the synagogue where Rebecca Gratz worshipped, were lay ministers, who led services and officiated at weddings and funerals. After Abraham Rice, the first ordained rabbi in the United States, made his way to Baltimore, he wrote Leeser, asking if there was some way to compel "every married Jewish lady" to go to the *mikveh*. We do not have Leeser's response, but it is doubtful that he answered yes.[63]

In America, even traditionalist leaders like Leeser recognized the need for some religious accommodations. Soon after he arrived in Philadelphia in 1829, Gratz and other women in the synagogue asked him to deliver weekly sermons in English. The men of the board of the congregation opposed the move, but he prevailed and began preaching on Sabbaths.[64]

Synagogues cropped up wherever Jewish immigrants found a foothold in the new nation as it extended from sea to sea, and with them, the impetus toward reforming Judaism that had surfaced in Charleston gained traction. Laymen and the rabbis who followed Abraham Rice, among them the architect of American Reform Judaism, Isaac Mayer Wise, experimented further with modernizing Judaism. As the Reformed Society of Israelites had done, these men first eliminated prayers, shortened services, and added English readings and sermons. Some congregations followed Beth Elohim, installing organs. Into the twentieth century, Reform worshippers sang hymns composed by Penina Moïse, without knowing she was their author.[65]

Reformers introduced other changes to adapt and American-ize Judaism. Since Christian men doff their hats, out of respect, on entering a church, Jewish men began doing the same, eliminating the skullcaps they typically wore—if not always, as Jewish custom prescribes, then at least in synagogue. Where there were enough Jews in a town or city to argue over the organ and skullcaps, the community divided along religious lines into two or more syna-gogues. Eventually, the distance among these different expressions of Judaism would widen as Reform Jews accepted as binding only Judaism's moral laws and preserved only those ceremonies and rit-uals that elevated and sanctified their lives.

As Judaism began changing in Europe and the United States, some rabbis and laymen began scrutinizing women's roles. For example, with men and women singing together in churches, some Jewish congregations copied them. They invited women to join their choirs to inspire the worshippers with four-part harmony accompanied by the organ. Unsurprisingly, the innovations sparked dissent.

Soon another instance of women's power to disrupt surfaced. In 1851 Isaac Mayer Wise introduced mixed seating. His new congre-gation had recently purchased a church. Rather than renovating it to build the women's gallery, husbands and wives sat together in its pews. Wise boasted that he had begun "the emancipation of the Jewish woman . . . in Albany." However, it is likely that economy rather than any burning desire to equalize women's status propelled this radical departure. As other synagogues followed Albany's lead, whether families sat together or men and women sat separately during services eventually marked the dividing line in America between the branches of Reform and Conservative Judaism and Orthodoxy.[66]

At the same time, confirmation for boys and for girls won fairly wide acceptance. Invented by reformers in Germany early in the nineteenth century as a replacement for bar mitzvah, the Jewish confirmation mimicked the Christian, where the ceremony marked coming-of-age in the church. In the bar mitzvah, when a thirteen-year-old boy became an adult member of the congregation, he would be called to the Torah and might discourse on rabbinic interpretations of the text. Confirmation generally required the ability to answer questions on Judaism's principles and faith, to master a catechism as Christian youth did. Rabbis gravitated to confirmation, aware that the lack of an equivalent to a bar mitzvah for girls—bat mitzvah did not then exist—signaled that Judaism seemed to disparage the female sex. Confirmation thus opened a new avenue for Jewish girls' education outside the Hebrew Sunday schools.

In the first confirmation in America, in New York in 1846, sixteen boys and girls, who had been instructed for six months by their rabbi, Max Lilienthal, were confirmed during the holiday of Shavuot, which falls in May or June and commemorates the giving of the Torah on Mount Sinai. Even rabbis, not considered reformers, embraced confirmation for its educational value.[67]

The ceremonies varied widely. Boys and girls were confirmed at the same age, although according to Jewish tradition, girls reach maturity at age twelve. But at their confirmations, the children might be thirteen, fourteen, or fifteen. The ceremonies gave new meaning to the holiday of Shavuot. They were widely attended, frequently lavish spectacles. At that first one in New York, reportedly fifteen hundred people came to see those sixteen boys and girls confirmed. In some Reform synagogues, confirmation replaced bar mitzvah; in others, it did not.

Emily Fechheimer (later Seasongood) recalled her 1864 confirmation in Cincinnati by Rabbi Wise. He had left Albany a few years before for what was then dubbed "the queen city of the west," where he remained for the rest of his long career. Hundreds of confirmation class photos lining the corridors of synagogues across America suggest that she was wearing a white dress, as Christian girls did at communion, as she and her classmates filed solemnly into the sanctuary. The girls carried bouquets that they placed on the pulpit as offerings. Emily recited a poem in English, and, according to Rabbi Wise, the children led the service, taking the Torah out of the ark and pledging to live according to Judaism's sacred precepts. Afterward Emily returned home to receive congratulations and display her gifts, including a silver filigree bouquet holder, in the parlor.[68]

Other Jewish leaders were also enlarging women's religious lives. New York Rabbi Morris Raphall published the first American prayer book for "Maidens, Brides, Wives, Mothers" in 1852. He modeled its English prayers for moments of joy or "trial, incidental to their sex," on the *techines*, European books of Yiddish prayers women recited as they baked the Sabbath challah and surfaced from the *mikveh*. In 1869 a group of rabbis meeting in Philadelphia decided that, instead of only being acted upon, the time had come for the bride to speak in the service and to give her groom a ring. These modest developments affecting women's religious experiences were welcomed by some, denounced by others. But they did not satisfy the spiritual yearnings of all.[69]

MARRIAGE IN 1821 brought Rachel Lazarus to Wilmington, North Carolina. Its Jewish community was so tiny that it could not muster the quorum of ten men required for prayer. The Lazaruses observed Sabbaths and High Holidays in private at home. One Yom Kippur, Rachel, disregarding the custom that only men read the service, conducted it herself. But on Sundays, seeking community and religious inspiration and convinced that they could worship their God anywhere, the Lazaruses joined their neighbors in the pews of St. James Episcopal Church.

Rachel, contrasting those services with Jewish worship, became increasingly dissatisfied. She yearned to study the Bible, like her Christian neighbors, and to hear explications of its lessons. Finding little to sustain her soul in Judaism, she was drawn to Christianity. As she spoke of her newfound love for Jesus, a rift cracked the bedrock of her home. Her husband threatened that, if she were to convert, he would take their children away. That was more than Rachel could bear until, on her deathbed, she received baptism. Rachel Lazarus, born a Jew, died a Christian.

Still, other American women found their way to Judaism. Caroline Hamlin's Quaker family traced their roots in the New World to 1637, just three decades after an English colony was founded at Jamestown. Marcus Spiegel had left Germany after the failed revolution of 1848. Peddling on the byways of Ohio, he met Caroline, and they wed. After a time spent studying Judaism, German, and auspiciously, Jewish cooking, Caroline converted. She raised their five children in her adopted faith.

"Write . . . long loving letters . . . to a Soldier"

IN FEBRUARY 1862, from Paw Paw, Virginia, Marcus Spiegel wrote to his beloved wife Caroline: "write . . . long loving letters . . . to a Soldier . . . whose whole soul is home, home, Sweet home." Two months earlier he had enlisted in the Union Army. The Spiegels' separation mirrors one of the paramount experiences of women, North and South, Christian and Jew, during the Civil War. As men went off to war, they left behind wives, mothers, and daughters. While the greater number of American Jews lived behind Union lines, women, whether of the Union or of the Confederacy, found themselves carrying unexpected responsibilities and sustaining their cause, as their great-grandmothers had during the Revolution.[70]

Of the more than two million men who fought in the Civil War, only eight to ten thousand were Jews; of these, two to three thousand fought for the Confederacy. Southern Jewish women stood with their neighbors in supporting their states' rights to secede. When South Carolina left the Union, Penina Moïse wrote that the patriots of the "Palmetto State . . . [would] engage hand to hand / Any foe that dare enter its gate." Miriam Moses Cohen, one of the nieces Rebecca Gratz raised, married a southern slaveholder and moved to Charleston and then to Savannah. She too came to defend the South, condemning abolitionists for wanting to destroy its way of life. Catherine Ezekiel, mother of the sculptor Moses whose memorial to the Confederates stands in Arlington National Cemetery, sent him off to war. She "would not own a son who would not fight for his home and country." Northern Jewish women supported their side. The mother of Fifth Kansas Cavalryman August Bondi told him that, as a Jew, he was obliged to defend the Union "which gave equal rights to all beliefs."[71]

Northern women rarely suffered war's horrors or the material deprivations Southerners faced under blockade as the war dragged on. Southern women discovered just how much the lives they had known before the war depended on the protection of their men and on the labor of the enslaved people those men managed. For Southern women, the war meant rage against the Union and its occupation as the Union advanced. For women North and South, it meant launching hundreds of women's organizations to do all they could to help their soldiers.

The rare Civil War diary of a Jew in her teen years living in New Orleans, the largest city in the South, offers a glimpse into the world of the Confederacy. Growing up, Clara Solomon became convinced that the South must triumph or perish. She followed the war and its battles closely. She ached as her father was called away to supply the troops in Virginia. Clara joined her schoolmates in packing boxes of bandages, medicines, and preserves to send to the wounded in hospitals, and she read, with tears streaming down her cheeks, the long lists of the dead printed in the paper.

For Clara, the fall of New Orleans and its occupation by Yankee troops brought great humiliation. She railed against Gen. Benjamin F. Butler, the commander of the occupation, confiding to her diary: "If he could only have as many ropes around his neck as there are ladies in the city & each have a pull! Or if we could fry him!"[72]

She was not the only New Orleans Jewish woman to wish harm to the ruthless "Beast" Butler who resorted to violence to bring hostile civilians under control. As the women of New Orleans refused to be cowed, General Butler waged war on the honor of Southern womanhood. He ordered that any woman showing "contempt for any officer or soldier of the United States" be "treated as a woman of the town [prostitute] plying her avocation." If the women would not behave like ladies, he would treat them just as they behaved, and prostitutes were sometimes arrested.[73]

Eugenia Levy Phillips, a "fire-eating secessionist in skirts," faced off with Butler. Describing herself as a weak, wretched woman, Mrs. Phillips—wed when she was sixteen and bearer of nine children—was imprisoned twice for her Confederate sympathies. The first time, suspected of espionage in Washington as war broke out, she whispered to her Irish maid to destroy her correspondence even as soldiers were searching her home. The second time, in New Orleans, Butler charged her with mocking the funeral procession of a Union officer. When she retorted that she "was in good spirits" that day, the general became so outraged that he sentenced her to be imprisoned at Ship Island, a disease-ridden, bug-infested sandbar off the coast.[74]

Phillips was not the only ardent patriot in her family. Her sister Phoebe Pember also served the Confederacy. During the war, women North and South, bereft of breadwinners and living in economies with labor shortages, took up paid employment. The U.S. publication of Florence Nightingale's *Notes on Nursing* made the occupation respectable for women. The Confederate Congress, recognizing the superior care the wounded received when women did the nursing, created matrons' positions in military hospitals. Pember, a thirty-nine-year-old widow living unhappily with relatives, leaped at the chance to change her lot.

Although southern women, like Rachel Lazarus's sister Emma Mordecai, visited the wounded in hospitals, genteel ladies mostly eschewed matron's positions as an assault on their delicacy and refinement. In contrast, Pember embraced the hard work of keeping house, cooking, and nursing thousands of men. She killed chickens to make soup, guarded food against wanton pilfering, hired and fired staff, and won the "wars of the whiskey barrel," giving the matrons control over the Civil War's chief painkiller. She wrote letters home for illiterate soldiers and read the Bible to comfort the ill. She dressed wounds and eventually became inured to the dead.[75]

Surely she sensed the antisemitism spiking during the Civil War. Christian teachings, across the centuries, blamed the Jews for murdering Jesus. When Christianity became dominant in Western civilization, governments and churches punished the Jews for

that crime and for stubbornly remaining Jews rather than accepting Christianity. Sometimes those punishments took the form of
violence. More often they came as legislation limiting where Jews
could live and the kind of work they could do, accompanied by stereotypes depicting Jews as avaricious, greedy, and conniving.

These ideas so permeated America that antisemitism, a term
coined in Europe only in 1879, was a fact of life for America's Jews
since they first set foot on its soil. In 1654 New Amsterdam's governor Peter Stuyvesant tried to eject the Jews who had just arrived,
calling them members of a "deceitful race—such hateful enemies
and blasphemers of the name of Christ." The pastor of the Salzburg
Lutherans, who came to Savannah in the colonial period and break-
fasted with Benjamin and Perla Sheftall, counted them as friends.
He planned to preach to them Christ's gospel and bring them to
the light.[76]

While Emma Lazarus recalled the expulsion of her ancestors
from Spain, Penina Moïse had no need to look to the past. In "Lines
on the Persecution of the Jews of Damascus," she envisioned the
agony of thirteen members of that community, imprisoned and tor-
tured, accused, in 1840, of murdering a Christian monk to use his
blood for religious purposes.[77]

But America's Jewish women did not have to look to history or
overseas to experience antisemitism. Their children might stumble
on a verse in Mother Goose: "Jack sold his egg / To a rogue of a Jew
/ Who cheated him out / Of half of his due." The American Sunday
School Union's The Young Jew explained that Jews had no country
of their own, God having punished them for disobedience. In the
1855 novel The Prince of the House of David, which reportedly sold
between four and five million copies, its author, an Episcopal priest,
addressed "the daughters of Israel, the country-women of Mary,"
hoping to persuade them "that this is the very Christ."[78]

Eras of anxiety, disappointment, and insecurity fuel antisemitism. The Civil War saw the worst period in the United States to
date. Newspapers north and south accused Jews, "the people whose
ancestors smuggled for eighteen centuries," of profiting from the
war. By far the worst episode was General Ulysses S. Grant's 1862

General Orders No. 11, expelling the "Jews, as a class," from the vast Department of Tennessee, then under his command that stretched from southern Illinois to the Gulf of Mexico. In Paducah, Kentucky, in the rush to leave, one mother, it was said, almost left her baby behind; two dying women could not be moved and had to stay in the care of a neighbor. Although President Lincoln countermanded the order, the legacy of an expulsion on American soil painfully echoed Jewish experience across the ages.[79]

Unsurprisingly then, during the war, Jewish women tended to mask their Jewish difference. Emma Mordecai fled embattled Richmond, the capital of the Confederacy, where she taught Hebrew Sunday school, for the safety of her Christian sister-in-law's farm on the city's outskirts. There she read the Jewish service quietly in her room on Saturdays and, on Sundays, occasionally went to church with her sister-in-law.[80]

Pember avoided telling those she worked with that she was a Jew. Instead, she voiced her hatred for the Yankees. But one evening, after a woman requested a "Yankee Skull" for her trinkets, she broke her silence. Turning to the company, she confessed that she was glad to have been born in a faith that did not command, love your enemies. She even jested that, until the war ended, they should all join her church.[81]

As the war turned against the Confederacy, the situation in Richmond, where Pember was posted, became increasingly desperate. When the city was evacuated in April 1865, she stayed, with pistol cocked in her pocket, to do her duty. She continued to nurse the sick until all had either convalesced or died, her vocation at an end.

WOMEN'S WARTIME experiences in the North mirrored those in the South. Anxiously, they too awaited news of their loved ones. They nursed the wounded, although no northern Jewish woman left a wartime record to match that of Phoebe Pember.

Northern women also organized to do their part, as had Clara

Solomon's schoolmates. In Quincy, Illinois, nineteen-year-old Annie Jonas (later Wells), whose father Abraham Jonas was a friend of Abraham Lincoln, became treasurer of the Needle Pickets, a soldiers' aid society representing the town's leading families. Before the war, her neighbors would have met at church in sewing and missionary societies that excluded Annie. Now they could work together to support the war. That she was elected treasurer was a sign of their esteem.[82]

The Needle Pickets met regularly to roll bandages. They "scraped lint," running a knife over stretched linen to gather fibers to dress wounds. Monthly dues, substantial enough to limit membership to the town's elite, raised funds. The Needle Pickets helped the wounded—donating lard, honey, butter, thread, Bibles, and prayer books to Quincy hospitals, including the "Negro hospital"—and to the widows and children Union soldiers left behind.

Jonas was one of only four Jewish women to join the Needle Pickets. The daughter of a British-born father and American-born mother, educated in Quincy schools, she likely had more in common with its members than with the women of the local Hebrew Ladies' Benevolent Society, who were mostly German-speaking immigrants. Its members did the same kinds of war work and donated the funds they raised to the Needle Pickets.

Elsewhere, Jewish sisters in arms in Philadelphia, Boston, Chicago, and New York, where surely the women of the Lazarus clan were among them, packed care packages for soldiers and the wounded, no matter their religious creed. They too visited hospitals and the families of men away at war. They knitted earmuffs and sent crates of supplies filled with flannel shirts, pickles, envelopes, and pencils to army hospitals in the field.[83]

Their aid formed a tiny part of a far-reaching network of Northern women massed to sustain the largest military operation ever on American soil. Just as men from every sector of the Union took up arms, women—Christian and Jew, the well-to-do and those struggling to make ends meet—did their part for their cause. Much of their work was coordinated through the U.S. Sanitary Commission, established by the federal government to centralize local relief efforts. Philadelphia's Ladies Hebrew Association for the Relief of Sick and Wounded Union Soldiers sent its own representative to the commission.

In addition to directing the dispensing of supplies and medicines, the commission promoted patriotic fundraisers called sanitary fairs, modeled on women's antebellum charity and church fairs, among them Jewish women's own modest fairs. As fair frenzy took hold, Jewish women stood side by side with their neighbors, selling refreshments and homemade goods—pincushions, pot holders, and pencil cases—and staging entertainments. At the sanitary fair in the nation's capital, the Hebrew Society's table raised almost one-tenth of the total receipts for the day. "All honor to our fair Jewesses!" boasted *The Jewish Messenger* with pride.[84]

WOMEN MIGHT lobby on behalf of their husbands at war. In December 1861, eight months after the war started, Septima Levy, born in Charleston, married, in Philadelphia, Charles T. Collis, a Union soldier. Unfortunately, she says nothing about the romance that led her, a Southerner, to become a Northerner.

But she does recount her audience with President Lincoln. She asked him to promote her husband. The president responded that the soldier was too young to be a general. She shot back: "He is not too young to be killed in the service and make me a widow." Lincoln eventually did nominate Charles Collis to the brevet grade of brigadier general, but not until late in 1864. As the wife of a high-ranking Union officer, Septima joined her husband, and Mrs. Ulysses S. Grant, in the field at military headquarters, where she found life, with its dinners, balls, and races, quite gay.[85]

For many women during the Civil War, their paramount experience was not a meeting with the president or a sanitary fair but the absence of their men. Surely, Caroline Spiegel's experiences were typical. In her husband's absence, she had to run the household and manage its finances. Marcus let her know how much of his army pay he was sending home to help her budget. She asked him about money he was owed and how she should go about getting it. When he wanted a command in a new regiment, he asked his wife to intercede for him. She may not have braved meeting the governor, but he was promoted from captain to colonel.

She tried to ease her beloved's life in the field. The Quaker who had learned German cooking to become a Jewess sent her husband his favorite cookies. She had a family portrait taken so that Marcus could gaze upon his loved ones. For his part, Marcus managed to secure a furlough in time to be with his wife during the birth of their fourth child; a subsequent leave left her pregnant.

Yet the wartime separation challenged the marriage. Caroline confessed that she had "the blues." Marcus recognized "the Heroism" of his wife living on her own. When she pleaded for him to resign his commission and come home, the colonel lectured her on duty to country and wished his wife were "a little more incoraging as to [his] military career."

Caroline was not alone in wishing her husband would leave the battlefield. Historians find that, as the war dragged on, Union husbands and wives argued. Wives begged husbands to return to farms and businesses; men scolded that they had to do their duty.

That may partly explain why two years into the war, Northern women found their patriotism questioned. The war, fought mostly on Confederate soil, threatened Southern women with the loss of their men, their homes, and their way of life. Northern women, distant from battlefields, were relatively unscathed. *The New York Herald* credited the rebellion's persistence to the fierce courage and indomitable energy Southern women displayed for their cause and threw blame for the Union's failure to end the war at the feet of Northern women. Had they displayed comparable zeal in encouraging "a loyal and devoted spirit among us," the *Herald* continued, our side would have prevailed by now.[86]

The *Herald* was not the only paper voicing disparaging comparisons as popular opinion against the war rose. In the midterm elections of 1862, Lincoln's Republicans lost their majority in the House of Representatives over failure to bring a speedy end to the conflict. The Emancipation Proclamation, freeing the enslaved in the rebel states but not in slaveholding states in the Union, and the imposition of a draft further fueled the fires of discontent.

Republican men responded by establishing Loyal Leagues to promote the Union cause. Republican women created female counterparts. Among those active in the Woman's Loyal National League was Ernestine Potowski Rose, an abolitionist and the leading Jewish woman's rights advocate of her day.

IN 1851 the Polish Jewish immigrant Ernestine Rose addressed the Second National Woman's Rights Convention in Worcester, Massachusetts. There she demanded: "It is high time . . . to compel man by the might of right to give to woman her political, legal and social rights."[87]

Only a few years before in 1848 in Seneca Falls, New York, the woman's rights movement, one of the great reform movements of the nineteenth century, had launched, when some three hundred women and men, echoing the Declaration of Independence, resolved, "We hold these truths to be self-evident: that all men *and women* are created equal."[88]

Born in Russian Poland, a self-described rebel at age five, Ernestine Potowski learned to read the Torah and then to spurn its patriarchal teaching of "your urge shall be for your husband, And he shall rule over you" (Gen. 3:16). When she was sixteen, she refused to marry the man her father had chosen. She then sued her father to keep the money she had inherited at her mother's death, which he had intended to use for her dowry. She won her suit and left Poland behind. [89]

Stopping over in England, where she polished her English, she met the social reformer and freethinker Robert Owen and became one of his followers. She married William Rose, another of his admirers. The Roses sailed to America in 1836, intending to establish a utopian socialist colony to plant Owen's ideas in the United States. But instead of heading into the hinterlands, when they landed in New York, they stayed.

Almost immediately, Ernestine plunged into politics, campaigning against the laws that gave husbands control of their wives' property, the same statutes that Rebecca Gratz had to circumvent to protect the treasuries of female organizations. In these first years, when Ernestine likely bore two children, home and family took precedence, and she lectured infrequently. Unfortunately, those children died young, leaving her free to crisscross the country by stagecoach and railroad. Crowned by the press "Queen of the Platform" for her masterful oratory, Rose, an ardent abolitionist and atheist, became a leader in the woman's rights movement. Praising her courage, her devoted husband supported her uncommon career as a political activist and public speaker.

When, during the war, Northern women's zeal for their cause was questioned, woman's rights activists convened the National Convention of the Loyal Women of the Republic. There Rose demanded freedom and justice for women as well as for black people. The end of slavery, the necessity for religious freedom, and the urgency of woman suffrage became her abiding passions.

A woman of fierce intellect and uncompromising convictions, Rose was the only Jewish woman to win acclaim as a suffragist in her day. That she did so at a time when the woman's rights movement carefully distanced itself from black and immigrant women, whose presence might undermine their cause with the men who controlled the ballot box, was all the more remarkable.

Rose stuck out not only as an immigrant and a Jew but also as an atheist in the Protestant-inflected reform movements of abolition and woman suffrage. Yet the freethinker remained marked as a Jew, and eventually, as Emma Lazarus would later do, she took up her prolific pen in defense of the Jewish people.

During the war, when Horace Seaver, the editor of the abolitionist *Boston Investigator*, vilified Jews as "about the worst people of whom we have any account," Rose, smelling "genuine Christian brimstone," jumped to their vindication. The unbeliever would not endorse Judaism—she supported no religion other than rationalism—but in the face of prejudice and injustice, she vociferously defended Jews as honest and upstanding citizens. She told

Seaver, "I don't like your prejudice against the Jews, nor against any other people; and above all, keep your temper in an argument."[90]

When Ernestine Rose met calumny against the Jewish nation, she leaped to its defense. Unusual, not only among nineteenth-century woman's rights reformers but also among immigrant Jewish women of her day, Rose, championing justice, blazed a trail of activism later Jewish women would proudly follow.

"I do not murmur at God's will":
War's Aftermath

WAR's END meant different things to Jewish women straddling the great divide. For Emma Mordecai, the final days of the war were harrowing. As the Confederates evacuated their capital, Richmond went up in flames, and her sister-in-law's farmhouse shook as gunboats exploded on the river. Braving danger, Emma ventured into the city to retrieve valuables stored in a bank, but the smoke and fear that the Yankees would soon arrive forced her to turn back. The South's defeat left her feeling "as if there was nothing more to live for in this world," but she would not "murmur at God's will." Another southern Jewish woman was less accepting of her fate. A staunch believer in the institution of slavery, she bemoaned how abolition had ruined her life. She sorely missed having enslaved people wait on her and added that she detested white servants.[91]

War's aftermath left Ernestine Rose dissatisfied too but for very different reasons. Alluding to Lincoln's famed speech that "a house divided against itself cannot stand," she fumed that her house was still divided, but no longer between slave and free. Instead, after the Fourteenth Amendment, it was divided between the enfranchised—white and black men—and the disenfranchised—white and black women.

For Rebecca Gratz, war's end eased her continual agitation over the fate of her loved ones on either side of the divide. During the war, she had corresponded across enemy lines with her politically divided family. Seeking to preserve its unity, she veiled her Unionist predilections and instead foregrounded her love of family. Writing to her niece in Savannah, she took consolation in knowing that "there was no war in our own hearts."[92]

The preservation of the Union left Caroline Spiegel a widow with five children forced to turn to the state for assistance. The federal government's new pension law, the most extensive social welfare system yet enacted, gave military widows eight dollars a month, as long as they did not remarry, and an additional two dollars per child. But that was not enough to sustain her large family. Spiegel rented out rooms, took in sewing, and putting to good use those lessons in German Jewish cooking, fed her Jewish and German boarders.

The southern Jewish women we have previously met in this book rebuilt their lives. Clara Solomon married and raised four daughters. Eugenia Phillips wrote a memoir, returned to Washington with her husband, and outlived him by eighteen years. Within the contours of marriage, children, widowhood, and old age, these women returned to lives of more tranquil domesticity.

Widowed, Phoebe Pember took to writing, publishing a memoir and stories in magazines, like *Harper's New Monthly*, and traveling to Europe. When she died, she was reunited in a Savannah graveyard with the gentile husband of her youth.[93]

Other southern Jewish women perpetuated what unrepentant Southerners called the Lost Cause. Octavia Harby Moses, whose eldest son was killed in action the day Gen. Robert E. Lee surrendered at Appomattox, presided over Sumter, South Carolina's, Ladies' Monumental Association. It was one of many white women's groups organized to re-inter soldiers from shallow battlefield graves to Confederate cemeteries and, building memorials to them, to honor their dead. When some of those cemeteries refused to bury fallen Hebrew soldiers, they were interred in a Jewish military cemetery in Richmond, where the Hebrew Ladies' Memorial Association for the Confederate Dead erected its own monument. Appealing for funds, they anticipated that, in days to come, voices would rise again to slander Jews, and that this memorial, with the names of Jewish men who had sacrificed their lives, would silence those who dared to question Jews' loyalty to their cause.[94]

WHEN CONFEDERATES fired on Fort Sumter in April 1861, eleven-year-old Emma Lazarus was living a life of privilege in New York City. Four years later, days after Lee surrendered to Grant, she wrote an elegy about hearts irrevocably broken by the war. A few years later, on "The Day of Dead Soldiers," she counseled the mothers, sisters, and widows decorating with flowers their Union "heroes' graves," not to mourn with wild grief but rather to display quiet resignation and pride in those who "left their land a fame so wide." Speaking with empathy as a woman, displaying her patriotism as an American, Lazarus would soon also speak out as a Jew.

2

"Mothers in Israel"

THE AMERICAN JEWESSES

O N A DREARY Sunday afternoon in March 1882, a ferry carried Emma Lazarus to a windswept island in New York's
East River. There, where the city buried its poor and locked
away destitute immigrants and the insane, two worlds converged.
Encountering a desperate mother whose emaciated baby lay dying,
Lazarus met the first wandering Jews of a "new exodus," the survivors of Russian atrocities. There, in the imposing State Emigrant
Refuge on Wards Island, a descendant of America's Jewish women,
who was one of the best-known Jewesses of the day, met the future.[1]

Lazarus's great-grandmother Grace Nathan represented the
past, her world that of the tiny Jewish community of colonial days
and the republic's first decades. Lazarus stood for the present generation, many of them the daughters of tens of thousands of Central
European Jewish immigrants, who, having come of age in America,
called themselves and were called by others American Jewesses.

But on this day, coinciding with the Jewish holiday of Purim,
Emma Lazarus saw, for the first time, "a new kind of Jewess." This
sorrowing young mother, fleeing the mayhem unleashed against
Jewish communities after Tsar Alexander II's assassination, was the
vanguard of the more than two million Eastern European Jews who
found refuge in America until its gates slammed shut in 1924. They
presaged the future.[2]

Meeting the first of the "huddled masses yearning to breathe free," Lazarus would call for a great movement to support their emigration. But she could not have anticipated that this "new kind of Jewess" and her daughters would eventually overwhelm the earlier American Jewesses of her world.[3]

IF THE PENNILESS Russian mother represented a new kind of Jewess, who was the old? A few, like Lazarus, were descendants of Jewish families from colonial times, but most had shallower roots in America. Between 1820 and 1880, about 150,000 Jews left primarily from the German states of Prussia and Bavaria; Austria-Hungary's Silesia, Styria, and Moravia; Poland's Poznań; and Alsace on the Franco-German border, and set off for America. Many, speaking Yiddish, came from villages and hamlets where, for generations, men had earned their living in trade and peddling. Some fled angry neighbors, yelling at them to get out and threatening violence. Others were spurred by shrinking economic opportunities, the results of expanding industrialization and urbanization and sundry laws fixing the maximum number of Jewish marriages. Those conditions also pushed Jews from these same towns and hamlets into growing European metropolises where they learned European languages, especially German, acquired education, became upwardly mobile, and adapted Judaism to the modern world. Some of these urban Jews also came to America.

In the United States, the new immigrants fanned across the nation as it extended from coast to coast. Settling in frontier towns, some of which eventually became cities, they founded Jewish communities across the land. Those who stayed on the East Coast challenged the domination of the lone synagogue, whose Sephardic rituals seemed so foreign to their Ashkenazic ways. These new Jewish immigrants founded many different congregations, fracturing the prominence of earlier synagogues.

By 1840, there were 15,000 Jews living among seventeen million Americans. By the time Lazarus took that ferry to Wards Island,

forty years later, there were 250,00 Jews among America's fifty million citizens, a great growth but still only a half a percent of its
population.[4]

The American Jewess

ONE OF the Jewish women who came during this time was Rosa
Fassel Sonneschein. Born in 1847, the daughter of a well-respected
liberal-minded rabbi from the Czech lands, she grew up in a town
in Hungary. There she acquired the kind of education rabbis often
permitted their daughters as well as their sons, studying at home,
learning about Judaism from her father, and attending high school.
Family lore claims that when she was sixteen, she rejected the first
two suitors her father proposed. A year later, while visiting a married sister living in Croatia, she met the local rabbi, Dr. Solomon
Hirsch Sonneschein. He was eight years her senior. They wed,
and a year after that, she gave birth to a son, the first of their four
children.[5]

The family moved to a larger congregation in Prague, where
Rosa gave birth to two daughters. In 1868 they set off for America.

Sophie Schaar was another woman who married a rabbi, her former tutor, Benjamin Szold. Leaving Styria, in Austria, in 1859, the
two set off for Baltimore's Congregation Oheb Shalom. There, a
year later, she gave birth to Henrietta, the eldest of her eight children, all girls. Two died in infancy, another as a very young child.

Rosa Sonneschein and Sophie Szold were atypical of the new-
comers. Most of the Jewish women here and the new ones coming to America married businessmen. Leaving Europe to seek their
fortunes across the sea, many of these men started out as peddlers,
crisscrossing the continent with packs on their backs, scrimping
until they had saved enough to find a spot for a store or a depot.
Settling down and opening a business—whether in the frontier
communities along the Mississippi and Ohio rivers; in growing cities like New Orleans, Cincinnati, and Chicago; or in small towns
dotting the South and West—meant it was time to marry. Running

a store required at least two people, someone to man the counter and another to keep the books and acquire the goods or even cook food to sell.

But where to find a wife? The first step was a journey. Leaving businesses behind in the care of partners or selling off everything they had, believing they could start anew, some men returned to Europe to find a bride. After five years in America, Julius Brooks regaled his Silesian hamlet with stories of riches for the taking and Indians rampaging on the warpath. When his starry-eyed niece begged to go to America with him, he replied: "The only way you can come is to marry me." Not long after, he and his sixteen-year-old bride, Fanny, crossed the Atlantic.[6]

Others did not journey as far. When the High Holidays came, itinerant peddlers would descend on a nearby Jewish community, spending the ten days between Rosh Hashanah and Yom Kippur searching for a wife. In 1845 Michael Greenebaum left a small village in the Rhine Palatinate for the frontier town of Chicago. A few years later, having heard that his cousins, the Spiegels, had landed in New York, he headed east to visit. He returned to the Windy City, where Indians wrapped in blankets walked the streets, with his bride, Sarah Spiegel. Michael Greenebaum helped found Chicago's first Reform congregation while his wife began populating it by giving birth to ten children. Greenebaum also brought the rest of his clan over to Chicago where he expected his unmarried sisters to find good husbands. Surely in this land of promise, they would be wealthy.[7]

European Jewish mothers and fathers, with nine or ten children, sometimes sent daughters off on their own to join relatives or friends who had already crossed the ocean. Here the young women would find husbands, and no man expected them to bring a dowry. In a nation that had more men than women, just being female was enough of a dowry. American Jewish men also advertised in German Jewish newspapers for brides. But only the poorest of the poor would agree to marry a man she had never met and become a mail-order bride.

Moving across the country—to mining camps in California and

the western territories; to cities like Rochester, Mobile, Denver, and Santa Fe—these Jewish women crossed the plains in covered wagons, as Fanny Brooks did; rode sternwheelers up the Mississippi; and logged hundreds of miles by stagecoach and railroad. One young bride surely spoke for most when she said it felt as if she were going to the end of the world. In harsh new climates, in foreign terrain—among people born in Europe, Africa, North and South America—Jewish women, a tiny minority in this vast land, planted their roots in new soil, as Rosa Sonneschein was about to do.[8]

SONNESCHEIN'S FAMILY landed in New York. After a short stint while her husband led a congregation there, they settled in St. Louis in 1869. There he led Congregation Shaare Emeth, one of the largest Reform synagogues in the Midwest.

Meanwhile the cosmopolitan Rosa, with her dark hair piled high atop her head, her waist cinched into frocks bought on return visits to the continent, made a home, bore her last child, and interested herself, as was appropriate for a rabbi's wife, in local and Jewish affairs. She led the "Ladies' Meetings" and organized choral societies at the synagogue. As the wife of a prominent member of the local clergy, she socialized outside the Jewish community and participated in St. Louis's vibrant cultural life, a legacy of the many German-speaking immigrants who made the city their home.

An avid reader since childhood, Sonneschein brought her love of learning to the city's Jewish women when she founded, in 1879, the Pioneers—one of hundreds, if not thousands, of women's literary and culture clubs popping up. They advanced female education in an era when only a tiny minority of women attended college. The Pioneers was perhaps the first Jewish women's literary society in America, a forerunner of today's many book clubs. Its members not only read books, but they also discussed music, essays, and current affairs and embarked on programs of self-study, occasionally on Jewish themes.[9]

As the children grew, Sonneschein made her first forays into journalism. She published a few short stories and wrote a column, "Our St. Louis Letter," under the pseudonym D'Arwin in the newspaper *The Jewish Messenger*. D'Arwin wondered why, as Reform Judaism advanced, women had not simultaneously progressed in their synagogues. When D'Arwin disclosed of her own accord that he was a she, Sonneschein explained that she had deliberately taken a man's name because everyone knew that in matters of religion, no one paid any attention to what women said. She argued that the columns she wrote before anyone knew that she was D'Arwin proved that intelligence was not the province of one sex, and that the thoughts of a female writer carried power equal to that of any man.[10]

Meanwhile, at home, the marriage was deeply unhappy. Even before the birth of their last child in 1873, Rosa had confided to a confidant that her husband was unfaithful, that he seduced the servants, that he drank, and that their troubles had started years before. She would have taken the children and fled to Europe were it not for the grief that would have caused to her elderly father. So she stayed in the marriage, announcing that one day she would indeed walk out.[11]

Rosa too often behaved in ways considered improper for the wife of a clergyman. Tongues wagged over her extravagant dress and household excess. Her circle inappropriately included a divorcée and journalists. People gossiped that she went bowling and gadded about too much in society. Of course, that the friend she confided in was a man, others would have considered unseemly.[12]

By 1891, with her father long dead and the children grown—the youngest was then eighteen—the couple separated. In the years when grounds for divorce were required, Sonneschein abandoned her husband and went to live in Chicago. In April 1893 their divorce was finalized. She had not contested the decree. "I wished to be rid of him, not ruin him," she told her grandson.[13]

A month later Rosa spoke about Austrian newspaper women at the Public Press Congress's Women's Auxiliary, convened as part of the Columbian Exposition, the world's fair in Chicago that marked the four-hundredth anniversary of Christopher Columbus's voyage to the New World. Just a few days before, she had likely heard Susan B. Anthony remark that the time was ripe for women to run their own newspapers.[14]

In St. Louis, Rosa must have known woman's magazine publisher Annie Laurie Y. Orff. Orff, representing Missouri on the World's Fair Board of Lady Managers, tasked with organizing women's participation in the fair, handed out concessions to Missouri craftswomen wishing to sell their wares there. Apparently her only taker was Sonneschein. Not only did Sonneschein speak at the fair, but she also made and sold her own bags in the Woman's Building. The fair had over 28 million visitors. At its close, Sonneschein had netted $5,000, the equivalent of more than $125,000 in 2016. Two years later, perhaps inspired by Orff's publishing success, or by Anthony's call for women to set up their own presses, and likely by another event at the fair, a Jewish Women's Congress—where Michael and Sarah Greenebaum's fourth child, now Hannah Solomon, presided—Sonneschein took those monies and founded *The American Jewess*. It would support her and "connect with the cord of mutual interest" Jewish women across the nation. It became the nation's first English-language Jewish women's magazine. It would not be the last.[15]

BETWEEN 1880 and 1895, the number of magazines published in the United States had more than doubled. Readership soared to tens of millions by the time *The American Jewess* debuted in April 1895. It was not, however, the first periodical for American Jewish women. Forty years before, Isaac Mayer Wise launched the German-language *Die Deborah* to appeal to "priestesses on the domestic altar" who, from that privileged perch, exerted a quiet influence over every aspect of life. But *The American Jewess* was never intended only for priestesses in their homes.[16]

Like other women's magazines of the day, *The American Jewess* wrote about hearth and household, published fiction, and reported on health, education, and fashion. But it also spoke to those interested in women's emancipation. In its first issue, Sonneschein over-confidently proclaimed that the nation had freed woman from the shackles of political, legal, and social inferiority. She demanded that Jewish men do the same for the Jewess.[17]

Obliterating prejudice would free her to become a "New Woman!" When this new woman first sauntered onto the stage is uncertain, but by the 1890s, she was the subject of a wide-ranging conversation. She was a suffragist, clubwoman, college girl, single woman, reformer, breadwinner. She sped into the future on bicycles, the new craze of the 1890s, never again to return to the slower pace women had kept in earlier days. She swam rivers, sailed the seas, golfed, and fished. No sport was too manly for her. Her presence called attention to what seemed to be seismic changes under way in women's roles. The new woman, diagnosing what was wrong with confining women to home and family, prescribed the remedy: to seek public voice and personal fulfillment. Suffragist Susan B. Anthony, social reformer Jane Addams, and Woman's Christian Temperance Union president Frances E. Willard were all new women, and so were those venturing forth on Chicago's new elevated trains with children in tow or off to work.[18]

Endorsing the new woman, *The American Jewess* printed articles hailing woman suffrage, as Colorado, Utah, and Idaho gave women the vote, writing that, if mothers had the vote, they would be better able to educate their sons about government and politics. But giving women the ballot was only one aim of female emancipation. In the pages of *The American Jewess*, dress reformers liberated her from the corset, applauded her wearing low-heeled shoes, and advised female bicyclists to don bloomers. Reporting on the purported legions of new women in the workforce, the monthly showcased the Rosenfeld sisters' typewriting business, with their six offices and contract for a monumental legal index. Sonneschein endorsed equal pay for equal work for men and women, a law Congress would not enact until 1963, even if the current reality does not meet the law.[19]

Yet with a circulation of 31,000, surely most of them homemakers, *The American Jewess* prudently included ambivalent articles about women at work. The life of a female breadwinner is not necessarily enviable, wrote one journalist. Women who worked, but who did not have to, displayed unhealthy aspirations, wrote another.[20]

But when it came to reporting Jewish women's achievements and demanding for them full religious and social equality, Sonneschein refused to equivocate. She touted Jewish women marching out of their homes and working to help their people and their nation. *The American Jewess* featured glowing reports of women's leadership of Denver's National Jewish Hospital, Philadelphia's Jewish Maternity Association, and Cleveland's Jewish Orphan Asylum. It paid special attention to the achievements of the National Council of Jewish Women.[21]

As for the synagogue, Sonneschein lauded all that had already been done to promote women's equality. Confirmation gave boys and girls the same obligations. Reformers had wisely eliminated the offensive Orthodox prayer thanking God for not making a man a woman, and sensibly liberated women from the balcony.[22]

Yet more must be done. Where were the women on Reform's Sabbath school boards? It was high time for women, married and single, to vote in their congregations. Sonneschein surveyed a hundred Reform, Conservative, and Orthodox synagogues and discovered that not one name on their membership rolls began with anything other than Mr. ———. Widows, who paid for their pews, suffered "Taxation without Representation!"[23]

The American Jewess also reported on what would become a major battle in the long struggle for female religious emancipation, "The Jewess in the Pulpit." In 1890, on the eve of Yom Kippur, in Spokane, Washington, Ray Frank, a charismatic teacher and lecturer, addressed a packed house, boasting that tonight she was the only Jewish woman in the world, perhaps the first since the days of the prophets, called to preach. The press ordained her "the girl rabbi of the golden west." But of course, Ray Frank was never ordained a rabbi, and no Jewish woman in America would be for nearly a century.[24]

Writing about domestic culture through a Jewish lens, championing new roles for women, and demanding religious emancipation, *The American Jewess*, in its brief life, showcased the new woman to

American Jews, until financial troubles compelled its shuttering at the end of the summer of 1899.

~✂✄~

WHEN *The American Jewess* reminded its readers that they were expected, as their mothers and grandmothers had been, to marry, editor Sonneschein was merely reaffirming the reigning American paradigm. In 1873, in denying lawyer Myra Bradwell's petition to enter the Illinois bar, the U.S. Supreme Court ruled that woman's destiny, as fixed by the Creator and man, was "to fulfill the noble and benign offices of wife and mother." The court, conceding that unmarried women did not suffer the incapacities associated with motherhood, nevertheless ruled that society could not rest on unusual exceptions to the natural order. That order circumscribed women within the roles of wife, mother, and homemaker, ensconced within circles of family and friends, mapped by social class, local community, and faith.[25]

The Jewish women who came in the mid- to later 1800s kept house, shopped, cooked, raised children, married them off, and nurtured grandchildren until it was time for their generation to pass. In their early years as struggling immigrants, they also, of necessity, helped out in the family business. Some of them gained wealth. Later, looking back on those hard times from a Fifth Avenue mansion, one recalled how, even when her babies were just days old, she sat up in bed sewing buttons between stints of nursing. Another, celebrated by hundreds at her golden wedding anniversary, remembered the trials of those early years. But by the time she died in 1908, she had long worn the mantle of Mother in Israel.[26]

The appellation came from the Bible, where the prophetess and judge Deborah is called a "Mother in Israel" (Judg. 5:7). American Jewesses proudly laid claim to her laurel, boasting that, across the generations, a woman could hope for no better honor, no greater crown. The title denoted the Jewish variant of the Victorian age's celebration of wives, mothers, and homemakers. The era, named for Britain's Queen Victoria, who ruled an empire and was the mother of nine, lauded women for making their homes havens in a harsh world. It praised them for cultivating character, duty, and virtue in their children through order, self-reliance, hard work, responsibility, and education.

As a Mother in Israel, a Jewish woman dedicated herself to family—not just husband, children, and parents but also in-laws, siblings, aunts and uncles, cousins, nieces, and nephews. The women were to make sure that their families were close-knit. Outside her family, she did her utmost good to help the less fortunate, to use her beneficence to relieve the distress of the poor.[27]

AT HOME daughters trained for this future. Sophie Szold instilled in her brood a strong sense of duty and taught them the arts of sewing, canning, pickling, preserving, marketing, dusting, gardening, baking, and cooking. Her eldest, Henrietta, helped with her younger sisters, buttering their bread and mopping their faces, as her mother shuttled between the kitchen and the dining room. With her rabbi husband's salary, her mother did not need to manage alone. The Szolds relied upon a succession of maids and cooks; Maggie, Kate, and Rose were likely Irish immigrants. An 1890 survey of ten thousand Jewish families, most having lived in the United States for more than fifteen years, observed that 70 percent, like the Szolds, had servants.[28]

Outside the home, Jewish girls began spending more time in the schoolroom. But public schools spotlighted Jewish difference. Bible readings from the New Testament, recitation of the Lord's Prayer, hymns exalting the Trinity, and passages portraying Jews in the harshest light in readers, geographies, and history books permeated many a classroom. A teacher had no compunction about telling a young girl, her very best student: "I am sorry for you . . . it is your misfortune, not your fault, that you are a Jew."[29]

That teacher's comment illustrated the discrimination Jews faced when they left their enclosed worlds, whether these were European ghettoes or the portals of their American homes. In Western and

Central Europe, as the ghetto walls came tumbling down in the late eighteenth and early nineteenth centuries, Jews were emancipated not only from the ghettoes but also from anti-Jewish laws that had restricted where they could live and the work they could do. Now Jews rushed to assimilate and were pushed, by others, to do so. But assimilation meant very different things to Jewish men, Jewish women, and the Gentiles who knocked down those ghetto walls. Gentiles expected, that, liberated from the ghettoes and lured by opportunities formerly closed to them, the Jews would soon disappear as a distinct people. In this, they were not very distant from the pastors and priests who had preached conversion to the Jews for centuries.[30]

But Jewish men had very different hopes for assimilation. In Europe lured to the cities, in America enticed by the open frontier, they poised on the precipice between the past and the future. They wanted to turn their backs on the past with its anti-Jewish discriminations and reap the benefits that their new access to education, careers in business and the professions, and political engagement opened. But most, although not all, refused to abandon Judaism. Instead, they modernized it, reforming their synagogues and transforming their faith. For Rabbi Sonneschein, those transformations extended to preaching in a Unitarian pulpit and officiating at a marriage between a Jewess and a Christian. But Jewish men expected that their accommodations to assimilation—and many were far less radical than those of Rosa's husband—would lead not to the disappearance of the Jews but to the elimination of anti-Jewish prejudice.[31]

In this new modern world, Jewish women's role became setting a boundary on assimilation in their homes. Despite gaining entrée to the middle class, women, in Germany and America, remained out of the worlds of work and politics. Ensconced in their homes as keepers of the Jewish flame, orchestrating their families' observance of customs and traditions, Jewish women enabled their men going about their business to be Jews at home and men in the streets.[32]

Of course, religious observance varied. Some Jewish girls took music lessons on Saturdays and never went to Temple, as the Reform synagogues springing up were named. Others, upholding Jewish traditions, gathered with family on Sabbath eves as well as holidays, blessed the candles as Jewish women have done across the ages, and walked to and from synagogue, complying with the Sabbath laws that made it also a day of rest for their animals. At Purim, they welcomed merry masqueraders into their parlors. At Passover, they cooked matzo kugel. In the Szold household, Sabbath was observed scrupulously.

Jewish girls and women visited family graves before the High Holidays and sat in "church," as some called their Reform synagogues, all day on Rosh Hashanah and Yom Kippur. The Jewish New Year and Passover, a time for new clothes and festive meals when business as usual ceased, offered a glimpse of the piety of the old ghetto. Jewish girls studied their ancient faith in synagogue Sunday schools, modeled on the one that Rebecca Gratz had founded. There, carrying bouquets and dressed in white, they were confirmed, in a ceremony some recalled as the transcendent moment of their youth.[33]

Having, as girls, imbibed Christianity in their schoolrooms, other Jewish women saw no incongruity in lighting Sabbath candles and hanging stockings by a Christmas tree. Surely, there was no holiday tree in the Szold household. Still, Rabbi Benjamin Szold expected his daughters to become familiar with the New Testament, the better to understand America's dominant faith. Even women like Hannah Solomon, who did not celebrate Christian holidays, marked time by them. When a famous actor appeared in St. Louis, the presumably usually observant Rosa Sonneschein could not bear to pass up the chance to see him, even though he performed on a Friday evening.

Consequently, Jewish difference remained a given. Even before daughters would awaken to their duties as women, they socialized mostly with other Jews. They took it for granted that with scarce exceptions, their friends would be nice Jewish boys and girls. The reality was that, even as Jews assimilated into the modern world, they remained, as that antisemitic teacher's remark showed, a people set apart.

SOCIAL LIFE was tightly circumscribed within the fixed circles of family and home. In Hannah Greenebaum Solomon's generation—born in 1858, she had married businessman Henry Solomon, when she was twenty-one—Christians and Jews, who could afford it, had large homes, often allowing for the extended family, including parents and in-laws, to live together under one roof.³⁴

Their social world would pivot around the laughter, conversation, and food at their grand dining tables. The larder always had to be stocked. Family members might pop in before lunch or dinner and expect to stay for the meal. Sophie Szold's preserves and pickled meats fed scores of visiting scholars and communal leaders. One, a graduate student at the local university, dined every Sunday until he married Henrietta's sister Rachel.

Friday evenings the Greenebaum clan gathered; Friday mornings found Hannah Solomon shuttling between her desk and kitchen to prepare her famed sweet-and-sour fish. Noodle parties—the menu always the decidedly unkosher chicken, noodles, and ice cream—brought together her family; so did an annual ladies-only auction, where the women sold each other clothes they no longer wanted and donated the proceeds to charity.

Special occasions meant feeding larger crowds. The Greenebaums were sixty for supper on New Year's Eve. Sophie's daughter, faculty wife Rachel Szold Jastrow, hosting her husband's students, made enough chicken salad to feed ninety people. Then, of course, there were extended family visits. Hannah Solomon remembered the time her mother's younger brother, Marcus, who would later be killed in the Civil War, and Aunt Caroline Spiegel and their children came to stay for the summer.³⁵

Even with servants—who were more common in cities where a pool of immigrant women was willing to work as maids—making their homes social centers required enormous effort. Two cookbooks gave guidance for these well-off families. In 1872 Philadelphia's Esther Levy published America's first Jewish cookbook, the plainly titled *Jewish Cookery Book*, filled not only with recipes but also with words of advice for the homemaker about medicines, economizing, and sound domestic management.[36]

Levy reminded her readers that, in attending to their kitchens, they followed in the footsteps of the biblical Sarah, who had baked cakes for the angels who stopped, in the heat of the day, at Abraham's tent (Gen. 18:1–6). Her chapters on fish, soups, meats, poultry, bread, cakes, puddings, pastry, preserves, cheeses, wines, pickles, and foods for invalids avoided forbidden, unkosher foods. She instructed her readers to keep a proper Jewish home, to post passages from Deuteronomy on their doorposts, referring to the custom of affixing a mezuzah, a case holding parchment with biblical verses (Deut. 6:4–9, 11:13–21); to buy kosher meat, to salt and soak it to remove all traces of blood as required by the dietary laws; to burn a piece of dough when baking their Sabbath bread, fulfilling the commandment to set aside a portion of dough as the ancient Israelites had for their priests (Num. 15:20–21); to remove leaven at Passover, and to store the holiday's special dishes at its end.[37]

Their pristine homes required a white cloth on the breakfast table and a servant to present luncheon on a tray. The family breadwinners, husbands and sons, were to be welcomed at midday to a proper dinner of stuffed roast veal, stewed steak, and an array of side dishes, perhaps green peas and stewed turnips, with several salads. The evening's supper was the lighter meal: fish, bread and butter, hot biscuits, cake, fruit. Men's labor paid for the meal, the tablecloth, the servant. But taking charge of the kitchen, the larder, and the table was woman's affair.

Levy's recipes came from both Europe—*matzo kleis* soup and *luxion* (noodle pudding)—and America—succotash and cornbread. While the Sabbath required special preparations, she saved her most elaborate menus for Sundays when the menfolk, at home and resting, deserved a feast.

How many of America's Jewish women followed her directions is unknown. Her cookbook had a single printing. But Mrs. Bertha F. Kramer's *"Aunt Babette's" Cook Book*, with *Hints for the Housewife, Many of Which are not to be Found Elsewhere*, first published in 1889, went through at least eleven editions. Its title page bore a Star of David; it was published by a Jewish publishing house; and its Easter dishes included matzo kugel and notes for setting the table for the Passover seder. Appealing to well-to-do Reform Jewish women, who thought keeping a strictly kosher home passé, its index had an entry for "*Trefa*," unkosher foods, and there were recipes for oysters (stewed, fried, escalloped, and creamed), chicken croquettes made with a glass of rich cream, and barbecued rabbit. All were most definitely not kosher. Still, its recipes were "selectively *treyf*"—shellfish and ham were acceptable, lard and pork not—revealing the lingering influence of the Jewish dietary laws even for these modernizing Jewish housewives. *Aunt Babette*'s long success—the book remained in print for at least twenty-five years—rested on the excellence of its recipes. Bertha Kramer really was a good cook. It managed to appeal both to successful immigrants, who remembered many of its foods from their mothers' kitchens, and their American-born daughters, who needed advice on removing sandbags from soft-shell crabs, tips for making bacon bandages to cure sore throats, and instructions for making charoset—a mixture of apples, nuts, cinnamon, and wine essential to the Passover seder. Its long shelf life was also attributed to the limited competition it faced for more than two decades.[38]

CHERISHING German culture for cultivating the mind and the spirit, American Jewesses celebrated the music, literature, and art of the lands of their parents and sometimes themselves. Until the 1870s, most of Chicago's Jews spoke German. There New Year's Eve found its Greenebaum clan singing "Lauter Schöne Leut' Sind Wir" (Fine People Are We). In Madison, Rachel Szold Jastrow's copious bowls of chicken salad fed its German Society. German was the language of the Szolds' childhood home in Baltimore, and Henrietta attended German school, although her youngest sisters did not.

Outside the home, social life revolved mostly around a set of

Jewish institutions. For Hannah Solomon's family, they included the Zion Literary Society's lectures, theatricals, and musical recitals; Purim charity balls, Sinai Temple, and the Concordia Club, founded by affluent Jewish merchants when they were barred from gentile clubs. The oldest, New York's Harmonie Club, was established in 1852. On appropriate occasions, these exclusive, restricted spaces welcomed members of the opposite sex.

At such clubs, debutantes, the daughters and relations of club members, entered society just as gentile daughters did at clubs that excluded Jews. The purpose, in both, was the same: to meet, court, and mate young men from the right social set. *The Jewish Messenger* gave a glowing account of New Orleans Harmony Club's 1892 ball. Debutantes in gold-metal tulle and striped flower gauzes had traveled from Boston, Vicksburg, and Shreveport to dance to an orchestra, hidden from view behind a thicket of tropical plants, and dine at an elegant midnight supper. Writing as D'Arwin, still disguised as a man, Rosa Sonneschein observed the dazzling young ladies and smart young men at St. Louis's Harmonie Club's last ball of the 1885 social season. If possible, D'Arwin wrote, soon every one of those doe-eyed damsels would star in her own "realistic" drama, her wedding.[39]

Once a young woman came out into society and had her first season, she entered into the calling system, announcing her days at home to receive visitors. Myriad rules dictated when proper young men could call, how long they would stay, and how long the mother remained in the parlor. Notwithstanding the Constitution and the nation's laws, everyone knew that Jews called on Jews. Eventually, public spaces, like the men's social clubs and the new Young Men's Hebrew Associations, brought an end to the days of calling to court the Jewish women in the parlor. Yet still everyone, Jews and Christians, expected Jews to court only Jews.

Gentiles and Jews did mix on occasion—Henrietta Szold went to lectures at Johns Hopkins University and performances at the Peabody Conservatory. Hannah Solomon and her sister Henriette were the first two Jews invited to join the Chicago Woman's Club. Nevertheless, they mostly socialized among their own.

Hannah Solomon understood the impetus behind this social whirlwind of gentlemen in top hats and ladies whose billowing skirts swept the ground. Pioneers, like her parents, resolved to do all that they could to protect their children from ever knowing the hardships they had endured as new immigrants—and some, but by no means all, had acquired the wealth to do so.[40]

YET OTHER immigrant Jewish women, although we will never know how many, lived more modestly their entire lives. With their husbands, they ran groceries and dry goods stores. They had enough to eat, enough to raise their families, but they never became rich and grand from such enterprises. Married women—not only widows like Caroline Spiegel—ran boardinghouses and cooked for single men living in their towns to augment their incomes and pay the rent when the shop did not bring in enough. Other Jewish women worked as dressmakers and tailors to put a roof over their heads and food on the table.[41]

Still others found America not a land of opportunity but a land of adversity. Had they not, there would have been no need for those Hebrew ladies' benevolent and sewing societies to help the Jewish poor. The nineteenth-century Jewish writer Cora Wilburn, likely recalling her own experiences, writes, in her novel, *Cosella Wayne*, of a woman, coming to America, who started out as a lady's companion, "that misnomer for ceaseless drudge." Then she took care of children, watched over the sick, and took in sewing. Some days she had no money to make a fire, her threadbare clothes testifying to her life of destitution.[42]

FROM TALLAHASSEE, businessman Day Apte courted Atlanta's Helen Jacobus, writing her letters daily for several years before, at last, she agreed to marry him in 1909. Both were twenty-two. They had met in Atlanta where Day lived during his teen years.

Helen's parents were German Jewish immigrants; Day's came from Austria. That made them part of the city's established Jewish community.[43]

The bride-to-be spent the months before her wedding outfitting her new home, shopping for her trousseau, and being fêted in a round of parties and theater outings. The night before the big day, she collapsed in tears, nervous and fearful of leaving the only home she knew. But the wedding day found her glorious in a Directoire-style white gown, her bridesmaids in yellow satin. To the strains of Wagner's *Lohengrin* wedding march, she descended the stairs to the family parlor, and the rabbi joined the couple in marriage. Champagne and festivities made the celebration speed by. Then Mrs. Day Apte changed into her traveling dress, and the crowd sent the couple off to board a train bound for a honeymoon in Florida.

Writing in her diary in the summer of 1909 of the early days of her marriage, Helen likened them to a precious strand of pearls. On their first Sabbath eves together, her husband read her the biblical words that Jewish men have spoken to their wives across the ages: "A woman of valor who can find?" She rises before dawn and is never idle. She provides for her household, spinning wool, selling cloth, planting a vineyard. She gives generously to the poor and is pious. Wise, she knows that "beauty is illusory." Her husband and children sing her praises, her "worth is far beyond that of rubies" (Prov. 31:10–31). Kindling the Sabbath lights, Helen already began seeing herself as a Mother in Israel.[44]

But that did not mean that she immediately began bearing children. In the nineteenth century, married American women's birth rate declined dramatically—from an average of seven children in 1800 to three and a half by 1900. Women's magazines advertised pessaries—forerunners of the modern diaphragm—and douches to prevent conception. The invention of vulcanized rubber made condoms available. But the 1873 Comstock Act, named for Anthony Comstock, the founder of the New York Society for the Suppression of Vice, had a chilling effect. It made it illegal to sell, distribute, or mail obscene literature, including contraceptive information.

Comstock boasted of the enormous quantities of indecent materials seized, arrests made, and even suicides spurred by the law. In 1875, when he arrested Morris Bass, a Bavarian Jew, Comstock confiscated a large cache of 200 dozen condoms, twelve dozen pessaries, and other contraceptive paraphernalia.[45]

Nevertheless, statistics do not lie. American women were increasingly effective in controlling their reproductive lives. A campaign for voluntary motherhood condoned a married woman's right to refuse relations on the grounds that she would bear healthier, happier children if she wanted them. How widely this practice was accepted is unknown.

Jewish women's birth rate mirrored this decline. Immigrant Jewish women were far more likely to have larger families than their American-born daughters. Sarah Spiegel Greenebaum had ten children; Hannah Solomon had three. In 1900, in Portland, Oregon, of the German-born Jewish women over age forty, half had six children or more; of their daughters born in America, only 5.5 percent had that many.[46]

For Helen Apte, sex was too intimate to confide to her diary, but she openly confessed her conflict over contraception. On the one hand, she wrote, surely a woman cannot have a baby every year. On the other, she deemed it physically and morally wrong to prevent nature from taking its course. Ethical conundrum aside, given that she bore a single child four years after she married, she either did all in her power to prevent unwanted conception or had trouble conceiving.

If American Jewesses' birth rate matched that of American women, when they gave birth set them apart. A statistician made a startling observation: a significant proportion of the Mothers in Israel gave birth in December, January and June. He surmised that Jewish women were far more likely to conceive at Passover, which falls either in March or April, and during the fall High Holidays, when men, who were on the road buying and selling, were at last at home for longer visits.[47]

WHEN APTE LEARNED that a friend was pregnant, she prayed to God to bring her and her baby safely through this ordeal. This was no chance remark. Early in the twentieth century, in the United States, one mother died for every 154 live births, and the rate remained the same into the 1920s. In 1917 maternity was the second leading cause of death for American women aged fifteen to forty-five; only tuberculosis killed more.[48]

The perils of pregnancy and childbirth—toxemia, hemorrhage, and infection—claimed the lives of vigorous young women. Facing their confinements, as labor and delivery were then called, American Jewesses thought of those who had died giving birth. When defender of her people Rachel Mordecai Lazarus bore her four children, the first in 1822, the last in 1830, she must have trembled remembering how her thirty-three-year-old mother had died bearing her seventh infant in twelve years. The baby had died, too.

Well into the twentieth century, the risks of childbirth persisted. Addressing a Mother's Day luncheon in 1931, former first lady Edith Roosevelt told her audience that women descend into "the valley of the shadow of death" (Ps. 23:4) to get their children, and that even with excellent medical care, some never returned. That excellent medical care signaled that childbearing was evolving from a trial managed in the home by midwives and female friends and relatives into a medical procedure controlled by men in hospitals.[49]

When at last Helen Apte became pregnant, she was terrified. Was she strong enough to bring a healthy child into this world? She did not feel strong, and her organs were inflamed. A miscarriage threatened. The doctor confined her to bed. Her last four months were an agony of pain and fear. In July 1913 she was taken to the hospital before the baby was due. There her doctor induced labor, forcing, so Apte wrote, her daughter into this world, so that mother and child might both have a chance to survive.

That Helen Apte had her baby in a hospital was unusual in 1913. Even as late as the mid-1930s, more than half of all U.S. births still took place in the home. Between 1904 and 1911, social reformer Belle Moskowitz bore four children at home, despite problems experienced with her first birth. Reciting the Twenty-third Psalm over and over, she almost died delivering the first. With the last, the placenta separated prematurely. The doctor knew that performing a cesarean in the house would have killed her. Instead the baby bled to death.[50]

NOT EVERY GIRL intended to grow up to become a mother. When Julia Richman was eleven, this future New York City school superintendent announced: "I am not pretty . . . and I am not going to marry, but before I die, all New York will know my name!" Others who never wed—Rebecca Gratz, Penina Moïse, Emma Lazarus, and Henrietta Szold—were among the best-known Jewish women of their day.[51]

Not all chose this path. The story of Henrietta Szold's unreciprocated love for the younger scholar Louis Ginzberg became widely known. But Richman fulfilled her young ambition, and so did a discontented twenty-two-year-old Lillian Wald. Bored by her education of school, kitchen, and society, she yearned for serious work. That led her to nursing and the Lower East Side's immigrant Henry Street Settlement.

These single women pointed to a transformation under way. The many women left widowed by the Civil War had helped set it in motion. Although the number of single women seems to have held steady in the latter decades of the nineteenth century, attitudes toward them began changing. Buoyed by expectations unleashed by the suffrage movement, expanded female higher education, growing career opportunities for middle-class women—these women never seemed to be working-class—and new respectable living arrangements for single women in the cities, the new single woman announced that she had arrived.[52]

With *The American Jewess*'s very first issue, editor Sonneschein plunged into the fray, addressing her readers, those who intended to marry, if they had not already done so, and those who did not. In "Latch Keys for Women," the new bachelor maid, reveling in her freedom, displaced the gray-haired, spectacled, cranky old spinster. A correspondent to *The American Jewess*, proudly signing off as a Chicago Old Maid, saw nothing wrong with a woman past thirty traveling on her own to Europe.[53]

This enthusiasm for the single life rested on shifting ideas about the matrimonial state. At one time, *duty* was the word most often associated with the bonds of marriage. In the *Woman's Journal*, the official voice of the National American Woman Suffrage Association, Alfred T. Story, the author of the 1880 book *Woman in the Talmud*, reported that the rabbis opposed celibacy and expected all Jews to do their duty and marry.[54]

But now, more than duty, love became requisite for a successful marriage. Sonneschein, perhaps thinking of her own miserable experience, published articles asserting that women would be happier if they never wed instead of marrying men they did not love or, even worse, were unworthy of them. Such attitudes helped legitimize unmarried women. So too did the well-deserved reputations of several single American Jewesses—the Hebrew Sunday school leaders Ellen Phillips, Simha Peixotto, and Louisa B. Hart; the writers Mary M. Cohen and Josephine Lazarus, sister of Emma; the sculptor Katherine M. Cohen, Neighborhood Playhouse's Irene Lewisohn, and National Council of Jewish Women founder Sadie American. (Her father, an immigrant and a successful merchant, must have chosen that surname before her birth in 1862.) Their life's work and accomplishments won them admiration among American Jews and respect for the unmarried.[55]

How many Jewish women never married is unknown. In Portland, Oregon, in 1900, nearly a fifth of the cohort had not married by age twenty-five, the age by which most of their peers wed. Some single women, like Lillian Wald, lived, worked, and vacationed over the years with female friends. Letters between Wald and those friends convey their esteem, affection, and sometimes eroticism.[56]

Single Jewish women, those well known and the many leaving smaller legacies behind, lived lives that differed from preceding generations. Only one other group of Jewish women, albeit a very small number, also diverged sharply from the ideal Mother in Israel—those marrying outside the faith.

LATER in the American Jewish experience, the theme of intermarriage would occupy a prominent place. But that was not the case for Jewish women of the late 1800s.

By one calculation, between 1776 and 1840, more than a quarter of American Jews intermarried, but later that figure would shrink. Observers have long claimed that, for much of American Jewish history, Jewish men were far more likely to intermarry than were Jewish women. Surely the paucity of Jewish women on the frontiers roamed by the peddlers was a contributing factor. Trudging the byways of Ohio, Hannah Solomon's uncle, Marcus Spiegel, met and wed the Quaker Caroline Hamlin, who converted. But no precise statistics exist for Jewish intermarriages for later in the 1800s.[57]

An early twentieth-century study in New York City concluded that of all the ethnic groups surveyed, Jews had one of the lowest intermarriage rates. But it predicted that the longer Jews lived in America among Christians, the more likely they were to intermarry. In that survey, Russian Jewish immigrants had one of the lowest mixed-marriage rates, less than a single percent, but the intermarriage rate rose to over 4 percent for native-born Jews who married between 1908 and 1912 and had parents born in the United States.[58]

This report also revealed that intermarriage remained a gendered affair. First-generation German Jewish men intermarried at a rate triple that of their sisters. In the 1880s, out of the 16,000 Jews living in San Francisco, 163 men but only 39 women had reportedly married Gentiles.[59]

The American Israelite asserted that, while a hundred Jewish men would succumb to the charms of a comely Christian, not even one percent of American Jewesses would make the same mistake. Upstanding Jewish women purportedly had no interest in intermarriage; they believed they must marry into their own religion. They may have had fewer opportunities to meet Gentiles than did their brothers whose businesses brought them into contact with Christians. Women were also, so the stereotype asserted, more closely bound to their faiths and so were presumably more reluctant to risk leaving the fold.[60]

The few reports of Jewish women intermarrying raised alarms. One woman warned that acrimony and warfare between husband and wife surely follow such misguided unions. *The American Jewess* scolded a young woman who intended to marry a Christian and convert. Intermarriage was "risky," especially if the couple kept their respective religions, but conversion for Jewish women was "contemptible."[61]

Conventional wisdom held that intermarriage destroyed families. Barnard College founder Annie Nathan Meyer remembered parents who "cut *crear*," tearing their clothes in the Jewish mourning ritual known as *kriah*, grieving for their daughter as if she had died, after she eloped with a blue-eyed, redheaded Irishman. A young woman, an only child, killed herself rather than choose between the Christian she loved and her parents who forbade the marriage. When Helen Wise married James Maloney, a lawyer and son of a clergyman, *The New York Times* reported her father's anger on page one. No longer would "Cincinnati's foremost rabbi," Isaac Mayer Wise, recognize his daughter. The paper called the blond Helen "one of the most beautiful Jewesses in the city," noting approvingly that "the Hebrew cast in her features is scarcely discernable."[62]

Some parents found family more important than religion. Lillian Wald's parents reportedly did not object when their daughter Julia married in a cathedral and raised her children as Catholics. The San Francisco Jewish writer Emma Wolf recounted the story of an intermarriage in her 1892 novel *Other Things Being Equal*. It was so popular that it went through multiple printings and was praised in *The American Jewess* for its interfaith story about the triumph of love. The protagonist's father, described as always just and liberal, rejects his daughter after she marries out of the faith. But on his deathbed, he embraces her and her Christian husband, as she reassures him, "I am a Jewess and will die one."[63]

Another story, this one biblical, required diplomatic inter-

vention. At Purim, Sonneschein praised Queen Esther as a shining example of Jewish womanhood. But of course, this role model
had intermarried. Adroitly, Sonneschein argued that nevertheless
Esther's devotion to her people triumphed over all.[64]

Despite her father's wrath, Helen Wise Maloney returned with
her daughter to the pews of his Cincinnati temple and reconciled
with her father. Because her husband was indifferent to his faith, in
the Maloney household, she determined the religion, and she raised
her daughter as a Jew. Yet of the American Jewesses who intermarried, her story seems unique. Likely more followed the path of Julia
Wald Barry out of Judaism than that of Helen Wise Maloney into
the synagogue.[65]

"Women's sphere is the whole wide world"

AT THE END of the century, in the pages of *The American Jewess*, Sonneschein dubbed Hannah Solomon "a representative Jewess of America." By then, the thirty-seven-year-old Solomon had
joined the Chicago Woman's Club, published her paper "Our Debt
to Judaism," organized the Jewish Women's Congress, and become
the founding president of the National Council of Jewish Women.
Solomon would go on to work tirelessly for this powerful organization, which is still going strong in the twenty-first century. In
subsequent decades, she ran a Bureau of Personal Service in Chicago's seventh ward. She became treasurer of the National Council of Women, an umbrella organization of women's associations
around the country, irrespective of race, creed, or tradition, to
advance women's status and improve society. She even translated
for suffragist Susan B. Anthony when they were both delegates at
a conference in Berlin. At the same time, Solomon ran a household
that included her mother-in-law, widowed sister-in-law, bachelor
brother-in-law, and own three children. Sadly, she buried one of
them at the age of nineteen. Her commitments to public service and
devotion to home and family did make her an outstanding representative woman of her day.[66]

As Solomon was embarking upon public service, critics began expressing tremendous anxiety that such pursuits would lead to mayhem. Women would neglect their children, leave the mending undone, and abdicate their position as queens of the household. Accounting for her own success at balancing service to family and to humanity, Solomon told Sonneschein that, with an efficient use of time, any woman could manage both. That Solomon and other American Jewesses carved out national and international reputations for their social welfare vocations was not only the product of efficient time management. They entered into public life at a moment when great numbers of American women were pushing forward, clambering onto far larger stages than Solomon's mother, Sarah Greenebaum, could ever have imagined.

That they did so was the result not only of their own grit but also of changes transforming women's lives in the latter decades of the nineteenth century. The declining birth rate paved the way; changes in mortality patterns sealed it. To put it simply, women were living longer. In 1850 white female life expectancy in the United States was just under forty years; by 1900, it had jumped by 25 percent; in 1920, it reached fifty-seven years. The consequences are obvious: women spent a smaller portion of their lives pregnant and raising their children and had more years than before to fill after their children grew up.[67]

At the same time, new labor-saving devices entered the home. Near the end of the century, when the Solomons moved to a grand house on Chicago's Michigan Avenue, electric lights and telephones were just beginning to appear in the homes of the wealthy. Running water, refrigeration, processed and canned foods, and washing machines (although electric ones would not arrive until the twentieth century) eased homemakers' lives. Seeing articles in the burgeoning women's press—*Ladies' Home Journal* and *Good Housekeeping* appeared in the 1880s—about women taking up the call to service, more American women ventured into organizations to help others.

Sarah Greenebaum had also cared for the poor. She organized the women she had gathered to sew layettes for poor, expectant mothers into Chicago's first Jewish Ladies' Sewing Society. She joined the United Order of True Sisters Jochannah Lodge; it helped members who were widowed, gave boys in need new clothes at Hanukkah, and ran a free public kindergarten.[68]

Through these charitable associations, the women molded American Jewish life, sustained their people, shaped its future, and fulfilled the biblical commandment to care for the widow and the orphan (Ex. 22:22). Their independent activities complemented, and were no less significant than, those of their husbands, fathers, and brothers in venues like fraternal orders, such as B'nai B'rith.

But the immigrant Jewesses of Sarah Greenebaum's generation confined their communal efforts to the local. In the aftermath of the Civil War, with its enormous death toll, so many widows and other women on their own had to shoulder increased responsibilities. Out of those responsibilities, broad new avenues for women's activity sprang open.

⚜

IN THE EARLY 1890S, as the men and women of Chicago began planning for the fair, the Board of Lady Managers—the one Annie Orff, the publisher Sonneschein knew in St. Louis, joined—made certain that women would be well represented in its more than two hundred congresses. (Today we would call them conventions.) Because Jews had no female clergy and no national women's association to coordinate the Jewesses' participation, the lady managers asked Hannah Solomon to take the lead.

Beginning her search, she wrote rabbis around the country asking them to recommend knowledgeable women they knew. Then she wrote those women to see if they would come to Chicago to present papers. After her plans were well along, the rabbis arranging the Jewish Denominational Congress asked her to cooperate with them. She agreed so long as the women would have a significant role. Then, as she later wrote, the men recessed. When they returned to present their program, "lo and behold," Solomon exclaimed, there was not a single woman's name on it. So Hannah Solomon stood up, stomped off, and announced that the Jewish women would hold a separate congress.

For four days in September 1893, some two dozen women stood before overflowing crowds, lecturing as experts on Jewish history, culture, and society. So many people tried to cram into one of the sessions that the speakers had to read their papers a second time. The women discussed the ancient, medieval, and modern histories of Jewish women. They lauded Jewish mothers. They reflected on contemporary Jewish affairs, reported on their mission work, and denounced antisemitism. Sensing that this was a momentous turning point, one presenter proclaimed that never before, across the millennia, had women stood and raised their voices, addressing the world as powerful authorities on Jews and Judaism. The speakers signaled their departure from the past in another way. The name Hannah G. Solomon appeared in the program rather than the customary Mrs. Henry Solomon, although the press, covering the congress, added "Miss" or "Mrs." before each woman's name. At the end of the congress, those present founded the National Council of Jewish Women, elected Solomon president, and pledged to seek solutions to problems in philanthropy, religion, and education.[69]

Even as the council maintained that woman's responsibility was to her home and family, its members, mostly Reform Jews, took time away from those families to assist immigrants, study Judaism, and campaign for women's progress in the synagogue. In its first seven years, the council established thirteen immigrant mission schools, launched fifty-seven study circles (which Solomon likened to university classes for women), propelled seventy-two women onto Sabbath-school boards, and called for inaugurating Council Sabbath, when rabbis across the land would recognize congregants who were council members.[70]

Soon, however, religious controversies churned the organization. Some leaders championed the revolutionary notion, put forward by a few radical Reform rabbis, of moving the Sabbath from Saturday to Sunday, the day America rested. To keep the peace among its members, the council's energies pivoted away from divisive religious issues and more toward social welfare and immigrant aid, especially for girls and women traveling to America on their own.

In 1905 the council established a permanent aid station at Ellis Island, the gateway of dreams and tears, for over twelve million immigrants who ran a gauntlet of government inspections before gaining entry to the United States. Council agents, wearing blue armbands and speaking Yiddish and other languages of the Jewish arrivals, interviewed females traveling alone to make certain that they had safe places to go and did not get taken in by unscrupulous men. After these women settled in America, council volunteers checked in to see if all was well or if they needed help. By 1910, the National Council of Jewish Women was keeping tabs on immigrant girls and women in 275 cities, from Elmira, New York, to Los Angeles.[71]

The women's watch over single women propelled the council into the politics of the international campaign against white slavery. At the turn of the century, there was deep concern over the entrapment of young women into prostitution by networks of traffickers widely presumed to be run by Jews. A 1903 report from Polish Silesia concluded that "every link in this entire devil's chain," including the culprits and the victims, were Jews. A decade earlier, in western Ukraine, twenty-seven Jews stood trial for conning unsuspecting young women, promising them jobs and a trip to the United States, then shipping them to brothels in the Middle East and Africa instead. Many of the witnesses, who had escaped to testify, were Jews.[72]

The council crusaded against white slavery to wipe out this stain on world Jewry that ruined the lives of unsuspecting young women and provided fodder for antisemites. In a leaflet distributed in Russia and at Europe's seaports, the council warned young women setting off for America that men and women lurked about, offering easy, well-paid work. Some promised marriage; some duped naïve girls into fake marriages before dispatching them into prostitution. The leaflets advised them to ask for the Council of Jewish Women— it would find out the truth and offer assistance.

Later the council took up new causes. In 1922, two years after women won the vote, the Cable Act separated a woman's citizenship from that of her husband. Previously an American woman who married a foreigner lost her citizenship because his determined hers. Now the National Council of Jewish Women instructed immigrants who had become citizens and native-born women in their new civic duties and obligation to vote. Its members campaigned for birth control and peace. For Hannah Solomon, who became honorary president after a dozen years at its helm, its successes and forays into politics affirmed that she had been right to oppose the men at the Columbian Exposition who tried, and failed, to silence Jewish women. Looking back on all that had been accomplished, she reflected that men had told women that their sphere was the home, but that the last thirty years had proved "our boast that women's sphere is the whole wide world, without limit."[73]

BEFORE THE MODERN ERA, everyone knew who was a Jew. But once Jews left the ghetto behind, both Jews and Gentiles wondered how to define a Jew, what constituted the distinctiveness of this people. Some answered that Jews were the people whose religion was Judaism. But what then defined those who had no use for Judaism, who never set foot in a synagogue, who saw themselves as fully assimilated, even those who had converted to become Christians, and yet were still considered to be Jews by Gentiles and often other Jews.

In the late nineteenth century, many American Jews, confronting this enigma of Jewish particularity, decided that they were a distinct race. The term *ethnicity* had not yet emerged. The catastrophe of the Nazi rampage to eradicate the Jews lay in the future. For late nineteenth-century Jews, calling themselves a race—they also used the terms *nation* and *people*—resolved the paradox of defining who was a Jew.

Race signifies more than ethnicity. It announced that Jews differed not only culturally and religiously but also, sharing ancestry, biologically. "Different blood flows in our veins," asserted a noted rabbi. Since race is immutable, a racial definition provided solace for those worried about the Jewish future. Living in an era of blurring social boundaries between Jew and Gentile, Jews worried that the Jewish people might utterly disappear. But if Jews were a race, that could not happen.[74]

Unsurprisingly, Jewish men and women shouldered different responsibilities for the future of their race. Nature made men its supporters, Jewesses its propagators. Jewish wives and mothers— bearers of the next generation, educators of the young, mistresses of the household, guardians of traditions, hostesses of holiday celebrations—transmitted Jewish values to their children, preserved the distinctiveness of the group, and sustained the race.[75]

Sonneschein was in agreement: "The Jewess represents a race." Apte concurred, feeling the ancient pride of the race burning within her. But Irma Levy Lindheim, who later led the Zionist women of Hadassah and eventually settled in Israel, heard her rabbi insist that the essence of the Jewish people was religion. Just like Protestants and Catholics, Jews were unique only because of their faith. That was Hannah Solomon's position too. Traveling to Europe and North Africa, she met Jews of every color—black, brown, yellow, white—professing every shade of belief and every kind of culture. Never again, she was confident, could anyone think of the Jewish people as a race or a nation.[76]

Sonneschein and Solomon clung to opposing rails of Jewish definition. For other Jews, race and faith were indistinguishable. Sonneschein's deep interest in Jewish religious life worked against the dichotomy. Even as she defined the Jewess as a proud member of her race, she also expected her to awaken her religious spirit. Solomon repudiated the racial definition but recognized that, until the walls of the ghetto crashed down, Jews would be considered a separate people.[77]

American Jewesses connected the rails of race and religion by hammering in rungs of new women's associations, laying the foundations for their service to their people. Over time some of these organizations floundered and disappeared. Coming generations would repair some weakened crossbars and affix new ones between the rails. Erecting a ladder of organizations, Jewish women climbed the rungs to meet the challenges of their day: to conserve Judaism, safeguard the Jewish people, and rise to meet the future.

> *"To think of others is as natural to the*
> *Jewish woman as to breathe."*

IN *THE AMERICAN JEWESS*, Sonneschein proclaimed that nothing barred women from leaving their homes and venturing out into the modern world. By then women across America were stepping out into new arenas. A host of new women's associations dedicated to a plethora of causes had sprouted. Elizabeth Cady Stanton and Susan B. Anthony started the National Woman Suffrage Association in 1869. Two years later Jane Addams's Hull House, which became the model for settlement houses, community centers serving the poor and immigrants in their own neighborhoods around the country, opened its doors in Chicago. At the same time, tens of thousands of women were also joining women's clubs.[78]

Although many began, as had Sonneschein's Pioneers, as literary and culture clubs, some, like the Chicago Woman's Club, turned, after a time, from self-improvement to civic betterment. Displaying administrative, financial, and political know-how, club women established kindergartens and homes for fallen women, playgrounds, and vacation schools. They defended their interventions into public life as natural extensions of their maternal instincts. From caring for disadvantaged women and children, they leaped to concern for the health, safety, and welfare of all women and children. From there, they vaulted into the political fray, demanding government attention to sanitation, schools, and child labor. "Politics is housekeeping on a grand scale," declared Jane Addams.[79]

Solomon agreed. When, in 1905, the Chicago Woman's Club charged her with investigating the Illinois Industrial School for Girls, founded in the 1870s to care for orphans and delinquents, she discovered a shockingly decrepit institution, housing 125 anemic girls in an old soldiers' home. By the time she finished, she had built the new Park Ridge School for Girls and lobbied in Springfield, the state capital, for the money to pay for it. Solomon had indeed traveled the new route from homemaker to political activist.

Unsurprisingly, given how the women's club movement challenged traditional female roles, it came under attack. Consumer advocate Maud Nathan, a cousin of Emma Lazarus, recalled a cartoon of a clubwoman, lounging about with drink and cigarette in hand and reading a book, while her husband washed dishes and her scruffy children quarreled. Well aware of the controversy, in Solomon's profile in *The American Jewess*, Sonneschein shrewdly emphasized Solomon's exemplary devotion to her home. It even mentioned that Solomon remained a member of the sewing society her mother had founded.[80]

Solomon entered civic life just as a triad of explicitly Christian women's organizations appeared. Methodist and Baptist women, demanding that single women become missionaries, set up female missionary societies to support churches, hospitals, and schools at home and abroad. The Young Women's Christian Association helped working girls with its low-cost boardinghouses and employment bureaus. Frances E. Willard's Woman's Christian Temperance Union, with over 200,000 members, the largest women's organization of the day, expanded beyond protesting the consumption of alcohol into a do-everything society. It provided practical help to women, including prostitutes, fleeing abusive relationships and campaigned for international peace and woman's rights.

Jewish women were unlikely to join these evangelically tinged Protestant endeavors. When the Woman's Christian Temperance Union debated admitting Catholics and Jews to membership, Sonneschein saluted its broad-mindedness but regretted that the name *Christian* denoted a very limited sphere of interest.[81]

Of course, the Jewesses had inherited well-established traditions of benevolence. "To think of others is as natural to the Jewish woman as to breathe," affirmed Belle Moskowitz, the social reformer who repeated the Twenty-third Psalm during her difficult births. But now these Mothers in Israel organized on a grander scale than their predecessors had ever imagined. Convinced that they had independent and decisive roles to play to benefit their faith, their people, their country, and all mankind, American Jewesses, like their Christian neighbors, marched down three paths. They pushed open new byways into charity and philanthropy, the synagogue, and Zionism. Their organizations attested to the remarkable dedication and formidable powers of these women as they strode forward into the twentieth century.[82]

❧❦❧

SINCE THE DAYS of Rebecca Gratz, Jewish women had crossed religious lines, linking arms with Christians for nonsectarian benevolence and civic improvement. Solomon followed in that vein. So did many other Jewish women. Nevertheless, most Jewish women likely focused the greater part of their charitable energies on other Jews.[83]

When the *American Jewish Year Book* first appeared in 1899, it listed scores of Hebrew ladies' benevolent, fuel relief, widows', and orphan societies, as well as Daughters of Israel guilds and Deborah groups. Some were still called by their German name, like Israelitischer Frauen Verein. There were mutual aid societies and lodges, like Sarah Greenebaum's Jochannah Lodge. There were even lodges named for Martha Washington. These groups persisted into the twentieth century, but new Jewish women's organizations also emerged. The Young Women's Hebrew Association, the Volunteer Corps of Friendly Visitors, and Sisterhoods of Personal Service signaled that Jewish American women were embracing the scientific charity movement.[84]

Instead of injudiciously giving alms to the poor, scientific charity called for welfare workers to respond to appeals from the needy by investigating and then rendering personal service. The philosophy was that by meeting friendly visitors coming into their tenement apartments and at the neighborhood settlement house, the poor, internalizing the ladies' middle-class rationality and efficiency, would uplift themselves and no longer need assistance. The movement promoted overarching citywide Charity Organization Societies to coordinate local groups, eliminate duplication of effort, and end the abuses that occurred when generosity was not rationally managed.

Waving the banner of scientific charity, American Jewesses fielded an army of women who marched up tenement stairs to assess needs and staffed settlement houses and bureaus. They modeled decorum and gentility and demonstrated the importance of honesty, hard work, and efficiency for impoverished women. They called themselves mission workers, borrowing the term from Christian groups.

Heading into the immigrant ghettoes, occasionally driven by their chauffeurs, these women dove into the squalor of crowded streets and dilapidated tenements to do battle with "the three D's, Dirt, Discomfort and Disease." They offered encouragement in troubled times, a loan to buy food, and help in finding work. They came armed with a mop, a brush, a broom, and an eye for rearranging sparse furniture. The ladies bountiful brought much-needed material assistance, but the immigrants they helped were not blind to their condescension, even as most Jewesses probably never noticed their resentment. The Russian Jewish immigrant writer Anzia Yezierska, whose stories spoke to her own life, wrote in "The Vacation House" of the embarrassment one Jewish immigrant mother expressed as the women from the charities made her feel "cheap like dirt."[85]

Moreover, the number of impoverished Russian Jews crowding into American cities cried out for larger solutions. Cheery words of encouragement and well-intentioned advice offered too little. So American Jewesses set up industrial schools to teach girls sewing to prepare them to earn a living. They ran workrooms and employment bureaus, religious schools and social clubs, nurseries and kindergartens to watch the children of working mothers. They assisted probation officers with delinquents to prevent recidivism. They dispatched doctors, midwives, and medicines to the sick. Encountering desperate "lungers," people with tuberculosis hemorrhaging on Denver's streets, Frances Wisebart Jacobs, who helped establish the city's Charity Organization Society, campaigned for the sanatorium that bore her name before becoming the National Jewish Hospital.

In 1889, when New York's Temple Emanu-El established its Sisterhood of Personal Service, the women of the congregation, averred its president Hannah Einstein, turned away from personal preoccupations to wage war on poverty. At its tenth anniversary, the sisterhood heard reports about the thousands it had helped in the past year. The sisters had given an old man the tools he needed to work as a shoemaker. They had helped another open a delicatessen. The 178 students in their industrial school were learning not only sewing but also habits of thrift and charity. In the past year, the children, donating $329.46 to the Penny Provident Fund, had forfeited 32,946 pieces of candy.[86]

Some Sisterhoods of Personal Service ran settlement houses. By the early 1900s, there were over four hundred in the United States: in 1895 four were Jewish; by 1910, twenty-four were. With their libraries, clubrooms, lecture halls, and workrooms; classes in cooking and stenography, mothers' clubs, story hours, and Sukkot pageants, they helped transform the shiploads of Eastern European Jewish immigrants into Americans.[87]

In settlement house classes, like those in Rosa Sonneschein's hometown of St. Louis, sisterhood women taught what was then called domestic economy. They covered the basics of sweeping, dusting, scrubbing, lamp cleaning, dishwashing, and "the mysteries of ventilation, drainage, [and] disinfectants." If such lessons were intended to train the immigrants as domestics, they failed. For the most part, Eastern European Jewish immigrant women preferred the wages and autonomy of almost any other job.[88]

This charity work required enormous resources. In 1909 the New York Sisterhoods of Personal Service spent over $151,000, the equivalent of $4 million today. Much of it came from the Jewesses' businessmen-husbands. Their financial wherewithal provided the charitable dollars and paid for the servants who cared for children and home while their wives attended to mission work among the newest immigrant Jews that these well-to-do matrons called the "unenlightened."[89]

Other monies came from fundraising schemes. When the Milwaukee Settlement published a housekeeping manual with recipes, it became the immensely successful *Settlement Cook Book*. Its profit built Milwaukee a new settlement home.

But, since not every settlement house produced a best seller, American Jewesses organized charity fairs. In Newark, Washington, Chicago, St. Louis, Denver, and San Francisco, they brought together the well-to-do in great style for good causes and demonstrated to Christian neighbors that Jews were upstanding citizens who cared for their own.

At New York's 1895 Great Hebrew Fair, a thousand women sold art, gloves, perfume, and dolls and poured hot chocolate and sodas. Dressed as letter carriers, they delivered love notes, and dressed like gypsies, with hair bound in scarves, they told fortunes. Welcoming children to the fair, New York's mayor told them that if they were good Jews and Jewesses, they would grow up to care for the less fortunate among their people.[90]

After World War I, the Sisterhoods of Personal Service gradually closed up shop. Professionalized social work replaced their volunteers with trained experts, mostly men. Organizing the grand charity fairs became such an arduous undertaking that their moment in time passed. In 1936 the last Sisterhood of Personal Service home, that of New York's Temple Emanu-El, closed its doors.

Yet as this rung in the ladder of American Jewesses' associations broke, another, founded in these years, holds steady to this day.

WHILE THE Sisterhoods of Personal Service and the National Council of Jewish Women were facing outward, the synagogue sisterhoods were turning inward to their congregations. From Buffalo to New Orleans, Selma to Seattle, synagogues had long had ladies' auxiliaries. New ones kept cropping up, like the one at Washington Hebrew Congregation in the nation's capital. It was founded, in 1905, by Carrie Obendorfer Simon.

Born in Alabama, Carrie Obendorfer was raised in Cincinnati, where she graduated from the Conservatory of Music, taught Sunday school, and joined the National Council of Jewish Women after her mother established its local section. In 1896 Carrie wed Rabbi Abram Simon, a recent graduate of the city's Hebrew Union College. The couple moved to congregations in Sacramento and Omaha before settling in Washington, DC, in 1904. A year later she became the founding president of its Ladies' Auxiliary Society. Its goal was clear: to help the congregation, nothing more, nothing less. Sisterhood lore recalls that fifty women attended the founding meeting, pledged themselves to ten-cent dues, promised to help pay off the building's mortgage, and in the spirit of being the temple's homemakers, promptly recessed to polish the doorknobs.[91]

Sisterhoods set out to encourage religious life and inspire more members and their families to attend services. In some places, they promoted congregational singing. Their women taught Sunday school, visited the ill, and alerted the rabbi to families in distress. In Anniston, Alabama, the ladies' auxiliary not only installed the organ, but also first purchased the lot and built the building, giving the congregation a debt-free gift.[92]

Making the house of the congregation a home, the sisterhood arranged flowers for the sanctuary, bought furniture, served refreshments, and took charge of social life. The nineteenth-century *Schwesterbund*'s sewing circles, strawberry parties, and the like gave way to the sisterhood's lectures, bridge games, teas, dinner dances, children's seders, and charity bazaars. In its first seven years, Washington Hebrew Ladies' Auxiliary raised over $5,000 for the temple's sinking fund, the equivalent of over a hundred thousand dollars today. That the congregation's all-purpose sinking fund had $8,943.05 in 1913 demonstrates the magnitude of the sisterhood's contribution. Sisterhoods also set up synagogue libraries and later gift shops.[93]

Ladies' temple societies had been around for more than half a century. Only when the council began losing members, as it seemed to abandon its original aim for religious work to focus on immigrant welfare, did Carrie Simon light on the idea of uniting the ladies' temple societies into a powerful national organization dedicated to religious work. In January 1913, representatives from fifty-two Reform synagogues founded the National Federation of

Temple Sisterhoods, renamed, in 1993, the Women of Reform Judaism. Within the decade Conservative sisterhoods joined together in
what became the Women's League for Conservative Judaism; and,
not long afterward Orthodox women launched the Women's Branch
of the Union of Orthodox Jewish Congregations of America.

Uniting local organizations along denominational lines heralded
sisterhoods' coming of age and proclaimed, asserted Carrie Simon,
the power and influence of the modern American Jewess. With
twenty thousand members at its founding, the National Federation
immediately became the largest American Jewish women's organization of its day.

The women of sisterhood exerted influence beyond the portals of their congregations. In Cincinnati, Reform women built a
dormitory for rabbinical students and pioneered Sisterhood Sabbath, a day, at first, when the rabbi would preach about women or
a woman would address the congregation from the pulpit. Later,
on Sisterhood Sabbaths, women led both the Friday evening and
the Saturday morning services. In the early 1960s, Reform sisterhood women championed women's ordination a decade before any
American woman was called rabbi. The women of Conservative
Judaism opened a student house and, in 1941, published the hugely
popular homemaker's guide *Jewish Home Beautiful*. The Orthodox
Women's Branch made itself a force for traditional Judaism with
pamphlets like *Yes, I Keep Kosher*.

Women, historically marginalized in synagogue worship, ritual,
and governance—even as in some congregations, especially Reform
ones, they became a majority of worshippers—found new opportunities through sisterhood branches. Sisterhoods propelled them
toward leadership, giving them new roles within their congregations and wider movements. Two years after uniting the women
of Reform Judaism, Carrie Simon confidently proclaimed, "Woman's emancipation is no longer to be argued; it may be dreaded,
deplored, or defied. But it is to be reckoned with." It was not fully
reckoned with then, but sisterhoods became so integral to the welfare of American Judaism that their members boasted no congregation could manage without one.[94]

LOOKING BEYOND their horizon, some Jewish women's gazes fell across the world on Palestine. Zionism, an international movement for the reestablishment of a Jewish nation in the land where the ancient kingdom of Israel was, became, after helping the poor and supporting their synagogues, the third avenue of activism for America's Jewish women.

The Zionism that came into view in the late nineteenth century had multiple origins. It was rooted in Jews' deep longing to return to the Holy Land as expressed, over the centuries, in prayer. But now disillusionment with the unfulfilled promises of Jewish emancipation added urgency to those prayers. In Western Europe, where modern political Zionism first emerged, Jews, no matter how assimilated, were still marked out as Jews. Defining the Jewish people as a race, an idea that Sonneschein and Apte embraced, may have resolved the quandary of classifying the Jews, but it called forth a new form of anti-Jewish hatred, antisemitism.

The term, coined in Germany in 1879, refers to prejudice against Jews because they are members of an inferior and dangerous Jewish race. Antisemites charged that Jews were plotting to take control of the world and destroy Western civilization. These ideas gained traction in Germany and France as antisemitic newspapers and political parties trumpeted that Jews could never be loyal citizens. By 1895, the depth of antisemitism in Europe convinced the Viennese journalist Theodore Herzl that emancipation had failed and that Jews must have their own homeland. The movement to create such a homeland, widely associated with Herzl, was called Zionism. But he was not the first to imagine this solution to what everyone was calling the Jewish problem. Among his predecessors was Emma Lazarus.

In "The Jewish Problem," Lazarus wrote that both in the United States and in Europe—where emancipation had ostensibly abolished civic and legal restrictions, allowing Jews to become citizens of their nations—the "Jewish problem . . . as old as history" that began with Pharaoh's persecution of the biblical Israelites had merely assumed a new guise in her day. Jews were "still universally exposed to injustice, proportioned to the barbarity" of the nations in which they lived. The only solution, she argued, was for the Jews to have their own nation, to find a new Ezra to lead them home, just as the biblical Ezra had led Jews out of exile in Persia back to Jerusalem. To promote her ideas, she helped found, in 1883, the short-lived Society for the Colonisation and Improvement of Eastern European Jews.[95]

In the late nineteenth century, Zionism still had little support among American Jews. Rosa Sonneschein was an exception. On her frequent travels to Europe, she had met Herzl a few times and later claimed that, even as her Viennese hosts mocked his harebrained Zionist scheme, she was mystically drawn to his vision and embraced it from the start. By then, antisemitism had become rampant not only in Russia, where pogroms had broken out, but also in France. There a scandal rocked the nation after Capt. Alfred Dreyfus, a French Jew, was convicted, in 1894, of treason on false evidence. Antisemitism was also disturbingly rising in the United States, as resorts and social clubs that had once welcomed well-to-do Jews changed their policies. In 1877, in Saratoga Springs, New York, the Grand Union Hotel turned away the banker Joseph Seligman and his wife Babet, despite their having stayed at the hotel previously. Now the hotel had adopted a "No Israelite" policy, and others followed.[96]

With antisemitism proliferating, Sonneschein became a committed Zionist. She never expected all Jews to emigrate to Palestine as other Zionists did. Instead, she joined Herzl in embracing the dream of a land for the Jewish homeless, a refuge for the persecuted of her people. In 1897 she appointed herself the lone representative of the American press to the First Zionist Congress that Herzl convened in Basel, Switzerland. Her enthusiasm for the meeting did not preclude her from criticizing the Congress's disenfranchisement of its female delegates. Hers was, in the late 1890s, a rare voice championing Zionism to Jewish Americans. But already there was another who would leave an unforgettable mark on the movement.[97]

THE IDEA that the Jews needed their own homeland gained traction in America after 1914, when war broke out in Europe. Relief for war-ravaged Eastern European Jewry took on new urgency. In the United States, Zionists found a charismatic leader in the future Supreme Court justice Louis D. Brandeis, who emphasized Zionism's compatibility with the American ideals of justice and democracy. He exhorted that "to be good Americans, we must be better Jews, and to be better Jews, we must become Zionists!" Heeding his call, men joined the Federation of American Zionists, and women flocked to Hadassah, the Women's Zionist Organization of America. Hadassah was the brainchild of the leading Jewish woman of her age, Henrietta Szold.[98]

As we saw, Szold grew up in Baltimore learning *Kinder und Küche* (children and cooking) from her mother. As the eldest in a rabbinic family with no sons, she studied Hebrew and sacred texts with her father. By the time she was in her teens, she had become his assistant, translator, and editor.

Szold was the valedictorian of her graduating high school class. She had hoped to continue her education and published an essay calling on Baltimore to establish a women's college, since no Baltimore college then admitted women. Going away to school, especially for a firstborn daughter needed at home, was just not done.

Szold became a teacher. Highly intelligent, exceedingly organized, and able to work countless hours, for the next fifteen years she taught language, mathematics, history, and sciences in a private, nondenominational girls' school and Jewish subjects in her father's congregation.

Meanwhile, by the 1880s, the Baltimore Jewish community was changing as Russian Jews settled there. Szold shared with her father a love for the Hebrew language. Meeting immigrants, already immersed in its revival, that became a pillar of Zionism, they formed a literary society to read Zionist thinkers. Szold introduced the group to Emma Lazarus. When this society established the first night school in the United States to teach immigrants English, Szold became the principal. She raised money, hired teachers, and bought chalk, pencils, and slates.[99]

If her first career was that of educator, her second, that of writer and editor, was already under way. Under the pen name Sulamith, Szold published "Our Baltimore Letter" in *The Jewish Messenger* at the same time that Sonneschein was writing "Our St. Louis Letter" in it. In 1893 Szold became the first paid employee of the Jewish Publication Society of America: her title, secretary. Today the work she did as translator, indexer, fact checker, proofreader, statistician, administrator, and writer would be termed editor-in-chief. The books begun or guided to publication during her time at JPS—works of Jewish history, literature, and thought, children's textbooks, and the inaugural annual volumes of the *American Jewish Year Book*, with their lists of Jewish organizations and essays about Jews at home and abroad, and which continues to be published—left an indelible imprint on American Jewish life.[100]

A few years later, while continuing her work for the Jewish Publication Society, she and her mother moved to New York. There Henrietta studied at the Jewish Theological Seminary to deepen her knowledge of rabbinic literature, hoping to edit the papers of her father, who had died in 1902. Her request to sit alongside the men preparing to become rabbis had raised again, as Ray Frank had, the subject of women's ordination. But Szold reassured the seminary's leaders that she had no intention of becoming a rabbi.

In New York, Szold joined a women's Zionist study group and became part of the seminary's circle. She tutored its European faculty in English and edited their work. Spending countless hours with Louis Ginzberg, editing his magnum opus, *Legends of the Jews*, Szold, age forty-two, fell in love with the professor, thirteen years her junior. When, in the summer of 1908, he returned from his annual visit to his parents in Europe and announced that he had become engaged to an eighteen-year-old, Szold was devastated.

To help her get over her heartbreak, in 1909, Szold, accompanied by her mother, took a life-changing trip to Palestine. There she saw children with wreaths of flies circling their diseased eyes. She knew that when she returned to New York, she must speak of the filth, disease, and misery that she had seen. "What is the use of reading papers and arranging festivals?" her mother prodded, referring to

Szold's Zionist reading group. American Jewish women must take up practical work for Palestine. That practical work would engage Szold for the rest of her long life.[101]

In 1910 she became secretary of the Federation of American Zionists, a group founded in 1897. But worn out by her despair and the immense obligations of trying to bring order to the federation and her ongoing work for the Jewish Publication Society, she fell ill. In 1911 she had surgery, then a long convalescence.

In 1912 on Purim, Szold, then fifty-two, and thirty-seven other Jewish women met to lay the foundation for a new organization, an army of women dedicated to building up Jewish life and institutions in Palestine and promoting Zionism in America. They called their new organization the Daughters of Zion, Hadassah Chapter—naming the group for Purim's heroine, Esther, whose Hebrew name was Hadassah—and elected Szold president. Not long afterward the Daughters of Zion revised their name to Hadassah, the Women's Zionist Organization of America. Hadassah became Szold's third career.

SZOLD was a towering figure in her lifetime. Even after she moved, in 1927, to Jerusalem, where she set up the Jewish community's social welfare system, she remained an icon of American Jewish womanhood, her milestone birthdays celebrated by Hadassah groups in the United States until her death in 1945.

But she did not labor alone. Among Hadassah's other early leaders was Emma Gottheil, the daughter of Palestinian Jews and the daughter-in-law of Gustav Gottheil, rabbi at the prominent Reform synagogue, Temple Emanu-El, and a Zionist. When, in 1898, Emma Gottheil became a delegate to the Second World Zionist Congress, Sonneschein predicted that this time the men would not dare deny women the right to vote, and she was right. Later Gottheil broke from Hadassah, charging that Szold and her cohort had run its medical projects like a personal fiefdom. She established the Keren Hayesod Women's League to raise monies that the World Zionist

Organization, which was based in Europe, would distribute to its various projects in Palestine.[102]

A shared passion for Zionism and a commitment to doing essential work to build a Jewish homeland knit together its founders. Szold expected American Jewish women to grasp not only the necessity of a sanctuary for persecuted Jews but also their own need for a center of Jewish culture and vitality to inspire their lives and work. Writing, in 1915, to convey Hadassah's message to Reform's sisterhoods, she was sure that American Jewesses could not possibly turn their backs on Zionism and Hadassah's plans to see it realized. But of course, she was wrong. Most Reform Jews then did not embrace the Zionist dream.[103]

Not only Hadassah's aims were unique among the organizations founded by Jewish women; so were its members. Zionism crossed social and economic lines, and Hadassah did too. Workingwomen—teachers, shopgirls, stenographers, factory workers—also joined the organization. Working girls met in the evenings, the more well-to-do in the afternoons. Some even ran their meetings in Yiddish.[104]

Hadassah exported to the Jewish community in Palestine American women's successful social welfare projects. Its mission, to improve the lives and health of women and children, Jew and Arab, crystallized in 1913, when two American Jewish nurses sailed to Palestine, rented a house in Jerusalem, and hung a sign in Hebrew and English: "American Daughters of Zion, Nurses Settlement, Hadassah." In their first year, they saw five thousand patients. The settlement shuttered during the turmoil of World War I, but after the war, Hadassah returned with the American Zionist Medical Unit.[105]

Hadassah asked not only what America's Jewish women could do for Palestine but what Hadassah could do for America's Jewish women. America's Jewish women needed Zionism, in Szold's estimation, as much as Jews, hounded elsewhere, needed the Zionist homeland as a place of refuge. Hadassah connected American Jewish women to Jewish people around the world. It built up the medical and social welfare infrastructure of the future Jewish state. But it also built up American Jewish women by opening pathways for vital service to their people and propelling its leaders into the rough-and-tumble politics of the world Zionist movement.

DURING THE PROGRESSIVE ERA (1890–1920), the age of great social and political reform, a small group of America's Jewish women made activism for the Jewish community their springboard to wider action for all. As one woman explained, nothing precluded their turning their enormous energies to the great problems besetting the country.[106]

The very same forces that propelled Jewish women to aid penniless immigrants, fight against white slavery, and bring nurses to Palestine compelled social reformers, Christian and Jewish, male and female, to tackle a range of urban and national ills. Even before women could vote, the web of women's organizations bent on effecting public policy constituted an informal female dominion. Working across ethnic, religious, and racial divides, women joined forces to address the evils spawned by urbanization, industrialization, and immigration. They targeted inadequate education and health care, drew attention to intolerable working conditions, called for consumer protections, and demanded woman's rights.

Working tirelessly as professional volunteers, a small group of women, many in New York, won acclaim, locally and nationally, as leaders of reform projects. Their efforts to aid impoverished Russian Jewish immigrants had demonstrated to them the necessity for the larger solutions that would necessitate government intercession. Yet because care for their own people remained paramount even as they campaigned to better the lives of all, they stood apart, remaining a distinctive subgroup among the country's female activists.

Hannah Bachman had grown up in New York, the daughter of German Jewish immigrants who worshipped at Temple Emanu-El. She continued her membership after marrying William Einstein and in 1897 became president of Emanu-El's Sisterhood of Personal Service. She held that position for the next twenty-five years while also becoming president of the city's Federation of Sisterhoods. Dividing New York into districts and assigning one to each sisterhood, the federation centralized and coordinated their relief efforts. Einstein had knocked on doors in tenements where she met widowed and abandoned mothers who, forced to work, were unable to care properly for their children. She saw for herself their anguish when, having no other option, they placed their children in orphanages, where, if they were fortunate, they could visit them once a week.

To increase her work's effectiveness, Einstein took courses in criminology and sociology at Columbia University, which persuaded her that the nation's future rested on the stability of the family. It was thought that broken families bred juvenile delinquency. While orphanages kept children off the streets, fed them, and educated them, the regimented days with their clamoring bells were no substitute for a loving mother. Convinced that the state's abiding interest in its future citizens would best be served by allowing widowed mothers to stay out of the workforce and at home with their children, she entered into politics, campaigning for mothers' pensions. She became chair of the state's committee investigating relief for widowed mothers. Its report led to New York State's groundbreaking 1915 Widowed Mothers Pension Act, which gave qualifying applicants a state pension to care for their children at home. From its passage until her death in 1929, Einstein worked to implement the law and raise funds for widowed mothers who had been ruled ineligible for state pensions because their husbands had not been citizens.[107]

Lillian Wald, another of the era's social activists, became a nurse among the immigrant poor. Her "baptism of fire" came the day she hiked up a tenement's grimy steps to discover a Lower East Side mother hemorrhaging from giving birth two days before. Her experience led her, on her twenty-sixth birthday in 1893, to found the Nurses Settlement to provide public health care to the poor. Its nurses were on call seven days a week, twenty-four hours a day. In its first year, this troupe of visiting nurses treated 4,500 patients. They provided more than health care, pointing the unemployed to jobs and intervening on behalf of children having problems in school and with the police. In 1895, thanks to the generosity of the

Jewish philanthropist Jacob Schiff, Wald and the nurses moved into a larger house that became the Henry Street Settlement. It continued to provide health care but expanded into a full-fledged settlement house, with clubs for children and the first playground on the Lower East Side. Its social workers helped immigrants learn English and offered vocational training.

There Wald forged bonds with a broad coalition of activists bent not only on helping the poor but also on remedying urban and national problems. They campaigned for playgrounds, parks, and better housing; government-mandated safety and sanitation in the workplace; and special safeguards for workingwomen and children. The historic civil rights organization, the National Association for the Advancement of Colored People, was founded at the Henry Street Settlement. In the settlement's backyard, immigrant sewing girls gathered to unionize.[108]

Other Jewish women took on further roles in the public sector. As a young woman, Belle Moskowitz had dreamed of a career on the stage, but instead she ended up planning entertainments for immigrant Jews at the Educational Alliance, another historic settlement house on New York's Lower East Side. While raising a family, she also became active in the New York chapter of the National Council of Jewish Women.

She took charge of its Lakeview Home for pregnant and unwed Jewish mothers, which started in temporary quarters on Staten Island in 1905, as a place where "wayward girls are taught useful and better lives." By the time its permanent building was dedicated six years later, 150 unwed Jewish mothers had passed through its doors. They had learned how to care for themselves and their babies and acquired skills in housekeeping, laundry, and sewing that were intended to help them support themselves when they left the home. Several of its graduates, its founders reported with satisfaction, had even married.[109]

Another of Belle Moskowitz's projects for the Council of Jewish Women was lobbying the New York Assembly to license the dance halls that working-class girls frequented. The close dancing, flowing alcohol, tango teas—where shopgirls learned the sexualized

Argentinian dance—and links to gangsters had led to the pregnancy of many of the young women she met at the Lakeview Home. She campaigned to license dance halls, keeping minors and prostitutes out of them and closing them at 11:30 p.m. rather than at 3:00 a.m. It was her first foray into state politics, and her success brought her to the attention of New York's future governor Al Smith. She became his most trusted adviser, chief sounding board, and press agent during his unsuccessful presidential campaigns. When she died in 1933, from complications after a fall, at fifty-six, a bereft Smith called the death of this political trailblazer, one of the most influential women in politics of her day, "a disaster."[110]

At eleven years old, Julia Richman had announced that she would not marry, "but before I die, all New York will know my name." She led the council's Sabbath School Committee to establish mission schools to teach immigrant Jewish children their religion. Then, becoming a school superintendent on the Lower East Side, she instituted what a later generation would call English-language immersion. Unfortunately, she went too far in strictness, telling teachers that children lapsing into their native tongues should have their mouths washed out with soap. The idea of allowing only English to be used in the classroom, however, was a smart one. Richman, not surprisingly, angered many immigrant parents, but her peers praised her loyalty and devotion to her community.[111]

Two sisters, Maud Nathan and Annie Nathan Meyer, cousins of Emma Lazarus, trod different paths to reform. Intelligent, ambitious, and needing higher education to further those ambitions, Annie Nathan took the exams that would admit her to Columbia's Collegiate Course for Women. She had studied secretly because she knew her father would oppose her going to college. When she announced that she had passed the exams and planned to enroll in the Collegiate Course, her father tried to stop her. She would never marry, he said: husbands "hate intelligent wives."

Established in 1883, the Collegiate Course admitted females to Columbia but did not permit them to attend class. Instead they met once a semester with each of their professors and were given assigned readings. At the end of the term, the women sat for the same exams that their male "classmates" were taking. Annie Nathan never forgot her despair when she saw their questions. She had done the reading, but the tests were based on the forbidden lectures. Frustrated, she quit the course.

Annie Nathan did marry, and her husband, a physician, fifteen years her senior, never objected to her secluding herself to write each morning, even if that meant that she was discourteous, refusing to be interrupted by anyone who unwittingly came calling during her writing time. She became a prolific author of essays, novels, plays, and a memoir.

But Meyer never forgot her dream of women's higher education. A casual meeting with Columbia's chief librarian propelled her, still in her twenties, on the path to establishing a women's college in Manhattan. She launched a campaign to make that dream a reality, contacting every person who might help, either financially or by positively influencing others. She gave talks and interviews, wrote letters and editorials, and persuaded well-known New Yorkers, including a bishop, to write articles supporting a woman's college. She buttonholed every member of Columbia's board of trustees to win their support and signed the lease for the new school's brownstone. In October 1889 her work bore fruit when the women's college Barnard, named for Columbia's tenth president, Frederick A. P. Barnard, admitted its first class. She remained active in its affairs for the rest of her life.[112]

Meyer's elder sister Maud Nathan championed woman's rights not by founding a women's college but by striving to improve the lives of workingwomen and campaigning for female suffrage. Early in her marriage to her first cousin Frederick Nathan, she reveled in the life of a well-to-do society wife, spending her mornings practicing her singing, her afternoons shopping and visiting friends, and her spare time volunteering in her synagogue, where she was the founding president of the sisterhood. But the death of her only child drove her to find a cause into which to throw herself. She joined the New York Consumers League, which urged shoppers to improve the lives of factory women sewing in sweatshops and of salesgirls who waited on the well-heeled in department stores while standing on their feet sixty hours a week. Nathan was the league's president for over a quarter century.

The Consumers League told the women of New York that they were responsible for the terrible working conditions and that they could use the power of the purse to fix them. It called for setting living wages throughout the garment industry and wanted working girls and women to have a voice in determining them. It established minimum standards for stores—shortened hours, evening closings, seats behind the counters, and half-holidays in the summer—and then published a list of the complying stores and asked consumers to support them. Nathan, who had once spent afternoons buying whalebones and crinolines to send to her dressmaker, said that if women would shop in stores certified by the Consumers League, no shopgirl would ever "faint before their eyes."[113]

Opposing her sister Annie, who was anti-suffrage, Maud wrote letter after letter to those with the power to change the law and grant women the vote. She reasoned that in a democracy, all the people elect their leaders; "Ergo, either we are not living in a democracy or else women are not people."[114]

Nathan and Meyer may have disagreed about suffrage, but they were joined in confronting antisemitism. At the time, apartment rentals and jobs were openly advertised for Gentiles only. When young, Annie had clipped articles about antisemitic incidents and pasted them in her scrapbooks, and she had also personally experienced antisemitic slights. Even Barnard's official histories limited her role in its founding. Perhaps her outspoken opposition to woman suffrage, which she broadcast in The New York Times, was awkward for the women's college. She knew, though, that some considered her being Jewish undesirable for Barnard's founder. In the 1930s, as antisemitism crescendoed at home and abroad, Meyer, a prolific writer, used her pen to expose Americans who shared what she called Hitler's "insane hatred" for her people.[115]

Maud Nathan, too, encountered antisemitism. In 1920, at a suffrage meeting in Switzerland, she heard a delegate blame Jewish profiteers for postwar suffering. That contretemps uncannily presaged late twentieth-century Jewish feminists' confrontations with antisemitism in the international women's movement.[116]

Nathan felt that her combination of volunteer interests—embracing Jewish particularity as well as universal needs—made her a pioneer among Jewish women for venturing beyond the Jewish community to serve the country. But Hannah Einstein, Lillian Wald, Belle Moskowitz, Julia Richman, and her own sister Annie Meyer proved that she was not alone among America's Jewish women in serving both her Jewish and her national communities. In towns and cities across the United States, Jewish women like Denver's Frances Wisebart Jacobs and Chicago's Hannah Solomon, grappling with the hodgepodge of the era's problems, also earned a place in the network of female movers and shakers who ventured beyond philanthropy into politics. Nevertheless, caring for other Jews and defending them against calumny continued to set them apart, even as they tried to make the world a better place for coming generations.[117]

IN 1914 war broke out in Europe, a war that Wald, a pacifist, strenuously opposed, considering it a violation of the current generation's obligation to do better for the next. The Great War, as World War I was then known, pitted the Allies (England, Belgium, France, and Russia) against the Central Powers (Germany and the Austro-Hungarian and Ottoman empires). It eventually engulfed the entire continent, stretched to Palestine, and swept up millions of Jews, both soldiers and civilians, in its horrific path.

Initially the United States remained neutral, as Americans vociferously debated their nation's future, weighing militarism over pacifism. Then German submarines began attacking American merchant ships in the North Atlantic, and President Woodrow Wilson asked Congress to declare war on Germany, which it did on April 6, 1917. U.S. involvement lasted but nineteen months; still, four million American men went to war, while American women, including Jews, took up the war work they could do from home shores.

But before we turn to America's Jewish women and the Great War, we must spend more time with the "new kind of Jewess" that Emma Lazarus discovered on Ward's Island. On many occasions, the more settled and the more recent Jewesses had crossed paths. They had met on the docks at immigrant reception stations, at the train depots the weary travelers passed through, in the settlement houses on the Lower East Side, across the counters of department stores, and at rallies protesting miserable working conditions. Although their paths had crossed, these two groups of Jewish women—those who had been settled in the United States for generations and their Eastern European immigrant distant cousins—lived parallel lives. Having peered into the world of American Jewesses, we want to visit with the women whose journeys from the shtetl to the United States turned them into America's new Jewish women.

3

"A new kind of Jewess"

EASTERN EUROPEAN
JEWISH WOMEN IN AMERICA

MMA LAZARUS DIED long before New York's imposing immigration reception station, Ellis Island, opened in 1892. Lazarus had encountered that sorrowing young mother whose baby was dying at New York's Ward's Island. Although the poet did not know it at the time, this "new kind of Jewess" was the vanguard of a wave of 25 million immigrants who were about to change the face of America. Among them were Italian sewing girls, Polish meat packers, Irish lady's maids, and Japanese picture brides. Propelled from their homes by poverty and drawn to America's "golden door" by dreams of economic opportunity and freedom, they were carried across the ocean in steamship steerage.

Their numbers included an astounding 2.5 million Jews, about a fifth of the world's Jewish population, and nearly half of them were women. A few tens of thousands sailed from the Ottoman Empire and Mediterranean lands; some were the descendants of Jews who, like Lazarus's ancestors, had been expelled from Spain centuries before. Others came from Hapsburg Galicia and Romania. But three-quarters were Jews fleeing the shtetls and cities of the Russian Empire, which years before had gobbled up the shtetls and cities of the Kingdom of Poland.

One of them was Bessie Abramowitz (later Hillman). Born Bas-

Sheva Abramowitz in 1889 in a village in the Pale of Settlement—the westernmost provinces of the Russian Empire where Jews were permitted to live—she was the fourth of ten children. Her father, a commission agent at the railroad depot, tramped the countryside selling goods that he bought from merchants passing through; her mother fed those merchants and other passengers at their large home, which doubled as an inn. Private tutors taught Bas-Sheva and her siblings; hers even gave her Karl Marx to read. But her real schooling came from her mother, who was raising her to follow in her own footsteps to become a proper Jewish wife and mother. Surely, Bas-Sheva also helped out at home and not only with the chores and younger children but also at the inn.[1]

In her early teens, perhaps because she wanted to earn money to journey to America, she left the village to work, most likely in the burgeoning garment industry in a nearby town. Then at the age of fifteen, overhearing her parents and a matchmaker planning to marry her off to the butcher's son, she pleaded with her father not to force her to do this terrible thing, as she saw it. Instead, she and a "sister," most likely a cousin, joined the throngs of Russian Jews streaming westward. Claiming she was twenty-one, with twenty-four dollars in her pocket, and the address of another "sister" in Chicago, Bas-Sheva boarded the SS Rotterdam bound for New York. Twelve days later, in December 1905, after a voyage filled with the tumult of the steerage throngs, she disembarked at Ellis Island.

Abramowitz had fled an arranged marriage, but violence drove other Jews across the sea. Pogromniks burned one young girl's family alive while she was in the outhouse, leaving the devastated fifteen-year-old to cross Europe alone on foot to catch a boat bound for America. While waves of pogroms periodically erupted, the struggle to earn a decent living, made ever more hopeless by a welter of antisemitic restrictions and limitations, propelled most of the Jewish emigrants to pack up and leave.[2]

Despite the myth enshrined in Jewish memory that tradition ruled the Old World, it was very much a world in transition. The writer Israel Joshua Singer, one of the millions of Jewish immigrants to America, recalled seeing his pious mother, Bathsheba, weeping in their Polish village of Leoncin, as she read the eighteenth-century *The Rod of Chastisement,* a book detailing the terrible fates await-ing sinners. It told of mothers who, having neglected to shield their bosoms while nursing, had their breasts impaled on fiery hooks in Hell. But the winds of change that brought Abramowitz to read Karl Marx and refuse the arranged match testify to the impact of modern ideas and the transformations under way. Consequently, new kinds of Jewesses, not just "a new kind of Jewess," were mak-ing their way to America in the decades after 1880.[3]

Unlike some immigrant groups, most Jews came to America to stay. Poverty propelled fathers to set off on their own. Rose Pines (later Cohen) was just a toddler when her father, to avoid the tsar's draft, left Vilkomir, in Lithuania, then part of the Russian Empire, and sailed for America in 1913. He left his wife on her own, to run the shoe store and to raise their three children under the age of three. Heading to Baltimore where his wife had two sisters, he expected soon to bring over his family.[4]

Decades later children like his remembered their hungry, bitter childhoods without a father or a father's income. Relatives tried to help, but they had their own large families. Daughters needed dowries, and sons needed bribes to escape military service. Children left school to learn a trade; sons were apprenticed to cobblers and tailors, daughters to dressmakers and milliners. When a distraught wife no longer had money for wood to heat the stove, after the creditors had taken every-thing she owned, and after she had borrowed all her relatives would lend, she set off to the charities, tears streaming down her cheeks.

They turned to tears of joy the day ships' tickets for America arrived. Now the wife had to sell whatever belongings remained, to liquidate a business if she had one, and to find an agent to help her, with squabbling children in tow, steal across the border. (Acquir-ing passports meant navigating a government minefield that most immigrants wisely shunned.) She would guard over her brood as they journeyed on foot, by cart, or by train; see them through sundry inspections; propel them up the gangway; and watch over them amid steerage's disorder and seasickness, until at last "the big woman with the spikes on her head" came into view. Then she still had to overcome the hurdle of passing U.S. immigration inspection; failure would mean returning across the sea. A woman traveling alone, as mentioned, faced another danger: white slavers lurked to rape her or trick her into a false marriage before dispatching her to a brothel on the other side of the world. No wonder Abramowitz traveled in the company of her "sister."[5]

But for some like Rose Pines, her siblings, and her mother, the Great War, with its terrible disruptions, intruded. Rose, born in 1911, was too young to remember how Russians, Germans, Lithuanians, Poles, and Bolsheviks turned Vilkomir's streets into a battleground. In 1918, in the great influenza pandemic, her mother died. The children ended up living with their paternal grandparents in the small town of Tauregin, where Rose's grandfather was a rabbi, and where, Rose recalled, men earned a few pennies delivering buckets of water suspended from a pole laid across their shoulders.

The half-orphans remained there until 1922. Then, even as the United States was already setting its first immigration quotas, their father managed to arrange for visas. Gliding into New York harbor, Rose, her sister, and her brother, accompanied by an uncle, entered the Promised Land at Ellis Island and reunited with the father they scarcely remembered.

"Becoming an American lady!"

IN AMERICA, arriving Jewish immigrants often had Yiddish in common. A majority lived on New York's Lower East Side, while others settled where well-to-do American Jews lived: in Boston, Philadelphia, Baltimore, Columbus, Chicago, and Sioux City. Immediately, many of the newest immigrants, mocked as greenhorns, began reinventing themselves as Americans.

For married women, that meant discarding the *sheitel* (wig) and kerchief that modest Jewish women, reserving all their beauty for their husbands, donned the day they wed. While an attack on the *sheitel* was already under way in the shtetl, many, perhaps most, married women there still covered their hair.

In America the attack became a full-fledged assault. Sending home passage for his family, Israel Antin, who had landed in Boston three years before, demanded his wife step onto the road to progress and leave her wig behind. In America, daughters, chagrined by their old-fashioned mothers, plotted, pleaded, and cajoled them to put away the wig and kerchief. Not everyone did; my great-grandmother did not. One old-fashioned woman, refusing to give up her wig, reflected, "It's rather late to begin sinning." But others surprised their husbands, who, returning home from work one day, found their wives with their hair smartly styled by their daughters, and applauded them: "Already you are becoming an American lady!"[6]

"Becoming an American lady" required abandoning the old country dress. A woman wearing a kerchief on her head, an ankle-length calico dress covered by an apron, layers of petticoats, a large shawl, thick woolen stockings, and clumsy, heavy shoes was clearly a newcomer fresh off the boat in serious need of new American clothes. Israel Antin's daughter, Mary, who would grow up to write a memoir of her first years in Boston, *The Promised Land*, recalled the "fairy godmother," a neighbor, who took her uptown to a dazzling palace, with the curious name "department store," where she acquired her first real machine-made American clothes.[7]

Another child, landing in New York, figured it must be a holiday: all the children were wearing shoes and stockings. "If it weren't a holiday, they'd be barefoot," she exclaimed. But American girls and boys wore shoes and stockings every day; their mothers put off their wigs; and their older sisters swept up their hair into great puffs piled atop their heads. Over those puffs, immigrant mothers and daughters, if they could afford them, perched fancy hats of silk and straw decorated with feathers, ribbons, and roses. Not only did all respectable American women wear hats, but they changed them to suit the season's fashion and the occasion: daytime's straw boater just would not do for an afternoon suit.[8]

Jewish immigrant girls and their mothers learned about fashion from working in the clothing industry. Not long after Bas-Sheva Abramowitz landed in New York, she boarded a train for Chicago.

There, renamed Bessie, she moved into a boardinghouse on Halsted Street, west of the Chicago River, in the ward dubbed the immigrant ghetto, and began working as a hand-button sewer in a garment shop, one of tens of thousands of immigrant Jewish women hunched over their work in tenement sweatshops and clanging factories. Whether they stitched until their aching fingers bled or stood all day behind the counters of stores selling clothes and sundries while their feet swelled, their uniform was the skirt and the shirtwaist, a blouse that buttoned, like a man's shirt, down the front. A working girl could afford several relatively inexpensive shirtwaists. Pairing them with her one dark-colored tailored skirt and the right hat for the season, she had her wardrobe.

Immigrant mothers, who grew up wearing their best only on Sabbaths and holidays, complained about how much their daughters spent on clothes. To buy a new hat, working girls went for weeks subsisting on lunches of dry cake and little else. After all, they reasoned, a girl must have clothes if she were to be presentable.

"Broom, washtub, and pot": Keeping House and Raising a Family in Jewtown[9]

A CACOPHONY assaulted immigrants, just off the boat or train, heading into the crowded city streets: the clatter of horse-drawn carts, the rattle of elevated trains and streetcars, the whir of sewing machines spilling out of open windows, the screech of wheeled clotheslines on roofs, the singsong of boys learning the *alef-beis* of the Hebrew alphabet, the scales of girls practicing piano, the shouts of newsboys hawking papers, and the shrill voices of women bargaining over pushcarts. Amid the clamor and the crowds, in run-down immigrant neighborhoods that some Americans called ghettoes or Jewtowns, America's newest Jewish women began making homes.

As the immigrants poured in, urban tenement construction boomed. But the purportedly new and improved dumbbell tenements failed to alleviate the worst abuses of the older railroad flats, with their stifling, windowless interior rooms. Narrow air shafts, meant to bring light and ventilation into rooms facing the sides, cinched these walk-ups into their dumbbell shape. But with buildings six stories high, windows overlooking the air shafts got little light and air, and the passages, which could not easily be accessed for cleaning, became dumping grounds for garbage.

Trudging up four or five dark, steep flights of stairs, immigrant Jewish women set up house. Their apartments had one or two bedrooms, a parlor, and a kitchen with a gas stove. To the immigrant wife, seeing a flame appear at the strike of a match and cooking without chopping wood, hauling coal, or taking out the ashes was a marvel. The parlor doubled as a workroom: there many families and their workers stitched during the day. Tenants from the four apartments on each floor shared the two toilets in the hall. A mezuzah on the doorpost, a *pushke* (charity box) on the table, and candlesticks on a shelf for Sabbath eves signaled that this was a Jewish home.

Rarely did a family live alone. New York's housing inspectors reported that three, four, five, or more people slept in a single room, stretched out on makeshift beds of boards balanced between chairs or even on the floor. It was not that families were so large but rather that boarders, along with roaches and bedbugs, inhabited the tenements.

Despite the ghettoes' overcrowding and the buildings' shabbiness, Jewish settlement house workers preached, as we saw, middle-class housekeeping to immigrant wives. They lectured on the arts of dusting and of napkin rings, on the proper washing and drying of glassware—immediately, to avoid spots—and on the imperative to fold the tablecloth neatly at the end of each day. Such expectations conveyed to the immigrant housewife, who shuttled from broom to washtub to pot, that her work was never done.

Sadly, for too many there came a day when there was nothing to put in that pot. The careful housewife, who had squirreled away a little money for hard times, dipped into her stash. But others—the single, divorced, and widowed who lived close to poverty's edge— declined into abject misery, at a pace recorded by pawnshop tickets.

One by one their possessions disappeared, starting with the gold watch and ending with all but the woman's last shirtwaist. Nurse Lillian Wald had wanted to send a mother and her seven children to a charity picnic, but the children were almost naked. Mothers, reduced to boarding in someone else's apartment, put their children to sleep on the floor and took in washing—an exhausting job that required boiling vats of water on the stove and hauling baskets of heavy, wet clothes to lines on the roof. Widows, often at the bottom of the heap, reluctantly surrendered their youngest children to orphanages, where they could see them for an hour on Sundays. After a despondent young woman whose children were starving discovered that neighbors had left food on her doorstep, she, utterly ashamed, slit her own throat.[10]

Her despair over her starving children cut to the core of the immigrant Jewish mother's charge. Her chief responsibility was to stretch the money coming in to feed her family. America offered immigrant Jews access, if they had money, to an abundance of foods, old and new. Foods once reserved for Sabbaths and holidays— blintzes, strudel, knishes, and meat—became the stuff of everyday fare. Friday mornings found immigrant mothers in their kitchens frying onions, peeling carrots, and chopping up carp that had been swimming the day before. As they cooked Sabbath dinners— challah, gefilte fish from that carp, chopped liver, chicken soup, roast chicken, meat with potatoes and onions, carrot and prune *tzimmes*, and fruit compote, washed down with seltzer, port wine, and tea—they were feeding their children not only food but also heritage, making for them memories of their origins, their history, and their people meant to last a lifetime. But the existence of kosher soup kitchens, like the one the women ran at Philadelphia's Congregation Keneseth Israel, and local Jewish charities' annual tallies of what they spent on milk, eggs, and butter, point to the cruelties of immigrant poverty amid American abundance.

The imperative of the Jewish dietary laws escalated the centrality of food for these women. Probably most Eastern European Jewish mothers never mixed milk and meat, never cooked shellfish or pork, bought only kosher meat, and kept separate dishes for dairy, meat, and Passover. But some, after they came to the United States, gradually abandoned these traditions. Perhaps they lived where kosher meat was not easy to obtain. Others, in the next generation, no longer cared. One woman wrote her sister that if their mother was not coming to her home for Passover, she would leave the holiday dishes in their box. "But," she cautioned, "please do not tell Mother."[11]

Pushed to become Americans, pulled by the Jewish traditions of their past, these new kinds of Jewesses followed different paths into America. Pious women lit Sabbath candles and prayed that their children would never desecrate the Sabbath. Some wives held on to traditions even as their husbands abandoned them. Mary Antin's father believed that a wife must follow her husband's law in all affairs. Yet even as he kept his store open on the Sabbath, he did not meddle with her kosher kitchen and Shabbos candles. On the High Holidays, he bought her a synagogue ticket but sent their children to school. His wife could do as she pleased, so long as it did not interfere with the family's march into becoming American.

When immigrant Kaila Grobsmith, who became the well-known travel writer and memoirist Kate Simon, was growing up, her mother would polish the furniture with lemon oil and make gefilte fish on Fridays. As the Sabbath descended, covering her hair as a proper married woman should, Kaila's mother lit the candles and recited the ancient prayer blessing God who commanded the kindling of the Sabbath lights. But one Sabbath eve, in the midst of the prayer, she suddenly stopped, tore off her headcloth, and blew out the candles. Turning to her astonished family, Kaila's mother exclaimed: "No more. I never believed it, I don't now. And I don't have to do it to please my mother, or anyone, here." She never lit candles again. Yet afterward, Kaila recalled, Friday nights still smelled of lemon oil and fish.[12]

Buying kosher poultry and meat raised its own set of challenges. According to a 1915 study, butchers routinely lied: only 40 percent of those purportedly selling kosher meat actually did. But there was no way to tell. Kosher meat was then, as today, expensive.[13]

Housewives watched every penny and prided themselves on buying the freshest fish and unbruised vegetables at bargain prices.

Rising prices angered mothers, the family's household managers, who always felt that catastrophe lay just around the corner. The slack season in the sweatshop, a sudden illness, or the death of a husband could plunge a family over the edge into dire poverty.

In charge of the family's shopping, they needed those pennies saved not only for an impending disaster but also for the children's new clothes for the High Holidays. Passover, when observant Jews eat off dishes other than those used the rest of the year, became the occasion to dump old, chipped crockery and buy new that could be used until the next Passover came around. If things were going well, immigrant housewives treated themselves to some cut glass to put in a china closet and bought, on an installment plan, a secondhand piano. That piano signified immigrant achievement and dreams for the future. "Für Elise," thumping from an apartment in the afternoons after the children returned from school, announced that this family was on the road to becoming real Americans.

If the housewife budgeted very carefully, the family could enjoy another American indulgence, a vacation, escaping the heat of Chicago's summer streets for Lake Michigan's South Haven and leaving Newark and Philadelphia for Asbury Park on the Jersey shore. But the grandest of all the Jewish vacation playgrounds was New York's Catskill Mountains. Affectionately dubbed the Borscht Belt, for the beet soup Russian Jews ate, it began as a Jewish immigrant adventure in farming, spurred for some by the same ideas that led Zionist Jews to drain Palestine's swamps, and, for others, by the summer heat and too many restless children.

In 1914, after failing at several businesses, immigrants Malke and Asher Grossinger bought a run-down Catskills farmhouse without electricity, heat, or indoor plumbing. When it became apparent that they could not make a living farming, they began taking in paying guests. Making blintzes by the hundreds so that no one would ever leave the farmhouse hungry, the boardinghouse became so successful that, five years later, the family sold it and bought a hotel. A web of Catskills hotels, boardinghouses, bungalow colonies, and *kuchalayns*—where guests did their own cooking over a propane stove and shared an icebox while the owner nagged that they used too much of her gas and water—bloomed. During the week, this Jewish vacationland was a world of women and children; husbands and fathers trekked up by train for the weekends.

But of course, not every immigrant mother enjoyed a vacation or found happiness in America. Some endured and lived in service to a dream, the dream that her children would succeed in the golden land. She prayed that, in coming to America, God had led her on the right path, that in this free country, her children would become decent people. If they were healthy and happy, if her daughters married well, if her sons became good providers for their own families, then, with pride tinged with relief, she would be able to announce: "Now I come to say with all my heart that I have it good. I am happy with America."[14]

But the golden land also defaulted on its promises. By the time one mother and her four daughters arrived to join her husband and two sons, she found the men in the advanced stages of tuberculosis. Within a few years, they died, and so did her eldest daughter, in childbirth. "America, the land of abundance," wrote her grandson, the physician Sherwin Nuland, "had provided her with an abundance of sorrow . . . the nation of opportunity stole her dreams and returned them tearstained and desolate."[15]

To LIVE, to keep a roof over one's head, to put food on the table, to save, as Bessie Abramowitz did—for ships' tickets to bring over siblings and to send money back to needy parents—husbands, fathers, daughters, and sons went out to work. Immigrant wives and mothers rarely did. In these years, only a tiny percentage of white married American women were working for wages outside the home. While immigrant Jewish mothers were most definitely working, most did not go "out to work."

The heart of the Jewish immigrant economy, in New York and in cities like Philadelphia, Baltimore, and Abramowitz's Chicago, was the garment industry. Before they married, young immigrant women worked in the needle trades' sweatshops, workshops, and factories. But when they married, they left the factory behind, just as their mothers had. Jewish husbands did not want their wives under the thumb of some foreman. Without a grandmother or mother around to help with the children and with the oldest daughter in school or in the factory, immigrant mothers had to mind their children on their own. So they did not go out to work; work came to the home. Working mothers rocked the cradle while they sewed piecework in the parlor, getting up from their machines to fix lunch for family and workers on the same stove where the pressers were heating heavy irons.

Those not sewing were most likely selling something. If the family had a storefront, they lived in rooms behind, and a working mother could shuttle from the pot on the stove to the babies, from the babies to the customers at the counter.

Immigrants understood that, in America, married men did not let their wives go out to work. But as long as husband and wife were working together in their own business, they could work day and night. And they did, keeping the store open every day of the year, except on the High Holidays, and sending their daughters home to light the Sabbath candles because the breadwinning housewife had to man the shop. Working in your own store did not bring shame, as it did when a wife went out to work in a factory. After all, "if you had to help out in the store, you were still home."[16]

"Helping out" was what wives did. Of course, no one helping out—not wives, not sons, not daughters—was paid for their work. Selling groceries, butter and eggs, fruit, fish, candy, herring, and pickles straight out of the barrel; waiting on customers, keeping the books, and ordering supplies—that was helping out. In South Baltimore, where Rose Pines lived with her father and siblings, one of her aunts helped out in the family's wholesale dry goods business; Rose's future mother-in-law helped out at her family's soda fountain. This was the family economy.

Whether they sewed piecework at home, lived behind the grocery, or hawked tin cups and sewing needles, cherries and damaged eggs off pushcarts, at one time or another, most immigrant Jewish women also took in boarders. Cooking for and cleaning up after paying boarders—often young male immigrants who had no idea how to cook for themselves—was hardly working. After all, these wives were already keeping house for the family. What difference did a few more mouths make?

Boarders helped pay the rent. Anzia Yezierska, dubbed the Cinderella of the sweatshops after one of her novels set in the Jewish ghetto was made into a silent film, wrote, in another, about a wife worrying about the rent. Her self-centered scholar husband wanted the parlor for himself. She insisted, "Only millionaires can be alone in America." The front room had to be rented out, and if she cooked supper for the boarders, they would earn even more.[17]

Working wives and mothers sustained their families. But when the calamity of death, illness, divorce, or desertion fell, Jewish women found themselves in dire straits.

"A Gallery of Missing Husbands": *The Family Rent Asunder*

A 1909 White House conference praised home life as American civilization's finest achievement. The United Hebrew Charities boasted of Jewish families' love and domestic harmony. But such idealizations belie the truth.[18]

A disabling illness or a husband's death could send a family spiraling downward. Rose Schneiderman would grow up to champion labor rights and shape landmark legislation, first under President Franklin Delano Roosevelt and then as New York State's secretary of labor. But when she was a child and her father died of the flu, leaving her pregnant mother with three children, the family survived only because a charity sent food. There came a day when that was no longer enough, and her mother was forced to send her brothers to the Hebrew Orphan Asylum and her baby sister to an aunt. It took her mother years to earn enough money to retrieve her sons from the orphanage.[19]

Death and incapacitating illness were not the only disruptors of Jewish family life. Marriages broke apart then for the same reasons that they have across the years. A neighbor whispered, *Your wife has taken up with the boarder.* A wife who signed her letter "Deceived" had believed in her husband of twenty-three years "the way a religious Jew believes in God"—until she met his mistress. For other couples, the years when an ocean had separated them proved insurmountable. While she languished in the old country, he had gone out dancing and much more with other women. The day she landed at Ellis Island, they no longer recognized each other. He had become an American who, disregarding Jewish custom, shaved his beard. She was a greenhorn from the old country. Ending the marriage was the only way out.[20]

Divorce, of course, was not unknown in the old country and in the new, as the example of Rosa Sonneschein proved. American divorce rates were slowly rising. In 1860 one in a thousand marriages ended in divorce; by 1920, nearly eight did. In the United States, divorcing immigrants, bound to Jewish tradition, required not only a state court to decree the end of the marriage but also a *get*, a Jewish bill of divorce written by a rabbi. Without the former, if either remarried, they could be arrested for bigamy. Without the latter, the ex-wife who hoped to remarry under the *chuppah*, the wedding canopy, never could. But divorce cost money and also required a legal ground, like adultery. Divorce was the way the leisured classes dissolved their lawful wedded unions; desertion was how some men of the poorer classes ended theirs.[21]

Under Jewish law, only a husband can divorce his wife. If he disappears but there is even the slightest chance that he might be alive somewhere, she remains an *agunah*, chained to a marriage that in effect has ended but from which she cannot be released to marry again.

Desertion plagued other groups too, but Jews viewed the problem as a nefarious blight on their people. Jewish communal leaders faulted abandoned wives, accusing them of frigidity and sloppiness. No wonder husbands went missing, they charged, when homes were dirty, children were neglected, and meals were inedible; no man would walk out on an affectionate wife who respected her husband as a Jewish daughter should.[22]

But of course, marital breakdown could be the fault of the wife, the husband, or both. Infidelity, incompatibility—exacerbated by the distance that grew when the husband immigrated first—and poverty lay at its roots. One impecunious St. Louis father pawned his wife's watch and hit the road, leaving two dollars on the dresser and a note saying he would let her know when he found a place where he could earn a living. But too many husbands never let their wives know.[23]

Deserted wives who could work and whose children could work managed on their own for as long as they could. But when someone fell ill, or had her wages slashed, or lost a job; when the boarders decamped; when in the slack season no one needed their laundry or windows washed; when everything but the bed had been pawned, and the kindness of neighbors was stretched thin, then the abandoned wife appealed for help.

That Jewish communal leaders felt compelled to establish the National Desertion Bureau testifies to the dimensions of the problem. Although many deserted women never appealed for its aid, by 1922, at the end of its first decade, it had seen more than twelve thousand cases. The bureau hunted down the rogues who had come to America, married, fathered children, and then vanished without a trace and those who, already fathers, came first, brought the family over, and then disappeared. Yiddish newspapers published the runaways' names and photos in a "gallery of missing men."[24]

If the bureau could track the scoundrels down, its staff expected reconciliation, but some abandoned wives, remembering their husbands' abuse, did not want reunion. They just wanted their men to give them the *get* and liberate them from the chains of Jewish law. One historian, studying a sample of National Desertion Bureau cases, found that its success rate at reunification and getting men to support their families was a measly 3.3 percent. But until the federal government stepped in during the Depression with the Emergency Home Relief Bureau, the only recourse for abandoned Jewish wives and mothers, pushed over the economic brink, was the National Desertion Bureau.[25]

SEXUAL ABUSE and prostitution in the Jewish ghettoes also betrayed the myth of domestic tranquility. Kate Simon wrote powerfully of how, as a child, her older male and female cousins, boarding with the family, molested her. Others remembered their fathers crawling into their beds at night. One, Maimie Pinzer, pointed to her uncle who abused her when she was just a girl.[26]

While the National Council of Jewish Women was crusading against international white slavery, prostitution was flourishing in its own American cities. How many were Jewish is unknown, but with names like Channala, Celia, Fanny, Rosie, Yetta, Sarah, and Sadie, many of these women were Jews.

Although illegal, prostitution was a thriving business. Graft kept corrupt politicians and police looking the other way as brothels operated openly across America. A few fancy houses catered to government officials and a wealthy clientele. In less exclusive settings, madams and pimps collected a dollar or two for each girl's trick. At the bottom of the system, in dank cellars, older and diseased prostitutes serviced clients for considerably less.

In the first decades of the twentieth century, Manhattan had an estimated 15,000 prostitutes servicing 150,000 men daily. Workingwomen, desperate to buy bread during the slack season or to supplement their insufficient wages, were sometimes starved into the business. One sewing girl defended herself: she could not live on five dollars a week. Some Jewish women turned to prostitution after their husbands deserted. On Allen Street, in New York's Jewish ghetto, prostitution was so much a part of the immigrant world that the pimps and madams had their own Hebrew benevolent society and burial plots in a Brooklyn cemetery.[27]

Historians believe that entrapment occurred only for a minority of the women who became prostitutes, that the vast majority were neither dragged nor drugged into the profession. Nevertheless, stories abound of immigrant Jewish women being ensnared. In New York, a recent immigrant, a sewing girl, met an older woman who claimed to be a matchmaker. She said, "Pretty girls could wallow in pleasure if they made the right friends." The young woman had no idea what she meant. The "matchmaker" handed her over to "bandits." They raped her, locked her up, beat her, and forced her into prostitution. Eventually she escaped and told her story.[28]

Some young women unwittingly fell in with "cadets," good-looking, sharply dressed young men, on the prowl for women. They met at the dance halls that Belle Moskowitz crusaded to license in order to protect them. A cadet courted a girl, promised her marriage, and then seduced her, or raped her when she resisted. Sometimes he even married her under a *chuppah*, in a wedding where his buddy, a fake rabbi, officiated. Once she was ruined, he threw her into a brothel, where she was beaten into submission. Then he went hunting for his next victim.

Some prostitutes managed to get out, although often into no less dire circumstances. They became ill, and their pimps threw them out onto the street. One, urged by a neighbor to be a good girl and get a job in the factory, committed suicide by swallowing carbolic acid.[29]

Maimie Pinzer, whose uncle raped her, was thirteen when her father was murdered. Her mother, who once had two servant girls to help her care for the house and five children, now had to scrounge for a living. She forced Maimie to quit school to take care of the house and the children while she worked. When her mother would not give her any spending money, Maimie found a job as a salesgirl in a department store. Dating young men she met there, she took off with one for a few days. When she returned home, her mother was so furious that she had her jailed. Terrified, she begged to be let out of her cell. A jailor agreed in return for, as Maimie wrote, taking "all sorts of liberties with me." Perhaps that moment crystallized her utilitarian view of sex. Declared "an incorrigible child," she spent the next year in a Magdalen home, a reform school for wayward girls. From age fourteen to eighteen, she lived with a lover in Boston and did sex work. Of the times when she thought to leave this life behind and go back to a lawful job, she wrote: "I just cannot be moral enough to see where drudgery is better than a life of lazy vice."[30]

Pearl Adler's family sent her, the eldest, to America, expecting to follow. The outbreak of World War I scuttled their plans. By the time the United States entered the war, Pearl, now Polly, was sewing soldiers' shirts in a factory. Her foreman asked her out and raped her. When he learned that she was pregnant, he fired her. She had an abortion.

A few years later she and a gangster struck a deal. She would let him use her apartment to meet his married girlfriend if he would pay the rent. Soon his friends were also using the flat, and Adler, who had never thought of becoming a madam, began procuring women for them. Although by 1925, Jewish social reformers would declare, with relief, that New York City had seen a 40 percent decrease in Jewish women arraigned for sexual offenses, Polly Adler's business flourished, despite periods in jail, until the end of World War II. Her professional assessment: "Neither depressions nor wars have an adverse effect on the whorehouse business."[31]

"Education: It makes you feel higher"[32]

THIRTEEN-YEAR-OLD Maimie Pinzer had loved school. When disaster struck, she had to leave it behind. A quarter century later, writing in a letter, the last trace that remains of her life, she still yearned to return to the classroom. Although Pinzer and Rose Pines lived utterly different lives, they shared immigrant Jewish daughters' passion for "education: It makes you feel higher."[33]

The public school was, as superintendent Julia Richman ensured with her ban on Yiddish, the place immigrant children became Americans. In South Baltimore, eleven-year-old Rose, who had studied Hebrew and mathematics in the old country, squeezed herself into a desk meant for a second-grader on her first day in school. Then mastering English, she leaped across the grades, vaulting through grammar school and continuing on to high school.

In elementary school in the Bronx, Kate Simon excelled in all subjects except math, her nemesis. Alas, those poor math grades were decisive. At the end of sixth grade, she would not advance to the accelerated junior high and from there to high school, where girls could take either the curriculum leading to a teacher-training col-

lege, then called a normal school, or the regular college prep program. Instead she marched off with the other rejects to a commercial
course to prepare for office work, still a big step up from the factory.
Fortunately for Simon, her teachers, detecting the gifted writer in
the child, intervened and transferred her to an academic high school.

At a time when most American teens did not attend high school,
social welfare reformers established industrial schools in the immigrant ghettoes to teach Jewish boys carpentry and mechanics, and
to teach their sisters sewing, tailoring, and millinery, stenography,
typewriting, and bookkeeping. These schools propelled their graduates into better jobs—in a dressmaking house rather than basting
shirtwaists, in an office rather than standing hours on end on a shop
floor. Although these schools also taught cooking and housekeeping
to train Jewish girls for domestic service, those courses found few
takers. Young Jewish women had not come to America to become
servants. While working in someone else's home meant no dreaded
factory layoffs and enough to eat, it also meant only one evening
and every other Sunday free.

Even as Jewish girls trained for better jobs, they were still
expected to work only until marriage. When former president
William Howard Taft came to congratulate the Lower East Side's
Hebrew Technical School for Girls on its success over the past
thirty-four years, he favorably noted that less than 15 percent of
its graduates had not yet married. Its alumnae, he added, were fortunate. Earning a decent wage, they had not had to accept the first
man to propose. They could wait for the right one to come along.[34]

Public and industrial-training schools were not the only places
for learning. In Camden, New Jersey, after sophomore Minnie Seltzer had to quit high school to go out to work, she promised her
parents that she would finish at night. Immigrants like Minnie,
exhausted after a long workday, skimping on sleep and skipping
a real supper break, pushed themselves to night schools, like the
one Henrietta Szold had established in Baltimore. There they studied English; some finished grammar school; others high school; and
some even tried to master the algebra, physical science, and Latin
required for college entrance exams.[35]

Free public libraries, with their thousands of books, were also for learning and, as Kate Simon happily recalled, never had any tests. And on any night in Jewish ghettoes around the country, the settlement houses, unions, and socialist and Zionist clubs sponsored speeches on almost any topic imaginable. In Chicago, Bessie Abramowitz lectured on woman suffrage. In New York, Jewish daughters and mothers heard talks on the Roman emperors, how to become an American, Hegel's dialectic, and electricity.[36]

JEWISH IMMIGRANT women passed their burning desire for education on to their daughters and granddaughters. Hewing to a lifelong road of learning and reading became a distinguishing trait of America's Jewish women. Referring to the biblical laws, the ancient Israelites were commanded: "Thou shalt teach them diligently unto thy children" (Deut. 6:7). Across the ages, that meant educating males, not females. Boys growing into men spent lifetimes in study. Girls learned to read and write enough to run a home and a business, as Bessie Abramowitz's mother had. If they yearned for more, there were few opportunities.

But America's free public schools opened up a new world. They made education a dream within the reach of some. Nurse Lillian Wald observed that Jewish immigrants were sending not only their sons but also their daughters to school. There, as Henrietta Szold observed, the girls were learning "pretty much" the same things as the boys. Immigrant Jewish women knew that education could lead to a better job in an office rather than in a factory. And if the need to earn a living impeded their dreams, they would make sure that their children fulfilled them. The longing for education was so powerful that one immigrant, who spent her life sewing blouses, called it her only goal in life.[37]

For many immigrant girls, like Minnie Seltzer, dreams of schooling bumped up against the reality of the family's daily grind. She left school because she could no longer bear watching her parents struggle to put food on the table. School might be free, but who would support the family? A working daughter knew what was expected: at the end of the week, she turned her unopened pay envelope over to her mother, the family manager; in return, she received an allowance, enough to cover carfare and to put aside a little toward new clothing.

Age and sex determined who went to school and who went to work. Older sisters tucked away their childhoods and set off for the workshop first. Because Mary Antin's older sister Fetchke, known now as Frieda, headed straight into the factory, Mary, the younger, went off to school.[38]

Jewish girls also knew that they would have to sacrifice their educations for their brothers. Boys had to finish school; they needed a career, a solid position in life. Girls would eventually marry and be supported by husbands whose educations and success rested on their sisters who had made the same sacrifices. Dutiful daughters worked as cashiers in nickelodeons and sewed shirtwaists so that their brothers could finish high school, college, and sometimes even law school.

Ultimately, age (younger children stayed in school longer than their older siblings), the family (if both parents were alive and well), and economic advancement made all the difference for Jewish girls' educational aspirations. By the 1920s, they were attending high school and college in disproportionately greater numbers than other American women. By 1934, over half of the students at Hunter, New York's free college for women, were Jews. Rose Pines went on to college.[39]

*"It was not only our arms and time we sold
but our souls too."*

SIX DAYS A WEEK workers rose in the dark to a shop where they hunched over sewing machines for ten, twelve, even fourteen hours a day in the busy season, then went home in the dark. In shops that were freezing in the winter and stifling in the summer, bombarded by the sounds of machines roaring, the power belt hissing, the foreman hollering, workers kept up a brutal pace. They sewed shirtwaists and skirts, dresses and caps, corsets and undergarments, vests and neckties. Bessie Abramowitz started out sewing buttons. The firebrand labor leader Clara Lemlich (later Shavelson) sewed shirtwaists. She recalled, "It was not only our arms and time we sold but our souls too."[40]

A second industrial revolution in the late nineteenth century had lit up America's streets and workshops and advanced new ideas about mass production, mechanization, and worker efficiency. It had pulled huge swaths of workers to expanding urban centers, whose shops and factories needed an inexhaustible supply of men and women to turn their machines' wheels.

Here Eastern European immigrant Jews carved out a unique economic niche. They came ashore on a Friday; by Monday, they were bent over a sewing machine, working in the needle trades.

Clothing production had been subdivided into small steps. A single shirtwaist passed through many hands before it was finished. One worker cut the cloth, another was the baster; one sewed the sleeves, the next the collar; others sewed buttons on by hand; then there were the finisher and the presser. What the immigrant sewed depended on who they were. Men cut cloth and were pressers; women were basters, sewers, and finishers. Men made cloaks; women sewed shirtwaists and kimonos; men and women made suits.

Hour after hour, day after day, a worker bent over her machine, sewing cuff after cuff, working as fast as she possibly could, for if she could not keep up the pace, another would take her place.

This task system strained workers' nerves, aged young faces, dulled minds. Workers could lose their jobs for talking; they were not allowed to sing. Sometimes a needle would break. Sometimes it would pierce a hand. Then a working girl lost precious time and income while the wound was clumsily sewn, scarring her for life. In a Chicago knitting shop, management, claiming the girls lingered in the lavatories, took off their doors. But why would this be necessary? The girls needed to make money, "and no one could earn money sitting in the toilet."

At the end of the day working girls were searched to make cer-

Bessie Abramowitz Hillman, leader of Chicago garment workers' strikes, and Sidney Hillman, president of the Amalgamated Clothing Workers of America. *The Day Book*, September 30, 1915, Chicago, Illinois. *Courtesy of University of Illinois at Urbana-Champaign Library.*

Rose Pines Cohen (right) with her sister Leah Pines Zaid, her father Nathan Pines, and her brother Milton Pines in the early 1940s. *Courtesy of the family of Rose Pines Cohen.*

Portrait of Grace Mendes Seixas Nathan by Henry Inman, c. 1820.
*Pen and ink on paper, 3 × 2¹/₂ in. Collection of the American Jewish Historical Society,
New York, New York, and Boston, Massachusetts.*

Emma Lazarus. *From* Emma Lazarus Poems, *in the Clifton Waller Barrett Library, Accession #8827 to 8827-a, Albert and Shirley Special Collections Library, University of Virginia, Charlottesville.*

Rosa Sonneschein. *From* The American Jewess, *March 1896, vol. 2, no. 6.*

Henrietta Szold (second row, center) at a graduation in 1942. *Collection of the American Jewish Historical Society, New York, New York, and Boston, Massachusetts.*

The Adolph Weiss family, along with three neighbor children, lived on the Lower East Side. They made garters during weekday nights when there was a lot of work for the Berger Company. The youngest worked until nine p.m., including seven-year-old Mary, while the rest stayed up until at least eleven p.m. Taken by Lewis Wickes Hine on February 27, 1912. *Library of Congress, Prints and Photographs Division, LOT 7481, no. 2881.*

Women raise their hands, pledging to support the shirtwaist strike and walk the picket lines for its success. This action brought risks of violence from police and hired thugs, and it put the women in conflict with judges, lawyers, employers, and sometimes their families and other workers. November 1909. *Courtesy Kheel Center, Cornell University.*

Marching through cold rain and mud, protesters hoped to rally support. Signs call for fire drills in every shop, closed shops with union contracts, and an end to political graft and to days spent working in fire traps. 1911. *Courtesy Kheel Center, Cornell University.*

Crowd gathered in front of butcher shop during meat riot, New York, c. 1910.
Bain News Service. Courtesy Library of Congress, Prints and Photographs Division, LC-B2-995-11.

"Gentiles Only" sign at Beverley Beach in Mayo, Maryland, c. 1948–58. *Collection of the Maryland State Archives, Rudolph and Alice Stevens Torovsky Collection, MSA SC 3571-1-256.*

Mah-jongg at bathing beach, Wordman Park Pool, June 20, 1924.
Library of Congress, Prints and Photographs Division, LC-DIG-npcc-11609.

Miss America Bess Myerson, center, poses with her two sisters, Helen Myerson, left, and Sylvia M. Grace, after walking off with the honors at the annual beauty pageant held at Atlantic City, New Jersey on September 8, 1945. *AP Photo/Sam Myers.*

American Red Cross Canteen Corps from the *Newport News*, 1942.
Taken in front of the Red Cross Building in Virginia. *Courtesy of the
collection of the Peninsula Jewish Historical Society.*

"This woman's place is in the House . . . the House of Representatives!: Bella Abzug for Congress," created between 1971 and 1976. *Library of Congress, Prints and Photographs Division, LC-USZ62-109588.*

Female faculty, students, rabbis, and cantors at the
Jewish Theological Seminary, New York, in 1994.
© Frédéric Brenner, courtesy of the Howard Greenberg Gallery, New York.

Heather Booth playing guitar for Fannie Lou Hamer and others during the Freedom
Summer Project in Mississippi, 1964. *Photograph by Wallace Roberts.*

Some of the several thousand Chabad women who took a "class picture" during a 2015 weekend in Crown Heights. *Photograph by Nechama Kotlarsky.*

Ruth Bader Ginsburg (first row, third from left) with her confirmation class at East Midwood Jewish Center in Brooklyn, New York, 1946. *Courtesy of the Archives of the East Midwood Jewish Center, Inc.*

Combined Jewish Appeal luncheon, Miami, 1950s. *Courtesy of the State Archives of Florida.*

tain they had not stolen anything. For those who finished garments by hand, the day was not over. Going home, they ate a quick supper and then threaded a few hundred needles before bed. After all, workers were paid by the piece, not for their time, and threading needles took time. In slack season, they sat there all day with little to do and took home less. Periodically, the foreman would arbitrarily cut the piece rate to make a greater profit. No wonder a Chicago paper described "piecework" as "one of the modern slaveries that blindfold and gradually murder workers."[41]

In New York, Boston, Chicago, and Baltimore, the needle trades expanded exponentially as machine-manufactured garments came to replace those sewn by hand. Jews sewed alongside Italians and Greeks, but Jewish immigrants dominated the industry's workforce; in its epicenter on New York's Lower East Side, in 1897, 75 percent of the garment workers were Jews. They stitched away for the husbands of the well-off American Jewesses and for Russian Jewish immigrants like themselves who, arriving a decade or even just a few years before, had accumulated a little capital and started their own shops.[42]

Not everyone worked in a factory or workshop that sold directly to retail. To keep prices at rock bottom, manufacturers contracted some piecework to middlemen, who then subcontracted with small workshops in tenement apartments that, by day, doubled as sweatshops, where the husband, his wife, their children, and a few hired hands stitched together.

By 1900, five million American women worked for wages outside the home; by 1920, 7.5 million did. Most were under twenty-five, and three-quarters were single. In cities around America, women in factories wove textiles, canned peaches, packed meat, and rolled cigars. But the greatest number of immigrant Jewish daughters and their American-born sisters who went out to work found jobs in the garment industry.[43]

The religiously observant did not want to work on the Sabbath, but they often had no choice. Some were lucky; their bosses closed up shop on the Jewish day of rest and kept it open on Sundays. But once factories began dominating the industry after the turn to the twentieth century, it became increasingly difficult to avoid working on Saturdays. An immigrant father might lay down the law: his daughter would not work on Shabbos. But by the time he awoke, she had left for the factory. She knew that her family would starve without her wages, and that, according to the rabbis, "A life in jeopardy overrules the Sabbath."44

Workers' wages depended on the kind of work they did. But even when men and women performed the same task, girls earned less, sometimes less than half of what a man made. "Learners" earned least of all. A twelve-year-old girl, fresh off the boat, was taught to baste sleeve linings; her pay was fixed at three dollars a week. Even after she mastered her task, she was still considered a learner, the lowest paid worker in the shop, except, of course, for the children who trimmed threads from finished garments from dawn until dark during busy season. Because the learner knew nothing but basting sleeve linings, she dared not look for another job, and she could not learn a skill that would lead to better wages.

NOT UNTIL the last quarter of the twentieth century was the term *sexual harassment* coined. But no matter what it was called, immigrant Jewish women knew it when they faced it. With young men and women working together in the shop, flirting helped pass the time, making the hours less dreary. A male worker might invite a girl out, treat her to dinner and dancing, upbraid his co-workers whose coarse jokes made her cry, and after seeing her home for some time, eventually propose. Surely some workshop romances led to the *chuppah*. But just as often, young women found the sexualized atmosphere of the shop menacing. Workingmen, degraded by deadening jobs, exerted power over the only group beneath them, the shopgirls. They felt free to insult them and drag some, like Polly Adler, down to ruin.

No laws protected a sixteen-year-old girl from the foreman who pinched or stroked her body each time he passed, or the co-worker who tickled her and made lewd remarks. Nothing stopped a boss from demanding that a shopgirl go to dinner and spend the night with him at a hotel. Once an observant young woman dropped her thimble. Her boss grabbed it, put it on her finger, recited the marriage blessing, and then stomped on a lightbulb, just like the groom breaking the glass at the end of the Jewish wedding. Terrified, she fled to her rabbi: was she really married to that brute?[45]

When catcalls and vulgarity rained down, working girls just hung their heads. What else could they do—quit their jobs? Labor organizer Pauline Newman, who remembered her own struggles against her boss's propositions, thought the solution was to educate girls to defend themselves. Occasionally, during strikes, female workers added to their demands that they be respected as ladies. But in these years, little attention was paid to this problem that had no name.[46]

"Strikes were . . . valiant, glorious, and justified battles."[47]

AN 1898 newspaper clipping contrasted the very different lives of a society lady and sewing girl.[48]

LIFE OF SOCIETY WOMAN	LIFE OF LADIES' TAYLOR
9 A.M. / Arises.	5 A.M. / Arises.
9:30 A.M. / Breakfast.	5:15 A.M. / Breakfast.
10:30 A.M. / Goes riding or bicycling.	5:30 A.M. / Begins work.
12 NOON. / Sees dressmaker, &c.	12 NOON. / Dinner.
1:30 P.M. / Luncheon.	12:30 P.M. / Resumes work.
3 P.M. / Reading, correspondence or charitable work.	
4 P.M. / Driving in Park.	
5 P.M. / Tea.	6 P.M. / Supper.
6:30 P.M. / One hour dressing for dinner.	6:30 P.M. / Resumes work once more.
7:30 P.M. / Dinner followed by dance or opera.	9 P.M. / Quits work, unless the rush is very great.
11:30 P.M. / Supper.	
1 A.M. / Goes to bed.	11 P.M. / Goes to bed.

The ladies' tailor's life of drudgery helped give rise to a powerful Jewish labor movement. Angry Yiddish-speaking immigrants organized to demand a better life. For these workers, the American dream envisioned in the old country had broken in the new. Grinding poverty, grueling working conditions, and merciless exploitation propelled workers into the labor movement and spurred many to socialism and other left-wing politics, with their promises to end poverty and care for all. The result was an immigrant Jewish labor movement inextricably intertwined with leftist views.

As immigrant Jews joined unions, marched on picket lines, staged protests, cheered socialist candidates, read the radical Yiddish press, and paraded on May Day, they joined forces in a broad workers' movement. In the clothing industry, labor unions with large Jewish memberships, like the International Ladies' Garment Workers' Union (ILGWU) and the Amalgamated Clothing Workers of America, anchored one wing. In New York, the United Hebrew Trades, founded to organize Yiddish-speaking Jews in every industry—the milk wagon drivers and bedspring makers— fixed another.

The Arbeter Ring—the Workmen's Circle—established in 1892 as a mutual aid society to provide workers with strike funds, sickness benefits, and burial costs, became a nationwide fraternal order. Although its founders included men and women and although it admitted women as members, gender dynamics in this socialist brotherhood shunted most females into women's clubs. There members' wives and workingwomen advanced their own working-class projects, raising money for Yiddish schools and opening children's summer camps, and honed the same skills—setting agendas, running meetings, public speaking—that American Jewesses were developing in the National Council of Jewish Women and in Hadassah.

The Workmen's Circle championed women's equality, convinced that men could never be liberated while women remained enslaved. Husbands were to mind the children one night a week so that their wives could go to club meetings. But married women received benefits only through their husbands, never in their own right, and Workmen's Circle medical insurance did not cover pregnancy, childbirth, or female illnesses.

Radical intellectuals, speaking about economics, political theory, science, and literature to socialist clubs and mutual aid societies, advanced the greater labor movement's agenda. The immigrant Emma Goldman lectured, in Yiddish, to workers about poverty, injustice, government oppression, free speech, and women's economic and social freedom. An anarchist, she opposed all forms of government. Her public speeches about birth control and sexual freedom violated the Comstock laws and frequently landed her in jail. Eventually she was deported as an immigrant alien. Leaders of women's socialist clubs, like the Workingwomen's Society (Arbeterin Fareyn), pleaded with workers' wives not to undermine strikes, as mothers desperate to feed hungry mouths sometimes felt the need to do. They must not let their men go back to work until the bosses gave in to the strikers' demands.[49]

The Yiddish left-wing press was another force. Adella Kean Zametkin wrote the women's column in *Der fraynd* (*The Friend*), the Workmen's Circle paper as well as the column "From one woman to another" in the Yiddish newspaper *Der Tog*. She dispensed advice about housekeeping and raising children and shared her thoughts on the exploitation of the workers she called slaves. "But the plight of his wife is much worse because she is the slave of the slave," she wrote. At the end of the day, her husband came home to his dinner and to put his feet up, "but who ever saw a worker's wife rest?"[50]

The most influential of all the socialist dailies was the *Forward* (*Forverts*), established in 1897. It became, by the 1920s, with its circulation of a quarter of a million, one of the most widely read foreign-language newspapers in the United States. Its articles advanced labor politics, interpreted the nation to the immigrants, and advised them on how to become Americans.[51]

Female readers were surely drawn to its advice column, *Bintel Brief* (Bundle of Letters), where immigrants, like "Deceived" and the one tricked by the "matchmaker" into prostitution, unburdened their hearts to the worthy editor. One anxious wife who, after eight years of marriage, had not had a child, asked whether, if she was still barren two years hence, her husband could divorce her in an American court of law as she knew he could do in a rabbinical court. Another wrote out of desperation: she and her husband had divorced but, after three months, realized that they had made a grave mistake and wished to remarry. But he was a *kohen*, a descendant of the priests in the ancient Jerusalem Temple, and rabbinic law prohibits a *kohen* from marrying a divorcée.[52]

The *Forward* also ran a woman's page. There writers addressed timeless matters—love, marriage, and raising children—and slanted their take on public affairs to educate their readers about socialism. The solution to women's meager earnings was unionization and a governmentally mandated minimum wage; replacing private kitchens with cooking cooperatives would eradicate women's indenture in the kitchen. The page advised working-class wives to eschew the frivolous card playing typical of women whose husbands' success afforded them too much leisure. They expected workers' wives to know better, to spend their leisure time advancing their educations and joining clubs to improve society.

The Jewish labor movement strove for decades to convince workers, male and female, that unions were the only tool powerful enough to compel management to improve industrial conditions. Its various components laid the groundwork for a wave of major strikes in the garment industry early in the twentieth century, and militant Jewish women, like Bessie Abramowitz, stood fast on their frontlines.

"When," said the teacher to one of the pupils, a little working-girl from an Essex Street sweater's shop, "the Americans could no longer put up with the abuse of the English who governed the colonies, what occurred then?" "A Strike!" responded the girl promptly.[53]

IN 1886 a wave of strikes shuttered New York's garment industry, but a strong union movement failed to emerge, and workers won few lasting concessions. At the turn of the twentieth century, the U.S. Industrial Commission reported that on the Lower East Side, there was always a rumor of a strike happening somewhere. Still it took a decade of labor unrest, sparked by New York's November 1909 uprising of twenty thousand shirtwaist makers, most of them Jewish women, to organize the needle trades around the country. When it comes to the labor movement, working-class Jewish women occupy a special place in its history; their agitation giving rise to the notion of industrial feminism. The term was coined in 1915 to explain the preceding six years of workingwomen's militancy as in city after city, young women in their teens and early twenties turned off their machines, pinned on their hats, and calmly walked off the only job that kept them from starvation to demand an end to worker exploitation and deplorable working conditions. Bosses told them, "If you go on strike, you won't be able to live." They retorted: "At forty-nine cents a day I'm not living much now. I might as well starve fighting as starve working."[54]

The chain of strikes began with the Lower East Side's shirtwaist makers. In September 1909, workers at the Triangle Waist Company and at Leiserson's spontaneously, or so it seemed, walked out. In truth, for months, seasoned activists, among them Pauline Newman—who, just a year before, at seventeen, had been the Socialist Party candidate for New York's secretary of state—and Clara Lemlich had been recruiting workers to the union in these shops. At Triangle, where 60 percent of the workers were Jews, the rest Italians, and most were female, workers sat in large lofts at long rows of sewing machines. When Triangle owners got wind that their workers were organizing a union, they announced layoffs. The next day, after Triangle advertised for new workers, the union knew it was a lockout. Its members hit the picket lines.[55]

Lemlich, usually described as a frail teenager, was actually a twenty-three-year-old veteran organizer who had already been fired for leading strikes at other shops. At Leiserson's, she had convinced the male cutters and drapers that for a strike to succeed, female workers had to be organized. The strikers turned for help to the ILGWU, founded in 1900. By 1909, its Local 25, where Lemlich sat on the board, had only a hundred dues-paying members and the grand sum of four dollars in its treasury. The local's weakness affirmed what male unionists took as gospel: there was no sense in wasting resources to organize women; they did not join unions, and even if they did, they would soon get married and quit.

Lemlich, all too familiar with this scorn for women workers, knew that, just as employers paid female workers less than they paid men, when workers struck, the union paid married men strike benefits; women, even those supporting widowed mothers and younger siblings, got nothing. The same was true for the women who worked for the union. When Pauline Newman learned that the union paid her less than it paid male organizers, she quit, although she eventually returned to her post.

Union ambivalence about female workers propelled the striking shirtwaist makers to turn elsewhere for help, to the college girls and well-heeled members of the Women's Trade Union League. Founded in 1903, it allied progressive reformers and working-class women. After its president, Mary Dreier, walked the Triangle's picket line, where she was punched by a strikebreaker and arrested, the ensuing publicity alerted the public to corrupt policemen closing their eyes to the hired thugs and prostitutes, who, with fists swinging, charged picket lines, knocking striking girls to the pavement. Then police vans hauled the bleeding strikers off to court, where they were either fined for disorderly conduct or sentenced to the workhouse. Clara Lemlich was a veteran of these battles; arrested seventeen times, beatings had left her with six broken ribs.

As the Triangle and Leiserson's strikes continued into the late fall, Local 25 pushed for a general strike in the shirtwaist industry. But the ILGWU hesitated. General strikes were costly and difficult to coordinate, and union leaders doubted that female shirtwaist makers had what it took to sustain one.

Nevertheless, labor leaders called a public meeting on the evening of November 22, 1909, at Cooper Union. As speaker after speaker equivocated about calling a general strike, Lemlich pushed her way forward. In a torrent of Yiddish, she demanded: "What we are here for is to decide whether or not to strike. I offer a resolution that a general strike be declared—now." In a moment of high drama that would live on in labor movement memory, her passion swept the room. The chairman of the meeting, Benjamin Feigenbaum, turned to the crowd overflowing the hall: "Will you take the old Jewish oath?" Thousands of hands shot into the air as the workers vowed— echoing the biblical words, "If I forget thee, O Jerusalem, may my right hand wither" (Ps. 137:5)—the solemn labor oath, "If I turn traitor to the cause I now pledge, may this hand wither from the arm I raise!" The next morning fifteen thousand shirtwaist workers walked off the job. Two weeks later, fifteen thousand Philadelphia shirtwaist makers, urged on by Rose Pastor Stokes, who, at the age of eleven, had begun her American life rolling cigars in a Cleveland sweatshop, struck out of sympathy for their sisters in New York. By strike's end, between 20,000 and 40,000 (estimates vary) shirtwaist makers had shuttered 450 shops and spurred an entire industry to revolt.[56]

Over seven hundred strikers were arrested in the first month. The Women's Trade Union League posted bail. The league, which advocated woman suffrage, believed that workingwomen's problems were the direct result of female oppression. Its leaders viewed the strike as a powerful expression of the woman's rights movement and used it as a platform to advance their demands for government oversight of industrial problems. Praising the strikers' self-sacrifice and bravery, the league raised funds to feed strikers' hungry families and held rallies to draw attention to the walkout. When Helen Taft met some of the strikers, she promised that she would tell Papa about the terrible conditions of the working girls; Papa was President William Howard Taft.[57]

The strike united women not only across class lines but also across ethnic and religious divides. A sixteen-year-old Italian striker reported that her priest came around to tell the Italian girls that if they struck with the Jewish girls, they "would all go to hell— excuse the language." But she remained steadfast. Italians comprised only a small percentage of the strikers, and the same was true for the American-born: three-quarters were immigrant Jews, the vast majority female.[58]

The workers wanted a fifty-two-hour work week, higher pay, and overtime pay; an end to fines, if they inadvertently spoiled goods; and a closed shop, committing the manufacturers to hire only union labor. When the strike ended almost three months later, workers in some shops, especially those in the smaller ones that had settled early, had won all their demands, but in others, where the owners had united in opposition to the workers, they had won only some. The strike was not an unparalleled success, but it had proved that tens of thousands of Jewish girls and young women could sustain a strike. Their tenacity and bravery forced union men to reassess their attitudes toward workingwomen.

The industrial feminism spurred by the shirtwaist makers' strike went beyond the bread-and-butter issues then at the heart of the labor movement. As Rose Schneiderman, who eventually became president of the Women's Trade Union League, put it: "The woman worker wants bread, but she wants roses too." Certainly working-class women and men, Jews and Christians, wanted better wages, shorter working hours, decent working conditions, safe work spaces, the bread of life. But workingwomen wanted roses too, to fill their lives with more than deadening hours of labor at their machines. They wanted to improve their minds, to have access to culture, to enjoy moments of beauty. The Jewish women leaders of "the 1909 vintage," as Pauline Newman styled them, like Newman herself, Lemlich, and Schneiderman, would devote the rest of their lives to helping workingwomen earn their bread and smell the roses too.

BUT 146 WORKERS would not live to smell the June roses in 1911. Instead on March 25, they perished in the deadliest industrial fire in New York City's history. On the first Saturday of spring, just as the closing bell rang at the three-story Triangle Waist Company—on the eighth, ninth, and tenth floors of the Asch Building on Washington Place, within walking distance of its workers' tenements on the Lower East Side—a fire broke out in a scrap bin. The factory prohibited smoking, but the skilled cutters, who knew just how to lay out a pattern with minimum waste and whose knives could slice through many layers of cloth in one sweep, took liberties. As

the best paid workers in the shop, they arrogated to themselves the privilege of breaking the rules. Later a fire marshal would speculate that someone had tossed a still-lit match or cigarette into the scrap bin, igniting the blaze.[59]

Workers grabbed buckets of water kept nearby for just such an emergency, but they could not stop the flames. The fire hoses in the stairwells had no pressure, and little water came out. As the fire spread, pandemonium ensued: first on the eighth floor where the fire had erupted, then on the tenth after the eighth-floor book-keeper called up to management, and at last on the ninth where unsuspecting workers knew nothing until, to their horror, flames shot up the air shaft. Workers crushed against exit doors that only opened inward. Management had locked many of the doors so that no worker could leave without being checked to make sure she didn't steal a scrap of fabric. Some workers rushed to the elevators, usually reserved for management, whose brave operators made as many runs as they could until the fire spread. Others who could not squeeze into the cars jumped into the shafts, hoping to ride to safety on top of the cars. Instead they died there. The factory's Jewish owners—who in years past had collected insurance on several fires, all of which had oddly broken out when no one was in the shop, and who would be acquitted of all criminal charges connected with this one after their attorney planted doubts about whether they knew the exit doors were locked—clambered up the stairs to the roof and over it to the safety of the next building. Some ran to a flimsy fire escape that inexplicably ended just above a basement skylight without access to the street; it collapsed under the weight of the frantic workers.

As the inferno spread, others rushed to the windows. The fire department's tallest ladder did not even reach to the eighth floor. Some leaped into firemen's nets. One woman hit a net, got up, walked a few feet, and then fell down dead. After others smashed through the nets onto the pavement, the firemen abandoned them. Faced with the agony of burning, workers jumped anyway. One young man, wearing his hat, guided several women onto the windowsill, then helped them step away from the building, as if he were handing them "into a street car instead of into eternity." Then he too leaped. Within half an hour, 146 victims were dead, 123 of them female, many in their late teens and early twenties, who had no chance to escape. As the police gathered up the bodies, they recognized some from the picket lines of 1909. Others were scarred beyond recognition, so that relatives searching for their loved ones at a makeshift morgue on a Manhattan pier were uncertain which body to claim. Six victims, so disfigured that no one even pretended to recognize them, were buried under a marker for the unidentified. A century later an amateur historical sleuth unearthed their names.[60]

In the fire's aftermath, the Lower East Side grieved. For six hours, in a bone-chilling rain, a hundred thousand workers in thin shoes, many without umbrellas, some without hats, wound their way through the streets in a mourners' parade. First came the fire's survivors, young women, pale and trembling. Behind them marched the Shirtwaist Makers Union, followed by members of sixty Lower East Side unions. A quarter of a million men and women lined the city streets to pay their respects as the procession passed by.

The *Forward* filled its front page with a cri de coeur by Morris Rosenfeld, poet of the sweatshop and the slum.

> *There will come a time*
> *When your time will end, you golden princes.*
> *Meanwhile,*
> *Let this haunt your consciences:*
> *Let the burning building, our daughters in flame*
> *Be the nightmare that destroys your sleep,*
> *The poison that embitters your lives,*
> *The horror that kills your joy.*[61]

Rosenfeld gave voice to the masses whose grief erupted in fury over the cavalier attitude to workers endangered by filthy firetraps. The shock spread from the grieving masses of immigrant women and men to mobilize a coalition of activists. Two months after the fire, at a meeting at the Metropolitan Opera House, Rose Schneiderman excoriated the uptown crowd: "We have tried you good people of the public and we have found you wanting. . . . This is not the first time girls have been burned alive in the city." Schneiderman was right: just four months before the Triangle fire, twenty-five workers had died in a blaze in a four-story factory in Newark, New Jersey. There too frenzied young women had leaped to the pavement. New York's fire chief had warned that this could happen in his city too. Furious over workers who died untimely deaths, who were maimed in the workplace each day as public officials looked the other way, Schneiderman raged on: "I can't talk fellowship to you who are gathered here." Only a powerful labor movement could save the workers. The Triangle Waist Company tragedy added fuel to the firestorm of labor activism surging since the Uprising of the Twenty Thousand.[62]

It propelled forward a coalition of Progressive uptown women and men, working-class activists, and politicians to cross class, party, and religious lines and demand that the government step in to safeguard its workers. They convinced the New York State legislature to create a commission to investigate the factories. Two years later New York State passed a raft of legislation—requiring automatic sprinklers in high-rises, ordering fire drills, directing all doors to be unlocked and swing outward—which, had they existed on March 25, 1911, would have saved lives. Rose Schneiderman considered New York State's Industrial Code a living memorial to those sacrificed on the altar of the Triangle fire. The Jewish workingwomen who sparked the Uprising of the Twenty Thousand and those who had died in the horrific Triangle Waist Company fire had stirred the nation's conscience to demand justice and safety for its workers.

꧁꧂

THE UPRISING of the shirtwaist makers in New York emboldened workers around the country, in Chicago, Philadelphia, Baltimore, Cleveland, Boston, and beyond. It spread across the garment trades as well, from shirtwaist makers to those sewing men's suits and cloaks, women's underwear, and wrappers. Tens of thousands of workers—Jewish women, Jewish men, Italian women, and others—headed for the picket lines. In the winter of 1913, eight thousand women in Manhattan and Brooklyn who basted wrappers and kimonos, some of whom earned as little as five dollars a week, struck at the same time as tens of thousands of other garment workers in New York City. The protests reached all the way to women making corsets in Kalamazoo, Michigan, and women sewing buttons in Muscatine, Iowa—and to Bessie Abramowitz stitching men's suits in Chicago.[63]

In September 1910, when Abramowitz's Hart, Schaffner, and Marx foreman announced that he was cutting the piece rate a quarter of a cent, she and a few other girls put down their needles, picked up their hats, and marched out. Their spontaneous walkout sparked a four-month mass strike of 35,000 workers that crippled the industry. It won Abramowitz the moniker "Hatpin Bessie" because, when "mounted coppers" charged into picketing strikers, she jabbed their horses with her hatpin.

Widely recognized as a leader of the strike, she was soon working full time organizing women for the United Garment Workers union. But as its leaders appealed to the rank and file, urging "decent American women" to join them "in their struggle against the Jews" who were trying to take over the union, a floor fight for control broke out. In October 1914, Abramowitz and more than a hundred delegates stormed out and founded the Amalgamated Clothing Workers of America. Bessie nominated fellow immigrant, garment cutter, and strike leader Sidney Hillman to be its president. No one knew that the two—whose photos were paired in the press as Chicago's labor leaders—were secretly engaged. They had met at a boardinghouse not long after Simcha (Shimkhe) Hillman, a revolutionary socialist who had done time in the tsar's jails and who considered his yeshiva studies fine preparation for his career as a labor leader, arrived in Chicago.[64]

On May Day 1916, as workers around the world marched in solidarity, Bessie Abramowitz and Sidney Hillman linked arms, announcing their engagement to the world. Two days later they wed in a synagogue. Since Sidney had been working in New York,

Mrs. Sidney Hillman resigned her position and relocated. The couple agreed that only one of them should take money from the union. For the next three decades, Bessie Hillman worked for the Amalgamated without pay.

By the time these great revolts ended, the garment industry was among the best organized in the nation, and tens of thousands, if not hundreds of thousands of Jewish women—among them Pauline Newman, Clara Lemlich, Rose Schneiderman, and Bessie Hillman—had played major roles in making that happen.

"No wonder we started rioting. We can't starve
without a protest of some kind."

THE MILITANCY of the shirtwaist makers was not a transitory, isolated phenomenon. Even though, in due course, most would leave the job once they married and became mothers, raising a family did not stop Jewish women from protesting injustice. Many immigrant Jewish women and their American-born daughters remained activists throughout their lives, especially when their families' welfare was in danger.

In New York, on May 15, 1902, immigrant Jewish mothers, furious at the soaring price of kosher meat, broke into butcher shops, grabbed the meat, threw it on the streets, doused it with kerosene, and set it aflame. The boycott's ringleaders were in their thirties, forties, and even early fifties. Arrested, one told the judge, "We're not rioting. Only see how thin our children are." The New York kosher meat boycott spurred Boston women to start their own on May 23. A few years later, on a hot summer day in South Philadelphia, twenty thousand women, "maddened . . . to a pitch of frenzy" by rising kosher meat prices, mobbed butcher shops and pelted the police with rotten eggs. By day's end, not a pound of meat had been sold, but ninety-two women had been arrested and charged with assault, battery, and inciting to riot.[65]

The 1902 New York kosher meat boycott, while empowering the immigrant Jewish women, was a qualified success. The wholesalers, whose rate hike had spurred it, rolled back the price of meat, for a while. But kosher meat boycotts continued to erupt in New York and elsewhere, demonstrating that, even when meat prices dropped, they would rise again.[66]

In early 1917, with the United States sending basic foodstuffs to the war overseas, all food prices skyrocketed. When potatoes went from five to ten cents a pound and onions from fourteen to eighteen cents, New York's Jewish women spearheaded a potato and onion strike that spread to vegetables, fish, and poultry. They overturned pushcarts, shut down markets around the city, beat up shoppers, battled police, and shuttered six thousand kosher poultry shops. "No wonder we started rioting," said one housewife. "We can't starve without a protest of some kind."[67]

Rent strikes were another way Jewish women protested. During the economic depression in the winter of 1907–8, union organizer Pauline Newman galvanized a band of four hundred fuming New York City women to canvass building by building, on the mostly Jewish Lower East Side, telling tenants to withhold rent until the landlords cut the rate. Fighting evictions, women, armed with brooms and ashcan covers, stood fast on stoops, where they clashed with police. Meanwhile in Chicago's Jewish ghetto, where Bessie Hillman lived, immigrants organizing a tenants' union sent young girls out into the streets, hoisting placards in Yiddish and English reading, "Rise against the tyranny of the landlords," to call their neighbors to a meeting to declare a rent strike.[68]

In 1918, with America fighting overseas, landlords profited from the wartime housing crunch by increasing rents month by month, for tenants who had stayed for years but had rented by the month. In Brownsville, Brooklyn, the rent for an apartment that was $13.50 a month when the United States entered the war in April 1917, was three dollars higher a year later. "The last time the agent asked for more rent," said Mrs. Aaron Stein, "we could stand it no longer." The tenants struck and then most of them left, but she refused to pay the latest rent hike and refused to move out. One Sabbath, she returned from services to find her family's possessions, including her dinner, strewn on the sidewalk. She then paraded in front of the building, stage-whispering to anyone hunting for an apartment, "Rent Strike, Lady," as policemen loomed menacingly nearby.[69]

Kate Simon recalled her Bronx neighbors—women who had named their sons "Solly, Benny, and Davy" at birth but who renamed them "Leninel, Marxele, and Trotskele" for the Communist heroes Vladimir Lenin, Karl Marx, and Leon Trotsky—banging on the door, yelling "The Cossacks are here!" That was their signal. The landlord's goons had arrived to evict yet another tenant, and they were calling their neighbors to arms.[70]

Consumer protests would erupt again and again in working-class Jewish neighborhoods in the years ahead, whenever price gouging, selfishness in hard times, or the economic realities of supply and demand compromised Jewish mothers' ability to feed the kids and pay the rent. Whether such activism was born out of the roots of Jewish tradition, with its prophetic call for justice, out of memories of persecutions of the past, or out of dreams woven from the cloth of America's promises of freedom and equality, Jewish women exercised their right to protest.

JEWS WANTED women to have the vote, declared *The Woman Voter*, a journal published by the Woman Suffrage Party of New York, in 1915.[71]

Of course, not all Jewish women wanted women to have the vote. We have already seen how the sisters Annie Nathan Meyer and Maud Nathan disagreed. Annie Nathan Meyer had even helped persuade the National Council of Jewish Women to defeat a resolution endorsing suffrage for women. By the time former president Theodore Roosevelt met the best-selling memoirist Mary Antin, he had become an ardent woman suffrage champion; she surprised him by opposing it.[72]

But by the twentieth century, many, likely most Jewish women, supported suffrage. Leaders of some Jewish women's organizations, those prominent in the labor movement, and others whose names were known only within their local communities, lent their voices, enthusiasm, and energies to the cause. The days when Ernestine Rose stood out as the lone Jewess calling for woman suffrage were long gone. Whether these women debated young men in a settlement house, shocked their mothers by speaking on street corners, or counted national suffrage leaders as friends, Jewish women, like Hillman, were crusading for women to get the vote. In 1913, before she married, she had addressed a Chicago public forum on what different racial groups thought about the question. We do not know who else spoke that evening, but German Catholics and Irish Protestants tended to oppose suffrage, while Italian and Irish Catholics were more favorably disposed.[73]

Jewish organizations, however, came late to supporting female suffrage. Not until 1917 did the Workmen's Circle and Reform rabbis endorse it, but that year the National Council of Jewish Women declined to do so, even though its leaders, like Hannah Solomon, were widely recognized as advocates. As Congress debated a constitutional amendment, Hadassah leadership telegraphed President Woodrow Wilson to point, with pride, to how the Zionist congresses had given women the vote years before.[74]

The battle for woman suffrage was waged on two fronts—state by state and in the nation's capital. By 1920, nineteen of the forty-eight states had granted women some measure of suffrage. Those in the West, where a Jewish daughter daringly canvassed in front of a Montana saloon, had taken the lead, and a few midwestern states had followed.[75]

In 1915 a suffrage referendum failed in New York. In New York City, all five boroughs voted against it. In 1917 the men of New York headed to the polls again to decide whether to give their mothers and sisters, wives and daughters the vote. Eastern European immigrant Jewish women campaigned for the ballot, organizing neighborhood suffrage associations, holding open-air meetings, demonstrating in front of factories, and canvassing house to house to find out how each male citizen intended to vote. They created a powerful momentum for woman suffrage among New York's Jewish men. Clara Lemlich, a founder of the Wage Earners' League for Woman Suffrage, gave speeches perched on a soapbox outside factory doors. Pauline Newman harangued housewives hurrying home from the market, urging them to talk to their husbands. Writing in the Workmen's Circle newspaper, Adella Zametkin, recapping suffrage history since the 1848 Seneca Falls convention, argued that votes for women were long overdue.[76]

Suffragists had drawn a straight line from women's political powerlessness to the deadly Triangle fire. Explained one garment worker: "The ballot used as we mean to use it will abolish the burning and crushing of our bodies for the profit of a very few."[77]

But Rose Schneiderman doubted that women at the ballot box would make much difference. After all, working-class men had voted for decades, and little had been accomplished. Nevertheless, she campaigned for suffrage widely and even sailed to Europe for international suffrage meetings.[78]

Not all Jewish men were receptive. Socialists yelled at Newman: "Why don't you go home and wash the dishes?" Workers pelted Lemlich with rotten tomatoes.[79]

Although no one likely noted it at the time, when the votes were tallied, they proved that men in Jewish neighborhoods had turned out en masse to enfranchise women. That their wives and daughters had argued and cajoled, and that the Jewish labor unions, the *Forward*, and the New York State Socialist Party had supported female suffrage, proved decisive. After all, their leaders argued, how could any immigrant who had fled oppression in the Old World to become free in the new deny a square deal for women on Election Day?

When at last the federal constitutional amendment passed in 1920, America's Jewish women cast their ballots, many for the first time, despite New York women winning the vote in 1917. The National Council of Jewish Women added to its projects for Americanizing the immigrants teaching women what they needed to know to become citizens and vote. Members ran citizenship-training classes and distributed the council's pamphlet *What Every Woman Should Know About Citizenship*. In the years ahead, some women, among them Henrietta Szold, would continue the international battle for woman suffrage, taking it to the Yishuv, the Jewish community in

British Mandate Palestine. Others would point to the Nineteenth Amendment as they reiterated demands voiced since the 1890s in *The American Jewess* for women's full membership in their synagogues. But now they added that women should sit on their boards of trustees and even become the congregation's president.[80]

SUFFRAGE affected every Jewish woman who became a citizen. Birth control affected every woman who was, as a later generation would put it, sexually active. The 1873 Comstock Act had made disseminating any literature or devices that could be used to prevent conception illegal. But women all over America were controlling their reproductive lives as the nineteenth century's declining birth rate proved. The struggle to decriminalize access to birth control constituted a broad social movement. Not until 1936 did courts overturn the law, ruling that the government could not interfere with physicians providing contraception. But similar laws persisted, the last voided, in 1965, when the Supreme Court ruled, in *Griswold v. Connecticut*, that prohibiting contraception violated a constitutional right to marital privacy.

The face of the nation's birth control movement was the public health nurse Margaret Higgins Sanger. One of eleven surviving children, out of her Catholic mother's eighteen pregnancies, Margaret married a German Jewish immigrant. Although the Sangers divorced, Nurse Sanger worked closely with many Jews in the birth control movement.

She despaired over the chief method of birth control of her day, illegal abortion. By the end of the Civil War, almost all states, where abortion had once been a crime only after quickening (when the fetus's first flutterings were detected), ruled abortion at any stage of pregnancy illegal. In the 1890s, American doctors estimated that there were two million abortions a year; a later study surmised that about half of all pregnancies ended in abortion.[81]

Women desperate to end their pregnancies sat over pots of steaming onions, drank herbal concoctions, swallowed drops of turpentine, rolled down stairs, plunged into scalding baths, and pushed shoe hooks into their uterus. When these methods failed, they lined up on Saturday evenings outside the ghetto apartments of the neighborhood's abortionists.

Kate Simon remembered children returning home from school to find that Dr. James had stopped by and that their mother was in bed, resting. That was, of course, very odd. Mothers did not rest, and they had not been ill when the children set off that morning. Later Simon learned that Dr. James was a skilled gynecologist and abortionist, a member of the patrician New England James family, and that her baby sister had been born only because the careful doctor had refused to give her mother a fourteenth abortion. And that was not even the neighborhood record.[82]

On the Lower East Side, Nurse Sanger nursed back to health twenty-eight-year-old Sadie Sachs, the mother of three under the age of five, who had nearly died from a self-induced abortion. Mission accomplished, Sanger was leaving when she overheard Mrs. Sachs begging her doctor to tell her how to avoid getting pregnant again. Laughing, he replied, the only sure thing to do was to "tell Jake to sleep on the roof." Three months later Sanger returned to the Sachses. This time Mrs. Sachs had paid an abortionist, and the abortion had killed her.[83]

In composing the story of her life, Sanger made this event her epiphany. Whether or not Sadie Sachs was a real person or a dramatic representation of the women Sanger saw, senseless deaths from dangerous abortions set Sanger on her path. For her, nothing was as important to improving women's lives as severing the inevitable link between sexuality and reproduction. Only effective birth control could liberate women from long years of pregnancy.

Sanger recognized that Jewish women would be especially receptive to sex education and birth control if they knew about it. But how little immigrant Jewish women knew was appalling. In 1917 Dr. Morris Kahn, of the New York City Department of Health, disregarded the penal code to conduct a survey of what women knew about birth control at clinics in the city's poor neighborhoods. His study, published in the *New York Medical Journal* and reprinted by

Margaret Sanger, surely included Jewish women. He found that, out of the 464 women interviewed, 192 knew nothing about contraception, and the rest knew little that was useful.[84]

But the Comstock laws meant that when Emma Goldman, who had studied nursing and midwifery, distributed her pamphlet, *Why and How the Poor Should Not Have Many Children*, which had been translated into Yiddish, she was arrested. A Viennese-trained psychiatrist published a Yiddish book on birth control. It went through four editions before authorities realized the indecency of the work.

In the fall of 1916, Sanger rented a storefront in the Jewish and Italian immigrant neighborhood of Brownsville, Brooklyn, and, with her sister Ethel Byrne and Russian Jewish immigrant Fania Mindell, opened the first birth control clinic in America. Mindell had no medical training, but she spoke Yiddish and had income from her own small shop. Advertising in English, Yiddish, and Italian, canvassing the mothers at the babies' dispensary across the street, the clinic attracted hundreds of women. Hoping to circumvent the Comstock laws, the women did not dispense contraceptives. But the condoms and pessaries, usually prescribed for prolapsed uteruses strained by multiple pregnancies, that they recommended could be purchased at the pharmacy. Ten days after they opened, the vice squad raided and arrested the three. Mindell, charged with selling Sanger's purportedly obscene *What Every Girl Should Know*, which the judge ruled was what "no girl should know," was convicted and given the choice of paying a fine or going to the workhouse. She chose the fine. The three's convictions, their appeals, Ethel Byrne's terrible force feeding during her workhouse hunger strike, and the attendant publicity laid the groundwork for greater access to birth control information and devices.

In the 1920s the movement gained traction, and a network of birth control clinics emerged; by 1929, there were twenty-eight; by 1932, there were 145. Bessie Moses, one of the few Jewish women to become a physician then, opened the first Bureau for Contraceptive Advice in Baltimore and much later shared the stage with Margaret Sanger when they were both honored by Planned Parenthood.

Jewish women's organizations supported mothers' clinics for family regulation in several cities. The one in Detroit served few Jewish clients; presumably, by then, most Jewish women got their birth control from their doctors, but the clinic dispensed birth control to others, including African Americans, albeit at segregated hours.[85]

Making birth control widely available became an expression of Jewish women's politics; using birth control became an indispensable element of twentieth-century American Jewish family life.

War and Peace

IN AUGUST 1914 a conflict in the Balkans ignited a global war pitting the Central Powers of Germany and the Austro-Hungarian and Ottoman empires against the Allies: Britain, France, Belgium, and Russia. From the first, long before the war crossed the Atlantic and the United States entered alongside the Allies, America's Jewish women and their families were fearfully and inextricably connected to its horrors.

Much of the fighting between Germany and Russia took place in the very cities and shtetls where so many of the Eastern European Jewish immigrants had been born and where their extended families, and sometimes their wives and children, still lived, awaiting steamship tickets. Perhaps as many as two hundred thousand Jewish civilians caught up in the war zones were killed or maimed, their towns ravaged by shocking barbarism: murder, mutilation, rape, scorched-earth withdrawals, and pogroms. Viewing the Jews as enemy aliens, tsarist armies deported, mostly on foot, without carts even for the aged and ill, more than a half-million Jews into Russia's interior.

The letters that had once sailed back and forth across the Atlantic ceased, and many in America lost track of their families across the sea. Russia made a separate peace with Germany in December 1917, but the war raged on for almost another year. A new wave of calamities—revolution, civil war, and the 1918 flu epidemic— further disrupted the links between American Jews and the families they had left behind, as the war interrupted plans to bring over family members.

On the home front, the Jewish community divided over the war, its protagonists, and the possibility of U.S. intervention. As long as America sat out the war, American Jewesses could retain loyalties to Germany. But after 1915, when German submarines began attacking American shipping, that became increasingly untenable as the United States leaned toward the Allies, and the nation began debating the risks it faced if it refused to prepare to defend itself in a world at war.

In truth, American Jews were less pro-German than anti-Russian. Jewish immigrants hated the tsar and all that the Little Father symbolized: antisemitic laws, the degradation of the Pale of Settlement, the pogroms, and Russia's dreaded conscription. Immigrant Jews wanted Germany to crush the tsar.

The onset of hostilities prompted some American Jewish women to call for mediation and peace. Lillian Wald and Rose Schneiderman, who had long worked with Progressive leaders, like Jane Addams, joined a coalition of suffragists, settlement house workers, society women, women's club officers, and leaders of the Women's Trade Union League to march for peace. Wald helped found the American Union Against Militarism at the Henry Street Settlement, just one of a number of new organizations hell-bent on keeping the United States out of the conflict. Rosika Schwimmer, a fiery Hungarian-Jewish feminist, landed in the United States in September 1914 with mediation plans endorsed by women in thirteen different countries and managed to persuade Henry Ford to send a Peace Ship of American delegates to a mediation conference in Stockholm.

Others, however, took a different stance, unconvinced that preparing for war meant inviting war. Maud Nathan, sadly remembering that only a year before the Daughters of the American Revolution had dispatched her to present flags at the Peace Palace at The Hague, resigned her membership in the American Peace Society.[86]

Jewish immigrants also divided on the question of preparedness and intervention. Socialists and union leaders called for peace; others understood the need to prepare to intervene if provoked. The two sides fought it out in the immigrant ghettoes, in the pages of the Yiddish press, on soapboxes, and at public rallies in the streets.

When the tsar abdicated less than a month before the United States entered the war, Jews cheered. A few months later, when a national draft was called, it spurred painful memories of tsarist conscription. Immigrant Jewish women rallied against conscription. "Red Emma" Goldman was arrested again, this time for counseling young men to avoid the draft.[87]

Ultimately, with a quarter-million Jewish men in the U.S. Armed Forces, mothers and sisters, wives and lovers watched with anxiety from the home front, where they supported the war in women's ways. America's Jewish women raised money for Jews suffering in the war zones in Palestine and Eastern Europe. Maud Nathan, having no sons to send off to war, knit mufflers, sewed hospital gowns, volunteered at the Red Cross, collected clothing to send overseas, and raised money for refugees. The wife of a fabulously wealthy Jewish industrialist sent a thousand dollars to the National League for Woman's Service, which was coordinating women's relief work; it was reportedly the largest single donation received.[88]

Jewish women sold war bonds, bought war savings stamps, conserved food and fuel, frugally managed their households, and skipped unnecessary luxuries to show their patriotism. Those living near army training camps welcomed soldiers into their homes on Sabbaths and holidays. Jewish women chaperoned dances and teas, where Jewish soldiers could meet Jewish girls.

The war brought new opportunities for some. Women temporarily took over jobs vacated by men, working as drivers, secretaries, clerks, and telephone operators for civilian and military concerns. This war was the first in which U.S. women officially served in some branches of the armed services. Here and there a Jewish woman's name pops out as a navy yeomanette or a battlefield nurse.

Irma Lindheim's fourth child was but five weeks old when she enlisted for active service in the army's Motor Corps. Driving her own Cadillac, smartly dressed in the regulation uniform, with a knotted tie, a belted jacket, and a brimmed cap atop her head, she rushed from the Bowery to Long Island, checking on servicemen who reported ill, answering to the bark of her commanding officer, and ferrying a former world-class boxer to his recruitment speeches. This future Hadassah president surely spoke for America's Jewish women when she boasted about women's sacrifices and how they fought "along with the men to make the world safe for democracy," certain that "this was the war to end all wars, the last war to be experienced by mankind."[89]

IT WAS NOT the last war experienced by mankind. Nevertheless, World War I portended a turning point for American women. Many expected a reward for their wartime sacrifices—the vote. The war brought other changes for America's Jewish women as well. When, in November 1917, Britain proclaimed the Balfour Declaration, supporting a Jewish home in Palestine, Zionist women and men cheered. A few years after war's end, America, after years of debate, would close its open gates. The end of massive Jewish immigration transformed the American Jewish community. The rigid divide between the two kinds of Jewesses blurred. In the years ahead, America's Jewish women would encounter wider worlds as the nation roared through the twenties, sank into Depression in the thirties, and turned again toward war in the forties.

4

"Woman is looking around and ahead"

WIDER WORLDS

UGUST 26, 1920, ushered American women into the modern age. With the ratification of the Nineteenth Amendment, women across America, at last, had the vote and seemed ready to make changes everywhere. Flappers bobbed their hair. Women danced in public, played sports, flashed across the silver screen, and in 1921 not only voted but also paraded, for the first time, in the Miss America pageant. But of course, most American women, and most of America's Jewish women, were neither flappers, nor movie stars, nor beauty queens. Instead they stayed on paths trod before them, living out their lives as wives and mothers, workers and activists. Soon the modern age would repave those paths and the women would blaze new ones.[1]

Nineteen-twenty was also the year Gerda Kronstein (later Lerner) was born in Vienna. Later, this pioneering scholar of women's history, who had fled the Nazis to make a new life in the United States, would see this year as a turning point for American women. Urban living and new consumer goods made women's work of feeding their families and cleaning their homes easier than before. Greater access to birth control and better medical care improved maternal health, and infant mortality declined. Children spent more time in school. People outside the family circle—visiting nurses and aides in homes for the aged—helped care for the ill and the elderly.[2]

If the modern age promised greater freedom and ease to American wives and mothers, it also seemed poised to deliver on the new notion of feminism, a word so rarely used before the 1910s that it was often spelled with a capital F. Unleashing pent-up expectations for what women could do and achieve, feminism promised new possibilities.

The 1920s also marked a turning point for American Jewry. During World War I, Jewish immigration had slowed to a trickle. After the war, even as Eastern European Jews were desperate to flee the disruptions and violence of pogroms, revolutions, and new wars, the United States set its first immigration quotas based on national origins, the percentage of immigrants and their descendants from any given country in the U.S. census of 1910. There was no Jewish quota per se, but the law curtailed immigration from Russia and Poland. In 1921, with the Emergency Quota Act going into effect only in the second half of the year, just under 120,000 Jews entered the United States. A year later that number was cut by more than half. Rose Pines assumed that she and her siblings had gotten visas in 1922 only because immigration officials prioritized family reunification. By 1924, when the census base year was pushed back to 1890, before most of the Eastern European Jews had landed, Jewish immigration was cut to ten thousand. The gates barely propped open would, within a decade, transform American Jewry from a predominantly immigrant community into one whose majority was native born.[3]

Hence, in the years after World War I, American Jewesses and their daughters and granddaughters and the newer Eastern European immigrant Jewish women and their second-generation American-born daughters faced the modern age together.

"She's a wonderful mother—she gave the children everything she didn't have."

IN THE 1920S, Jews, including immigrants whose decades of hard work had propelled them into the lower echelons of the middle class, were on the move, abandoning crowded neighborhoods for more open metropolitan streets. In New York City, where half of America's Jews lived, public transportation sped them to the outer boroughs; by 1930, over a million Jews—about a quarter of American Jewry—lived in the Bronx and Brooklyn. Beyond its horizon, where the other half of America's Jewish women lived, Jews were on the move too. By the time Bessie Hillman decamped for the East, Chicago's Jews were leaving their Maxwell Street ghetto for the new neighborhood of Lawndale.[4]

On grand concourses and tree-lined parkways, new Jewish neighborhoods arose in cities across America. Christians lived here too, but in many neighborhoods Jews constituted not just a plurality but, as in Lawndale, a majority. Jews could not live anywhere they pleased. Landlords openly advertised apartments as "sensibly priced, sensibly built, sensibly restricted," or more bluntly, no Jews or dogs.[5]

In their new neighborhoods, whether in the latest art deco buildings or in the labor unions' workers' cooperatives, this era's Jewish women created comfortable havens for their modern American families. Gone were the boarders' cots set up in the kitchen, the sewing machines of workers that had turned the fourth-floor walk-up into a sweatshop. Instead, these apartments testified to Jews' climbing up the rungs of the middle class. The most luxurious, in buildings where doctor husbands practiced, offered all the latest conveniences—steam heat and electric lights, parquet floors and sunken living rooms, refrigerators and elevators, grand entrances and courtyards, day-and-night switchboard service, and a dumbwaiter to whisk baskets of laundry from the basement to clotheslines on the roof.

Other Jewish women, married to garment workers, shopkeepers, or civil servants, lived more modestly. But they too viewed the sunlight streaming into their new flats in multifamily homes or coops, as workers' cooperative apartments were called, as a real step up from the squalor of immigrant pasts. In the Bronx, Rose Hatkin could feel grateful for her three-room domain that held her two brass candlesticks carried all the way from Poland, an icebox, a cabinet for meat and dairy dishes, and an inkwell, a souvenir from her Niagara Falls honeymoon.[6]

Family, friends, and institutions stamped these neighborhoods as indelibly Jewish. When Lawndale's Jewish women stepped out of their apartments, they shopped, aired their babies, and visited with their mothers, sisters, and in-laws in a landscape dotted with synagogues and Jewish schools, social clubs, and community centers. At its peak, Lawndale's sixty synagogues nestled alongside the Jewish hospital, the Jewish orphan home, the Jewish home for the aged, and even Hebrew Theological College, all constructed in the 1920s.[7]

More than public institutions marked these landscapes as Jewish. Alongside the movie houses and the Woolworth's five-and-dimes were stores and shops bearing Jewish names—Epstein's Ideal Market, Harry's Meat Market. Dairy restaurants, cafeterias, delis, and kosher bakeries and butchers announced that these were Jewish neighborhoods. If anyone still had any doubts, they only had to see how, for three days each autumn, on the High Holidays, business ground to a halt as women—the lucky ones in mink stoles—watching over children in their holiday finest, strolled home from synagogue calling out "*Gut yontif*, have a good holiday."

In many homes, housewives lit candles on Friday evenings. Their Thursdays were for *einkoifen far shabes*, shopping for the Sabbath, the day the housewife battled with the butcher. Passover still meant an exhaustive spring cleaning, washing the windows, banishing the remnants of leavened bread, taking out the good Passover dishes, and cooking foods eaten only on the holiday.

Synagogue sisterhoods valorized Sabbaths and holidays in their "Jewish Home Beautiful" pageants, their spotlights shining on tables laden with candlesticks, silver, and cut crystal. One was even performed during the 1939 New York World's Fair. During World

War II, the military used *The Jewish Home Beautiful,* a book published by the national sisterhood of Conservative Judaism, as its field guide to Jewish observance.[8]

But only some held on to these ways. In Los Angeles, the immigrant mother of the future Communist organizer Peggy Dennis dispatched her daughter on Sundays to socialist, not Hebrew, school and, scandalously, sent her to public school, as Mary Antin had gone, on the Jewish holidays. On the other side of the continent, Irma Lindheim, the former World War I Motor Corps first lieutenant, was hosting some religiously observant guests for dinner. Confirmed in a Reform temple, she knew zilch about Jewish dietary laws. So her husband explained that the first-course oysters would have to go, but he forgot to tell her that smelts stuffed with lobster were also *verboten.* Her guests thought the fish course delicious.[9]

Yet surely most Jewish women of this era fell somewhere between the poles of devotional observance and ignorant or defiant repudiation. Being Jewish was less about God or synagogue than about a way of living. As one Baltimorean, remembering the aromas of her mother's kitchen, put it: "Jewish feeling was in your home." For this generation, being Jewish meant chicken soup cooking on the stovetop in an apartment in a Jewish neighborhood, with grandparents, aunts, uncles, and cousins living nearby. It meant buying butter cookies at a bakery, often run by a Jewish neighbor and his wife, even if the owners did not bother with rabbinical supervision. It meant shopping with sisters and sisters-in-law in a department store whose Jewish name blazed boldly above its entrance for a dress to wear to the Hadassah luncheon. Defining being Jewish for this generation was imprecise, perhaps because it rarely needed to be articulated. Jews knew who they were; so did those who turned them away from hotels and refused to rent them apartments.[10]

~❄~

A RIGID gender divide ruled these gilded ghettos. "My father never carried groceries on the street," recalled the daughter of a prosperous Bronx doctor.[11]

Her father never carried groceries because men and women lived in two different worlds. Men worked, paid the rent, and gave their wives grocery money. Women did the shopping, the cooking, and the cleaning and raised the children. In 1920 only 9 percent of all married American women earned wages; more would go out to work in the years ahead. Of course, the wives running stores with their husbands or managing their husbands' medical offices never earned wages. Yet whether a woman's work was only in the home or also in the family business, the man's hours—when he got up to go to work, when he came home—set the day's boundaries. That had not yet changed, but Jewish marriages did differ from those of the past.[12]

New views of female sexuality and its place within marriage became popular in the 1920s. Some writers daringly asserted that women's sexual desires were no different from men's. Earlier, the "sex radical" Emma Goldman had raged about women's right to passion and challenged the sexual double standard subordinating women within the "insurance pact" she derisively called marriage. This generation would not act on her radical notions. Nevertheless, new ideas about making marriage modern shaped Jewish women's expectations.[13]

Among these modern notions were shifting attitudes toward birth control. Although the Comstock laws criminalizing the dissemination of birth control were not overturned until 1936, a patchwork of new state legislation allowing physicians to prescribe contraception already made it increasingly acceptable and accessible. A journalist quipped that by the 1920s, American couples were violating the Comstock laws "hourly" and sustaining a multimillion-dollar contraceptive industry crowned by *Fortune* magazine as one of the most prosperous new businesses of the 1930s.[14]

By all accounts, women, not men, were the nation's leading consumers of contraceptives. Ladies' magazines advertised douches, the most popular form of female birth control even though they didn't work, by promising to resolve that "most frequent eternal triangle: A HUSBAND . . . A WIFE . . . and her FEARS."[15]

But Jewish women did not have to read ladies' magazines to

learn about birth control. Their mothers warned them just before they married, "Don't be in a hurry," or "You have to know how to take care of yourself"; they might even, with embarrassment, hand them a douchebag. Friends whispered: *The druggist sells something.* Husbands knew about rubbers. Doctors prescribed diaphragms.[16]

Modern Jewish women used contraceptives when they wed, stopped when they wanted to have their first child, and then used them to space out their children. If birth control failed, there was always abortion as a backup. It was illegal, but for the most part, the well-to-do could get one from a sympathetic obstetrician in a hospital or office. The U.S. birth rate continued to drop, from 3.17 expected births per woman in 1920 to 2.45 in 1930. But Jewish women were having even fewer children. Those who married between 1925 and 1934 had an average of only 1.7 children.[17]

Successful birth control ushered in the notion of companionate marriage. Widely discussed in the 1920s, it called for mutual respect and for wives to find pleasure in sex. Thanks to effective and available birth control, sex decoupled from motherhood became the glue of these most modern marriages.

Moreover, not all Jewish women were waiting until marriage to have sex. The American-born daughters of Jewish immigrant mothers had met their husbands outside their homes, at school, at dances, or on vacation; they had dated before they wed. Flaunting older notions of promiscuity, some, many surely after they were engaged, had premarital sex.

Companionate marriage even paid lip service to the notion of domestic equality, but Jewish wives knew that their job was to keep house, to make it a home. Mondays were for vacuuming, Tuesdays for washing, Wednesdays for ironing, Thursdays for shopping. Every day was for dusting, straightening, carpet sweeping; cooking breakfast, lunch, and dinner; and washing up. Fridays were for dismantling the stove, stripping the beds, polishing the candlesticks, and skimming the fat off the soup while listening to the radio. Many Jewish women, and not only the well-off, did these tasks with the help of black women hired to scrub floors and wash windows. Even during the Depression, Jewish women who could afford it hired help, sometimes finding women on street corners that the NAACP called "slave markets." There poor black women, often recent immigrants from the rural South to northern cities, having left their own children at home, sold their labor for thirty cents an hour, sometimes even for less.[18]

Having finished the day's chores or having left her help in the apartment, the Jewish housewife set off to shop, "a wild adventure where she who did not elbow was elbowed out." Before refrigeration became the norm, milk, bread, cheese, and butter had to be purchased daily. On Mondays and Thursdays, she bought canned goods, meat, chicken, and staples. Every housewife had her own favorite butcher, chicken, vegetable, and fish man. Returning home laden with heavy packages, she started cooking dinner: soups—pea, vegetable, or chicken—never from a can; fried, baked, or boiled fish; and roasted chicken, lamb chops, beef liver, or perhaps a meat loaf. With dinner ready, she changed into a dress and a clean apron—a housedress was unacceptable—to welcome home her breadwinner.[19]

Some kept the dietary laws, but others abandoned them even as more prepared foods—Aunt Jemima's pancakes and Hershey's Kisses—bore kosher certification. A Jewish wife might move bit by bit from keeping kosher to kosher-style to Jewish-style. At first, her kitchen held two sets of dishes to please her mother and mother-in-law, but already high on another shelf was a third set just for *treyf*, unkosher foods. Then she might stop buying kosher meat. Between 1914 and 1924, its consumption in New York City dropped 25 percent. Still, it took time to cross the boundary of buying sliced ham or topping off a steak with a pat of butter. Eating shellfish was an easier barrier to cross than cooking a pork chop. Somehow shellfish seemed less repellent; pork was still seen as vile.[20]

Marketing was not the Jewish housewife's only shopping. She had to buy the housedress she wore for cleaning, the nice apron she put on to greet her husband, clothes and shoes for herself and her family, and all sorts of goods—pots and pans, furniture and knick-knacks, appliances and wallpaper—for her home. As new products enticed women to become America's primary consumers, America's Jewish women labored at shopping. Dressing in the latest fashion and buying new things signified that they and their families had economically arrived.

One place to shop was in the grand palaces of the downtown department stores. Some, like Hutzler's in Baltimore, where Rose Pines went, although never on Saturday, had grown from dry goods stores, founded by German Jewish immigrants, into fabulous emporiums. Others, however, headed downtown on the Sabbath. Meeting girlfriends for a bite at Hutzler's balcony or waiting for its delivery truck, knowing that if she changed her mind and wanted to return what she had just bought, the same truck would come back the next day, became part and parcel of Baltimore's Jewish girls growing up. Newark's Jewish women headed downtown to Bam's, which was Bamberger's. In New York they shopped for hose and clothes at B. Altman's. These splendid department stores promised Jewish women that they would enjoy the same courtesy and gracious service once rendered only to high, and gentile, society.

NOT ONLY were Jewish women having fewer children than their mothers had had and their gentile neighbors were having, but other things were changing about bringing children into the world. The idea of confinement, of retreating from view once a woman's pregnancy showed, a convention only the well-to-do had ever maintained, had gone out of fashion. By the 1920s, ready-to-wear maternity clothes had been in stores for at least a decade at Lane Bryant, founded by Lena Himmelstein Bryant.

In 1895, sixteen-year-old Lena Himmelstein set off for America on her own. Like so many other Jewish immigrants, she started out sewing. A few years later she married and had a son. When the baby was just a few months old, her young husband died. She bought a sewing machine and began stitching lingerie while rocking the baby in a one-room flat on the Lower East Side. One day a pregnant customer asked her for something "presentable but comfortable" to wear. A line of maternity clothing was born, and Lena, whose bank mistakenly recorded her name as Lane, became the founder of a multimillion-dollar business, whose stores around the country sold maternity wear and later plus sizes.[21]

Meanwhile, where America's women were giving birth was also changing thanks to twilight sleep. Pioneered in Germany and introduced into the United States in 1914, twilight sleep's cocktail of scopolamine mixed with morphine promised women that if they would deliver in hospitals under a doctor's care, they would "sleep" through labor and delivery. Although their bodies were indeed wracked by labor pains, twilight sleep induced amnesia so that women had no memory of them. One of the first Jewish mothers to deliver under twilight sleep, who had just given birth to her second baby at a Jewish maternity hospital, marveled: "If there is to be a third baby, this way is my choice." Even though physicians questioned its safety, the twilight sleep movement won adherents and led rapidly to a shift from home births attended by midwives to hospital deliveries managed by obstetricians. What had been highly unusual when Helen Apte gave birth in a hospital in 1913 was becoming the norm for a new generation of American Jewish women.[22]

Raising her children was the American mother's most important job. A Jewish mother might add a bit of inflection to it. When they were young, she got up early to clean before they woke, took them to the park to play, and then it was either home for lunch or a stop at the deli for a hot dog and cherry soda. She soothed their cuts and bruises, physical and metaphorical, nursed them when they were ill, and saw them off in the mornings on school days. A few hours later they came home for lunch. Then they went back to school and were home again at three p.m.

Now more than ever, though, children went on to high school. World War I had convinced Americans that education was key to the nation's strength. Across the country, high school enrollments surged 650 percent between 1900 and 1930.[23]

High schools steered students to different tracks. Vocational classes in shop, woodworking, and mechanics prepared boys to become men. Home economics classes in sewing, cooking, and domestic science trained girls to become wives and mothers. Girls never took shop; why would they? Everyone knew that classified ads read "Female Help Wanted," "Male Help Wanted." In 1920, in Bridgeport, Connecticut, more than half the Jewish girls surveyed were taking their high school's commercial course, learning to type, take stenography, and reckon the account books. A quarter were on the college track. A fifth were in the normal course that prepared them to go on to become a teacher, the ultimate ambition for a Jewish daughter.[24]

Mothers were ambitious for their sons, more reticent for their daughters. When a teacher told Kate Simon that she should become a music critic, she knew that "was too remote for a girl who had it dinned into her that Jewish goals had to be modest and those of a Jewish woman more modest still." Even high school girls who studied Latin and economics in the honors program were expected to get a job and go to work after graduation. It was fine for girls to work as bookkeepers, stenographers, and secretaries before marriage, and smart ones were expected to play dumb to catch a husband. Of course, daughters would live at home until then: "Girls didn't leave; they got married." A Jewish woman might work after she wed, especially if she was putting her husband through professional school. But those days would end when she became a mother.[25]

A husband sang his wife's praises: "She's a wonderful mother—she gave the children everything she didn't have." In the 1920s, "everything she didn't have" included gym, swimming classes, and sports for sons and daughters at Jewish community centers and—if they could afford it, even just barely—summers in one of the Jewish sleepaway camps founded after World War I. A 1916 polio outbreak in Brooklyn had spread terror across the Northeast, crippling over twenty thousand people. Until the polio vaccine was discovered and became widely available in 1955, epidemics erupted somewhere almost every summer. Because so many of those whose legs and lungs it paralyzed were the young, Jewish mothers did all they could to speed their children away from steamy city streets to the countryside's sunlit meadows.[26]

"Two dot" . . . *"Flower"* . . . *"East":*
Taking Life Easy

ONCE THE CHILDREN were in school and especially after they were grown, this era's Jewish women found greater leisure than their mothers had ever imagined. Housework, cooking, and shopping no longer filled most of their time. Of course, volunteering remained a crucial outlet for their energies. But so too did the weekly euchre or bridge club with relatives and friends who years before had shared immigrant trials. Now those with husbands well established in business, and with children either grown or self-sufficient, could take some time for themselves away from cleaning, cooking, and keeping house. They dressed up for their weekly game in second-bests, saving their first-bests for weddings and dinner dances. But even second-bests required nice jewelry, perhaps a gold breast pin whose diamonds, large or chip, attested to their husbands' fortunes.

If there was one leisure pastime that many Jewish women took up, it was, oddly enough, mah-jongg, the Chinese game of "a thousand wonders," played with tiles decorated with the exotic signs and symbols of the Far East. A mah-jongg craze swept the nation in the 1920s, and Jewish women plunged in. Discarding cracks and bams, picking up dots and easts, they embraced the game for its intellectual challenge and conviviality. Setting up card tables in living rooms, pulling out the mah-jongg set in synagogue lounges or on the lawns of summer bungalow colonies, they played, snacked, gossiped, and smoked—the cigarette industry was then deliberately targeting women. Hadassah and the sisterhoods hosted mah-jongg fundraisers. Into the twenty-first century, Jewish women continue to play mah-jongg. At a Manhattan club, whose three hundred regulars are mostly Jewish women, one can still hear: " 'Two dot' . . . 'Flower' . . . 'East' . . . 'Oy vey. Is it hot in here or is it me?' "[27]

Leisure also meant tuning in to the radio that had become, after its debut in the early 1920s, the most powerful form of media in America until television eclipsed it in the 1950s. Once a family acquired a radio—and by the late 1930s, most Jews, even poor immigrants still living on the Lower East Side, had one—it brought into their homes Bing Crosby, Amos 'n' Andy, and President Roosevelt's Fireside Chats. It also broadcast hours of weekly Yiddish programs.[28]

On Friday afternoons, Jewish wives cooking for the Sabbath heard appeals from orphans, yeshiva students, and the ill, an American variant of the shtetl's beggars who had knocked on doors before Shabbos looking for alms. Roasting and polishing to the *Yidish Froyen Program* (Jewish Women's Program), the women hummed along to *"Tsumisht, Tsutumult, un Farkisheft"* ("Bewitched, Bothered, and Bewildered"). Jean Gornish, known as "Sheindele *die Chazente"* (Sheindele, the Female Cantor), chanted prayers. Rabbis reminded their listeners to light candles at sunset and that profaning Shabbos would break up their homes.

The rabbi who boasted of his matchmaking skills advertised on Yiddish radio; so too did Manischewitz American Matzos and Kraft Oil, certifiably kosher of course. Those who used electricity on the Sabbath could tune in on Friday evenings to Jewish theater and film star Molly Picon's *I Give You My Life*. She opened each episode: "Hello everybody. Good Shabbos."

Radio, whose serial soap operas gave housewives a glimpse of the world beyond their living rooms, of downtown newsrooms and courtrooms, became an American cultural force. Gertrude Berg, known to millions as the immigrant Jewish mother Molly Goldberg, understood the power of "Radio America. Columbus discovered just a rock-ribbed continent, but, if you want to discover the real heart and mind of America, you've got to look for it on the air!"[29]

Berg's *The Rise of the Goldbergs*, one of the most popular radio shows of all time, projected that "real heart and mind" through a Bronx Jewish family in the Great Depression. The show, debuting a month after Wall Street crashed, ran for almost three decades, first on radio and then on TV. Berg, the first woman to produce, direct, write, and star in her own show, portrayed Molly Goldberg as a kindhearted immigrant Jewish mother famed for having "a place in every heart and a finger in every pie." But her on-the-air children, Sammy and Rosalie, were Americans. Like all parents, Molly and her husband wanted better lives for them. At Sammy's bar mitzvah, she told him: "Ve vant you to be somebody, and ve dun't vant ull our hops shoud be far notting."[30]

The joys, trials, and tribulations Berg wrote into her scripts for *The Goldbergs* transcended Judaism and the Jewish people even as, in 1933, the year Hitler rose to power, she brought a rabbi to lead a Passover seder on the air. Later TV audiences would see Molly praying in the synagogue's balcony. Her portrayals of warm ethnic family life and its struggles touched her listeners. The show demonstrated that the immigrants the nation had welcomed had become Americans, even if they spoke English with a thick accent. But for Jewish women—whether they were closer in age to Molly or to her daughter Rosalie—the show hit other chords. As one wrote to Berg, the Yom Kippur episode "gave a tug at my heart strings."[31]

America's other great pastime drew women out of their living rooms and into picture palaces. By 1930, the movies were selling eighty million tickets a week to a nation of 120 million. Sitting in the dark, Jewish women misted up as Al Jolson's Jack Robin, the cantor's son, crooned "Blue Skies" to his mother in *The Jazz Singer*. They laughed at screwball comedies and sighed over Fred Astaire twirling Ginger Rogers around the ballroom. Al Jolson was Jewish; Fred Astaire and Ginger Rogers were not. But the movies featured other Jewish actors—the Marx Brothers, the silent film vamp Theda Bara, the risqué "Last of the Red Hot Mamas" Sophie Tucker, and the Ziegfeld Follies' Fanny Brice. Forty feature-length Yiddish films made before the cataclysm of World War II destroyed that industry drew audiences too. For Kate Simon, the movies were her gateway into the America that lay beyond the borders of her Jewish Bronx: "We learned how tennis was played and golf, what a swimming pool was and what to wear if you ever got to drive a car . . . and of course we learned about Love, a very foreign country like maybe China or Connecticut."[32]

"A shande my daughter should marry a shaygetz."

IF LOVE was a foreign country, sometimes it led, not to the states of China or Connecticut, but to the land of Christianity. One Sabbath eve in 1939, a Chicago rabbi denounced a recent spate of intermarriages. But the Jewish intermarriage rate in the 1930s was scarcely 3 percent. In the next decade, it began to rise when, during the war, young Jewish women and men went places, did things, and met people they never would have met before. As more young Jewish men married out than their sisters, rabbis blamed Jewish daughters' materialism for driving their brothers into gentile arms. Nevertheless, by 1950, just 6.7 percent of Jews had intermarried.[33]

Rabbis were not the only ones concerned about mixed marriage. Social scientists produced mounds of research proving that, when two people from different backgrounds wed, their marriages were far more likely to fail. For these experts, nothing doomed a marriage like religious difference. The housewife Rebecca Mack's expertise came not from a survey but from living in "that valley of tears caused by intermarriage." In her memoir, she warned the guileless about to follow in her sad footsteps that sooner or later their husbands would curse "You God-damn Jew," and that their children would pay the price, as had her four, of growing up in a family warring over two religions.[34]

But young Jewish women had no need to look to rabbis or experts to hear that like should marry like. They just had to listen to their mothers. Scholar Keren McGinity, whose own prenup, in the early 1990s, with her Irish Catholic ex-husband had stipulated that their future children would be raised as Jews, interviewed Jewish women who intermarried decades before. Half a century later, they painfully recalled the wars their mothers waged against their marriages. Sarah Pene fell in love with a Catholic who, oddly enough, worked in a Jewish bakery. He agreed to convert, but her mother sent him packing, telling him to go find a nice Italian girl. Defying her mother, Sarah married her sweetheart but in secret, just as Phila Franks had done nearly two centuries before. When Sarah's mother found out, she threw her daughter out of the house. It was three years before they would speak again.[35]

Eleanor Hatkin fell in love with Charlie Greco. Charlie's Italian mother showed her how to make eggplant parmesan just as she had taught her Jewish sister-in-law. But Eleanor's mother, Rose, who had brought home that inkwell from her own honeymoon, was an indomitable force. To Charlie, she said, "You not marry my daughter." To Eleanor: "A *shande* my daughter should marry a *shaygetz*," a disgrace that she would marry a gentile. The day the pair announced that they would wed, Rose threatened, "If you do it, I jump off the roof." Rose didn't. Instead Eleanor broke her engagement. A year later she married Lenny Schulman. Charlie wed Selma Rubenstein.[36]

While the intermarriage rate remained low in America, intermarriage was, as Rose Hatkin's threat made clear, a family crisis. Still, it was not yet the existential threat to the Jewish future that it would become decades later when its rates skyrocketed. In 2013, 17 percent of Jews who married before 1970 had intermarried, but more than 50 percent who married between 1995 and 2013 wed non-Jews. Yet across the decades, Jewish identification could persist in mixed families. For some, the religious divide might blur into Unitarianism. For others, the December crossroads meant a Christmas tree and Hanukkah candles. One intermarried mother made sure that her pediatrician circumcised her three sons on the eighth day, just as Jewish tradition requires; surely, she was not the only one. The Cracow-born cosmetics giant Helena Rubinstein (no relation to Selma) took a Russian prince for her second husband, but she was buried by a rabbi.[37]

After World War II, more Jewish women, like Selma Rubenstein, did marry outside the faith. But marrying Jewish had never guaranteed a happy ending, even if social scientists claimed that Jews married to Jews divorced less often than Protestants married to Protestants. Eleanor Hatkin's marriage to the suitably Jewish Lenny Schulman was annulled, a far easier way to dissolve a marriage back then. Even if Jewish couples were not divorcing, they were not necessarily happy. New York's Jewish Arbitration Court heard a regular litany of marital complaints. She couldn't live within their means and was a lousy housekeeper. He didn't trust her and was a mama's boy. Rebecca Mack blamed intermarriage for her misery, but Selma Rubenstein's marriage to Charlie Greco lasted until his death almost forty years later.[38]

"Everything a woman does successfully
in business or professional fields is a step forward
in making the home a better place":
Jewish Women at Work

HOME AND FAMILY occupied most American women in these years. But the Great War had opened new opportunities for women, and with economic changes permanently transforming the way Americans did business, more women than ever before went out to work, and more of them were married. In 1920 less than a quarter of the women working for wages were married; now that figure began climbing slowly. It even seemed possible to combine marriage and a professional career. While newspapers, including the Jewish press, ran stories about female magistrates and professors, 90 percent of all American women still worked in only ten different feminized occupations, and most were expected to choose marriage over career.[39]

The number of America's Jewish women, married or not, who were then working for wages is unknown. The uprisings in the needle trades of the decade before had swept hundreds of thousands of women, great swaths of them Jewish, into the garment workers' unions, America's largest group of organized female workers. But their female membership tended to turn over every five years as women quit the shop and the union when they married. Once these women were no longer dues-paying members, union leaders ignored these firebrands of the past. But of course, working-class women married to working-class men did not abandon their cause. They just displayed their convictions differently, doing all they could to help families and neighbors sustain strikes and recruiting for the union over backyard fences rather than perched on a soapbox.[40]

For some, marriage had not necessarily ended their working life. Workingmen and -women no longer came into their homes to sew. But in bedrooms and kitchens, women like Lonia Grobsmith, Kate Simon's mother, set up their sewing machines and made corsets and dresses to sell.[41]

Not all women left the factories and shops voluntarily. Tens of thousands were driven out as four million industrial workers lost their jobs in the depression of 1920–21. Then the ILGWU battled a reform movement making a power play that would have brought more women into leadership and strengthened the Communist Party's influence in the union. By the time the union finished purging its ranks in 1924, it had lost over seventeen thousand members. Female workers, once 75 percent of its membership, were now less than 40 percent.[42]

Not all Jewish women abandoned the unions, but those remaining in leadership, especially those who, never having wed, centered their lives around the union, found themselves increasingly embattled as the men in control, who had only grudgingly accepted female organizers and their agendas in the past, displayed even less enthusiasm for the "bread and roses" that women workers wanted.

Persistent, energetic, and smart, Fania Cohn had won a reputation in the ILGWU as an outstanding organizer, provoking strikes in the kimono and housedress industries in New York and then in Chicago, where she helped workers win a fifty-hour workweek with only a half-day of work on Saturdays. Elected the first female vice president of a major union, she made workers' education her raison d'être. Convinced that workers wanted to learn more than economics and union history and knowing, from her own life, how female workers thirsted after education, skimping on sleep to go to night school, she demanded that the union use its growing resources to feed that hunger for learning, for education to better oneself, to enrich life. She expected education to change men's deprecating attitudes toward female workers and to develop workingwomen's consciousness. Establishing a web of workers' schools around the nation, she saw hundreds of thousands enroll in their classes before she retired in 1962.[43]

But Cohn worked for the union in an era when there was an unwritten rule that only one woman could sit on its executive committee at any time, and unlike Bessie Hillman at the Amalgamated, she was never named head of her union's education department; her title remained secretary. Her critics, furious at deflecting resources away from pure unionism, derided her. She clashed so often with union president David Dubinsky that he called her his "cross to bear." Outraged, her colleague Rose Pesotta resigned from the union to dramatize male hostility to female activists. Were Cohn a man, she contended, everything would have been different. Economist Theresa Wolfson, one of the rare Jewish women in academia in these years, pinpointed the problem that workingwomen faced as "sex antagonisms." A later generation would rename it sexism.[44]

As Jewish women left the needle trades, younger ones, coming of age in the interwar years, graduated to office work. They joined the typing pool and became filing clerks, bookkeepers, stenographers, and personal secretaries. Office work was once the exclusive province of men, but at the end of the nineteenth century, as American enterprise expanded, it needed more and more clerks and typists, and typewriting, which had gained widespread acceptance only in the 1890s, had never been perceived as a man's job. This paved the way for a surge in the female clerical workforce. By 1900, over three-quarters of America's stenographers and typists were female; by 1930, almost all were.[45]

Why would young Jewish women gravitate toward office work? To put it plainly, office jobs were simply the best jobs most could get. They paid better than many other female jobs, and sitting at a typewriter, taking dictation, balancing a ledger, or even running a switchboard certainly beat sewing in a factory. So the day after graduation, young Jewish women put on their hats and gloves and set out on the streetcar for the office.

Commercial classes in school, like those where Kate Simon was first dispatched, had prepared them for office work. When Baltimore's Selma Litman wanted to take her school's college prep track, her older sister shot back: "What the hell they going to do when they grow up?" So even in college prep, Selma made sure to learn typing and shorthand, for unless female college graduates went into teaching, they were going to end up doing office work too.[46]

Jewish women who passed the civil service exam in dictation, transcription, and typing might head to Washington, which had been attracting female workers since World War I. Likely they knew that the government could not advertise that only Gentiles need apply, as private companies then did. Still, Jewish government girls met antisemitism at the office unless theirs happened to be headed by a Jew. During the 1930s, as the New Deal opened a few positions of power to women, Rose Schneiderman, by then a close friend of Eleanor Roosevelt's, was appointed to the National Recovery Administration's Labor Relations Board. In New York, Anna Rosenberg, who would later receive the Congressional Medal of Honor for her government service, became a regional director.

Jewish women also worked in these years in department stores as saleswomen, copywriters, buyers, and customer service agents, or in Jewish community centers and other Jewish organizations.

But no matter where women worked, the marriage bar blocked their advancement. It justified not only firing women who got married but also denying them promotions because one day they would marry and stop working, if not immediately, then definitely once the children arrived. Smart wives left their wedding rings at home when they set off for the day. The end result was that the upper echelons of corporate management, government, and executive positions remained out of bounds for most American women. Their office careers may have been better than working in a factory, but they remained dead-end careers.

The 1928 *Who's Who in American Jewry* shows just how rare it was for Jewish women to achieve prominence in their working lives. In nearly eight hundred pages, women are less than 6 percent of those named. More than a third of the women listed were social welfare and communal workers, surely the vast majority as volunteers. Others were writers and artists, singers and actresses. As for Jewish women in the professions and business, *Who's Who* records eight lawyers, seven professors, six doctors, one librarian, a zoologist, a publicist, and a publisher.[47]

Despite the paucity of female leaders in business and the professions, the Jewish press took great interest in these exceptional women. That their accomplishments were newsworthy signaled just how unusual they were. *The American Hebrew* reported on Pauline Steinberg's meteoric rise from a stenographer earning just seven dollars a week to vice president and director of the million-dollar Amolin Company. The paper also discovered Clarice M. Baright, who had been the only "girl" in her class of a hundred at New York University's law school. The Jewish Telegraphic Agency spotlighted Mrs. Peter J. Schweitzer, who, during the Depression, was running the Schweitzer family business importing "fine papers," actually cigarette papers, from a factory in France, as she had been doing for more than a decade since her husband died.[48]

Such reports always deliberately underscored their subjects' femininity and unbridled enthusiasm for traditional female roles. While the president of that million-dollar concern lauded Steinberg as "one of the finest brains in the country, regardless of sex," his words were buried under the headline: "Business Women Need Not be Mannish: Charm Plus Competence Is Asset in Modern Industry." Even as *The American Hebrew* announced lawyer Baright's becoming a magistrate, the paper quoted her: "Of course, women belong in the home. And everything a woman does successfully in business or professional fields is a step forward in making the home a better place." Mrs. Schweitzer, whose given name, Rebecca, never appears in the news release, described herself as "indifferent on suffrage" fifteen years after women got the vote and thought that "a woman should give her best efforts to her home and her children."

Still, not all successful Jewish career women so carefully dissembled. As President Calvin Coolidge was proclaiming "the chief business of the American people is business," a group of enterprising Jewish women, engaged in manufacturing, advertising, and selling products to women, proved that not only was women's business big business but also that it brought them unprecedented power, fame, and fortune.[49]

When, in 1912, the ladies' magazine *Vogue* endorsed the respectability of a little lipstick and rouge, it signaled a sea change, and the
cosmetics industry took off. Jewish women, like Helena Rubinstein
(née Chaja Rubinstein) and, later on, Estée Lauder (née Josephine
Esther Mentzer), built multimillion-dollar businesses by creaming
and coloring the faces of America's women.

Fashion entrepreneurs Hattie Carnegie (née Henrietta Köningeiser), and Ida Rosenthal had, like Lena Bryant, started out on the
Lower East Side. In the 1920s the "Carnegie look" and the "little Carnegie suit" became the standards for elegance and high fashion; later
Hattie Carnegie would design suits for the Women's Army Corps.

Rosenthal set out to solve a problem triggered by the flapper
dress. Unless a woman had a boyish figure—no hips, flat breasts—
she would have to bind her chest to wear the dress. Rosenthal
reasoned: "Nature made woman with a bosom . . . so why fight
nature?" Two cups hinged by a piece of elastic launched the
Maiden Form Brassiere Company (later Maidenform). During
World War II, when there were shortages of fabric, Rosenthal convinced the government that manufacturing bras was indispensable
to the war effort: women welding airplanes to win the war needed
their uplift.[50]

Frieda Loehmann, dressed in black and carrying cash in her
bloomers, pioneered a different style of shopping. She haunted
designer showrooms buying up samples and leftovers. Selling them
at a discount, first at her Brooklyn store and later across America,
Loehmann's represented "Jewish resistance to paying retail."[51]

Working in routine jobs as clerks and typists, Jewish women in
this era bought Helena Rubinstein cosmetics and Maiden Form bras
and, if they lived in New York, shopped for bargains at Loehmann's.
But in office jobs too, not just in the factories, some stumbled into
one of the problems that still had no name. When Selma Litman was
looking for a job, she had a "terrible experience." Meeting with a
prominent attorney, "he got a little . . . ," and she managed to escape
only with the help of someone who worked in his office. Another
time, when she was working late, her boss came in and "started that
same kind of thing." Again, she managed to flee. Bold and brash,

the next day she faced up to him: "You ever do anything like that again; I'm going to tell everybody." His response: "Nobody will believe you." After that, she refused to take dictation in his office, but she knew that he was right. No one would believe her, or if they did, they would not care.[52]

As for the sanctioned women's professions, the Jewish press touted nursing as the most womanly of all occupations. Some Jewish women followed in the footsteps of the Confederacy's Phoebe Pember, Henry Street Settlement's Lillian Wald, and the Hadassah nurses who had gone to Jerusalem. Among them was Bessie Abramowitz's niece, Luba Bat. A nurse in Warsaw before World War II, she survived Auschwitz. A chance meeting after the war in Paris with her uncle Sidney Hillman brought her to America. But she had lost everything in the war. Without her diploma, all she could be was a nurse's aide. Astoundingly, her Warsaw school records survived. She mastered English and passed New York State's licensing exam, and Luba Bat became a nurse in America.[53]

But nursing never appealed to large numbers of America's Jewish women. They sensed its tradition as a Christian profession, caring for body and soul; and frankly, Jewish mothers were not keen on raising daughters to change strangers' bedpans. Only one profession attracted so many Jewish women that they called it the Jewish profession, and that was teaching.

In the second half of the nineteenth century, teaching became a woman's job; by 1888, 90 percent of the teachers in the nation's cities were female. America's Jewish daughters heard the same lecture from their mothers that Kate Simon heard from hers: "Study. Learn. Go to college. Be a schoolteacher." Another Jewish mother, Bella Myerson, warned her daughters that they had better be able to earn their own living. Of course, they were expected to marry, but a husband could lose his job, become ill, die, or be no good: "If you had a profession, you could say the hell with him and walk out." Not until the late 1960s would a new generation of America's Jewish women begin climbing beyond that professional peak.[54]

From the interwar years into the first decades after World War II, a majority of New York City's public school teachers were Jewish women. While Jewish women certainly became educators elsewhere in America, New York City, with its sizable Jewish population and unparalleled opportunities for free higher education, was the place where Jewish women dominated the profession.

The path to the front of the classroom lay either through teacher-training normal schools or through liberal arts colleges, like New York City's tuition-free Hunter and Brooklyn colleges. They prepared Jewish daughters for the licensing exams that they had to pass after graduation before their names could appear on the roster of applicants for a teaching job. Applicants were judged not only on their lesson plans and understanding of child psychology but also on their height, weight, and patriotism. If they passed the written tests, they advanced to the dreaded oral exams, where their appearance, decorum, manners, and English-language pronunciation were evaluated. Antisemitism worked to exclude those who displayed even the slightest trace of a Yiddish cadence. In New York City, even in the 1920s, when a growing school population needed more teachers, almost half of those taking the licensing exams failed. During the Depression, with few new teachers needed, the number plummeted even further. In 1934 only 5 percent of all applicants for elementary school certification got their license.[55]

For those lucky enough to find a teaching position, New York was atypical in that it permitted teachers to combine marriage, family, and career. Elsewhere, female teachers had to resign when they married; of course, married male teachers had no such restriction. But in New York, the procession to mother-teacher changed after a 1913 lawsuit led the state court to rule: "If she cannot be removed because of her marriage, she cannot be removed because of an act that is a natural incident of her marriage." From then on, as soon as a New York teacher knew that she was pregnant, or until she could no longer hide the news, she had to take a two-year leave of absence. But when her maternity leave ended, she left her toddler with her mother or mother-in-law, sister or aunt, and returned to her classroom.[56]

As wives, mothers, and teachers, these Jewish women joined a debate already under way in American life. Early champions of a woman's right to work had sought an alternative to the economic necessity of marriage. But as more women graduated college, they reframed the question: could a woman have it all—love, home, children, and a career and income of her own? New York City was unusual for its day in permitting teachers to marry and raise a family. It made its female teachers anomalous. In 1930 less than 4 percent of all women in America were trying to combine white-collar careers with marriage.[57]

Female Jewish teachers broke other boundaries too. They carried into their profession their families' legacies of political and labor activism. In New York, Jewish women helped unionize public school teachers; they became local and national leaders in the American Federation of Teachers.

One historian made a striking observation about teachers and the making of the American Jewish middle class. As teachers, large numbers of Jewish women became professionals almost a generation before significant numbers of Jewish men entered the learned professions as doctors and lawyers. Antisemitism and quotas in medical and law schools had mostly blocked their professional aspirations. Jewish mothers told their sons, "Marry a teacher." She would always earn a good living.[58]

"This, too, was Judaism"

IN THE INTERWAR YEARS, women's roles in Judaism were in flux in all its major branches. The national associations of synagogue sisterhoods came of age. More Jewish women were becoming religious school teachers; a handful dreamed of becoming rabbis. Meanwhile Orthodox men tried to persuade married Jewish women in their childbearing years to obey the commandment to immerse monthly in a *mikveh*.

Reform Jews had long had mixed seating in their temples. Now Conservative Judaism, a relatively new movement rapidly expanding among Eastern European Jewish immigrants and their children who had left the ghetto behind, acknowledged that in a land where women could vote, separating them from men during prayer seemed archaic. As Conservative Jews built scores of new synagogues in the 1920s, they had to decide where women would sit in their sanctuaries. Some embraced family pews, hoping that, if wives sat with their husbands, the men would not schmooze (chatter) so much during services. Others experimented with three sections: one for mixed seating, one for men, and one for women. Those that retained the traditional woman's balcony found that, as membership expanded, women overflowed the gallery, making their way down to the sanctuary, first to a separate roped-off section and eventually to places next to their husbands, family, or friends.

Sometimes Jewish women agitated for change. For thirty years, Washington, DC's, Conservative congregation Adas Israel rejected mixed seating. But more and more women, ignoring hostile glares, tested the waters. By 1927, a number daringly sat with their husbands during the late Friday evening services. This American substitution—and therefore somewhat irregular—for the sundown Sabbath eve service was invented to accommodate workingmen returning home after sunset on Fridays. Then some women stepped out of their place on Sabbath mornings, but never on holidays. Finally in 1951, in the congregation's new building, mixed seating became the norm.[59]

The growth of the Reform, Conservative, and Orthodox synagogue sisterhood federations implicitly, if not explicitly, acknowledged what the National Federation of Temple Sisterhoods had called "the increased power which has come to the modern American Jewess." In hindsight, these sisterhoods upheld a divide in American Judaism. Even when men and women inhabited the same spaces, they had markedly different roles. Yet some of those roles were beginning to shift.[60]

A sign of that shift was the coming of bat mitzvah. For centuries, bar mitzvah marked the moment when a thirteen-year-old boy became a man, required to observe all the commandments. But in March 1922, on a Sabbath morning, the New York rabbi Mordecai Kaplan called his eldest daughter, Judith, then age twelve and a half, to the pulpit. Bar mitzvah boys chant the weekly Torah portion from the sacred parchment scroll; Judith read hers from a printed book. Years later she wrote of her grandmothers' reaction. "In-law," said her maternal grandmother, "talk to your son. Tell him not to do this thing!" Her father's mother answered: "You know a son doesn't listen to his mother. You talk to your daughter. Tell *her* to tell him not to do this thing!" In the end, the thing was done, and Judith Kaplan (later Eisenstein) became a bat mitzvah.[61]

This first bat mitzvah failed to start a trend; a decade later only six Conservative synagogues offered girls bat mitzvah. But after World War II, it proliferated, and by 1960, almost all Conservative and Reform congregations permitted celebrating a girl's coming of age, even if how they did that differed from a boy's bar mitzvah. Eventually bar and bat mitzvah ceremonies became indistinguishable in Conservative and Reform synagogues. Bat mitzvah crept into Orthodoxy too, but in synagogues where a partition separates men and women during prayer, bar and bat mitzvah remain distinctly different.[62]

Bat mitzvah became routine, but it never transformed women's place in the synagogue. After bar mitzvah, boys could be called up to the Torah, counted in the *minyan* (the quorum of ten required for public prayer), and become rabbis. For girls, a bat mitzvah signaled the first and last time that anyone thought she would stand before the congregation, except perhaps at her son's bar mitzvah. It augured no revolution in Judaism.

A radical change, however, had crept into the teaching of bar and bat mitzvah boys and girls. In Jewish tradition, recalled one Jewish educator, "we girls were not taught like the boys, we were treated like a flock of sheep." But in America, Jewish teaching underwent, to the consternation of some, the same feminization that had occurred in public schools. From the first, students at Jewish teachers' institutes were predominantly female, and among them was Rose Pines.[63]

When Rose was fifteen, a teacher in the local Talmud Torah—the community afternoon school—quit, and she found herself in front of the classroom teaching the first-grade Hebrew class. In 1930 she graduated high school and won a scholarship to study accounting at Johns Hopkins University evening business school. One of only ten women in a class of more than ninety, she remembered a teacher carping, "What in the world are you women doing in this class? You should be home in the kitchen," not taking up a spot from a man who needed it.[64]

After a year's study, she began looking for work but was devastated to find that every employer expected half days on Saturdays. For a religiously observant young woman like her, Sabbath meant a Friday evening dinner of gefilte fish, chicken noodle soup, and roast chicken. Saturday mornings were spent at *shul* (synagogue), followed by a Shabbos lunch. Even when she told a prospective employer who was Jewish that she would work an extra hour every day, giving him four hours for the two and a half that she would have worked on Saturdays, he told her that he was sure that if she explained the situation to her father, he would let her work on Saturdays. But working on the Sabbath was out of the question, and not just because of her father.

Pines knew how to type and take shorthand, but she did not want to be a secretary. Instead, she entered Baltimore Hebrew College and Teachers Training School, which was founded in 1919 to prepare teachers for the next generations of the city's Jewish children. Her diploma, certifying her as a "teacher in Israel," declared her ready to teach all levels of Hebrew language and reading, Jewish laws, customs, and history, and to tutor boys for their bar mitzvahs. Although men held the reins of Jewish educational leadership, in the classrooms where the children sat, the teachers were more often than not females like Rose. After all, Jewish teaching was, for the most part, part-time and poorly paid.

Female Jewish educators reinvented Jewish education for the American scene, pioneering Jewish camping and integrating fine arts, dance, and music into their schoolrooms. They developed educational programs for Jewish women's organizations and wrote thousands of primers, textbooks, histories, curricula, and children's books. In an era when it was common for women to marry men who had the professions they wished for, female Jewish educators often married rabbis who shared their passions. Together these couples transmitted Jewish traditions, Hebrew language, and Zionism to the next generations.

Jewish women could become Hebrew teachers, but they could not become rabbis. A debate over women's ordination had opened in the late nineteenth century, an unanticipated by-product of the woman's rights movement, which, even at its 1848 Seneca Falls Convention, had railed against men for monopolizing the learned professions. After World War I, a handful of women advanced what had, up until then, been a rhetorical discussion, by seeking ordination for themselves. Among them was Irma Lindheim, whose knowledge of Jewish practice, as we saw, was once so abysmal, she thought lobster was kosher. None were allowed to became rabbis.

But what they did after their dreams of ordination foundered shows the tectonic plates of American Judaism slowly shifting. When Martha Neumark's (later Montor) dreams of becoming a rabbi were foiled, Reform's Hebrew Union College certified her as a Sunday-school principal. When, instead of completing the rabbinical course, Irma Lindheim became national president of Hadassah, she told Henrietta Szold that she felt that she had "been ordained, more truly so, even, than had I been confirmed as a rabbi." For now, just so long as women set out to guide Jewish children or to lead Jewish women, few disputed their right to Jewish leadership.[65]

One private area of women's observance was also undergoing review: immersion in a *mikveh*. The Philadelphia *mikveh*, built in the 1780s, seems to have been little used. But with great masses of Eastern European Jews coming to America, numerous "kosher bathing places" were built; New York's health officials estimated there were about forty in the city on the eve of World War I.[66]

Still, in the eyes of some Orthodox, too many Jewish women ignored this essential commandment. So rabbis and scientists touted the health benefits of regulating marital relations. Jews built model ritual baths, furnished with hair dryers. Someone suggested putting a *mikveh* in the home disguised as a dressing table. One daughter remembers being puzzled: her mother would leave the house say-

ing she was going out to see a friend, then return home with wet
hair. Another recalls being told, "Grin and bear it . . . this, too, was
Judaism."[67]

"A place for Jewish womanhood in the affairs of the country": Jewish Women's Politics[68]

FROM GALVESTON, Texas, the National Council of Jewish
Women's local section proclaimed its Ten Commandments: "1st: I
am the Council who brought the Jewish Women before the eyes of
the world. . . . 4th: Many days hast thou for bridge, Mah-Jong or
movies—but the second Tuesday is thy regular meeting day." As
caring for children took up less time, as women lived longer, and as
most in the middle class and above did not linger in the workforce
before the 1980s, hundreds of thousands of American women, Jewish and gentile, looking for purposes beyond their families, joined
female associations. Across America, they hoisted banners for an
array of social service projects and political causes that were as
diverse as they themselves were. In these settings, the new voters
weighed in, by the tens and hundreds of thousands, on the great
affairs of their day—Prohibition, immigration reform, the League
of Nations, the World Court, international peace, care for the aged,
fair labor standards, slum clearance, and civil rights. Women paid
especially close attention to legislation that could affect them, like a
wife's right to retain her citizenship even if she married a foreigner
and uniform marriage and divorce laws.[69]

Perhaps surprisingly to later generations, many women's organizations in this era, the National Council of Jewish Women among
them, refused to support the Equal Rights Amendment. Introduced into every Congress between 1923 and 1970, the amendment guaranteed, irrespective of sex, equal rights under the law.
But many women, like Bessie Hillman, opposed it, fearing that it
would strike down, as unconstitutional, legislation for which they
had fought so hard, that protected the health and welfare of the
nation's women.[70]

Jewish women banded together in droves. In the interwar years, they established at least a dozen new national associations—the Conference Committee of National Jewish Women's Organizations (1929), the Women's Division of the American Jewish Congress (1933), B'nai B'rith Women's Supreme Council (1940)—even as older groups like Hadassah grew and added "junior" divisions for younger members. Overlapping memberships make it impossible to know just how many Jewish women joined these organizations. But it is likely that at one time or another, most affiliated with some Jewish group.

Did Jewish women's associations, with their resolutions calling for world peace and supporting a federal anti-lynching bill, have an impact? The answer is occasionally. In the 1920s the National Council of Jewish Women was one of several organizations lobbying successfully for the first federal funding for prenatal and infant health care. But more significantly, in their associations Jewish women found a platform for their collective voice.[71]

If, as Americans, Jewish women took stances on the political issues of the moment, they especially took up matters of concern to the Jewish people. Their associations objected to a literacy test for immigration. They decried employment discrimination at a time when it was perfectly acceptable for businesses to refuse to hire Jews. A 1941 presidential executive order barred government contractors from discriminating in hiring based on race, color, or national origin, but not until the 1964 Civil Rights Act were private employers prohibited from employment discrimination based on race and religion, among other factors. Jewish women's organizations called for exceptions to the immigration quota system. In 1939, after the British severely restricted immigration to Palestine, just as the Nazi noose around European Jewry was tightening, the Conference Committee of National Jewish Women's Organizations, representing a quarter-million women, urged President Roosevelt to condemn the policy. Although FDR expressed his concerns to the State Department, he issued no public statement.[72]

This burst of energy announced Jewish women's determination to take to the stage as actors in contemporary Jewish affairs: reconstructing European Jewry after the Great War, advancing Zionism, opposing Nazism, and confronting antisemitism. The emergence of these organizations, their struggles to control their own funds and projects, and their determination to assert autonomy from Jewish men, even when their separate associations shared similar objectives, highlight the fraught sexual politics of American Jewry.

IN 1895, when Henrietta Szold proclaimed that she was a Zionist, a Jewish newspaper called this "a sentiment almost too profound for an American woman." But this profound sentiment came to define hundreds of thousands of American Jewish women. In Zionism, they sought solutions to problems confronting Jews around the world.[73]

In the interwar years, Hadassah evolved into an independent dynamo. As the Yishuv, the Jewish community in Palestine, was growing, Hadassah played roles, large and small, in developing it. Early Hadassah leaders understood that Zionist women had to unite if they were going to compel Zionist men at home and abroad to give them a seat at the Zionist table. The key to control was massing women behind Hadassah, and the key to that was targeting women who had joined the many other Jewish women's organizations. By 1926, the tiny group founded in 1912 had 27,000 members, the same number as the male Zionist Organization of America. A decade later, when the men's membership plunged during the Depression, Hadassah's had grown. After World War II, knowledge of the Holocaust's devastation and awareness that a quarter-million of Europe's surviving Jews were living in displaced persons camps propelled more women to join. By 1948, Hadassah, a quarter-million women strong, stood at the pinnacle of American Jewish organizations.[74]

Building up health care in the Yishuv was one of its main projects. Less than a decade after establishing, in 1918, the first nurses' training school there, its graduates manned many of the clinics and medical stations that the Hadassah Medical Organization had set up. The flagship Hadassah Hospital opened on Jerusalem's Mount Scopus in 1939.

At home, Hadassah's social activities were geared to fundraising and to growing membership: Card parties, picnics, Hanukkah toy teas, and competitions to sign up the most new members. Five hundred circles sewed linens and clothing for Palestine. Hadassah's monthly newsletters reported from around the nation on Chicago's tithe campaign, on Henrietta Szold's midwestern tour, on circuit physicians treating Arab and Jewish children for trachoma, and on how, in Laredo, Texas, a float showing Hadassah nurses won first prize in the George Washington Birthday parade.

Its shift beyond projects aimed at women and children—the infant welfare stations and the Tipat Halav (Drop of Milk) pasteurized milk distribution program—transformed Hadassah from an organization of women helping women and children into a body that created an indispensable element of the future state, a health-care system for all its citizens—men, women, and children, Jews and Arabs, alike.

In the United States, appealing to middle-class, English-speaking Jewish women, Hadassah advanced Supreme Court Justice Louis Brandeis's conviction that good Jews were Zionists, and Zionists were Americans. Newark, New Jersey, Hadassah leader Sarah Kussy linked America's past to the Zionist future: Zionist pioneers were tilling the soil and building a nation just like the Pilgrim fathers had done in America.[75]

Hadassah entered into politics as it battled a Zionist Organization of America faction that tried, throughout the 1920s and into the 1930s, not only to control the women's funds but also to dictate the arenas of their activism. What these men wanted was "a Jewish women's movement—auxiliary, complementary, aiding and comforting the main stem of the movement." When they did not get that, they charged that it was "impossible to work with Hadassah, that they are arrogant, that they nag, that they interfere in things which are none of their business."[76]

Initially, the Depression affected Hadassah's projects overseas, but in 1935 Hadassah rallied and raised today's equivalent of $7.5 million and added twenty-one new chapters, as the Nazis' persecution of the Jews converted many Jews to Zionism. This set the stage for Hadassah's declaration of independence from the Zionist Organization of America. A year later, for the first time in its history, Hadassah submitted its own slate of delegates to the World Zionist Congress, the international organization dedicated to advancing the dream of a Jewish national home. As it neared its first quarter century, Hadassah had come of age, heralded as an equal player in the worldwide Zionist movement.[77]

Hadassah was not the only women's Zionist organization standing up to domineering men. In 1924 a Palestinian rabbi from the international Mizrachi Organization of Religious Zionists, whose members were Orthodox Jews and Zionists, traveled to New York and told the Orthodox women of Ahios Mizrahi (Sisters of Mizrachi) to hand over the funds they had raised—for him to dispense. In reply, Bessie Gotsfeld, one of its leaders, announced that she herself would go to Palestine to figure out how to spend that money. The Sisters of Mizrachi decided not only to establish a girls' technical school in Jerusalem but also to become the independent Mizrachi Women's Organization of America (today AMIT).[78]

Mizrachi Women's aims dovetailed with the politics of religious Zionists who wanted to control education in the Yishuv. But men were not interested in educating religious girls. After all, how much education could they need? Elementary school would suffice. Then they would either help out at home or hold menial jobs until destiny led them to marriages and families of their own. But as Americans, Gotsfeld and Mizrachi Women, having other ideas about female education, established vocational schools to prepare religious girls for careers as dietitians and nutritionists. While Mizrachi Women cooperated with Hadassah during and after World War II, especially for the children's refugee rescue project Youth Aliyah, Gotsfeld made sure that the engulfing Hadassah did not swallow Mizrachi Women.

Other organizations brought together socialism and Zionism.

The male-dominated American Poalei Zion Party, founded in 1905, claimed, just like other revolutionary groups, that it had emancipated women. But with the singular exception of a female secretary on its board, women sat on the sidelines and took care of the children. In 1925, taking a lesson from the women organizing around them, Yiddish-speaking, working-class immigrant women, similarly bent on building up the Land of Israel as a socialist state, founded Pioneer Women (today Naamat U.S.A.). Its Yiddish language and socialist politics set it apart from Hadassah, which never affiliated with any Zionist political party. So too did a conscious feminism committed to realizing the full potential of working-women at home and in Palestine, and a close relationship to the Yishuv's Women Workers' Council. Party men tried to stop Pioneer Women from emerging, claiming that an independent group would deplete their strength since women could join Poalei Zion branches. But Pioneer Women would not be stopped.[79]

From Palestine, the Women Worker's Council sent emissaries to America to meet with Pioneer Women. Rahel Yanait Ben-Zvi, who would one day be Israel's first lady, was the first. Goldie Meyerson followed, and at some point, she and Bessie Hillman, two labor leaders, met. Pioneer Women, increasingly English-speakers by the 1940s, staged a skit about Meyerson coming to America: "Phooey on the men! When it comes to doing the actual work, leave it to the women, so Goldie Meyerson came to get the money herself." Goldie Meyerson would change her name, and the world would know her as Golda Meir. But as Goldie Meyerson, she left the United States in 1921 bound for Palestine.[80]

Born in Russia, Israel's future prime minister grew up in Milwaukee. Meir is one of the two best-known American women to live out their Zionist dreams in the land of Israel. Henrietta Szold, who spent most of her last quarter century there and who called those years the grand adventure of her life, was the other. But they were just two of five thousand American Jewish women who settled in Palestine before World War II.[81]

They included other Hadassah leaders. Irma Lindheim headed for Palestine in 1933 with her five children and eighty-year-old mother-in-law, leaving behind a mansion on Long Island to live in a hut on a kibbutz. In New York, poet Jessie Sampter had run Hadassah's School of Zionism. In Palestine, she adopted a Yemenite baby and lived with a woman. Their unconventional lives in the Zionist experiment defied all expectations.

Religious women who moved to the Yishuv followed customary paths, marrying and raising families, but they lived in Jerusalem, Safed, and Tiberias, which they considered holy cities. Zionist *chalutzot*, pioneers, went off to *kibbutzim*, agricultural collectives, where, to become accepted, they had to prove their worth. Meir remembered how stunned the *kibbutzniks* were that an American girl could do farm work. Still, when she spread a white sheet over a table on Friday evening and put flowers on it, she was accused of " 'bourgeois' weakness."[82]

Bringing to the Zionist project American know-how, these women tackled problems in the Yishuv, working on refugee relief and immigration. Henrietta Szold was elected to the Yishuv's National Council and tasked with shaping a nationwide system of social welfare. Hadassah expats supervised playgrounds and distributed clothing. During the violent 1936 Arab uprising, Hadassah's school lunch program stretched to feed thousands of refugees and volunteers.

Golda Meir best summed up the American immigrants' commitment to the Zionist project on the ground in the Yishuv in Palestine. In a letter written not long after she landed there, she reflected: "Of course this is not America and one may have to suffer a lot economically. There may even be pogroms again, but if one wants one's own land, and if one wants it with all one's heart, one must be ready for this."[83]

"I needed that 85 cents an hour very badly at that time": The Great Depression

THE STOCK MARKET crash on Black Tuesday, October 29, 1929, ushered in the United States's Great Depression. A year later, when the Bank of the United States failed, one-fifth of New York's Jews lost their savings, quickly adding more hardship to the Jewish community.

In 1932 more than a quarter of American households had no employed worker. In cities the average American family income plummeted almost 40 percent by 1933. Stenographers who had once made forty dollars a week were now making sixteen and lucky to have any job at all.

Women on their own, including educated "business girls"—and surely there were Jewish typists, stenographers, and clerks among them—were out of work and out of luck. Women lost their jobs at a higher rate than men, and, if they had no husband or father to support them, they soon lost their savings and their apartments. Eventually, overstaying their welcome with similarly desperate friends and relatives, they might find themselves out on the streets. Until 1934, only families with dependent children were eligible for emergency home relief. The Jewish newspaper *Forward* reported on a mother who sued her four sons: "Once they married, they forgot that their mother must also live."[84]

The crisis signaled not only major financial setbacks but also the collapse of rising expectations. Jews' belief that America promised an upward trajectory into a better future was crushed. As for their hopes for the next generation to advance even further, Jewish parents watched as their children stalled out on the educational and economic byways of a land that had once vouchsafed bright futures for those born here who studied and worked hard. For America's Jewish women, the Depression was most of all a time of uncertainty. Jewish wives and mothers asked, *Should we try to go back to work?* Single women wondered, *Can we afford to marry? to have children?* When Jewish women looked beyond their homes and families, they saw a world not only in trouble but also making trouble for Jews. They saw the signs of rising antisemitism—not only in Nazi Germany but also in the rising populist politics of the United States. In this time of global depression, where did America's Jewish women stand? How did they cope?

There is no single story of America's Jewish women in the Great

Depression, although given that great numbers of America's Jews were white-collar workers, Jews, as a group, weathered the crisis better than those forced to take to the road when they lost farms and homes. As in every group, some went hungry, and wives economized. Fortunately, food remained cheap. Families could eat three-day-old bread. They might have chicken only on Shabbos and eat more of the cheaper dairy meals. The Depression became, in the long-life stories of Jews who had come to America as impoverished immigrants, another crisis that they would have to weather. Some Jewish women ended up on relief doled out by the charities, but they did everything possible to avoid not only that fate but also the shame of having their neighbors know. Nevertheless, some successful Jewish businesswomen and those starring on stage and screen were lucky; their careers shielded them from the Depression's effects.

When families could no longer pay the mortgage on their homes, they moved in with relatives, or they rented, to the dismay of fastidious housewives, a grimy fourth-floor walkup. When they could no longer pay the rent, they organized strikes to reduce it. In the Sholem Aleichem Bronx co-ops, the families set up a fund to pay half the rent for those who had lost their jobs until they could find work, expecting their landlord, Louis Klosk, to wait for the rest. When, in August 1932, he evicted forty tenants anyway, the building went out on strike. Young women, among them Bella Myerson's three daughters, including Bess, the future Miss America, walked the picket line. As Bess Myerson recalled, "If a family was evicted, someone took the children, someone else took the living-room sofa, another neighbor housed the mother and father until they could find jobs and provide for themselves again."[85]

The writer Faye Moskowitz remembers her mother feeding the tramps who found their way to her door in a small town outside Detroit. The hungry who stopped there on Friday evenings got a kosher Sabbath meal. "It's a mitzvah to feed the poor," her mother said. Occasionally, she even managed to send the men on their way with a quarter from her *knippl*, a stash of cash she kept in a cocoa box.[86]

The Depression forced wives, who had long ago left the workforce, to return to it. When husbands could no longer support their families on their own, everyone chipped in. Once again America's Jewish women peddled goods, cooked for boarders, watched other people's children, and stitched away in their kitchens. Some returned to the factory and the shop. A Jewish mother who worked in a bakery while her children were in school, said, "I needed that 85 cents an hour very badly at that time." Jewish mothers' return to the workforce undermined their sense of place in the middle class, so entrenched by now that it persisted even when incomes were propelling them down the economic ladder. Working wives confirmed just how remote the dream of the male breadwinner supporting his stay-at-home wife and children had become.[87]

As for Jewish women now graduating college—and since the 1920s, Jewish women were going to college two to three times more often than their Christian counterparts—the prospects for employment were bleak. "It was a relief to be graduated," wrote Lucy Dawidowicz, who finished Hunter College in 1936. But after applying to countless employment agencies and sitting for the Civil Service and Board of Education exams, she could not get a job. This future historian ultimately found part-time work at Macy's.[88]

Anzia Yezierska, whom we met before, had once audited a Columbia University seminar taught by the influential philosopher John Dewey. In the 1920s, Hollywood had beckoned her to turn her books *Hungry Hearts* and *Salome of the Tenements* into silent films. But by the 1930s, she was back in New York, a struggling writer once again, one of the fortunate ones hired by the Works Progress Administration, the ambitious New Deal program that put millions of unemployed Americans to work.

The national marriage rate fell, but it dropped even more precipitously for Jews as the Depression dampened hopes for the future. Now a combination of economic constraints and family obligations led young couples to delay marriage. One evening Rose Pines met fledgling lawyer Moses J. Cohen at a Hebrew-speaking group. He walked her home that night and for the next five years from ballparks, ice hockey rinks, and meetings of young religious Zionists, just one of the warring Zionist factions in their Baltimore hometown. Together they heard President Roosevelt urge Baltimore's youth "to dream dreams and see visions" of "a greater and finer America." That they waited five years, until 1937, to marry may well have been a consequence of the limited prospects the young faced during the Depression.[89]

When those couples, Jewish and gentile, did marry, they postponed parenthood. Rose and Morris Cohen's first child was born in 1941, four years after they wed; their third and last, in 1949. Jewish family size had been decreasing before the Depression, and this generation of Jewish women continued on that path, giving birth to fewer children than their predecessors.[90]

THE DEPRESSION fueled the fury of those whose politics were to the left. As the socialist immigrant and young mother Rose Chernin encountered Hoovervilles of the unemployed and homeless sleeping in boxes and eating rotten food, long lines of pinched faces shivering outside soup kitchens, and desperate women and men hawking apples on every corner in New York, "there seemed to be no hope." On May 7, 1930, thirty-five thousand men, women, and children thronged New York's Union Square in a demonstration, organized by the Communist Party, for the unemployed. As the crowd chanted "jobs or wages," mounted police, swinging blackjacks, charged. Amid the "screams of women and cries of men with bloody heads and faces," Chernin ran for her life. That battle evoked a visceral memory: "It seemed we were standing in a village and the Cossacks were riding down." That was the day Rose Chernin joined the Communist Party. For her, Communism was a woman fighting injustice.[91]

The legacy of Jewish immigrant left-wing politics had waned in the 1920s. The Red Scare of 1917–20 had targeted subversive aliens. Union activist Rose Pesotta was arrested and "Red Emma" Goldman deported. Even American-born settlement worker Lillian Wald was targeted, her name published alongside that of Jane Addams on a list of those believed to hold radical views dangerous to the government. Meanwhile many Jews moving up from the working class had abandoned left-wing associations. Those who remained active in left-wing politics were mostly immigrants. In Russia, they had distributed subversive literature for the Bolsheviks. In America, they organized union workers, were beaten bloody by the cops, and were drawn to the Communist Party, like Rose Pastor Stokes, its national secretary of Women's Friends of Soviet Russia.[92]

At the onset of the Depression, the Communist Party U.S.A., founded in 1919, had less than ten thousand members. But its ranks swelled, especially after 1935, when the party embraced the Popular Front, making common cause with others on the left to defeat fascism. Branding Communism as democratic, progressive, and a bulwark against social injustice, the party's new slogan became "Communism is Twentieth Century Americanism." Riffing on Justice Brandeis's words about American Jews and Zionism, the playwright Lillian Hellman, who briefly joined the Communist Party, wrote that to be a good Jew and a good American, every Jew must be anti-Fascist.[93]

About one hundred thousand Jews passed through the party in the 1930s and '40s; nearly half its membership was female; almost half was Jewish. Communism called for a workers' revolution that would not only overthrow capitalism but end racial and religious prejudice. Its universalism, its promise to assimilate Jews in the new Communist brotherhood, attracted Jews, especially those who repudiated Jewish particularism and parochialism.

Communists were never more than a tiny fraction of America's 4.5 million Jews, but their fierce commitments to revolution and class struggle and the price they paid made them seem far larger than their numbers. In the early 1930s, Peggy Dennis, who had gone to socialist school on Sundays, lived in Moscow working with her husband for the Comintern to advance the Communist revolution around the world. When the Comintern posted the couple back to the United States, it ordered them to leave their Russian-speaking five-year-old son behind in a Soviet nursery. The family never lived together again.[94]

In the 1930s a new generation of radicalized Jewish women—

college students and office workers, writers and artists, like Hellman—were attracted to the party, and some stayed even after the Soviet Union stunned the world with its alliance with the Nazis in 1939, when the two countries agreed to divide Poland between them in the coming war.

Immigrant Jewish women had long banded together whenever high prices and social injustice jeopardized their ability to feed, clothe, and shelter their families. The catastrophes of Depression-era working-class life propelled the Communists to send women, many of them Jewish, out into the neighborhoods to organize working women's councils and unemployed councils "to fight like hell."[95]

The solution to eviction became a posse of Jewish housewives barricaded in an apartment, wielding kettles of boiling water, threatening to scald anyone coming up the stairs to move out the furniture. When a neighbor was crying after the sheriff carted out her worldly goods, the answer was not to take her and her family in but to mobilize neighbors to pick up the furniture and carry it back upstairs. With the neighborhood as their primary political turf, militant Jewish women, unafraid to sock the cops, stood at the forefront of rent strikes. Men might have organized the strikes, explained the Jewish daily *Forward*, but women were "the fighters, the picketers, the agitators." Not all women protesting evictions and striking against high prices in the 1930s and '40s were card-carrying Communists. But those who were raised children who played worker versus boss rather than tug-of-war and sang of laborers carrying the revolution forward into the future. They would be dubbed "red-diaper babies."[96]

Turning mothers into political activists was not hard when there were babies. Mothers would do almost anything to get a better life for their children. After one organizer went into the home of a woman who was ill, cleaned her house, bathed her children, and fed them a kosher meal, the neighbors formed their own working-class women's council.[97]

In 1935, convinced that wholesalers were hoarding meat to drive up their profits, Clara Lemlich Shavelson, whose fiery speech had spurred the 1909 Uprising of the Twenty Thousand—and who was by now a married Brooklyn housewife and mother—had become a Communist. She spearheaded a boycott shuttering the city's butcher shops that started in New York's Jewish and African American neighborhoods and spread around the nation. Then she marched down to Washington at the head of a housewives' delegation to lay the blame for the rising prices at the door of the secretary of agriculture.

Ultimately, this working-class "nationwide housewives uprising" lowered the costs of food and rent in many places and forged a coalition of women—white and black, rural and urban, Christian and Jew—into a political force. It realized Shavelson's dream of a movement sweeping the country. By the end of World War II, this consumer movement, fighting like hell, had increased support for federally funded public housing, led to investigations into profiteering, and brought about governmental regulation of food and housing costs.

"We and They": Antisemitism at Home and Abroad

IN THE 1930S life for Jews in Europe became not just difficult but perilous. In July 1930 every Jewish home in Balaceano, Romania, was smashed; a year later in Salonika, Greece, fifty-four Jews saw their homes burned to the ground. In January 1933, when Hitler came to power, college student Lucy Dawidowicz—who worked at Macy's after graduation—recognized the moment "as a dangerous crossing in history." Within just a few years, Nazi state-sponsored antisemitism brought the expropriation of Jewish property, the revocation of Jews' citizenship, and the shocking *Kristallnacht* pogrom on the night of November 9–10, 1938, when Nazi thugs torched 267 synagogues, smashed and looted 7,500 Jewish shops, and sent 30,000 Jewish men to concentration camps. Elsewhere right-wing and fascist governments enacted laws limiting Jewish economic and political rights. Outbursts of anti-Jewish violence erupted in Poland. In Italy, the 1938 racial laws dismissed Jews from all public positions and prohibited them from studying in Italian schools.[98]

Antisemitism was not only the norm in Europe, it was also a fact of life in the United States. Lucy Dawidowicz recalled the polarization she felt: "We were raised to know that the world was divided into two irreconcilable groups: We and They. *They* were the non-Jews, who hated us and wished to destroy us. But *We* would prevail," she was convinced.[99]

American Jews did prevail, but they did so amid antisemitism that had waxed and waned in the long history of the United States and that was once again on the rise. Living in a boardinghouse in Tampa, Helen Apte, who we first met as a young bride, overheard her neighbor demand that their landlady turn out the "stinking Jews."[100]

The most notorious episode of popular antisemitism played out in the city where she had come of age and wed. In Atlanta in 1913, the Jewish pencil factory manager Leo Frank was convicted, on highly circumstantial evidence, of murdering thirteen-year-old Mary Phagan, and sentenced to hang. Georgia's governor John Slaton, whose conscience would not let him rest if Frank were executed, commuted the sentence to life imprisonment. Not long afterward a mob snatched Frank from jail and lynched him. He left behind his wife, Lucille, who grieved the rest of her life for him. Frank's wrongful conviction and horrific death cast a long shadow over America's Jews. For years, Helen Apte noted the anniversary of his lynching in her diary.[101]

In the 1920s the industrialist Henry Ford introduced Americans to the nefarious antisemitic ideas then circulating in Europe about a world Jewish conspiracy. Ford's *The International Jew: The World's Foremost Problem* charged that Jews controlled the world's finances, incited radical political movements, and conspired to foment revolutions and wars to kill Christians and enrich the Jewish people. The book, from such a prominent American figure, enhanced antisemitism's respectability. Jews, even those with money, were routinely excluded from neighborhoods and resorts, from business and professional settings. Many colleges and universities limited the number of Jews they admitted.

Antisemitism in America surged during President Franklin

Delano Roosevelt's administrations. Fifty years earlier, as social reformer Maud Nathan had recognized, prejudice against Jews was not much of an issue. But now, as more than a hundred antisemitic groups flexed their muscles, what was called "the Jewish problem" had become an urgent question. Antisemites blamed "the Jews" for the Depression, charged that they controlled the media and the government, and accused FDR of promulgating a "Jew Deal." A whisper campaign even called the Episcopalian secretary of labor Frances Perkins, the first woman in the cabinet, a Jew, but Henry Morgenthau, Jr., secretary of the treasury, was the only Jew in FDR's cabinet. Detroit's Father Charles Coughlin ranted against Jews to an audience of millions on the radio. Cincinnati's Ethel Groen was president of the Mothers of Sons Forum, one of dozens of groups comprising the isolationist mothers' movement, whose five to six million members were determined to keep America out of the war and their sons safe. Groen's forum called for "the downfall of the British and the elimination of the Jews." Whether she meant eliminating Jews' influence or their expulsion or destruction is not clear.[102]

Antisemitism was obvious and blatant, a condition of life for Jews that went well beyond the official and unofficial exclusions from neighborhoods, schools, and jobs. Even living in predominantly Jewish neighborhoods could not shield women and their families. Their children still came home from school crying that they had been called dirty Jews.

In 1942 in *She*, a "magazine for the modern woman" published briefly in New York, an anonymous "Jewess" described how antisemitism targeted her children. Her daughter had wanted to vacation with a friend, but the hotel responded that she "probably would not find the company there for which [she] was looking." Her son wanted to be a chemist, but that industry did not hire Jews. Looking across the ocean to Germany, this Jewess concluded, "It Can Happen Here" too.[103]

She then surveyed its readers; 75 percent condemned anti-Jewish feeling and wanted to eliminate it. But readers' ideas about what caused antisemitism showed just how deeply entrenched it was. They blamed antisemitism on the Jews: Jews refuse to blend in; they are arrogant and clannish. All they care about is money, and they cheat customers. Said one woman, if Jews expected to live in Christian lands, they had to let their children learn Christianity and make up their own minds about their future; let the children choose to assimilate into the Christian American melting pot.[104]

Not only Gentiles aired their prejudices. Confessing "I, too, am a Jewess," one of *She*'s readers directly addressed Jewish women. She told them that if they wanted Gentiles to accept them, then they had to become like them. Clean up the ghettos. Stop forcing themselves upon "more cultured" people; that was what made Gentiles put up restriction signs. She urged Jews, presumably like herself, who were "more advanced than the rest of the race," who knew how to display reserve and tact, to help the rest of their people learn how to behave in a gentile world.

Antisemitism at home was inextricably linked to the international situation. When the Rutgers University Board of Trustees called more than sixty witnesses to investigate charges of Nazi sympathies in the German department at the New Jersey College for Women (later Douglass College), the investigation spilled over into an inquiry into antisemitism at the school. One professor testified that the former dean had refused to hire Jews. Yet Jewish students and recent graduates displayed reticence. They asserted that they had never faced antisemitism or been discriminated against as Jews on campus. Perhaps, once they were on campus, they had never faced prejudice. But when their dean, Margaret Corwin, who admired Nazi educational reforms, met with members of a Jewish women's group, she urged them to refrain from encouraging their daughters to apply to the college.[105]

Pulitzer Prize winner Edna Ferber, author of *Showboat* and *Giant*, described a nasty confrontation with antisemitism during a dinner in the pine forests of Michigan. When her host proclaimed, and the guests immediately concurred, that money-grubbing Jews schemed to take over the world, Ferber revealed that she was a Jew. A stunned silence followed, and she saw "such hatred as I never before have seen on human countenances."[106]

This best-selling author was secure enough to stand up for her people. But antisemitism led others to try to escape Jewish visibility even if they did not necessarily abandon Jewish identity. Although changing Jewish names seems to have been more common for men than for women, careers in the public eye persuaded many to do so, including actor Betty Perske, whose professional name was Lauren Bacall.

Others changed their noses. When the popular comedian Fanny Brice had a nose job in 1923, a wit quipped that Brice had "cut off her nose to spite her race." Desiring invisibility, wanting to blend in, to look like everyone else in an era of heightened antisemitism led to a surge of rhinoplasties. Those having nose jobs then and later were disproportionately Jews.[107]

Antisemitism also compelled a reappraisal of deeply held political convictions. After World War I's carnage, numbers of Jewish women had embraced the causes of international peace and disarmament. Now these women found themselves torn in two. Whether they were members of Jewish women's organizations that had passed resolutions calling for disarmament or individuals in the Women's International League for Peace and Freedom, Jewish women were caught in a bind. They believed war was evil, that it was mankind's greatest scourge. Yet by remaining silent in the face of Nazism, "we stamp ourselves as traitors of the race." The National Federation of Temple Sisterhoods' executive director Jane Evans persisted in her pacifism, convinced that one could fight evil without slaughtering the person who disagrees with you. But others who had long campaigned for peace realized that too few were seeing "the problems of one . . . [as] the problems of all." Unable to just stand there, to watch Hitler devour Europe, and seeing antisemitism as the first step on the road away from democracy that would end in totalitarianism, they accepted the coming war as vital to save their people.[108]

In May 1933 a hundred thousand Americans marched in New York to protest Nazi Germany's attacks on Jewish shops. Poalei Zion's

Goldie Meyerson—not yet renamed Golda Meir—and Hadassah's Rose Halprin addressed the crowd. But participating in the wave of protests that followed was not enough for many Jewish women. In 1933 Louise Waterman Wise, an artist and the wife of the influential rabbi Stephen S. Wise, established the American Jewish Congress's Women's Division. Standing up to antisemitism at home took its middle-class wives and mothers, decidedly not militant types, out into the streets, where they collared good Catholics on their way to mass to ask them to stop Father Coughlin's Jew-baiting.[109]

The Women's Division manned the front lines of an economic boycott of German goods. Declaring war against those importing and selling German products, these women, hoisting placards reading "Nazi Goods Are Soaked in Jewish Blood," picketed local shops to stop housewives from buying the German goods on their shelves. At the height of the busy Christmas retail season on New York City's Madison Avenue, an angry shopkeeper called the police to stop the white-haired Louise Wise from protesting in front of his store.[110]

By the time Hitler came to power, Cecilia Razovsky, born in St. Louis to poor Jewish immigrants, had led the National Council of Jewish Women's immigrant aid for a decade. In a world where many now marked time as before Hitler or after, she poured all her energy into rescuing Jews from the Nazi maelstrom. Even before war broke out, as German intentions became clear, Jews all over the continent were trying to escape. Between 1933 and 1943, as more than 150,000 European Jews took refuge in America, Razovsky mobilized Jewish women to help them.[111]

The road to America was paved with obstacles. Desperate would-be immigrants had to prove to American consuls abroad that if they were given visas, they would not become public charges. Because the Nazis plundered Jewish property and levied heavy emigration taxes, immigrants needed Americans, preferably close relatives, to sign affidavits swearing that if the refugees fell on hard times, their sponsors had the financial wherewithal to support them. "Sign an affidavit and save a life," campaigned the Women's Division. Anna Hertzberg, a Baltimore rabbi's wife, went from neighbor to neighbor begging them to sign affidavits for those trapped in Europe and raising money for the refugees who had made it to America.[112]

Yet the coveted affidavit was only one of the steps needed for a visa. German-born Edith Frank had two brothers in America who got affidavits for her two daughters. But even with them, Margot and Anne never got their American visas. Much later Anne's diary would be published and tell of her life hiding in an Amsterdam attic for more than two years until she, her mother, sister, father, and the others hiding with them were arrested. Months after that arrest, Anne Frank died, at the age of fifteen, from disease and starvation, in a Nazi concentration camp.[113]

FOR THE REFUGEES who were fortunate to make it out of Europe and become America's newest Jewish women, the years of living in fear ended. In America, they were safe, but they had left loved ones in Europe or flung across other ports of the globe. Still, no matter how anxious the refugees were about their families elsewhere, they had a job to do; they had to become Americans as quickly as possible.

Once again Jewish women stepped up to help. In Baltimore, where German liners docked, local women met the émigrés; found them places to live, a few sticks of furniture, and some pots and pans; and pointed them to employment opportunities, synagogues, and English classes. One day in March 1939, two Baltimore women met a ship refueling en route to Bolivia. Climbing aboard to see if anyone needed assistance, they found eighteen-year-old Ingeborg Cohn and her parents. She beseeched them to help her marry her boyfriend who had already escaped Germany, was living in Richmond, and had come to meet her ship in Baltimore. One woman got her husband, a judge, to waive the state's forty-eight-hour waiting rule on marriage licenses; the other found a rabbi. When the ship sailed the next day, Ingeborg Cohn Weinberger was aboard. Her husband, who could now help her get preference for an American visa, remained behind.[114]

In America, German Jewish women who used to spend their days embroidering and playing the piano, but were stunned to see "Gentiles only" signs here too, rolled up their sleeves and went to work. Finding a job even during the later years of the Depression was not easy, especially for those not proficient in English, but women's homemaking skills gave them an edge over refugee men in the workplace. Women could work in private homes, restaurants, and hotels as housekeepers, cooks, and maids. When, a year after her shipboard wedding, Ingeborg Weinberger's visa for America arrived, she returned to Baltimore to live with her husband. There she worked as a waitress, masseuse, exercise instructor, camp counselor, salesgirl, and office worker.

Émigré psychoanalyst Helene Deutsch, who fled the Nazis and later published the groundbreaking *The Psychology of Women*, understood the enormity of this economic and social downward spiral, of how the refugees had to close the curtains on their European pasts and reinvent themselves in America. Perhaps women met the decline in their status with greater equanimity than men. Émigré men who had been businessmen or professionals, who had owned and managed factories, now worked in other people's factories, washed dishes, and cleaned hospital corridors. They experienced an even greater loss of self-esteem. That they needed their wives' wages to make ends meet upset the bourgeois norms of the working husband supporting his stay-at-home wife.[115]

But women who had been physicians, lawyers, and psychoanalysts in Germany and Austria, and who found work in America caring for children and chopping vegetables, also experienced the high costs of exile. Two-thirds of the émigré female physicians, facing biases against foreigners, Jews, and women doctors, never managed to practice in America.[116]

The new Americans included over a thousand Jewish refugee children, whose parents were so desperate to save them that they sent them across an ocean knowing that they might never see them again. Clutching a single suitcase and, for the youngest, perhaps a teddy bear, these children were met in America by ladies from a committee, organized by Cecilia Razovsky, and then dispatched across the land to other ladies from other committees, who took them in hand and placed them in foster homes.

Hadassah responded to the desperate need to save Europe's Jewish children with Youth Aliyah, a program conceived in Germany even before Hitler's rise to power. It sped Jewish children and adolescents to Palestine. There Henrietta Szold, energetic, efficient, and as effective as ever at age seventy-five, coordinated their resettlement. First Lady Eleanor Roosevelt became Youth Aliyah's honorary chairwoman.

In 1939 no one could have predicted the enormity of the disaster that lay ahead. But those who excoriate America's Jews for their failure to rescue Europe's Jews ignore what America's Jewish women did accomplish.

"*The world was going to change*": World War II[117]

DECEMBER 7, 1941, seared itself into American memory. Japan's attack on Pearl Harbor propelled the United States into the global conflict that had been under way since Hitler's Germany had invaded Poland two years earlier. Stunned by the news, Americans would remember the moment their nation went to war for the rest of their lives. On a bus, on a street corner, in a dorm room, in Sunday school, Jewish women heard: "We're at war! We're at war!"

But what did war mean? What would happen to the nation, its men, women, and children, and the Jewish women among them? The war recast American women as foot soldiers on the home front. As Jewish women, too, stepped up, they sensed, consciously or not, Jewish difference. This time it sprang not only from their public and private lives but also from the knowledge that this war threatened the survival of their people.

In kitchens across America, mothers and daughters, wives and girlfriends cried together as they cooked farewell suppers for their men. Jewish sons' and husbands' last meals at home saw tables laden with the men's favorite foods—brisket and roast chicken or pastrami sandwiches, kosher hot dogs, and salamis. Whether these were Jewish foods of the past or American variations did not matter. These were the foods that had kept these families together.

Just as the foods Jewish mothers and wives cooked as their men went off to war differed from those of other Americans, so too did the talismans they slipped into their soldiers' pockets: mezuzahs to wear instead of St. Christopher medals. But even if foods and talismans differed, the emotions of those left behind did not. The next morning, with tears or brave smiles, America's women saw their sons and brothers, fiancés and husbands off to boot camp and from there to war.

During the war, marriage rates spiked. One winter vacation, a rabbi's daughter had six proposals, not because she was so attractive, she reflected, but because "a lot of guys wanted to go away, knowing they had a gal." Having too many offers sometimes seemed worse than having none. Women's Army Corps Corporal Mollie Weinstein, an army medical intelligence secretary, juggled two marriage proposals and a couple of serious boyfriends. Later she married an army captain just three weeks after they met on a blind date.[118]

In wartime, women became not only war brides but also camp followers, trailing after their husbands from one stateside base to another. Cheerleader Pearl Nadel met sax player Jules Sachs in a New Jersey high school. She took the secretarial course; he was studying accounting. They got engaged. Then America went to war. Jules enlisted, and the air force sent him to Buffalo, New York. So Pearl, her parents, and her younger brother piled into the family car. In a single day, a rabbi, a dress, and a restaurant were arranged. The next evening, at the end of the Sabbath, the couple wed. By Monday morning, Jules was back on base. His wife followed him to training in Missouri and Wyoming, living in boardinghouses and hanging out with the other military wives, until her husband got his wings and shipped out. Then she returned home to New Jersey.[119]

One morning Pearl woke up crying hysterically. Something had happened to Jules. Not long afterward a telegram confirmed that his bomber had gone missing in action on November 11, 1944. The war bride had become a war widow.[120]

Not all husbands were sent overseas. Phyllis Fisher's was stationed stateside. In the fall of 1944 he announced that they would be moving, but he could not say where or what he would be doing. Days later she set up house on a desolate plateau in the New Mexican desert, one of thousands of idle wives mystified by husbands working on a project that officially did not exist. On August 6, 1945, she learned that, at Los Alamos, those thousands had made the atomic bomb dropped that day on Hiroshima.[121]

WHILE MEN showed their patriotism by going off to war, women displayed theirs with support, sacrifice, and stoicism. Stoicism meant exercising self-restraint, shoving desires to the back burner, and putting the nation first. Women would have to give everything to the war effort, the best-selling writer Fannie Hurst told the Federation of Jewish Women's Organizations.[122]

As wartime brought austerity and shortages, sacrifice meant not grumbling about rationing sugar and meat nor complaining about shortages of rubber and tires. It meant planting Victory Gardens and buying war bonds. Support meant Hadassah and Pioneer Women urging their members to register for civilian defense work, and Jewish women volunteering for the Red Cross: organizing blood banks, preparing care packages, taking home-nursing courses; and wearing its uniforms to Red Cross Sabbath.[123]

To free men to fight, women went out to work. The war demanded the mobilization of all available man- and woman-power. Nearly 50 percent of American women were employed at some point during the war, and for the first time in the nation's history, more married than single women were in the workforce.[124]

Americans sang of Rosie the Riveter, but when Jewish women found wartime jobs, they were more likely to be among the two million women working in office jobs than among those welding munitions on an assembly line. Still, even during the crisis, Jewish women faced discrimination. Before America entered the war, the navy recruited co-eds to become code breakers; it told Radcliffe College president Ada Comstock not to recommend any Jews since they might push America into the war. Comstock ignored the navy's not-so-subtle antisemitism and put two Jewish names on her roster of high-achieving women who should serve their country.[125]

Even as they took on men's jobs for the time being, Jewish women assumed that it was just a temporary interruption in their lives. War's end would surely right their natural course, from school to job, marriage, housewife, and motherhood. This generation of Jewish women knew that they were expected to marry Jewish, raise Jewish children, and live a Jewish life: "It's as if there was no other way. You never pondered about it, you never questioned why."[126]

BUT FOR THE DURATION, another way opened. Despite strong opposition—who would "maintain the home fires, who will do the cooking, the washing, the mending," a congressman snarled—World War II brought American women into the military. By war's end, more than 350,000 had served in the U.S. Armed Forces.[127]

It took guts for young Jewish women to enlist over their parents' objections. American Jews accepted that their young men would have to fight, but they could not fathom why a nice Jewish girl would want to go to war. But Marian Gold Krugman wanted to see the action, and in the back of her mind, joining the army was for her family. She had relatives in Poland.[128]

As the armed forces inducted women, young Jewish women signed up. Those who had been secretaries before the war served as stenographers and typists. In the military, though, women were taught new skills. Jewish servicewomen installed and repaired radio gear, became air traffic controllers, and flew planes transporting personnel and cargo. They were Morse code operators and weather observers; they drew secret maps, planned meals, and entertained the troops; one even painted artificial eyes for the wounded. Another deciphered Japanese codes. In civilian life, lawyer Eva Kritzer was an expert on international law. In the Women's Army Corps, she was deployed to the judge advocate general's division at the Supreme Headquarters of the Allied Expeditionary Force in the European Theater of Operations.[129]

And of course, some were nurses. Nursing on the front lines, with hospitals under bombardment, Jewish women cared for the wounded in the Pacific battles of Okinawa and Iwo Jima. Polish-born Frances Slanger returned to Europe in June 1944, wading ashore days after D-Day, to find seventeen trucks of injured needing care. A few months later, with the rain pouring down on her tent, she wrote by flashlight: "The GIs say we [girls] rough it . . . but . . . we can't complain nor do we feel that bouquets are due us. But you, the men behind the guns, the men driving our tanks, flying our planes, sailing our ships, building bridges . . . it is to you we doff our helmets." Shortly after she scribbled these words, an enemy shell killed her.[130]

Plane crashes and shells did not discriminate between Jews and Gentiles, but military service accentuated Jewish difference. The armed forces introduced servicemen and -women who had grown up in Jewish neighborhoods to an America that they had never known and scarcely imagined. The women faced officers known to make it rough for the Jewish girls. They heard: "Ain't no way I'm going to live next to a Jew." Northerners stationed in the South saw their first "Whites Only" drinking fountains. It took courage to stand up to antisemitism and Jim Crow. Women's Army Corps Captain Doris Brill, a Jewish teacher from Philadelphia, told restaurant owners that if they did not serve the Negro women under her command—she was in charge of black and white recruits—none of her women would eat in their restaurants.[131]

For Jews isolated in a sea of Gentiles, religious services allowed for Jewish difference. Stateside, after the base chaplain goaded Mollie Weinstein into attending Sabbath services, she discovered its upside: with only five girls at the service and the rest men in uniform, a lieutenant took her home. She ushered in the new year 5706 (1945–46) in Frankfurt am Main's bombed-out synagogue where the few survivors, walking in with heads held high, made her proud to be a Jew. Religious services even presented military women with opportunities they never would have had back home. In Italy, on Passover 1944, first lieutenant Mildred Scheier, the ranking Jewish officer, led the enlisted men's seder.[132]

But holidays also brought homesickness. On Yom Kippur in newly liberated Paris, Mollie Weinstein, writing on letterhead that the Nazis had printed during their occupation, told her mother that going to services would make her longing for home and family unbearable. So this enlisted woman spent that Yom Kippur in the office as if it were any other day.[133]

ON THE HOME FRONT, Jewish difference brought anguish and despair over the fate of European Jewry. As the war progressed, Jewish women heard speaker after speaker lecture that the Nazis wanted to exterminate Europe's Jews. In 1943 they learned that almost three million of their people had already been slaughtered.[134]

Hadassah joined the Joint Emergency Committee for European Jewish Affairs, as it urged the Allies to recognize that if they did not act soon, there would not be any Jews left in Europe to save. In the late summer of 1943, thirteen national Jewish women's organizations sent representatives to the American Jewish Conference as it demanded that the British rescind their closing of Palestine's gates to Jewish immigration and called for the establishment there of a Jewish commonwealth.[135]

Resolutions relayed American Jewish women's grief and distress. Their associations called for the Allies to work through neutral countries to save the remaining Jews and appealed to Congress to override the immigration quotas and bring the remaining Jewish children to America. But the harsh reality was that, this late in the war, few opportunities for rescue emerged. When they did, a handful of Jewish women sprang to action.[136]

After Germany invaded Poland, hundreds of thousands of Polish Jews escaped to the east, to the Soviet sector. In the spring of 1942, as a new route for the British and Americans to supply the Soviet Union opened in Iran, the Soviets dispatched some of those Polish citizens and soldiers there. Among them were 870 children who had become separated from their families as they fled east. Jews in the Yishuv and the United States wanted to get these Teheran children, as they were called, to Palestine. Henrietta Szold found them immigration certificates. Hadassah promised that Youth Aliyah would care for them. But the quickest way lay through Iraq, and Iraq refused transit visas to Jewish children bound for Palestine.

For months, a triumvirate of Hadassah leaders exploited every connection they had to government officials, diplomats, politicians, businessmen, and the press to make "the voice of the outraged women of Hadassah" heard. In New York, Jerusalem-born Hadassah resident Tamar de Sola Pool and Youth Aliyah chairwoman Gisela Warburg of the famed German banking family, who had escaped Nazi Germany just in the nick of time in 1939, and in Washington, Denise Tourover, who had grown up in New Orleans and earned a law degree in 1924, worked the back channels. Tourover appealed to Elinor Morgenthau, a close friend of the first lady and the wife of the U.S. Treasury secretary, to bring the matter to President Roosevelt. Finally, in January 1943, the British found a ship for the children. When the Jewish Agency for Palestine announced that the Teheran children were on their way, it overlooked Hadassah's part in the rescue, creating, so the furious women cabled, a calamity for their emergency fundraising campaign.[137]

A year later the maverick journalist Ruth Gruber stumbled on another opportunity to help some survivors. Having earned her doctorate in Germany at the unusually young age of twenty, and having already traveled to Siberia to report on Soviet Communism, Gruber became, during the war, special assistant to Secretary of the Interior Harold Ickes. In June 1944, not long after D-Day, President Roosevelt announced that the government was establishing a temporary shelter at Fort Ontario, in Oswego, New York, for refugees who had managed to make their way to southern Italy, which was then in Allied hands. When the German- and Yiddish-speaking, Brooklyn-born Gruber heard the news, she told her boss that she should go to Italy to escort the refugees to America. He approved, but she had to face down others: officials, who wondered how she could possibly deal with male refugees who would not listen to a woman, and her mother, who thought her daughter "crazy" for crossing the Atlantic while the Germans were shooting down planes and torpedoing ships. Just before Gruber set off, Ickes made her a "simulated general" so that if she were captured, she would, under the Geneva Conventions, be a prisoner of war rather than a civilian who could be shot as a spy.[138]

She met the refugees in Naples and from there sailed back to America with the boatload of the first Jewish men, women, and children who had variously survived concentration camps, spent years in hiding, and fought with the partisans. They were the harbinger of tens of thousands of survivors who would come to America at war's end.

BY THE TIME these survivors landed in New York harbor in August 1944, America's Jewish women were already planning for what their role would be in the postwar world. They knew that an Allied victory would not end the Jewish problem and that the catastrophe's survivors would be looking to them for help, even as they were looking among those survivors for any of their family members who had somehow pulled through.[139]

As the Allies advanced into Western Europe, American Jews also began developing plans to help the Jews overseas at war's end. The National Council of Jewish Women helped establish an index of the millions of displaced persons. Representatives from fifty women's organizations, including Jewish women's associations, learned about their present needs and possibilities for repatriation. Women collected millions of pounds of used clothes to ship to those who had survived the war and were living in displaced persons camps.[140]

On April 12, 1945, President Roosevelt died. On May 8 the Germans surrendered. With war still raging in the Pacific, Jewish women knew that they must continue the struggle for freedom for all, and especially for their own people who had suffered an unimaginable horror.

The end of the European war gave new urgency to Zionism. The future, insisted Hadassah's president Rose Jacobs, demanded the realization of the Zionist dream for a Jewish homeland. Pioneer Women looked ahead to Palestine becoming a Jewish commonwealth and to the past, shaping what later would be called Holocaust memory, as they dedicated a Tel Aviv school to the women who had fought the Nazis in the Warsaw Ghetto Uprising.[141]

In their dreams of freedom, America's Jewish women prepared to take up new responsibilities as they crossed the divide from a world of war to a world of fragile peace.

5

"Down from the pedestal . . . up from the laundry room"

INTO THE FUTURE

HEADLINES BLARED: "BRONX Girl, 21, Wins 'Miss America' Title." "Pair Silent to the End: Husband Is First to Die." "Boxing Fan Wins $64,000 Decision." "Nazi Victims Reunited." "Case of the Teenage Doll." "Women Endorsed as Reform Rabbis." The girl-band the Shirelles topped the music charts with "Will You Love Me Tomorrow?" A disgruntled suburban housewife decried the "feminine mystique." The women behind these headlines? Miss America Bess Myerson, convicted spy Ethel Rosenberg, quiz-show champ Dr. Joyce Brothers, Holocaust survivor Gerda Weissman Klein, Barbie's Ruth Handler, Reform Judaism's Jane Evans, songwriter Carole King, and journalist Betty Friedan. Very different women, they had one thing in common: all were Jews. Their names in the news revealed that despite powerful images of American women disappearing into their homes the minute the war was over, the first postwar decades were years of transition for American women. Over time those transitions would pave the way for a revolution that reverberates to this day. For America's Jewish women, nothing would ever be the same.[1]

"A housewife through my own inertia and DNA"

JAPAN'S SURRENDER in August 1945 brought the catastrophic conflict of World War II to a close. As soldiers returned stateside, as the Cold War between the United States and its erstwhile ally the Soviet Union heated up, Americans rushed headlong into an era of prosperity. Cold War anxieties elevated religion as the American way over godless Communism, planted the nuclear family at the center of the nuclear age, and after acknowledging women's wartime service, sent them packing back to home and family. On that powerful new medium television, cheerful wives, wearing dresses and pearls, welcomed their breadwinners home at the end of the day. Experts of all kinds touted that a woman's road to happiness lay in her meticulous housekeeping, in her bright and talented children, and alongside her loving and invariably wiser husband.

After more than a decade of depression, war, and deferred gratification, young couples, heeding these messages, rushed to the altar, embracing the promise of babies and a home of their own. In the 1950s, three-quarters of Jewish women married by age twenty-five, some propelled by panic as college commencement loomed. Putting a doctor, a lawyer, or as Eleanor Hatkin Schulman would, a podiatrist-in-training through school was the route to a better life. New York University junior Miriam Solomon was just nineteen when she eloped in the summer of 1945, destined, so the future *New York Times* food critic Mimi Solomon Sheraton ruefully recalled, to "become a housewife through my own inertia and DNA."[2]

Housing shortages forced these young couples to start out living with parents and in-laws. But as soon as they could, they made a beeline for homes of their own.

Some Jews stayed in the city but moved to its outskirts. An astounding 83 percent of Newark, New Jersey's, Weequahic High School class of 1958 was Jewish. These teens came of age in a middle-class Jewish area on the city's edge. Other Jews headed for the suburbs. There in ranches, split-levels, and colonials, mothers kept house while their husbands went off to work. Even as the American

Jewish population hovered at 3 percent, new enclaves, where Jews comprised 20 percent, even 40 percent, arose in Long Island's Nassau County and in suburbs outside other major cities, like Cleveland's Shaker Heights, Chicago's Highland Park, Boston's Newton, and Detroit's Oak Park. Still other Jewish families moved farther away to the warmer climates of the South and West, soon making Los Angeles and metropolitan Miami the second- and third-largest Jewish communities in the country.[3]

No matter where their new homes were, another generation of America's Jewish women was raising families and building communities. A mezuzah on the doorpost, a Hebrew calendar on the desk built into the kitchen for the well-organized housewife, a seder plate on the mantel, extra dishes stashed in the utility room for visiting relatives who still kept kosher signaled that these were Jewish homes.

In their bedrooms, women marrying young could limit their family size, thanks to effective and legal birth control, although the Pill did not come on the market until 1960. But these women were having more children than their mothers had. Between 1946 and 1964, 92 percent of all American women of childbearing age gave birth. The Baby Boom arrived. There was a Jewish baby boom too, but Jews had been having smaller families than their neighbors for at least two generations, and that stayed the same.[4]

THE SAME WEEK that Imperial Japan signed its treaty of surrender, Bess Myerson was crowned Miss America 1945. Born in the Bronx in 1924 to immigrant parents, she grew up in the working-class co-ops. Graduating from Hunter College, Myerson entered the Miss America pageant. Crowned Miss New York City, she headed to Atlantic City—where another contestant represented the state of New York—and, during pageant week, took the lead.

That a Jew was the front-runner months after newsreels had shown bodies piled high in German concentration camps evoked, for Jews, deep pride, and, for antisemites, fury. Judges got calls

warning them not to vote for the Jew. Pageant officials tried to persuade Myerson to anglicize her name. On the boardwalk, strangers
baring numbers tattooed on their arms told her, "You see this? You
have to win."[5]

When Myerson was crowned, shouts of mazel tov rang out in
the convention hall. Yet antisemitism dogged her. Three out of the
five pageant sponsors refused to use this Miss America in their ads.

After her reign ended, Myerson married and, with apartments
difficult to come by, moved in with her in-laws. A year later she
gave birth to a daughter.

She understood her generation's rush to wed. A life alone for a
Jewish girl was simply inconceivable. The future novelist Anne Bernays recalled that all her friends, no matter how smart, how ambitious, were looking for mates: "That's what you were expected to
do and that's what you did. You got educated, you married, you had
children."[6]

Bernays had the sequence down pat: school, husband, family.
But school came first, and for Jewish women like Mimi Sheraton,
Eleanor Schulman, and Bess Myerson, school meant college. Perhaps the desire for education incubates, and those Eastern European immigrant daughters who had yearned to learn passed their
longing on to their next generations. More than half the females of
Weequahic's Class of '58 went to college.[7]

As the veterans flooded into classrooms on the GI Bill, higher
education expanded, drawing in more women than ever before. "Is
College Education Wasted on Women?" asked *Ladies' Home Journal*. Not if they found husbands there, it answered, and during the
1950s, they did. A coed who was not going to go straight from
graduation day to wedding day and who was not prepared to teach
had better know how to type. Few workingwomen held executive
jobs. In fact, most college-educated women earned less than a man
with a high school diploma. Frankly, getting an MRS degree and
marrying a professional man seemed the best options for aspiring
American women. No wonder so many 1950s coeds dropped out
of college.[8]

But Joyce Bauer was not among them. She earned a B.A. and

M.A. by the time she became Mrs. Milton Brothers. While he completed medical school, she finished a doctorate. When she gave birth to her only child, this psychologist, convinced that a mother should stay home to care for her child, discovered that it was tough living on a resident's salary. Wanting to find some way to help, she tried out for the TV game show *The $64,000 Question*. Joyce Brothers already knew something about boxing, presumably because her husband liked the sport. He thought the novelty of a female boxing expert would win her a spot as a contestant on the show. When it did, Brothers, gifted with a prodigious memory, mastered an encyclopedia on boxing in a few weeks. After seven weeks on the show in 1955, she became the second person and the only woman to walk off with the top prize, a feat she repeated two years later on *The $64,000 Challenge*.

Her educational success pointed to the future for America's Jewish women. Of course, most never used their educations to become boxing experts or popular psychologists. But young Jewish women kept graduating from college at nearly double the rate of other American women. Having more higher education sets American Jewish women apart. College polished skills these Jewish coeds would use in the years ahead—how to hone an argument, speak in public, debate, and write.[9]

DR. JOYCE BROTHERS went on to have a remarkable career as a columnist, author, and TV personality. But few Jewish wives in these years reached her heights. Instead, one recalled her despair at graduating from star doctoral student to sloppy housewife. Another frantically burrowed under the blankets after her husband left for work, ignoring the baby rocking in his crib. These women could not understand what was wrong. After all, they had what they thought they had wanted: a husband, a home of their own, a child. Why weren't they happy? Looking back, Mimi Sheraton knew she had been lucky. Marrying a man while he was still in school meant that she had to work to support them.[10]

In the era of *Father Knows Best*, unhappy wives were expected to keep up appearances, to pretend that all was well. Divorcing was complicated. After divorce rates climbed in the 1920s, states made it more difficult to end a marriage by requiring grounds for divorce. In New York, until 1966, the only acceptable ground was adultery. After the war, divorce rates spiked again as couples who had rushed to the altar before he shipped out discovered how incompatible they were now that he was home.

Jewish communal leaders boasted that their people had higher marriage and lower divorce rates. Interestingly, Mimi Sheraton, Bess Myerson, and Eleanor Schulman ended their first marriages in the 1950s. Ten years after she had eloped, Sheraton headed to Mexico to divorce. When Myerson's husband of a decade became abusive, her parents, who had made sure that the Myerson girls had educations to fall back on should they ever need to earn a living, told her, "You don't leave a marriage. No matter what, you don't leave. Go back and make it better." Meanwhile her husband sued for custody of their daughter, and she feared that he, the breadwinner, would win. The notions of joint custody and co-parenting were virtually unknown then. When Eleanor Schulman saw the husband that she had put through podiatry school walk in with lipstick on his collar, she ended their marriage. When she remarried, her new husband bribed a rabbi to issue a *get*, the Jewish divorce, so that another rabbi could marry them.[11]

The dating and mating that led to their marriages were governed by that era's sexual double standard. Good girls dated and went steady but knew that they were expected to remain virgins at least until they wore, if not a wedding band, an engagement ring. Single women found it hard to get birth control, and it was even illegal for them to try to get it in some states. If the unwanted happened, there were three options—find an abortionist, give up the baby, or marry the father. When seventeen-year-old Carol Klein—better known as Carole King—got pregnant, she and her boyfriend dismissed the first option, never seem to have considered the second, and, as quickly as her parents could line up a *chuppah* and social hall, rushed into the third. Two years later, in 1961, the Shirelles recorded a song she and her young husband wrote. It famously asked: After "this moment's pleasure . . . will you still love me tomorrow?"[12]

As for abortion, it became even more difficult to obtain one after the war. Municipal authorities, who used to look the other way at the abortionists they would call for their own mistresses and sisters, and hospitals, which used to perform D&Cs without asking questions, reversed course. In cities across America, a campaign against crime targeted abortionists, and hospitals established abortion boards requiring women who were seeking to end their pregnancies to face down a committee of doctors, surely most, if not all, of them male.

But of course, women, married and single, kept having abortions. The evocative short story writer Grace Paley had two children under the age of three when she became pregnant again. She was so exhausted that she could not imagine another baby. Her friends gave her names. She had the abortion in a Manhattan doctor's office. A year later he went to jail. The next time she needed an abortion, she was told, "If you weren't married, I would risk it," but since she was, that doctor did not dare. The others she contacted sounded shady, and she was rightfully frightened. In the end, she had a miscarriage and no longer had to worry.[13]

In Phoenix, Miss Sherri was the beloved host of the TV children's show *Romper Room*. (In college, a sorority had pulled her bid after it called her mother for the name of their church and then discovered that its Jewish quota was filled.) In 1962, a mother of four and pregnant again, she realized that she had taken, during the pregnancy, thalidomide, a drug that caused terrible birth deformities. Her hospital's medical board approved a therapeutic abortion, but administrators, afraid of breaking the law, balked. So Sherri Chessen Finkbine called in the press, flew to Stockholm for the abortion, was fired by *Romper Room*, and became a public face of a nationwide debate on abortion reform.[14]

In their organizations, many Jewish women took up the call to liberalize abortion laws. In 1969 the radical feminist group Redstockings, whose founders were Jewish, spearheaded a speak-out in a church basement where women shared their stories of illegal abortions. In the audience sat a journalist. Five years later, when that journalist, Gloria Steinem, whose father was Jewish, launched *Ms.* magazine, it published a manifesto signed by fifty-three women, including Steinem and Paley, testifying to their illegal abortions. A third of the signers were Jews.[15]

Although Orthodox leaders excoriated abortion on demand and decried Jewish women's diminishing their people as reprehensible in light of the Holocaust, theirs was a minority voice. Overwhelmingly, American Jewish women and men supported abortion reform.[16]

Then there was a third option for an unplanned pregnancy— have the baby and give it up for adoption. In the decade when Miss Sherri led her rapt viewers to pray over their milk and cookies, "God is great. God is good. Let us thank him for our food," states mandated that adoptive parents have the same religion as the birth mother. In Rhode Island, the court ordered a Jewish couple to surrender the four-year-old that they had adopted as a week-old infant after his Catholic birth mother sought to reclaim him. Sadly for them, the odds of finding another Jewish child to adopt were not high. The head of New York's Adoption Services observed that, for every Catholic baby, there were three to four Catholic applicants, but that for every available Jewish infant, seven to eight families were waiting.[17]

Back then a high schooler who found herself pregnant had to leave school as soon as she began to show. Not until 1972 would a law mandating gender equity in federally funded educational programs abolish this sexual double standard that allowed only the fathers to remain in school. Some Jewish girls disappeared, gave birth, and a week later, relinquished their babies. Told to move on and forget, they never did. A college sophomore, a child of Holocaust survivors, married her baby's father when she got pregnant; but beaten down by their parents telling the couple that they were too young and too poor to care for an infant, she gave her daughter away. Decades later, meeting that daughter, she said that surrendering her had been like "somebody ripping out a piece of me for thirty-two years."[18]

She had got caught breaking the rules, but she, and most young Jewish women, still followed another rule of the Jewish dating and mating game: Dating and marrying Jewish men. Yet intermarriage was starting its climb from 7 percent in the 1950s to almost a third by 1972. Later it would rise to 50 percent or more. In the first postwar decades, intermarriage still remained more common for Jewish men than for Jewish women. Later that too would change.[19]

UNPLANNED PREGNANCIES were not the only eruptions in Jewish women's lives. The parents of Weequahic's class of '58 included fathers who deserted and gambled away the family's money, as well as mothers who became ill, died, or divorced. Surprisingly, almost half the class's mothers, subverting the middle-class prescription of the day, worked, even if much of that work—running a doctor-husband's office, keeping the family's shoe store books—was still close to home.[20]

A very different kind of disruption shattered the lives of America's newest Jewish women, Europe's displaced Holocaust survivors. In March 1961 *The New York Times* reported the surprising reunion at a women's philanthropy luncheon of Gerda Weissmann Klein of Buffalo, New York, and Mrs. Joseph—likely Hannah—Lushan of Newton, Massachusetts. They had last seen each other in a Czechoslovakian slave labor camp. Klein and Lushan were but two of the 140,000 Holocaust survivors who came to America after the war.[21]

Another was Hanna Bloch Kohner, who in 1953 was on the popular TV show *This Is Your Life*. Millions of viewers heard her story, of how she had left behind terror and tragedy to make a new American life with her childhood sweetheart. Courtesy of the program, she would remember that old life—her mother, father, and first husband were murdered in Auschwitz—with a gold bracelet whose charms marked happier episodes from her past.[22]

Not all the women who came to America as Holocaust survivors enjoyed fancy luncheons or were feted on television for the triumph of a life rebuilt in freedom. But for the survivors, even as they went about becoming Americans, marrying, making homes, and raising children, the murders of their loved ones hovered over their lives. Two weeks after Bessie Hillman's niece Luba arrived in New York, another of her aunts said, *Tell me everything that happened during the war. Do it now, and then never, ever speak of it again.*[23]

Luba Bat told her of the starving Jews in the Lemberg ghetto who had done whatever they could to survive. She spoke of the morning she ran to her sick husband in the hospital and found the building empty and silent, its patients carted off in the middle of the night to the gas chambers. She told of hiding in a bunker, surviving the ghetto's liquidation. After that, she wandered the fields and hid in latrines until she was arrested. She lied to the Gestapo, claiming she was a Christian, not a Jew. To get her to confess, an officer whipped her until blood ran down her naked body. When she didn't, he sent her to Auschwitz anyway, not as a Jew but as a Polish political prisoner. There, somehow, she managed to survive.[24]

Many survivors were told, as Luba Bat was by her aunt, to put all that behind them and get on with their lives. These survivors shaped the American contours of Holocaust memory. American Jewish women read the best seller *Anne Frank: The Diary of a Young Girl* and saw its Pulitzer Prize–winning play and Academy Award–winning film. But of course, Anne Frank was not a survivor. Luncheon attendee Gerda Klein was. In 1957 she published *All But My Life*, an account of her six years in the whirlwind of the Holocaust. One of just a few hundred to survive a death march of thousands, she married the lieutenant who liberated her. Forty years later a film about her life, *One Survivor Remembers*, won an Academy Award. Taking the Oscars' stage before millions around the world, she spoke in a voice laden with tears: "In my mind's eye, I see those who never lived to see the magic of a boring evening at home. . . . Why am I here? I am no better."[25]

When Holocaust survivors had families, so many of their children were affected by their parents' traumas that they formed a unique cohort dubbed the second generation. Whether born in Europe or in America, they grew up with the mysteries of their parents' past and a lack of grandparents, aunts, and uncles. The second generation sensed the atrocities a parent had endured reverberating across their own lives. They spent a lifetime trying to grasp, as one second-generation daughter explained, what it was like to have your entire world torn apart.[26]

THE WOMEN who had been poor, Jewish, and Communist in the 1930s were usually still poor, Jewish, and Communist in the 1950s, sacrificing for the cause, even when donating two dollars to the party meant the difference between chicken and beans for the children's dinner. Later some of these women would look back on the years of sacrifice with anger. Taught then to believe that men's work was more important to the revolution, they had always put their husbands' needs first and had spent hours feeding and cleaning up night after night for the people their men brought home from the party.

The arrival of FBI agents on the doorstep signaled that, during the Cold War, it was again dangerous to be, or to have ever been, a member of the Communist Party U.S.A. In Congress, the House Committee on Un-American Activities and the notorious senator Joseph McCarthy conducted hearings to ferret out Communist infiltration in every part of American life. These witch hunts ended up with people fired from jobs, in jail, and many lives in ruin. Rose Chernin, who had been terrorized by the mounted police in Union Square, was arrested, charged with conspiracy to overthrow the government, and spent more than a year in jail. Called before the Un-American Activities Committee, she had refused to name any other Communists.

Ethel Greenglass Rosenberg and her husband Julius were arrested in 1950 as Communist spies and convicted of conspiracy to divulge atomic secrets to the Soviet Union. They both maintained their innocence. During the trial, the press commented on her unchanging expression as the guilty verdict was announced. Her stoicism propelled President Dwight Eisenhower to conclude that this "recalcitrant character. . . . has obviously been the leader in everything they did in the spy ring." The case polarized Americans, and protests against the verdict erupted in the United States and around the world. Some thought Ethel, if not both, were innocent. The Rosenbergs' sons, ages six and ten, gave a White House security guard a letter for the president, pleading for clemency. None came. The Rosenbergs were executed in June 1953. To this day, the case remains controversial.[27]

Another group of women stood out as they were interested in settling down less with a nice Jewish boy than with a nice Jewish girl. Ideas about lesbianism have shifted over time. For most of Jewish history, lesbianism evoked little interest. The concept does not appear in the Hebrew Bible, although the Bible considers male homosexuality a capital crime. That a few rabbinic sources from late antiquity and the Middle Ages discuss female homoeroticism suggests an awareness of lesbian behavior. But not until the modern era did Jewish lesbians come into view. The plot of the 1923 Broadway play *God of Vengeance*, by Sholem Asch, centered on a lesbian relationship. The female protagonist of the 1946 novel *Wasteland* by Jo Sinclair, the pseudonym of Ruth Seid, was a lesbian.[28]

Part of the reason lesbianism was so long obscured from view is that well into the twentieth century, society accepted deep female friendships, even those expressed in passionate language, as utterly normal. Women who had never married, but whose educations and skills gave them the economic freedom to be independent, lived openly with devoted companions although they were not always open about their relationships being romantic. When, in 1917, labor organizer and rent-strike agitator Pauline Newman fell in love with Frieda Miller, a research assistant in Bryn Mawr's economics department, her companion-in-arms Rose Schneiderman, already living with a woman, told her that surely there were thousands just like them. Newman helped raise the daughter that Miller bore after an affair with a man when she and Newman were already together. Newman vehemently opposed naming their relationship lesbianism.[29]

When Alfred Kinsey published *Sexual Behavior in the Human Female* in 1953, he claimed that a quarter of white women experienced some "kind of homosexual response," but that aspect of the report seems to have garnered little attention then. As a child, Gerry Faier, an American-born daughter of immigrant parents, wanted to sit downstairs with her father in *shul* and wear a *talis*, a man's prayer shawl. His response: *"Dos tor men nisht. . . .* You're not allowed to do this." As an adult after the war, overcoming the guilt, embarrassment, and shame then associated with lesbianism, she left her husband and grown children for the subterranean culture of the lesbian clubs of Greenwich Village.³⁰

Greenwich Village was attracting another set of women, those linked to the Beats, a group of mostly male writers rebelling against postwar conformity. Spurning materialism and monogamy, they went, as Jack Kerouac had, "on the road," rebelling in their lives and art against postwar political and cultural conformity.

Several Jewish women were pulled into their orbit. On their road to the Beats, they had stopped elsewhere. Elise Cowen, not recognized until decades after her suicide in 1962 as one of that generation's underrated poets, had spent time at a Zionist training farm. The Austrian-born ruth weiss, who deliberately spelled her name without capitals, had paused inside a doorway just steps ahead of the *Anschluss* before escaping to America, where, in San Francisco, she claimed her place in the Beats' pantheon with her jazz and poetry.³¹

Hettie Cohen occasionally went to a Queens synagogue when she was not out shopping with her mother, who volunteered with the Girl Scouts and Hadassah and who wore mink into the city to see a show. Wanting "to *become*—something, anything, whatever that meant," other than her mother, she refused to return home after college to await her destiny. Instead, in the 1950s, she moved into Manhattan on her own. There in 1958, when thirty states had miscegenation laws, she fell in love with, married, and bore two daughters to the African American poet LeRoi Jones (later to rename himself Amiri Baraka). Raising her biracial children under her neighbors' stares, she lived a life very different from that of her mother. She and Jones divorced in 1964.³²

For these women, wrote Joyce Glassman Johnson, Kerouac's lover, their road became the avant-garde lives they chose, fleeing their conventional homes and the limited futures for which their educations had destined them to hang out and sleep with the Beats. They became a bridge to the women who came of age in the 1960s, when no one any longer questioned a young woman's right to leave home, live on her own, and make her way in the world.[33]

"How much time do you spend taking care of your husband?": Doing Politics in a Man's World

IN THE POSTWAR YEARS, being a Jew meant joining a Jewish organization. "Those were the days when, if you sat next to a woman, your first question was, 'Are you a member of Hadassah?' If the answer was 'No,' you signed her up on the spot." Jewish women certainly flocked to League of Women Voters' meetings. But they were also signing on to the same organizations their mothers and grandmothers had joined—the synagogue sisterhoods, Hadassah, and the National Council of Jewish Women.[34]

As hundreds of new synagogues were built around the country, sisterhoods requisitioned space for their gift shops. Before 1948, only one congregation had one. Now they became ubiquitous, stocking the electric menorahs, chocolate seder plates, and olivewood ashtrays made in Israel exhibited in Jewish homes. Bringing a piece of the Holy Land home became a political statement—women's way of demonstrating pride in the new nation Israel.

If importing Israeli objects and wearing bracelets jangling with charms earned by selling Israel bonds seem inconsequential political expressions, they were less so against the backdrop of the Cold War. In those years women's organizations were pressured to downgrade their missions from advancing women's rights to emphasizing their responsibilities as exemplary citizens who put family and home first. A patronizing man interviewing Rose Halprin, president of Hadassah's three hundred thousand members, read aloud on the air her dawn-to-dark calendar of Zionist work, then snapped: "How much time do you spend taking care of your husband?" His message was abundantly clear: volunteerism not only brazenly propelled women beyond their place, but also might even lead them to contravene it.[35]

A member of the Jewish Agency's delegation at the founding of the United Nations, Rose Halprin lived in Jerusalem between her two terms as Hadassah president. When, in April 1947, Arabs ambushed a convoy of doctors and nurses en route to Jerusalem's Hadassah Hospital and murdered seventy-eight, she broke the news to the members. After Israel became a state in May 1948, the hospital atop Mount Scopus, in territory controlled by Jordan, remained cut off. Hadassah's members responded by opening a second hospital in Jerusalem in 1961.

Hadassah focused on the infrastructure of the Jewish state. The National Council of Jewish Women confronted problems closer to home. As momentum for the civil rights struggle surged, its president called on members to cross the dividing lines of American life—race, creed, and color—to support integration. But in the era when McCarthyism suspected Communist influence everywhere, the Council, working with civil rights organizations, was, unknown to its leaders, under FBI surveillance. The House Un-American Activities Committee never subpoenaed its leaders, but its FBI file contained a Council publication warning against right-wing extremists.[36]

JEWISH HOMEMAKERS, hearing echoes of the cry for justice that had sent their mothers and grandmothers out on strike, poured their energies into grassroots politics. They joined associations for homeowners, tenants, and school parents. They championed racial integration and civil rights.

In Miami, on a warm Saturday evening in the summer of 1949, a Jewish housewife and civil rights activist was hosting a party for her brother who was leaving for medical school. Then policemen knocked, not to tell her to keep the noise down, but to "get them damn niggers outta here." Matilda "Bobbi" Graf replied that they were her guests. The cops warned her that angry neighbors might come over swinging baseball bats, and they would be too busy to come to her rescue. The next morning, her five-year-old found a note that the Ku Klux Klan had left on their door.[37]

Jewish women were also doing politics as they clamored to build schools, parks, and libraries in their new neighborhoods. Journalist and stay-at-home mom Betty Friedan thought that for her generation, lugging groceries and kids had taken the place of politics, but she made sure it didn't stop her. Editing, from her Queens living room, her garden apartment's newspaper, she turned it from a chatty newsletter showcasing recipes into a local political force that supported integration and decried "Rents Going Down All Over Queens—Except Here!" As Friedan put it, activist homemakers "were concerned about the Negroes and the working class, and World War III, and Un-American Activities Committee and McCarthy and loyalty oaths, and Communist splits and schisms, Russia, China, and the UN."[38]

In one more Jewish stronghold in Queens, Roberta Strauss, another Jewish housewife and editor, ran front-page stories in the *Glen Oaks News* denouncing all forms of bigotry, including antisemitism. When one of Hettie Cohen's boyfriends took her to meet his family, his father told him: "You can sleep with the Jew but never marry her."[39]

But it was the writer Laura Z. Hobson who blew open the unspoken pact on genteel American antisemitism with her 1947 novel *Gentleman's Agreement* and the Academy Award–winning film based on it. The daughter of Adella Zametkin, who wrote women's columns in the socialist press, Hobson, an independent career woman working in advertising, flouted convention by adopting a son after she divorced. Then, wanting him to have a sibling, she concealed her pregnancy and adopted her own child. In *Gentleman's Agreement*, her protagonist was a journalist pretending to be a Jew to expose the insidious discrimination against Jews in jobs, housing, and society. Using episodes taken from her own life, Hobson showed the bigotry of even those people who would never use the word *kike* and claimed to loathe prejudice. When the Jewish

Book Council named *Gentleman's Agreement* the best Jewish novel of the year, she declined the award. She believed hers was an American story, not a Jewish one.

But more than Zionism, more than community politics, more than antisemitism, in these years "The Bomb: like God, a central presence," hovered over all. With children learning to duck and cover in school, on November 1, 1961, fifty thousand American housewives contravened their place and went on strike. Calling to "End the Arms Race, Not the Human Race," Women Strike for Peace was born. Its housewives told the "real" politicians to end the nuclear arms race whose fallout was lacing their babies' milk with radioactive strontium 90. For their efforts, fourteen members, almost half with identifiably Jewish names, were subpoenaed by the House Un-American Activities Committee. A cartoon showed a congressman whispering: "I came in late, which was it that was un-American—women or peace?" A decade later Women Strike for Peace sent one of its leaders to the 92nd Congress. Bella Abzug, crediting her early feminism to the obstructed view from her synagogue balcony, defiantly campaigned: "This woman's place is in the House—The House of Representatives." She was not the first Jewish woman to walk those corridors of power. That was Florence Prag Kahn who, after her husband's death in 1924, occupied his seat for a decade.[40]

But when Kahn was in Congress, feminism was in the doldrums. By the time Abzug headed to Washington, a new wave of feminism was surging in American life, and American Jewish women marched at its forefront.

Feminism, Arising

AS THE 1950S gave way to the 1960s, change appeared on the horizon for American women. The advent of frozen TV dinners made the work of feeding their families easier. Female life expectancy increased yet again. Once the Pill came on the market, women had the most effective birth control womankind had ever known.[41]

Yet ideas about gender in the workplace seemed stuck in the past, as when a medical school dean arrogantly boasted, "Hell yes, we have a quota." But he was just stating the obvious. Although more American women than ever, and more married women than ever, were in the workforce, most were clerks, secretaries, teachers, and nurses.[42]

Certainly there were outliers in the 1950s as there had been before, among them Joyce Brothers and Ruth Handler. The daughter of Polish Jewish immigrants, Handler and her husband launched Mattel Toy Company. Watching her daughter play Mommy to a baby doll, she pictured a different doll, one that would allow a girl to imagine her future before she became a mommy. Struck by a doll that she had seen in Europe, in 1959 Handler brought to the toy market a voluptuous mannequin with a wardrobe for every concievable occasion. Tens of millions of dolls later, Barbie is still going strong, as is her boyfriend. Handler's two children were named Barbara and Ken.

Of course, a psychologist and a wildly successful toy manufacturer were rare exceptions. But in the Cold War, American leaders contemplated harnessing womanpower to beat the Soviets. In 1961, to examine the possibilities, a young John F. Kennedy established the Presidential Commission on the Status of Women. He appointed to its Committee for Protective Labor Legislation the veteran activist Bessie Hillman.

When the Hillmans married, they had decided, as we saw, that only one of them should take a salary from the union. For decades, Bessie had worked for the Amalgamated Clothing Workers of America without pay. She had unionized workers and galvanized strikes in Pennsylvania and Connecticut. In New York, she had organized black female laundry workers. During World War II, when government service called her husband to the nation's capital, the woman who asserted, "I was Bessie Abramowitz before he was Sidney Hillman," announced that she had a job to do and that she had no intention of leaving it to be a Washington society wife. Instead she stayed home to advise New York City on labor's role in civilian defense.

In 1946, after a massive heart attack felled her husband of thirty years, she opened a new chapter in her life: she became a vice president of the union. She joined a delegation of educators and labor leaders who went to Germany to see the conditions in the displaced persons camps. She visited Israel.

She also became increasingly exasperated by the lack of American women's progress in the labor movement. In 1961, at a conference on the problems of workingwomen, seventy-two-year-old Hillman excoriated union leaders for their sexism. By the end of that year, she had found a new platform to express her opinions in JFK's Commission on the Status of Women.[43]

Meanwhile, over in Reform Judaism, Jane Evans, National Federation of Temple Sisterhoods' executive director, decided that Reform women should also undertake a study: an examination of the paramount signifier of inequality in their world, the failure to ordain women rabbis.

Two years later both groups published their findings. The presidential commission's report, *American Women*, reaffirmed women's proper roles as wives, mothers, and housekeepers. But documenting inequities that women faced in the workplace, it endorsed items long on Bessie Hillman's agenda: paid maternity leave and childcare centers. Meanwhile, at their golden anniversary convention, a thousand Reform Jewish women resolved that it was time their movement decided, once and for all, the question of women rabbis. Both events became harbingers of a new movement for women's equality that was about to burst out in American life.

Looking back at those years of activism, what jumps out is the number of Jewish women leading the way. Friedan coined the term "feminine mystique," naming the malaise of women who despaired that there was nothing more to life than being a wife and mother; Sonia Pressman battled government lawyers ignoring complaints of sex discrimination; Gerda Lerner wrote women into history and persuaded her adopted country to acknowledge that past with an annual Women's History Month.

At the time, many of these women downplayed or ignored their Jewishness; sisterhood among all women mattered, not religion or ethnicity. History, family, education, and status primed them for leadership. But it was the discrimination that they had experienced not just as women but as Jews and as Jewish women that pointed many on the road to feminism. They may have considered Jewishness, the experience of being a Jew, utterly irrelevant to their lives. Yet as an artist's sampler in an exhibition at New York's Jewish Museum noted: "If you think you can be a little bit Jewish, you think you can be a little bit pregnant." As for facing discrimination from Jewish men, a feminist literary critic observed that the 1970s best seller *World of Our Fathers*, about the immigrant Jewish experience, made her realize that if Jews were the world's strangers par excellence, among Jews, women were the outsiders. The result was the advent of an American feminist movement unimaginable without Jewish women on its front lines.[44]

BETTY FRIEDAN, née Bettye Goldstein, a former Queens *Parkway Villager* editor, was no ordinary Jewish college graduate and suburban housewife. In the 1940s, as a writer for the United Electrical, Radio, and Machine Workers of America, she published the pamphlet *UE Fights for Women Workers*. Her years of activism for a union calling for women workers' rights informed, although she never credited it, the feminism she advanced, in 1963, in *The Feminine Mystique*. There she chronicled the boredom, discontent, and dismay of her generation of female college graduates confined to suburban homes she provocatively denounced as "comfortable concentration camps." Friedan blamed the media, social scientists, and others for propagating a feminine mystique, telling women to sublimate their own desires to nurture those of their husbands and children.[45]

She traced her feminism to the antisemitism that she experienced growing up as an assimilated Jew in the Midwest. In high school, all Friedan's girlfriends were invited to join sororities; she, the Jew, never got a bid. That rejection isolated her. Being marginalized, standing outside the dominant culture looking in, fueled her passion against injustice. From the discrimination she faced as a Jew, it was but a short leap to confronting the oppression she faced as a woman.

Calling for an end to women's subordination in the home and the workplace, *The Feminine Mystique* touched a nerve. From around the country, thousands wrote Friedan to say the book had changed their lives. At home, sisterhood women read the book, then met over lunch in the synagogue's social hall, to discuss: "What kind of woman are you? Betty Friedan will help you decide."[46]

Meanwhile Congress paved the way for change, first with the 1963 Equal Pay Act, which didn't end up solving the problem but was a start, and then with one of the most sweeping pieces of legislation outlawing racial discrimination in American history. Title VII of the 1964 Civil Rights Act made it unlawful for employers to discriminate in hiring on the basis of race, color, religion, national origin, and . . . sex. A year later the government established the Equal Employment Opportunity Commission to enforce the law. Its staff expected to litigate racial bias, so they were stunned when more than a third of the complaints filed in the first year claimed sex discrimination. Was it still legal for employers to advertise "Help Wanted, Male" and "Help Wanted, Female"? Could states continue to "protect" women by barring them from certain jobs? Could airlines routinely fire stewardesses, as flight attendants were then called, when they reached the old age of thirty-five?

The commission hired its first female lawyer, Sonia Pressman. As a child, she had escaped Nazi Germany. As a lawyer looking for a job, she had interviewed with a man who told her she could be his legal secretary. Now this exasperated feminist, infuriated by her bosses belittling the sex discrimination complaints, groused to Friedan that women needed their own equal rights organization. In 1966 Friedan became the first president of NOW, the National Organization for Women. Twelve percent of its founding members were Jews, at a time when Jews were 3 percent of the American population. Its birth heralded the arrival of a new women's movement in American life.[47]

Four years later Friedan spearheaded the Women's Strike for

Equality. On August 26, 1970, fifty years after American women got the vote, women around the nation rose up. How many actually went out on strike, covering their typewriters to shine a light on women's limited job opportunities, or left the beds unmade and dishes unwashed to underline inequality in the home, is unclear. But across America, tens of thousands, if not hundreds of thousands, turned out to protest, hoisting placards reading "Don't Cook Dinner Tonight—Starve a Rat Today" and "Repent. Male Chauvinists, Your World is Coming to an End." Marching down New York's Fifth Avenue, the crowd streamed into Bryant Park behind the New York Public Library. There they heard Friedan exclaim:

> In the religion of my ancestors, there was a prayer that Jewish men said every morning. They prayed, "Thank Thee, Lord, that I was not born a woman." Today I feel, feel for the first time, feel absolutely sure that all women are going to be able to say, as I say tonight: "Thank thee, Lord, that I was born a woman, for this day."

Nearly fifteen years later, telling this story to a group of American and Israeli feminists meeting in Jerusalem, Friedan recalled that she was startled by her own words. She claimed that she had had no idea that she even knew the prayer. At this defining moment of what became second-wave feminism, she stood before the world as an American, a woman, a feminist, and a Jew.[48]

"The difference between a bookkeeper . . . and a Supreme Court justice . . . One generation."

THE NEW WAVE of feminism wrought a revolution. Women won the right not to change their family name when they married and, while they were married, to get financial credit on their own. Jobs once routinely held almost exclusively by men opened to women. Women flooded into the professions that, until then, had only token female representation. In 1970, on the day *Newsweek* magazine published its cover story "Women in Revolt," forty-six of its female employees revolted. They filed a class-action lawsuit charging the magazine with sex discrimination. One of those forty-six, Lynn Povich, was one of the first girls in her shul to have a bat mitzvah.[49]

The Supreme Court legalized abortion. Rape was recognized for its ubiquity. Domestic violence and sexual harassment entered the lexicon, and so did the use of the nonmarital-status-defining *Ms.* Feminists ran for public office. They wrote literature and poetry, made movies, and appeared on TV. They created women's studies classes and programs. Title IX of the 1972 Education Act made colleges and universities offer their female, not just their male, students sports teams.

In 1971, when a twelve-year-old girl had to quit baseball because Little League barred girls from its teams, a Jewish college professor, Judith Weis, filed a sex-discrimination suit. In 1973 another Jewish woman, Judge Sylvia Pressler, ruled: "The sooner that little boys realize that little girls are equal," the better. Two Jewish women opened the nation's favorite pastime to America's girls. A seismic shift around gender issues began rolling across the country.[50]

Although often called women's liberation, the struggle for equal rights for women and women's liberation were two wings of the wider feminist movement. Feminists, like Friedan, sought equality before the law, in life and opportunity, and pursued legislative and political redress.

But for some feminists, equity would not cut it. They came to recognize women's systemic oppression through consciousness-raising groups. Sharing stories of childhoods, boyfriends, and housework, they found that the experiences they had assumed were isolated personal put-downs and restrictions were the collective experience of sexism. The personal became political, and the movement's slogan was born. Women's liberation homed in on the power struggles between the sexes everywhere—in the boardroom, the courtroom, the bedroom, and the kitchen. Arguing that gender roles—who made the beds, who sat in the typing pool, who had the corner office—were not fixed biologically but rather shaped by past and present society, women's liberation scrutinized everything that touched women's lives. Its leaders, many of them vociferous Jewish women like Susan Brownmiller, Alix Kates Shulman, and Marilyn Salzman (later Webb), reevaluated relationships and marriage, housework and children, sexuality and medicine, work and workplace, body image and fashion.

Lofting banners for both poles of the feminist movement, Jewish women left their marks.

In politics, Bella Abzug, in her signature hats, strode the halls of Congress. Thirteen when her father died during the Depression, she said kaddish at an Orthodox synagogue every morning for a year before going to school. In 1942 she went to Columbia University's law school because Harvard had rejected her application, telling her that it did not admit women. Before marrying, she and her husband agreed that she would continue to practice law even after they had children.

Political action director for a decade at Women Strike for Peace, she poured her energies into the campaign to reelect New York City's moderate Republican mayor John V. Lindsay. He expected her to ask for a political appointment in return. She wanted him to lead a movement against the Vietnam War. He asked her: *Why don't you go into politics and see for yourself just how hard it is?* She did.

Serving three terms in Congress from 1971 to 1977, Abzug announced, "We are coming down from our pedestal and up from the laundry room. We want an equal share in government and we mean to get it." Later, addressing a conference on Jewish women's empowerment in Jerusalem, she exclaimed that it was high time that a woman became president of the United States: "She could hardly do worse than the men have done."[51]

Abzug was not the only Jewish lawyer driving feminism forward. Growing up during World War II, aware of what was happening to European Jewry, while seeing signs at home reading "No dogs or Jews allowed," Ruth Bader Ginsburg understood what it meant to be an outsider, to be persecuted for no reason. By the time she applied and was accepted to Harvard Law School, fifteen years after Abzug's rejection, it admitted a handful of women. Still, the dean made her justify why she deserved a spot that could have gone to a man. "It's important for wives to understand their husband's work," she replied to quiet him.[52]

When her husband, the tax lawyer Martin Ginsburg, graduated Harvard Law two years later and took a job in New York City, she asked Harvard to confer her degree if she successfully completed her last year at Columbia. Harvard refused, and Bader Ginsburg earned her law degree at Columbia. After she graduated, Felix Frankfurter, a Jewish Supreme Court justice, refused to hire her as his law clerk; no one hired female law clerks, and he would not be the first.

When asked about the inspirations for her lifelong drive for gender equity, she quoted a teenager angered over women's inequality. "I'd really like to know the reason for this great injustice," read Ruth Bader Ginsburg from *The Diary of Anne Frank*. She also pointed to the "indignities" she experienced at Harvard.[53]

While a law professor at Rutgers–Newark, she agreed, at the urging of several female students, to teach one of the first classes on "Women and the Law." She then moved to teach at Columbia Law School. Next, she became director of the American Civil Liberties Union Women's Project and argued landmark cases that overturned some laws that had allowed for sex discrimination. In 1983 the woman who, thinking of her own mother, asked, "What is the difference between a bookkeeper in the garment district and a Supreme Court justice?" and answered, "One generation," became the second woman and the sixth Jew to ascend to the Supreme Court.[54]

Other Jewish feminists also wielded their typewriters for the cause. They were not drafting legal briefs and congressional bills. Rather, as rebels and protesters, journalists and writers, they wrote their rage onto the page. On March 18, 1970, for eleven hours, more than a hundred women staged a sit-in at the offices of the *Ladies' Home Journal*. At the magazine whose slogan was "Never Underestimate the Power of a Woman," they demanded that its male editor be fired and replaced with a woman. Among the demonstrators leading the way was Susan Brownmiller. A few years later in *Against Our Will: Men, Women, and Rape*, she made the startling observation that the threat of rape allowed all men to intimidate all women and keep them in a perpetual state of fear. She redefined rape, not as an act of lust but as a crime of violence. She traced her lifelong fight against violence toward women to what she had learned in Hebrew school about pogroms and the Holocaust.[55]

One night in 1967, a thirty-five-year-old former editor, secret writer, and stay-at-home mother of two young children was washing the dinner dishes when she heard some spunky twentysomething feminists on the radio. Jotting down the time and place of their next meeting, she showed up to hear them grouse about the injustice of restricting their lives and opportunities. "Well, I always knew it was unjust," recalled Alix Kates Shulman, "but no one had ever said it before." Her middle-class Cleveland Heights upbringing had prepared her to accept her fate as wife and mother married to a breadwinner. Now she transformed into an activist. Shulman sat in at the *Ladies' Home Journal* headquarters. She helped plan the 1968 demonstration at the Miss America beauty pageant where protesters crowned a sheep "Miss America" and tossed into a "freedom" trash can high heels and other implements of female torture. Although they never burned a bra there, from that day forward, feminists were called bra-burners.[56]

In 1970 Shulman published "A Marriage Agreement," a contract for husband and wife to split all household tasks 50–50, from waking the kids in the morning to "Wife strips beds, husband remakes them." *Life* magazine turned it into a cover story. Holding before her the rabbinic dictum, "You are not required to complete the task, but neither are you free to abandon it" (Pirkei Avot 2:21), she spent a lifetime advancing the women's movement.[57]

Another writer-activist, Gerda Lerner, as mentioned earlier, was just shy of her eighteenth birthday when the Nazis marched into Vienna and annexed Austria. Overnight she became an outcast. Then the Nazis imprisoned her and her mother under horrific conditions to force her father to sign over his property. Among the fortunate few released who managed to get exit visas, they went first to Liechtenstein and then to France. Gerda got a visa for America; her mother decided to stay in France. She never saw her mother again.[58]

In the United States, she married, raised a family, and began writing novels. In her forties, she earned a doctorate at Columbia and devoted the rest of her life to proving that women had a history. "My commitment to women's history," she wrote, "came out of my life, not out of my head." Lerner lobbied her adopted country to dedicate a week each year to women's history. In 1987 Congress made March Women's History Month.[59]

These names showcase only a few of the Jewish women leading second-wave feminism. Others, like Heather Booth, who, as a child, wanted to be a rabbi, arranged a friend's illegal abortion in college. Her act of defiance morphed into Jane, a clandestine referral service that helped ten thousand women find safe abortionists until the Supreme Court made abortion legal in 1973. Another group, the Boston Women's Health Book Collective—nine of its twelve founding members were Jews—was furious at male doctors patronizing female patients. Its members started teaching women to take control of their health. They published what they had learned as *Our Bodies, Our Selves* and launched an international best seller.

More places needed to be shook up. Marilyn Salzman was shocked when a Little League coach told her, "You can't try out. You're a girl." In January 1969, at a counter-inauguration rally held the day before Richard Nixon was sworn in as president, the would-be Little Leaguer, now grown up, stepped up to the microphone, expecting her friends in the antiwar New Left to cheer women's liberation goals of equality, abortion rights, childcare, and respecting women. Then all hell broke loose. Her male comrades screamed, *Yank her off the stage and rape her.* Traumatized, Salzman broke with the New Left. She and other antiwar activists brought to women's liberation what they had learned there—how to stage a protest, occupy an office, get the attention of the media, and operate a mimeograph machine. Later, she was thrown out of Senate hearings on the birth control pill when she shouted, *Why are only men testifying?*[60]

Another remembered a different question asked by her grad school housemates planning a party: *Must we invite the Jew?* It primed Florence Howe to fight against injustice. One of the many Jews among the throngs of northerners heading south to Mississippi Freedom Summer, English professor Howe slept on the floor of a shack to fight for civil rights. Striving to end one oppression led to striving to end another. When no publisher would issue the women's biographies that she wanted her students to read, she launched the still-extant Feminist Press.[61]

MEANWHILE women who were deeply committed to Judaism and Jewish life stopped checking their feminism on their way into Shabbat services, as they, modern Hebrew speakers, would have called them. Outside the synagogue, they were demanding equality in the home, the workplace, and society. Inside their houses of prayer, only men were on the *bimah*. With Jewish women trying to win parity in American life, the synagogue and the American Jewish community would need to change too, and the women advancing Jewish feminism would show them how.

This Jewish feminism burst forth in the wake of events of the 1960s. In June 1967 American Jews watched with alarm as armies from Egypt, Jordan, and Syria massed on Israel's borders. Six days after war broke out, they were euphoric over Israel's victory. For the first time in almost two millennia, Judaism's most sacred site, the remains of the Second Temple's Western Wall in Jerusalem, was in Jewish hands.

During the 1960s as well, the USSR continued its refusal to allow Jews to practice their religion. As courageous Jews there demanded to leave, especially after Israel's Six-Day War, American Jewish youth, angry over parents and grandparents who they believed had been silent during the Holocaust, took a lesson from the activism of the civil rights movement and began marching to "Let My People Go."

Meanwhile the Jewish counterculture, a variant of the wider antiestablishment movement of unconventional lifestyles, civil and human rights, and antiwar protests, put forward its own ideas about renewing Jewish life. It led some young Jews, seeking "Meaning," which they wrote with a capital M, to establish intimate study and worship groups called *havurot* (*havurah* in the singular), as alternatives to the grandiose synagogues they deplored from their childhoods.[62]

The women pointing the way to a Judaism reinvigorated by feminism felt torn in two. Feminism promised them equality; Judaism relegated them to second-class status in their synagogues. There women ran the gift shops, men the services. Reform Jewish women called for female rabbis; Reform Jewish men did nothing about it. Bella Abzug said kaddish, but no one counted her as part of the *minyan*, the quorum of ten men needed for prayer. Outside the synagogue, the Jewish community was also segregated. Women ran Hadassah and were shunted by men's organizations into auxiliary women's divisions.

Because Judaism's laws, rituals, Sabbaths, and holidays sat at the very core of these women's beings, feminist Jews had their own list to add to the long roster of discriminations women faced. They were angry at being marginalized in worship, barred from rabbinic text study, banned from religious leadership, and ruled incapable of initiating Jewish divorce. (Christianity also was encountering demands for equality, female ordination, and gender-sensitive liturgies at this time.)

Once again Jewish women challenged Judaism's rules and traditions. A small group of feminist activists, many raised as Conservative Jews, some of them members of the New York Havurah, organized a study group in 1971. They named it Ezrat Nashim, Hebrew for both "the help of women" and the "women's section" of the synagogue. Its members, already committed feminists, like Paula Hyman who, as a graduate student, had helped organize the women's caucus at Columbia University's history department, set out to investigate the historical and cultural forces that had fixed Jewish women's roles across the ages.[63]

When the members of Ezrat Nashim heard that the leadership of the New York and Boston *havurot* were going to have a joint meeting and that women were deliberately excluded in favor of an all-male gathering, the women exploded in fury. For three thousand years, they charged, half the Jewish people had been considered second-class. It was time for change. Their demands: Women must become equal members of their synagogues, something that Rosa Sonneschein had raised three-quarters of a century before. They must count in the quorum for a *minyan*. They must be able to lead services, initiate divorce, go to rabbinical school, and acquire positions of prominence in American Jewish life. The days of Jewish women standing on the sidelines and being confined to women's organizations were over.[64]

A year after Ezrat Nashim insisted that women count in a *minyan*, Conservative rabbis agreed to their demand. American Judaism had made a small move toward equality for women. It was a big enough story that *The New York Times*—the newspaper in the city with the largest Jewish population in the world—made it front-page news.[65]

Jewish feminism began gaining ground. In 1972, at the General Assembly of the Council of Jewish Federations, representing Jewish communities across America, Jacqueline Levine, president of the American Jewish Congress's Women's Division, pointed to the gross underrepresentation of women in communal affairs. The women in the audience gave her an ovation, while the men seemed utterly bewildered. The next year the Jewish counterculture's journal *Response* published Rachel Adler's essay "The Jew Who Wasn't There," decrying women's peripheral status in Jewish law. The journal's entire issue was devoted to voices from what was already called the "Jewish Women's Movement."[66]

In Reform and Conservative synagogues, Jewish women began wearing the prayer shawls that historically only Jewish men had donned. Women polished skills once learned for a bat mitzvah. Others, who grew up before Lynn Povich had hers, trained for their bat mitzvah as adults. Then Jewish women ascended the *bimah*, chanting the weekly Torah portions in lilting sopranos.

But the most striking change was not the women who climbed the stairs to the *bimah* from the congregation, but the ones whose entrance on Friday evening signaled that the rabbi had arrived, and the service would begin.

For a century, American Jews had been asking: *Could women be rabbis?* In the 1890s, when the woman's rights movement called for Christian women to enter the ministry, some American Jews wondered if there would also be female rabbis. As we saw, early in the twentieth century, when Henrietta Szold went to study at the Conservative movement's Jewish Theological Seminary, she and its leaders agreed that she could take classes there but not seek rabbinical ordination. In the 1920s, Irma Lindheim had studied for the rabbinate at New York's Jewish Institute for Religion, a liberal seminary that would later merge with the Reform movement's Hebrew Union College. But her path led not to the pulpit but to becoming Hadassah's president. She was not the only Jewish woman to seek rabbinical ordination in the 1920s and 1930s, but every brave challenger who tried to crash into this male bastion then and after World War II failed.[67]

With feminism arising anew in the 1960s, another group of contenders to become the first woman rabbi came forward. Sally Priesand, as her friends at a Reform movement Jewish summer camp knew, hoped to become "Rabbi Sally." In 1972 she was ordained at the Cincinnati campus of Hebrew Union College–Jewish Institute of Religion, becoming the first woman rabbi in American Judaism. Two years later the Reconstructionist movement, founded by Rabbi Mordecai M. Kaplan, who had shocked his mother and mother-in-law when he held a bat mitzvah for his daughter Judith, ordained its first female rabbi. In 1985 the Conservative movement began ordaining women.

Feminism also opened spaces for Orthodox girls and women to master the texts of Jewish law and tradition that they had never studied in the past. Intentionally or not, the learning they acquired set some on the path to the rabbinate. Today women called *rabba* or *rabbanit*—because, in the gendered language of Hebrew, rabbi is masculine—lead and preach as rabbis in some progressive Orthodox synagogues.

Touched by female rabbis in the classroom, on the *bimah*, over Shabbat dinner, and often at the most vulnerable moments of their lives—as they wed, celebrated newborns, rejoiced at a bar mitzvah, and mourned the dead—boys and girls, men and women encountered Judaism newly inflected by women's perspectives.

In rabbinical school, these women heard their teachers boast that Judaism had prayers for everything. But they knew, from their own lives, that it wasn't true. So they wrote a dazzling array of prayers and readings for all the spaces and places in their lives that the rabbis of old had missed, like going into labor and recovering from rape. They popularized new rituals to welcome infant daughters into the community. They reappropriated the *mikveh*, making it a place not just for observant married women to immerse monthly but a space whose healing waters would mark a milestone or bring closure to a crisis. They injected female perspectives into Jewish tradition where, for millennia, women had been silent or silenced.

Women rabbis were not the only ones spreading Jewish feminism. *Lilith*, the first Jewish feminist magazine, premiered in 1976. Named for Adam's first wife, who is named not in Genesis but rather in a cautionary rabbinic tale about the terrible fate awaiting a wife who refuses to obey her husband, the magazine is still published today. Its exposés of the gender gap in power and pay in Jewish organizations and a 1998 story of sexual misconduct by a well-known rabbi gave a Jewish slant to issues feminists were raising in American life.[68]

The winds of feminist change also wafted through the Jewish organizations. Hadassah and National Council of Jewish Women added women's health and reproductive rights to their core missions. The female auxiliaries to the men's groups, questioning their separate but purportedly equal status, began merging into the main bodies. But when B'nai B'rith decided to admit women, B'nai B'rith Women proclaimed its independence and morphed into Jewish Women International. Its leaders feared that were they to dissolve into B'nai B'rith, issues they championed, like girls' and women's physical safety, would be pushed aside.

Jewish feminism even crossed over to popular culture. In 1983 Barbra Streisand's *Yentl* hit the big screen. Based on a story by Nobel laureate Isaac Bashevis Singer, the film centers on a woman of marriageable age who yearns to study Torah but is denied the education she wants because of her sex. Much like the women of Ezrat Nashim, who explored Jewish texts to understand their assigned roles, Yentl asks why she can't be a Jewish scholar. After the death of her father, who surreptitiously taught her, she hacks off her braids, dons his clothes, and heads to a yeshiva. *Yentl*, appearing just as the Conservative movement closed its acrimonious battle over women's ordination, resonated with audiences around the world. Two decades after the film premiered, when Bernadine Healy, head of the National Institutes of Health, discovered that physicians treated men and women with coronary heart disease differently, she called the phenomenon the "Yentl Syndrome." Yentl, a character brought to life by an American Jewish feminist filmmaker, Barbra Streisand, had become an icon.[69]

Anita Diamant's wildly successful *The Red Tent*, published in 1997, also gained a wide feminist audience. In the novel, Dinah, the daughter of the biblical patriarch Jacob, whispers the stories she heard from her father's wives as each month, when they bled, they retreated to the red tent to share secrets with their only surviving daughter. Before publishing the novel, Diamant had written books casting a feminist lens on Jewish weddings and new ceremonies for welcoming Jewish babies. She was also a force behind Boston's Mayyim Hayyim, a *mikveh* open to new feminist rituals. Like *Yentl*, *The Red Tent* reached far and wide, selling millions of copies in twenty countries even before its movie tie-in. That the not-Jewish actress Julia Roberts named it one of the books that made a difference in her life in O *Magazine*, published by another well-known not-Jewish woman named Oprah, helped spread the word.[70]

IN ISRAEL, socialist pioneers laying the foundations of the future state rhetorically championed gender equity in their collective farms called *kibbutzim* and in the military. But Israeli women's reality belied the equality myth. On the kibbutz, they washed shirts and peeled vegetables. In the army, they were dispatched to combat support and service roles. Rather than propelling egalitarianism forward in Israeli life, gender segregation in these pillars of the state entrenched it.

Then the American Jewish feminists arrived. Marcia Freedman, an American immigrant from Newark, New Jersey, created one of the first consciousness-raising groups in the country. Elected to Israel's Knesset, its parliament, she championed feminist concerns.[71]

In the summer of 1984, the American Jewish Congress brought together American and Israeli feminists in Jerusalem. That was the meeting where Betty Friedan claimed that she had no idea that she even knew the Hebrew prayer where man thanks God for not making him a woman. *Lilith*'s editor came, and so did Jacqueline Levine. They were joined by a Talmud professor, who was a member of Ezrat Nashim, and a writer and rabbi's wife, who, like Carrie Simon before her, wanted women rabbis, but she wanted hers to be Orthodox. Their Israeli counterparts were politicians, academics, journalists, and educators. At the end of the conference, the Americans pointed out that the Israelis did not have to adopt their feminist ways but that they needed to recognize that the personal is political. The Israelis founded the Israel Women's Network to broadcast that message and advocate for women's equality.[72]

Yet at times, Jewish feminists meeting up with their counterparts felt not the solidarity of sisterhood but the sting of antisemitism. It came from Christian scholars who lauded Jesus as the first feminist because he let a woman hear his teaching—not noting he was a Jew—but who excoriated an ancient rabbi who said teaching a daughter Torah teaches her obscenity. Once again Christians, this time feminist Christians, placed Christianity as superior to Judaism. It came from colleagues in the National Women's Studies Association who asked how a feminist could call herself a Jew given Judaism's strong patriarchy. In 1981, when this four-year-old association announced that it opposed antisemitism against Jews and Arabs, its Jewish members were pained and angered. They believed anti-Israel bias blinded their colleagues to the depths of continued prejudice against Jews, including by Arabs.[73]

Jewish feminists attended conferences convened between 1975 and 1985 during the United Nations' International Women's Decade. The meetings discussed an array of difficult issues and dangers that girls and women around the world faced—including illiteracy, malnutrition, exile, war, sexual slavery, forced marriage, and wife beating. Thousands attended the official conferences as members, as did Friedan and Abzug, of their national delegations. Others came from nongovernmental organizations, like the American Jewish women's organizations, to the parallel open forums.

The first meeting in Mexico City was to discuss improving women's lot around the world. When Leah Rabin, wife of the Israeli prime minister, got up to speak, Jihan Sadat, wife of Egypt's president, started a delegates' walkout. Arabs, women from Communist countries, and some Asian and African delegates left the hall. Furious, Betty Friedan strode up to the podium to shake Rabin's hand.[74]

At that conference, the delegates from 109 countries overwhelmingly passed the "Declaration of Mexico." It endorsed "Zionism as racism" months before the UN General Assembly did. Israel and the United States voted against the declaration; nineteen countries abstained. Bella Abzug was infuriated.[75]

The next conference took place in Copenhagen in 1980. Reporting on its impact a year later in *Lilith* magazine, Regina Schreiber captured Jewish women's reactions. They reported that, whenever Israeli delegates attempted to speak, they were shouted down and even physically menaced. The women representing Jewish women's organizations and others known to be Jews "were in a state of shell-shock." They heard: "The only good Jew is a dead Jew. . . . The only way to rid the world of Zionism is to kill all the Jews." Friends warned Chaie Herzig, co-president of the Women's Division of the American Jewish Congress, not to carry its tote bag, as it would make her "a lightning rod." The author Sonia Johnson, whose support for the Equal Rights Amendment led the Mormons to excommunicate her, heard people say that having Jews, like Steinem, Friedan, and Abzug, in the U.S. women's movement gave it "a bad name." The conference closed with its Programme of Action. This time the report omitted the word *Zionism*. Calling for "solidarity campaigns with women struggling against colonialism, neo-colonialism, racism, racial discrimination and apartheid and for national independence and liberation" allowed for avoiding the charge of antisemitism.[76]

Worldwide feminism embraced all sorts of female difference. It proclaimed solidarity with black women, African women, Latina women, Asian women, ethnic women of all stripes, every kind of woman, but never Jewish women. In refusing to recognize the Jews as a minority, to grasp that Israel was founded to provide a haven for a people persecuted across the millennia whose millions had been murdered in the Holocaust, international feminism replicated old antisemitic tropes. Antisemitism and anti-Zionism in the women's movement propelled some American Jewish feminists who had long elevated gender above all other affinities to reconsider what it meant also for them to be Jews.

BUT AMERICA'S Jewish women had never unanimously embraced Zionism or unequivocally supported the State of Israel. As we saw, the membership of the National Council of Jewish Women was so divided on the question of a Jewish homeland in Palestine that, until World War II, its leaders had kept the subject off its agenda to avoid losing members. Then, confronted with the plight of Europe's surviving Jews who, having no homes and families to return to, wanted to go to Palestine, the council came, after the war, to support the establishment of a Jewish state as a place of refuge. By then, almost all Jewish organizations, even those that had earlier opposed Zionism to avoid raising questions about Jews' allegiance to America, were also calling for a Jewish state.[77]

In 1948 Reform Jewish women, who had earlier supported an art school in Jerusalem, hailed the establishment of the State of Israel. More women joined Hadassah. Then, as tensions mounted in the Middle East in the spring of 1967, American Jews feared that war between Israel and its Arab neighbors would end in a second Holocaust. Dread turned to relief when, as Lucy Dawidowicz reflected, Israel's victory "brought elation and pride, but, even more, release from tension, gratitude, a sense of deliverance."[78]

But not all felt pride and gratitude. In 1970, writing in one of the many underground publications of the antiwar and New Left movements, Sharon Rose, who described herself as a "nice Jewish girl from New York" and who had spent time on a kibbutz, announced, "I am not a Zionist." For her, liberation for Jews demanded liberation for all people. In Israel, she had seen Israeli Arabs digging ditches, their villages under military rule, and Jews who, despite their own history of exile across the millennia, ignored the Palestinians' right to self-determination.[79]

Rose's was an early voice of dissent from what was then still largely an American Jewish consensus supporting Israel. But in the years ahead, other American Jewish women would become part of a growing chorus of concern over Israel's expanding settlements, its treatment of the Palestinians, and its failure to achieve peace.

New left-wing groups, Breira and its successor, New Jewish Agenda, expressed unease at a time when mainstream Jewish organizations sustained the position that the Arabs planned to push the Israelis into the sea. In Nairobi in 1985, during the last of the international conferences of the UN Decade for Women, New Jewish Agenda activists Christie Balka and Reena Bernards handed out thousands of copies of guidelines for productive Arab-Israeli dialogue. They stated, "Israel will not be singled out as a unique violator of human rights. Nor will the Palestine Liberation Organization be singled out as a terrorist organization." Censuring Israel for its "racist policies," these activists constituted a vocal but small minority of America's Jewish women.[80]

They were in the vanguard of America's Jewish women, and not just those on the left, who have voiced dismay over Israel's treatment of the Palestinians. In April 2018, the actor Natalie Portman, who was born in Israel and who holds Israeli and U.S. citizenships, declined to appear in Jerusalem to receive the Genesis Prize, known as the Jewish Nobel. She refused to share the stage with Prime Minister Benjamin Netanyahu, who opposes the establishment of a Palestinian state. In the uproar following her announcement, Rachel Azaria, a member of the Knesset, urged Israelis to take Portman's stance as a warning sign. The actor, who made her directorial debut with the Hebrew-language film *A Tale of Love and Darkness*, was, Azaria said, "totally one of us." Portman used the power of her fame to send a message of disapproval shared by growing numbers of American Jews, especially among America's Jewish youth.[81]

⚜

EVEN AS feminism had an impact on many American Jewish women, much has still not changed. In Jewish schools, synagogues, and organizations, a glass ceiling hangs under executive positions. Too often, an old boys' club still insists that few Jewish women can lead. Jewish women wonder, *Have they ever bothered to look?*[82]

There are troubling encounters too. The executive director of a campus Jewish organization goes to breakfast with a donor. He starts the meal by putting his hand on her rear. He ends it by drawing her close, "saying he needed 'to grab a thing or two.' " What was the difference between Selma Litman, a secretary who had to flee her leering boss, and that executive director sexually harassed by a donor? Other than three-quarters of a century, nothing.[83]

In the Orthodox world, recalcitrant husbands hold their ex-wives hostage over the *get*. Since only men can give a Jewish divorce, they blackmail their wives to extort money or get the upper hand in a custody battle. If she refuses to pay or give in, he goes on with his life; she remains a grass widow, an *agunah*, unable ever to remarry under conventional Jewish law. Five years after a congressman's aide and his ex-wife divorced in an American court, he was still refusing to give her a *get* despite a social media campaign urging the congressman to tell his staffer to do the right thing.[84]

As for the Orthodox women who have become a *rabba* or *rabbanit*, or who will want to one day, the Orthodox Union, which exercises influence over four hundred synagogues, told its members point blank that, in their congregations, no Jewish woman may act like a rabbi, no matter her title. That some of their member congregations pushed back, refusing to fire the female spiritual leaders already working in their synagogues and that a few even hired new ones does not mean that all will defy the union's authority.[85]

The battle within Orthodoxy has carried over to Israel. Late in 1988 a thousand Jewish women from more than twenty countries convened in Jerusalem for the first international Jewish feminist conference on women's empowerment. That was where Bella Abzug announced that it was high time for a woman to become president of the United States.[86]

But it was an event outside the conference's agenda that still roils Israel decades later. On a chilly morning on the first day of December, seventy women from across the religious spectrum, many of them Americans, went to pray in the section reserved for women at the Western Wall. A partition separates men and women in prayer there just as it does in Orthodox synagogues. The service, led by American female rabbis, began peacefully. Then, as the women unfurled the Torah they had brought for the day's public reading, something that had never been done on the women's side of the plaza, ultra-Orthodox women surrounded and screamed at them, and men from the other side of the barrier climbed onto chairs to shout obscenities at them. The feminists managed to finish their service and left singing a song of peace. They had made history, despite the protest against their actions.[87]

Since then, women, including Americans who moved to Israel, have tried, and more often than not failed, to pray regularly at the Western Wall. They have confronted violence, been dragged off to jail, sought redress from the Israeli government and its courts, and garnered tremendous international support. Liberal American Jews have championed the right of the Women of the Wall to pray in Israel, wear prayer shawls, and read from the Torah, just as they do in many synagogues in the United States.

If feminists have been disappointed in the areas where the Jewish community has failed to fulfill their feminist aims, they remained stunned by the recent surge of antisemitism in the women's movement. International Women's Strike USA—a new feminist group roused to action after the election of Donald Trump—published a 750-word platform that sets "Justice for Palestine" at "the beating heart of this new feminist movement." Outraged by its singling out Israel for opprobrium, journalist Emily Shire asked in *The New York Times*, "Does feminism have room for Zionists?" Palestinian-American-Muslim activist Linda Sarsour, one of the organizers of the Women's March in 2017 that saw millions of women in the United States and around the world take to the streets the day after Trump's inauguration, pointedly responded: no. She told Shire that she could "either stand up for the rights of all women, including Palestinians, or none." By extension, she has dictated to the many Jewish women who are feminists and who include caring about Israel as part of their Jewish identities that they have to choose. They can be feminists or Jews, not both.[88]

"I have my priorities. I know who I am": Into the New Millennium

IN THE TWENTY-FIRST CENTURY, feminism and changes across America reconfigured Jewish households. A survey of America's Jews at the turn of the millennium found that a quarter of adult Jews had never married; a half-century earlier almost all had been wed. A 2016 study, which excluded ultra-Orthodox Jews, found that only 50 percent of American Jews age twenty-five to fifty-four were married.[89]

In 1971, just as Jewish feminism was dawning, Marshall Sklare, a prominent sociologist of American Jewry, wrote, "It is beyond belief that anyone would choose to be childless." In the twenty-first century, the rabbis of Conservative Judaism's law committee, reminding couples that, to fulfill Jewish law, they must have two children, told them to have a third to replace those lost in the Holocaust and increase the world's Jewish population. By the time these rabbis spoke, over a quarter of Jewish women at the end of their childbearing years had not had one. With so many educated Jewish women—in 2013, 56 percent had graduated college, 28 percent had postgraduate degrees, another quarter had some college—spending their twenties and thirties in school or businesses or careers, their delayed childbearing has caused, thought Sylvia Barack Fishman, another sociologist, an epidemic of unexpected Jewish infertility. Others had never wed and had not wanted to raise a child alone. Still others, despite Sklare's conviction, had never wanted any children.[90]

Jewish households now included women living together who, unlike Pauline Newman, announced loudly and proudly that they were lesbians and Jews and would seek to claim their place as both within the American Jewish community. Jewish lesbians published books, like Evelyn Torton Beck's 1982 *Nice Jewish Girls: A Lesbian Anthology* and the 2001 memoir collection, *Lesbian Rabbis: The First Generation*, edited by Rabbis Rebecca Alpert and Sue Levi Elwell. The journal *Bridges* emerged from a publication of the New Jewish Agenda's feminist task force. Published for two decades until its last issue in 2011, *Bridges* not only printed lesbian voices; its articles, stories, and poetry by multicultural, Sephardic, and working-class women drew attention to the diversity of America's Jewish women. Lesbians fought for and won the right to wed under a *chuppah*. Many joined a gay and lesbian synagogue, often led by a gay or lesbian rabbi, which cropped up in cities like New York and San Francisco. But for Orthodox Jews, the issue of sexual preference has proved far more fraught even as their sons and daughters voice their pain at their exclusion from the religion they grew up with.

In another way, the Orthodox remain distinct among America's Jewish women. They marry young: four-fifths have circled their grooms under the *chuppah* by age twenty-nine; only one-fifth of non-Orthodox American Jewish women have wed by then.[91]

Orthodoxy spans a wide spectrum. The modern Orthodox, university-educated, engage with the working world during the week but remain nestled within their communities for Sabbaths and holidays. At the other end of the spectrum, the ultra-Orthodox, including Hasidic Jews, live together in neighborhoods they call shtetls, just like in the Old World. Their distinctive dress sets them apart. Married women cover their hair with wigs or scarves because ancient rabbis saw women's hair as sexually enticing. Orthodox Jewish women feel that following the strict Jewish laws of female modesty brings them closer to God.

As children, the ultra-Orthodox went to girls' schools. Graduation day from high school meant not time to leave for college but time to get married. Teachers, neighbors, even professional matchmakers, a relic of the Old World that Bessie Hillman would have remembered, bring out rosters of prospective grooms. Now it is time to date. The couple meet in a public place—a hotel lobby, a kosher restaurant. They talk about their lives and the future. If they agree, a second date follows. If not, other prospects are trotted out. Somewhere between a couple's fourth and eighth date, a match is announced. Several months later, after a whirlwind of wedding planning, the bride becomes a wife. Generally babies follow. On the average, Orthodox Jews have four children. Among the ultra-Orthodox, a dozen or more is not uncommon.[92]

Hasidic Jews venerate female difference, assigning women an innate, elevated spirituality to explain why observant women are freed from the obligations fixed in time incumbent on Jewish men, like praying three times a day. Hasidic women extol their rich lives, filled with traditions, family, and community. They are proud that the first thing their children learn is not "Mary had a little lamb," but the Hebrew blessings over food.

Some women from the Lubavitcher sect, one of the many Hasidic groups, live outside the closed circles of their tightly knit world. They settle with their families in communities across the United States and around the globe. Often they hand out Sabbath candles on Friday mornings to Jewish women passing by. Emissaries to secular Jews, assimilated Jews, Reform and Conservative Jews, they seek to persuade them to study Jewish texts and observe more of God's commandments, which they believe will hasten the coming of the messiah. When a Lubavitcher emissary, living amid the temptations of Los Angeles, was asked how she managed not to stray, she responded with a laugh, "I have my priorities. I know who I am."[93]

AMERICA'S NEWEST Jewish women came from the Soviet Union. Their families had not left Russia when Rose Cohen and Bessie Hillman had. Instead, they stayed behind. Somehow members of their families survived the ravages of the Russian Civil War, Stalin's purges, famine, world war, the Holocaust, and postwar antisemi-tism. After Communist leaders denounced Stalin's crimes, a crack opened, and some Soviet Jews began meeting in secret to learn Hebrew and celebrate Jewish holidays. Then, emboldened, they demanded the right not just to live as Jews in the Soviet Union but to emigrate to Israel. Some secretly hoped that, if they did get out, they would manage to get to America instead of Israel. Crying "Let my people go," American Jews, including those angry students from the 1960s counterculture, heard their plea. A groundswell for a powerful human rights movement followed.

Jewish women across America stepped up. Every day for twenty years, rain or shine, Jews held a vigil in front of the Soviet Embassy in Washington. Betty Miller, a Washington wife and mother, whose volunteer work included reading and responding to some of the millions of condolences Jacqueline Kennedy received after the pres-ident's assassination, began overseeing from her home the work of a DC committee to save Soviet Jewry. She learned the hard way what happened when protesters got too close to the embassy: she and her son were arrested.[94]

Armies of housewives organized, marched, wrote, and demon-strated to draw attention to the refuseniks, who had applied for visas to leave the Soviet Union but had been denied. The refuse-niks lived out their days in terror, fired from their jobs, liable to be arrested at any moment.

American bat mitzvah girls and bar mitzvah boys "twinned" with Soviet children denied their own Jewish coming-of-age cere-mony. In 1982 a ninth grader from North Miami Beach, who liked to collect stationery, wrote to her "twin." Over the past year, she had sent her letters, a Passover card, and a Hanukkah present of writing paper. *Had they ever arrived?* wondered Sheryl Sandberg. Decades later the notion of needing paper to connect has become obsolete. By then both were on Facebook. Sandberg was its chief operating officer. Her "twin" Kira Volvovsky was a Web designer in Jerusalem. They are not Facebook friends, but Volvovsky's father and Sandberg's mother are.[95]

But not all refuseniks and Soviet emigrés went to Israel; many came to America. Carrying memories of Soviet antisemitism, of the discrimination conjured by passports marked "Jew" that kept them out of universities and good jobs, one mother told her daughter never to reveal that they were Jews even to their Chicago neighbors, but of course, everyone knew they were. They arrived as stateless refugees with no winter coats, wearing cast-off clothes, learning English—another generation whose lives had been disrupted by antisemitism and emigration.[96]

As in the past, the families had left for the sake of their children, seeing no future for them as Jews in the USSR. For many of those children, the American dream became a reality. Yet the deprivations of life in the USSR still haunt some. One successful Soviet American daughter, remembering the food shortages of her childhood, finds herself suppressing the urge to steal all the croissants from the breakfast buffet every time she stays in a hotel.[97]

Other twenty-first-century American Jewish women, knowing who they are, assert proudly their varieties of Jewish difference. Their ranks include Israelis, who have left one Promised Land to live, temporarily or permanently, in another. Others emigrated from Hungary, Cuba, Ethiopia, Iran, or Iraq. They brought to their new American homes the memories, cultures, and foods of the lands of their birth.

Some, raised as Christians, were stunned when they learned that they were Jews. Madeleine Albright was just two when her family fled Prague for England, steps ahead of the Nazis' invasion. There she was raised as a Catholic. In January 1997, just as she was about to become the U.S. secretary of state, Albright learned from a journalist that more than twenty of her relatives, including three of her grandparents, had been murdered in the Holocaust. Madam Secretary was shocked to discover her Jewish ancestry.[98]

There are also Jewish women of color—blacks, Asians, and mixed race—like Rabbi Angela Buchdahl, the daughter of a Jewish American father and Korean Buddhist mother, named by *Newsweek* as one of America's fifty most influential rabbis. Other American Jewish women spent years asking, "What was a nice Jewish girl like me doing in a man's body?" before taking the journey to become female.[99]

THE DIVERSITY of today's Jewish women would have amazed Bessie Hillman and Rose Cohen. If they looked, they would still find women rushing to complete their Sabbath preparations before sundown on Fridays. They'd find others spending Sabbath mornings wrapped in prayer shawls praying with their congregations. Yet others, who never set foot in a synagogue, they'd find buying matzo and gefilte fish when Passover rolls around each year.

They'd see many carrying forward the powerful legacy of America's Jewish women in politics, gravitating to liberal causes that would have made their grandmothers and great-grandmothers proud. Some, having honed their political chops in Jewish organizations, were leapfrogging from them to run for Congress in 2018. They'd find others still dedicated to the century-old Jewish women's organizations, which continue to be places for America's Jewish women to study sacred texts, play mah-jongg, read in book clubs, and raise their collective voices for issues that matter to them—domestic violence, sexual abuse, women's health.[100]

America's Jewish women today include rabbis, Orthodox feminists, devout Hasidim, and lesbians; ardent Zionists, Israelis, and twenty-, thirty-, and fortysomething-year-olds who first visited Israel courtesy of Birthright's free trips. America's Jewish women continue their roles as daughters and daughters-in-law, mothers and mothers-in-law, wives, grandmothers, aunts, singles, and widows. They are also real estate moguls, philanthropists, artists, writers, doctors, lawyers, and corporate chiefs.

If Bessie Hillman and Rose Cohen could ask them what it means to be a Jewish woman today, they would hear myriad answers. For some, Jewishness, the everyday experience of being Jewish, is the rock at the core of their lives. For others, it is an incidental matter, perhaps a source of pride, that occasionally pops up. For still others, that they are Jewish or half-Jewish or quarter-Jewish is utterly irrelevant.

But one thing binds America's Jewish women together: all have a share in the story of their collective American Jewish female past. To paraphrase the Pulitzer Prize–winning playwright Wendy Wasserstein, an American Jewish woman of the recent past, they are lucky to have been born into such material.[101]

ACKNOWLEDGMENTS

WRITING A BOOK that is the product of a lifetime of learning and thinking, research and conversation, means that it is impossible to single out everyone whose guidance, chance remark, or email pointed me to a new source, thought, or sentence. I can only mention some of those who helped me over these many years.

At American University, my intellectual home since graduate school, my colleagues in the department of history and the Jewish studies program, especially Richard Breitman, Michael Brenner, and Lisa Leff, have inspired me with their own outstanding scholarship. Former senior vice-provost Kay Mussell and Dean Peter Starr encouraged and supported the work. I also benefited from conversations with Kate Haulman, the transcription expertise of Lauren Duval, the insights of Lauren Strauss, and a host of undergraduate and graduate students who, for decades, have helped me run the Jewish studies program and track down sources.

Colleagues of various learned, scholarly, and public history societies have immeasurably shaped my thinking. They include the members of the Association for Jewish Studies and its past and current executive directors, Rona Sheramy and Warren Hoffman; the American Jewish Historical Society and its Academic Council;

the Jewish Women's Archive, its Academic Advisory Board, and its executive director Judith Rosenbaum; the National Museum of American Jewish History, its leaders Gwen Goodman, Ivy Barsky, and Josh Perelman, and the other members of our founding historians team—Michael Berenbaum, Jonathan Sarna, and Beth Wenger.

Archivists and librarians, scholars and researchers, have answered my queries quickly and efficiently. I thank Kevin Proffitt, Joe Weber, and Gary Zola at the American Jewish Archives; Boni Koehler and Susan Malbin at the American Jewish Historical Society; Sharon Horowitz at the Library of Congress; Alan Cooperman and Gregory A. Smith at the Pew Research Center; Adele Heaney at the St. Louis Public Library; John C. Konzal at the State Historical Society of Missouri; Yael Robinson at Yad Vashem; and Samantha Gainsburg, Norman Goda, Karen Pastorello, Marc Lee Raphael, Jane Rothstein, Rabbi Jeffrey Stiffman, and Mary Ellen Zuckerman.

This book exists because several people believed—when I doubted—that I would write it. The first is the eminent scholar Jonathan Sarna. For more decades than he must care to remember, he has been advising me about this project. At the end of the academic year, the busiest time for professors, he read and critiqued the entire manuscript. As if that were not enough, he introduced me to Carolyn Starman Hessel, executive director emerita of the Jewish Book Council. From the moment we met, she began championing this book. She told me what was wrong with earlier drafts and how to fix them. Were it not for her advice and a serendipitous meeting with the Washington, DC, writer Scott Seligman, Peter W. Bernstein would never have become my agent. His shaping of the proposal was spot on, and it led me to Norton, where I have had the immense good fortune of working with the incomparable Amy Cherry. Having an editor with her experience and gifts is something too few authors ever experience. I am one of the lucky ones. It is a privilege to acknowledge also assistant editor Remy Cawley, editorial assistant Zarina Patwa, publicity assistant Caroline Saine, and the entire Norton team.

Friends and family, near and far, dance with us at weddings, dine at our holiday tables, and whether they knew or not, contributed to my thinking about this book. I am grateful to Sue Brett and Rob Shesser, Carol and Jeffrey Folkerth, Carol Weissbrod and Norman Gold, Glenn and Debbie Nadell, and my mother, Alice Nadell.

It is the tradition of acknowledgments to save the most important for last, and I happily follow it. Acknowledgments in my earlier books reveal that my children, as children will, have grown and continue to ground me. My son, Yoni Farber, has not only brought us a new daughter, his wife, Rachael—who shares my enthusiasm for the subjects of this book—but also his laughter and good sense. My daughter, Orly Farber, now wears the white coat of a physician-in-training and has joined the ranks of our family's published writers. She has grown to become my most valued reader and guide to the em dash. Finally, I thank, with boundless love and gratitude, my husband, Edward Farber, another of our family's writers, who has shared my journey, not only to this book but also the one of our lives across these many decades.

NOTES

Prologue

1. On Lazarus and Nathan, see Esther Schor, *Emma Lazarus* (New York: Nextbook/Schocken, 2006).

Spelling, whether that of poetic license or of colonial-era letters, written before dictionaries standardized orthography, reproduces the original unless otherwise noted.

For the most part, this book uses women's married names rather than their maiden names.

2. Emma Lazarus, "By the Waters of Babylon: Little Poems in Prose, I. The Exodus (August 3, 1492)," in *Emma Lazarus: Selected Poems*, ed. John Hollander (New York: Library of America, 2005), 91–92.

3. Grace Nathan, in *The American Jewish Woman: A Documentary History*, ed. Jacob Rader Marcus (New York: Ktav, 1981), 72.

4. Quoted in David de Sola Pool, "Some Letters of Grace Seixas Nathan, 1814–1821," *Publications of the American Jewish Historical Society* 37 (1947): 204; Emma Lazarus, "In the Jewish Synagogue at Newport" (1867), in *Selected Poems*, 9–10.

5. Quoted in Pool, "Some Letters of Grace Seixas Nathan," 204; Emma Lazarus, "Destiny" (1856), in *Selected Poems*, 66–67.

6. Lazarus, "Florence Nightingale" (1867), in *Selected Poems*, 4–5.

7. Nathan in Marcus, *American Jewish Woman*, 73.

8. Pool, "Some Letters of Grace Seixas Nathan," 203–4.

9. Lazarus, "In Exile," in *Selected Poems*, 77–79.

10. Lazarus, "Phantasies II: Aspiration," in *Selected Poems*, 29–30.

11. Nathan in Marcus, *American Jewish Woman*, 74.

Chapter 1: *"Many are the blessings I partake of"*

1. Arnold Witznitzer, "The Exodus from Brazil and Arrival in New Amsterdam of the Jewish Pilgrim Fathers, 1654," *Publications of the American Jewish Historical Society* 44, no. 2 (December 1954): 80–97.

2. Grace Nathan to Mrs. I. B. Kursheedt, New York, June 4, 1821, Nathan Family Papers, P-54, Box 1, Folder 2, American Jewish Historical Society, New York.

3. Leo Hershkowitz, "Original Inventories of Early New York Jews (1682–1763)," *American Jewish History* 90, no. 3 (September 2002): 278–79.

4. Hershkowitz, "Inventories," 297–301. The inventory mentions Five Books of Moses with ornaments.

5. Ellen Smith, "Portraits of a Community: The Image and Experience of Early American Jews," in *American Jewish Women's History: A Reader*, ed. Pamela S. Nadell (New York: New York University Press, 2003), 18–19.

6. Holly Snyder, "A Sense of Place: Jews, Identity, and Social Status in Colonial British America, 1654–1831" (PhD diss., Brandeis University, 2000), 217–18.

7. "C.P. & N. Raguet," *Pennsylvania Gazette* (Accessible Archives), August 23, 1780.

8. Doris Groshen Daniels, "Colonial Jewry: Religion, Domestic and Social Relations," *American Jewish Historical Quarterly* 66, no. 3 (March 1977): 392–94.

9. Isaac Seixas to Hayman Levy, November 13, 1778, in *The American Jewish Woman: A Documentary History*, ed. Jacob Rader Marcus (New York: Ktav, 1981), 21–22; Edith B. Gelles, ed., *The Letters of Abigaill Levy Franks, 1733–1748* (New Haven: Yale University Press, 2004), 117.

10. Mark Abbott Stern, *David Franks: Colonial Merchant* (University Park: Pennsylvania State University Press, 2010), 94, 104–5, 209n15.

11. Benjamin Rush, June 27, 1787, in Marcus, *American Jewish Woman*, 37–39.

12. Yiddish, one of several unique Jewish languages, is based on German, written in Hebrew characters, and was spoken by Jews from Central and Eastern Europe.

13. Snyder, "Sense of Place," 367.

14. Snyder, "Sense of Place," 351; Aviva Ben-Ur, "The Exceptional and the Mundane: A Biographical Portrait of Rebecca Machado Phillips (1746–1831)," in *Women and American Judaism: Historical Perspectives*, ed. Pamela S. Nadell and Jonathan D. Sarna (Hanover, NH: Brandeis University Press, 2001), 52, 61; Joyce Myers, March 21, 1805, in Marcus, *American Jewish Woman*, 63.

15. Malcom H. Stern, "The Sheftall Diaries: Vital Records of Savannah Jewry (1733–1808)," *American Jewish Historical Quarterly* 54, no. 3 (March 1965): 249.

16. Laura Arnold Leibman, *Messianism, Secrecy and Mysticism: A New*

Interpretation of Early American Jewish Life (London: Valentine Mitchell, 2012), 40.

17. I thank Jonathan D. Sarna for this suggestion.

18. Manuel Josephson, May 21, 1784, in Marcus, *American Jewish Woman,* 34–36.

19. Laurel Thatcher Ulrich, *Good Wives: Image and Reality in the Lives of Women in Northern New England, 1650–1750* (New York: Knopf, 1982), 35–50.

20. David de Sola Pool, *Portraits Etched in Stone: Early Jewish Settlers, 1682–1831* (New York: Columbia University Press, 1952), 226.

21. Frances Sheftall, March 3, 1780, in Marcus, *American Jewish Woman,* 28–29.

22. Pool, *Portraits,* 406; Snyder, "Sense of Place," 229.

23. Karla Goldman, *Beyond the Synagogue Gallery: Finding a Place for Women in American Judaism* (Cambridge, MA: Harvard University Press, 2000), 42, 99.

24. Gelles, *Letters of Abigaill Levy Franks,* 105.

25. Pool, *Portraits,* 341–42.

26. Gelles, *Letters of Abigaill Levy Franks,* 7.

27. Rebecca Samuel, 1792(?), in Marcus, *American Jewish Woman,* 43; Holly Snyder, "Queens of the Household: The Jewish Women of British America, 1700–1800," in Nadell and Sarna, *Women and American Judaism,* 24–25.

28. Samuel Urlsperger and George Fenwick Jones, eds., *Detailed Reports on the Salzburger Emigrants Who Settled in America* (Athens: University of Georgia Press, 1968), 60, 70.

29. Snyder, "Queens of the Household," 16–17.

30. Sheldon Godfrey and Judith Godfrey, "The King vs. Moses Gomez et al.: Opening the Prosecutor's File, over 200 Years Later," *American Jewish History* 80, no. 3 (Spring 1991): 397–407.

31. Gelles, *Letters of Abigaill Levy Franks,* 68.

32. Gelles, *Letters of Abigaill Levy Franks,* 123–26.

33. Jonathan D. Sarna, *American Judaism: A History* (New Haven: Yale University Press, 2004), 27–28; Anna Barnett, November 13, 1794, in Marcus, *American Jewish Woman,* 53.

34. Shinah Schuyler, December 17, 1791, in Marcus, *American Jewish Woman,* 48–49; Smith, "Portraits of a Community," 17.

35. Rachel Gratz, August 3, 1779, in Marcus, *American Jewish Woman,* 24; Miriam Gratz, June 2, 1777, in Marcus, *American Jewish Woman,* 11.

36. Ben Marsh, "Women and the American Revolution in Georgia," *Georgia Historical Quarterly* 88, no. 2 (Summer 2004): 174; Abigail Minis, October (?) 1779, in Marcus, *American Jewish Woman,* 26–27.

37. Cecil Roth, "Some Jewish Loyalists in the War of American Independence," *Publications of the American Jewish Historical Society* 38, no. 2 (December 1948): 89, 98–103.

38. David T. Morgan, "The Sheftalls of Savannah," *American Jewish Historical Quarterly* 62, no. 4 (June 1973): 348–61; Frances Sheftall to Mordecai Sheftall, July 20, 1780, in Marcus, *American Jewish Woman*, 28–29.

39. Quoted in Sarna, *American Judaism*, 35.

40. Rebecca Franks, 1778–1781, in Marcus, *American Jewish Woman*, 14–20.

41. Simon Gratz to Richea Gratz, August 5, 1793, in Marcus, *American Jewish Woman*, 50.

42. "From the 2nd Volume of Minute Books of Congn: Shearith Israel in New York," *Publications of the American Jewish Historical Society* 21 (1913): 154–55.

43. Quoted in William Pencak, *Jews and Gentiles in Early America, 1654–1800* (Ann Arbor: University of Michigan Press, 2005), 72–73.

44. David de Sola Pool and Tamar de Sola Pool, *An Old Faith in the New World: Portrait of Shearith Israel, 1654–1954* (New York: Columbia University Press, 1955), 287; John Adams and Abigail Adams, *Familiar Letters of John Adams and His Wife Abigail Adams, During the Revolution: With a Memoir of Mrs. Adams,* ed. Charles Francis Adams (New York: Hurd and Houghton, 1876), 172.

45. Pool and Pool, *An Old Faith in the New World*, 287–88.

46. Emily Bingham, *Mordecai: An Early American Family* (New York: Hill and Wang, 2003).

47. Rachel Mordecai Lazarus to Maria Edgeworth, August 7, 1815, in Marcus, *American Jewish Woman*, 80–81.

48. Penina Moïse, "La Musée," *Godey's Magazine and Lady's Book*, February 1845, 58. The "tribe" Moïse refers to is the Greek gods.

49. Penina Moïse, *Secular and Religious Works of Penina Moïse, with Brief Sketch of Her Life* (Charleston, SC: Charleston Section, Council of Jewish Women, 1911), 136.

50. Moïse, *Secular and Religious Works*, 177.

51. Quoted in Bette Roth Young, *Emma Lazarus in Her World: Life and Letters* (Philadelphia: Jewish Publication Society, 1995), 44.

52. Rebecca Gratz to Maria Gist Gratz, October 12, 1834, in *Letters of Rebecca Gratz,* ed. David Philipson (Philadelphia: Jewish Publication Society, 1929), 210, at Jewish Women's Archive, "Rebecca Gratz," https://jwa.org/womenofvalor/Gratz.

53. Thanks to Kate Haulman for sharing her research on the Philadelphia Ladies Association.

54. Joseph Jacobs, "The Original of Scott's Rebecca," *Publications of the American Jewish Historical Society* 22 (1914): 53–60.

55. *The Constitution of the Female Association of Philadelphia, for the Relief of Women and Children, in Reduced Circumstances* (Philadelphia: Jane Aitken, 1803), 12–13, https://collections.nlm.nih.gov/bookviewer?PID=nlm:nlmuid-2554009R-bk.

56. Ladies' Hebrew Relief Sewing Association of Philadelphia, 1861, in Marcus, *American Jewish Woman*, 244–45.

57. Dianne Ashton, *Rebecca Gratz: Women and Judaism in Antebellum America* (Detroit: Wayne State University Press, 1997), 100–1; Pool and Pool, *An Old Faith in the New World*, 360–61.

58. Anne M. Boylan, *Sunday School: The Formation of an American Institution, 1790–1880* (New Haven: Yale University Press, 1988), 11.

59. Ashton, *Rebecca Gratz*, 149–54.

60. The following is based on Reena Sigman Friedman, *These Are Our Children: Jewish Orphanages in the United States, 1880–1925* (Hanover, NH: Brandeis University Press, 1994), esp. 1, 46, 111–12, 115, 155.

61. Robert V. Wells and Michael Zuckerman, "Quaker Marriage Patterns in a Colonial Perspective," *William and Mary Quarterly* 29, no. 3 (July 1972): 427.

62. Quoted in Ashton, *Rebecca Gratz*, 195.

63. Quoted in Shari Rabin, *Jews on the Frontier: Religion and Mobility in Nineteenth-Century America* (New York: New York University Press, 2017), 65.

64. Ashton, *Rebecca Gratz*, 124.

65. Dianne Ashton, "The 1842 Hymnal of Penina Moise," in *Religions of the United States in Practice*, ed. Colleen McDannell (Princeton: Princeton University Press, 2001), 1:108–21.

66. Quoted in Jonathan D. Sarna, "The Debate over Mixed Seating in the American Synagogue," in *The American Synagogue: A Sanctuary Transformed*, ed. Jack Wertheimer (New York: Cambridge University Press, 1987), 371.

67. David Resnick, "Confirmation Education from the Old World to the New: A 150 Year Follow-Up," *Modern Judaism* 31, no. 2 (May 2011): 213–28; Laura Yares, "Say It with Flowers: Shavuot, Confirmation, and Ritual Reimagination for a Modern American Judaism," *Shofar* 35, no. 4 (Summer 2017): 1–19.

68. Emily Fechheimer Seasongood, n.d., in Marcus, *American Jewish Woman*, 176.

69. Quoted in Moshe Davis, *The Emergence of Conservative Judaism: The Historical School in 19th Century America* (Philadelphia: Jewish Publication Society, 1963), 421n123.

70. Marcus M. Spiegel, Frank L. Byrne, and Jean Powers Soman, eds., *Your True Marcus: The Civil War Letters of a Jewish Colonel* (Kent, OH: Kent State University Press, 1985), 51. The following discussion of the Spiegels is based on this work.

71. Quoted in Robert N. Rosen, *The Jewish Confederates* (Columbia: University of South Carolina Press, 2000), 50, 225; Dianne Ashton, "Shifting Veils: Religion, Politics, and Womanhood in the Civil War Writings of American Jewish Women," in Nadell and Sarna, *Women and American Judaism*, 81–106; August Bondi, *Autobiography of August Bondi* (1910), in *Memoirs of*

American Jews, 1775–1865, ed. Jacob Rader Marcus (1955; rpt., New York: Ktav, 1974), 2:203.

72. Elliott Ashkenazi, ed., *The Civil War Diary of Clara Solomon: Growing Up in New Orleans, 1861–1862* (Baton Rouge: Louisiana State University Press, 1995), 419–20.

73. Quoted in Drew Gilpin Faust, *Mothers of Invention: Women of the Slaveholding South in the American Civil War* (Chapel Hill: University of North Carolina Press, 1996), 208–10.

74. Bertram W. Korn, *American Jewry and the Civil War*, 3rd ed. (Philadelphia: Jewish Publication Society, 2001), 195; Eugenia Levy Phillips, in Marcus, *Memoirs of American Jews, 1775–1865*, 3:161–96.

75. Pheobe Yates Pember, *A Southern Woman's Story* (1879; rpt. n.p.: Nabu Press, 2010), 86.

76. Peter Stuyvesant, September 22, 1654, in *American Jewish History: A Primary Source Reader*, ed. Gary Phillip Zola and Marc Dollinger (Waltham, MA: Brandeis University Press, 2014), 10–11; Urlsperger and Jones, *Detailed Reports on Salzburger Emigrants*, 65.

77. Moïse, *Secular and Religious Works*, 270–72.

78. Quoted in Leonard Dinnerstein, *Anti-Semitism in America* (New York: Oxford University Press, 1994), 18–19, quoted in Louise A. Mayo, "The Ambivalent Image: Nineteenth-Century America's Perception of the Jew," in *Essential Papers on Jewish-Christian Relations in the United States: Imagery and Reality*, ed. Naomi W. Cohen (New York: New York University Press, 1990), 112.

79. Quoted in Korn, *American Jewry and Civil War*, 193; Jonathan D. Sarna, *When General Grant Expelled the Jews* (New York: Nextbook/Schocken, 2012), 6–7.

80. Ashton, "Shifting Veils."

81. Pember quoted in Rosen, *Jewish Confederates*, 300. She alludes to Matt. 5:44.

82. Cynthia Francis Gensheimer, "Annie Jonas Wells: Jewish Daughter, Episcopal Wife, Independent Intellectual," *American Jewish History* 98, no. 3 (July 2014): 83–125.

83. Korn, *American Jewry and Civil War*, 120–21.

84. Barbara Kirshenblatt-Gimblett, "The Moral Sublime: Jewish Women and Philanthropy in Nineteenth-Century America," in *Writing a Modern Jewish History: Essays in Honor of Salo W. Baron*, ed. Barbara Kirshenblatt-Gimblett (New Haven: Yale University Press, 2006), 36–54; "District of Columbia," *Jewish Messenger*, May 6, 1864, 134.

85. Septima M. Collis, *A Woman's War Record, 1861–1865* (New York: G.P. Putnam's Sons, 1889), 19–22.

86. Quoted in Nina Silber, *Daughters of the Union: Northern Women Fight the Civil War* (Cambridge, MA: Harvard University Press, 2005), 1–2.

87. Paula Doress-Worters, ed., *Mistress of Herself: Speeches and Letters of*

Ernestine L Rose, Early Women's Rights Leader (New York: Feminist Press, 2008), 97, 329.

88. "Declaration of Sentiments and Resolutions, Seneca Falls, 1848," in *Feminism: The Essential Historical Writings*, ed. Miriam Schneir (New York: Vintage Books, 1972), 77 (emphasis added).

89. On Rose, see Bonnie S. Anderson, *The Rabbi's Atheist Daughter: Ernestine Rose* (New York: Oxford University Press, 2017).

90. Doress-Worters, *Mistress of Herself,* 314.

91. Quoted in Myron Berman, *Richmond's Jewry, 1769–1976: Shabbat in Shockoe* (Charlottesville: University Press of Virginia, 1979), 196–97; Bertram W. Korn, "Jews and Negro Slavery in the Old South, 1789–1865," *Publications of the American Jewish Historical Society* 50 (March 1961): 194.

92. Quoted in Ashton, "Shifting Veils," 99.

93. Pheobe Yates Pember, "The Ghost of the Nineteenth Century," *Harper's New Monthly Magazine*, December 1, 1879, 251–60.

94. Robert N. Rosen, "Jewish Confederates," in *Jewish Roots in Southern Soil: A New History*, ed. Marcie Cohen Ferris and Mark I. Greenberg (Waltham, MA: Brandeis University Press, 2006), 126.

Chapter 2: *"Mothers in Israel"*

1. Esther Schor argues that Lazarus wrote an unsigned account of her visit: "Among the Russian Jews: A Visit to the Refugees on Ward's Island," *New York Times*, March 26, 1882, 12; see Esther Schor, *Emma Lazarus* (New York: Nextbook/Schocken, 2006), 125–27.

2. "Castle Garden," *Harper's Weekly*, May 27, 1882, 330–32.

3. Emma Lazarus, "The New Colossus," in *Emma Lazarus: Selected Poems*, ed. John Hollander (New York: Library of America, 2005), 58.

4. Jonathan D. Sarna, ed., *The American Jewish Experience*, 2nd ed. (New York: Holmes & Meier, 1997), 359.

5. On Rosa Sonneschein, see Jane Heather Rothstein, "Rosa Sonneschein, the *American Jewess*, and American Jewish Women's Activism in the 1890s" (M.A. thesis, Case Western Reserve University, 1996); David Loth, "The American Jewess," American Jewish Archives, Small Collections 11770; and Carole B. Balin, "Unraveling an American-Jewish Synthesis: Rosa Sonneschein's The American Jewess, 1895–1899" (senior thesis, Wellesley College, 1986).

6. Eveline Brooks Auerbach, *Frontier Reminiscences of Eveline Brooks Auerbach* (Berkeley: Friends of the Bancroft Library, University of California, 1994), 22.

7. Hannah Solomon, *Fabric of My Life: The Autobiography of Hannah G. Solomon* (New York: Bloch, 1946), 5–9.

8. Linda Mack Schloff, *"And Prairie Dogs Weren't Kosher": Jewish Women in*

the Upper Midwest Since 1855 (St. Paul: Minnesota Historical Society Press, 1996), 36.

9. Laura D. Jacobson, "The Pioneers: The First Literary Society of Jewish Women in America," *American Jewess*, August 1895, 240–42; Rosa Sonneschein, *The Pioneers: An Historical Essay Read Before the Society of Pioneers at Their Annual Entertainment, May 18, 1880* (St. Louis: Woodward, Tiernan & Hale, 1880).

10. D'Arwin, "Our Milwaukee Letter," *Jewish Messenger*, June 19, 1885, 2; Sonneschein disclosed her identity; "Our St. Louis Letter," *Jewish Messenger*, May 8, 1885, 5.

11. Diary of August Binswanger, entry for November 14–16, 1871, American Jewish Archives, MS-0234.

12. Diary of August Binswanger, entry for June 29–July 2, 1872, American Jewish Archives, MS-0234.

13. "A Noted Rabbi Divorced," *Weekly Intelligencer* (Lexington, MO), April 8, 1893, 4; Loth, "American Jewess," 7.

14. "Press Congress Closed," *Salt Lake Herald*, May 28, 1893, 1; "Three Speeches of Susan B. Anthony at Columbian Exposition, 1893," Rutgers University, http://ecssba.rutgers.edu/docs/sbaexpo.html#may27/.

15. Mrs. Chas. (Anne) P. Johnson, ed., *Notable Women of St. Louis, 1914* (St. Louis: Woodward, 1914), 171–73, https://archive.org/details/notablewomenofstoojohn; "Press Greetings," *American Jewess*, May 1895, 100.

16. Martha H. Patterson, ed., *The American New Woman Revisited: A Reader, 1894–1930* (New Brunswick, NJ: Rutgers University Press, 2008), 2; Maria T. Baader, "From 'the Priestess of the Home' to 'The Rabbi's Brilliant Daughter': Concepts of Jewish Womanhood and Progressive Germanness in *Die Deborah* and the *American Israelite*, 1854–1900," *Leo Baeck Institute Year Book* 43 (1998): 60.

17. *The American Jewess* is available at https://quod.lib.umich.edu/a/amjewess/. I attribute unsigned articles to Sonneschein; Rosa Sonneschein, "Salutatory," *American Jewess*, April 1895, n.p.

18. Sarah Grand, "The New Aspect of the Woman Question," *North American Review* 158, no. 448 (March 1894): 270–76; see, inter alia, "The New Woman," *American Jewess*, July 1895, 185.

19. See, inter alia, Pauline S. Wise, "Successful Business Women," *American Jewess*, May 1895, 67–70; Rosa Sonneschein, "Editorial," *American Jewess*, November 1897, 93.

20. Ada Robek, "Women as Breadwinners," *American Jewess*, May 1899, 4; Max B. May, "Women in the Law," *American Jewess*, July 1897, 176–77.

21. Rosa Sonneschein, "Editor's Desk," *American Jewess*, December 1895, 174–75; "Jewish Maternity Association of Philadelphia," *American Jewess*, October 1896, 49; "The Jewish Hospital at Denver, Colorado," *Ameri-*

can Jewess, November 1897, 83–84; "Jewish Orphan Asylum, Cleveland, O," *American Jewess*, October 1896, 50.

22. Sonneschein, "Editor's Desk," *American Jewess*, May 1895, 103–4; Sonneschein, "Editor's Desk," *American Jewess*, June 1895, 153–55.

23. Sonneschein, "Editor's Desk," *American Jewess*, June 1895, 153–55; Sonneschein, "Editor's Desk," *American Jewess*, April 1895, 47–51; Sonneschein, "Editor's Desk," *American Jewess*, November 1895, 111–12.

24. Rebecca J. Gradwohl, "The Jewess in San Francisco," *American Jewess*, October 1896, 12.

25. *Bradwell v. The State*, 83 U.S. 130 (1872).

26. Bertha Badt-Strauss, *White Fire: The Life and Works of Jessie Sampter* (New York: Reconstructionist Press, 1956), 5–6; Rosa Stein Miller, Biographical Sketch by Jacob Miller, January 1909, handwritten, in "One Hundred Year Anniversary Book, Congregation Rodeph Shalom" (Philadelphia).

27. Louise Mannheimer, "Jewish Women of Biblical and of Medieval Times," in *Papers of the Jewish Women's Congress* (Philadelphia: Jewish Publication Society of America, 1894), 17.

28. John S. Billings, "Vital Statistics of the Jews," *North American Review* 152, no. 410 (January 1891): 71–72.

29. Nina Morais, "Jewish Ostracism in America," *North American Review* 133, no. 298 (September 1881): 268–69.

30. Paula E. Hyman, *Gender and Assimilation in Modern Jewish History: The Roles and Representation of Women* (Seattle: University of Washington Press, 1995), 10–49.

31. Benny Kraut, "A Unitarian Rabbi? The Case of Solomon H. Sonneschein," in *Jewish Apostasy in the Modern World*, ed. Todd M. Endelman (New York: Holmes & Meier, 1987), 272–308; Ed Reiss, "Rabbi Solomon H. Sonneschein: A Controversial Figure in Reform Judaism" (student paper, University of Missouri–St. Louis, n.d.), American Jewish Archives, Small Collections, 11776.

32. This paraphrases the penultimate line of Yehudah Leib Gordon's poem, "Awake My People."

33. Irma L. Lindheim, *Parallel Quest: A Search of a Person and a People* (New York: Thomas Yoseloff, 1962), 63.

34. Steven Ruggles, "Multigenerational Families in Nineteenth-Century America," *Continuity and Change* 18, no. 1 (2003): 139–65.

35. Alexandra Lee Levin, "The Jastrows in Madison: A Chronicle of University Life, 1888–1900," *Wisconsin Magazine of History* 46, no. 4 (Summer 1963): 248.

36. Susan Strasser, *Never Done: A History of American Housework* (New York: Pantheon Books, 1982), 162–64.

37. Esther Levy, *Jewish Cookery Book, on Principles of Economy, Adapted for Jewish Housekeepers . . .* (Philadelphia: W. S. Turner, 1871). Separating a piece of Sabbath dough and burning it is one of the three commandments

incumbent on Jewish women. "Taking challah" recalls ancient Israelites' giving a portion of their dough to the priests in the Jerusalem Temple. The other women's commandments are lighting candles on Sabbaths and holidays and adhering to the laws regulating marital relations.

38. Bertha Kramer, *"Aunt Babette's" Cook Book, Foreign and Domestic Receipts for the Household* ... (Cincinnati: Bloch, 1889); Barbara Kirshenblatt-Gimblett, "Kitchen Judaism," in *Getting Comfortable in New York: The American Jewish Home, 1880–1950*, ed. Susan L. Braunstein and Jenna Weissman Joselit (New York: Jewish Museum, 1990), 77–86.

39. "Local News: New Orleans," *Jewish Messenger*, December 2, 1892, 3; D'Arwin, "Our St. Louis Letter," *Jewish Messenger*, April 17, 1885, 5.

40. Solomon, *Fabric of My Life*, 41.

41. Hasia R. Diner, *A Time for Gathering: The Second Migration, 1820–1880* (Baltimore: Johns Hopkins University Press, 1992), 81–84.

42. Quoted in Jonathan D. Sarna, "The Forgetting of Cora Wilburn: Historical Amnesia and *The Cambridge History of Jewish American Literature,*" *Studies in American Jewish Literature* 37, no. 1 (2018): 76.

43. Helen Jacobus Apte, *Heart of a Wife: The Diary of a Southern Jewish Woman*, ed. Marcus D. Rosenbaum (Wilmington, DE: Scholarly Resources, 1998).

44. Apte, *Heart of a Wife*, 6.

45. Nicola Kay Beisel, *Imperiled Innocents: Anthony Comstock and Family Reproduction in Victorian America* (Princeton: Princeton University Press, 1998), 45.

46. William Toll, *The Making of an Ethnic Middle Class: Portland Jewry over Four Generations* (Albany: State University of New York Press, 1982), 53–54.

47. Billings, "Vital Statistics of the Jews," 75.

48. Judith Walzer Leavitt, "Under the Shadow of Maternity: American Women's Responses to Death and Debility Fears in Nineteenth-Century Childbirth," *Feminist Studies* 12, no. 1 (Spring 1986): 136; Rebecca Jo Plant, *Mom: The Transformation of Motherhood in Modern America* (Chicago: University of Chicago Press, 2010), 124.

49. Quoted in Plant, *Mom*, 118.

50. Elisabeth Israels Perry, *Belle Moskowitz: Feminine Politics and the Exercise of Power in the Age of Alfred E. Smith* (New York: Oxford University Press, 1987), 58–60.

51. Quoted in Selma Berrol, "Julia Richman," in *Jewish Women: A Comprehensive Historical Encyclopedia* (Jewish Women's Archive, 2009), https://jwa .org/encyclopedia/article/richman-julia.

52. Julissa Cruz, "Marriage: More Than a Century of Change" (Bowling Green, OH: National Center for Family and Marriage Research, 2013), https://www.bgsu.edu/content/dam/BGSU/college-of-arts-and-sciences/ NCFMR/documents/FP/FP-13-13.pdf.

53. Rosa Sonneschein, "The Woman Who Talks," *American Jewess*, April

1895, 39–40; "Latch Keys for Women," *American Jewess*, January 1899, 25; "Answers to Queries," *American Jewess*, June 1896, 496.

54. Rudolf Glanz, *The Jewish Woman in America: Two Female Immigrant Generations, 1820–1929* (New York: Ktav, 1976), 2:95; Alfred T. Story, "Woman in the Talmud," *Woman's Journal* 11 (Boston, August 14, 1880): 261.

55. L. Josephine Bridgart, "In Defense of the Single Woman," *American Jewess*, January 1897, 164–66.

56. Toll, *Making of Ethnic Middle Class*, 52.

57. Malcolm Stern, "Jewish Marriage and Intermarriage in the Federal Period (1776–1840)," *American Jewish Archives* 19, no. 2 (November 1967): 142–43.

58. Julius Drachsler, "Intermarriage in New York City: A Statistical Study of the Amalgamation of European Peoples" (PhD diss., Columbia University, 1921), 43–44, 46–49.

59. Jacob Rader Marcus, *To Count a People: American Jewish Population Data, 1585–1984* (Lanham, MD: University Press of America, 1990), 28; Glanz, *Jewish Woman in America*, 2:98.

60. Glanz, *Jewish Woman in America*, 2:97.

61. Esther Ruskay, "Intermarriage," in *Hearth and Home Essays* (Philadelphia: Jewish Publication Society, 1902), 58–62; Rosa Sonneschein, "Answers to Queries," *American Jewess*, July 1896, 556.

62. Annie Nathan Meyer, *It's Been Fun: An Autobiography* (New York: Henry Schuman, 1951), 12; "A Clandestine Marriage," *New York Times*, May 31, 1878, 1.

63. "Emma Wolf," *American Jewess*, September 1895, 294–95; Emma Wolf, *Other Things Being Equal* (Chicago: A.C. McClurg & Co., 1916), 213.

64. Rosa Sonneschein, "Editorial: Queen Esther," *American Jewess*, March 1898, 296.

65. Anne C. Rose, *Beloved Strangers: Interfaith Families in Nineteenth-Century America* (Cambridge, MA: Harvard University Press, 2001), 115–18.

66. Rosa Sonneschein, "Mrs. Hannah G. Solomon," *American Jewess*, April 1895, 26–27.

67. Michael Haines, "Fertility and Mortality in the United States," EH.Net-Economic History Services, https://eh.net/encyclopedia/fertility-and-mortality -in-the-united-states/.

68. Hattie Greenebaum, "Sarah Greenebaum biography, 29 April 1950," American Jewish Archives, Small Collections 4333; Joy Kingsolver, "True Sisters: Records Reveal the Achievements of the Johanna Lodge," *Chicago Jewish History*, Fall 2001, 10–11.

69. "The Jewish Women's Congress," *American Hebrew*, September 15, 1893, 626; Sadie American, "Organization," *Papers of Jewish Woman's Congress*, 218–62.

70. Hannah G. Solomon, *A Sheaf of Leaves* (Chicago: Printed privately, 1911), 53, 210.

71. Sadie American, "National Council of Jewish Women, Report to the

Senate Immigration Commission," 61st Congress, 3d session, S. Doc. 764, *Reports of the U.S. Immigration Commission: Statements and Recommendations Submitted by Societies and Organizations Interested in the Subject of Immigration* (Washington, DC: Government Printing Office, 1911) 32–51.

72. Keely Stauter-Halsted, "'A Generation of Monsters': Jews, Prostitution, and Racial Purity in the 1892 L'viv White Slavery Trial," *Austrian History Yearbook* 38 (2007): 25–35.

73. "American Jewish Women in 1890 and 1920: An Interview with Mrs. Hannah G. Solomon," *American Hebrew*, April 23, 1920, 748ff.

74. Eric L. Goldstein, "'Different Blood Flows in Our Veins': Race and Jewish Self-Definition in Late Nineteenth Century America," *American Jewish History* 85, no. 1 (March 1997): 29–55.

75. Rev. Dr. Henry Berkowitz, "Woman's Part in the Drama of Life," *American Jewess*, May 1895, 63–66.

76. Rosa Sonneschein, "The Woman Who Talks: The Jewess at Summer Resorts," *American Jewess*, June 1895, 139; Apte, *Heart of a Wife*, 93; Lindheim, *Parallel Quest*, 43; Solomon, *Fabric of My Life*, 194.

77. Friedrich Kolbenheyer, "Jewish Blood (Continued)," *American Jewess*, June 1896, 453; Sonneschein, "Editor's Desk," *American Jewess*, June 1895, 155; Solomon, *Sheaf of Leaves*, 29.

78. Sonneschein, "Salutatory."

79. Quoted in Lucy Delap, *The Feminist Avant-Garde: Transatlantic Encounters of the Early Twentieth Century* (New York: Cambridge University Press, 2007), 148.

80. Maud Nathan, *Once Upon a Time and Today* (New York: G. P. Putnam's Sons, 1933), 150; Sonneschein, "Mrs. Hannah G. Solomon."

81. "Searchlight on Woman," *American Jewess*, November 1895, 100–1.

82. Quoted in Perry, *Belle Moskowitz*, 14.

83. Faith Rogow, *Gone to Another Meeting: The National Council of Jewish Women, 1893–1993* (Tuscaloosa: University of Alabama Press, 1993), Appendix A.

84. Cyrus Adler, ed., *The American Jewish Year Book 5660: September 5, 1899 to September 23, 1900* (Philadelphia: Jewish Publication Society of America, 1899), 34–270.

85. Minnie D. Louis, "Mission-Work Among the Unenlightened Jews," in *Papers of the Jewish Women's Congress*, 177; Anzia Yezierska, "The Free Vacation House," in *Hungry Hearts* (1920; rpt. New York: Signet Classic, 1996), 78–91.

86. "Emanu-El Sisterhood of Personal Service," *American Hebrew*, November 24, 1899, 73ff.

87. Miriam Heller Stern, "Ladies, Girls and Mothers: Defining Jewish Womanhood at the Settlement House," *Journal of Jewish Education* 69, no. 2 (Fall/Winter 2003): 22–34; Marjorie N. Feld, *Lillian Wald: A Biography* (Chapel

Hill: University of North Carolina Press, 2008), 69. The fall holiday of Sukkot signifies the end of the harvest and commemorates the forty years the biblical Israelites wandered in the desert.

88. "In the World of Charity," *American Jewess*, July 1895, 206.

89. Felicia Herman, "From Priestess to Hostess: Sisterhoods of Personal Service in New York City, 1887–1936," in Nadell and Sarna, *Women and American Judaism*, 157.

90. Quoted in Barbara Kirshenblatt-Gimblett, "The Moral Sublime: Jewish Women and Philanthropy in Nineteenth-Century America," in *Writing a Modern Jewish History: Essays in Honor of Salo W. Baron*, ed. Barbara Kirshenblatt-Gimblett (New Haven: Yale University Press, 2006), 41.

91. Pamela S. Nadell, " 'The Synagog Shall Hear the Call of the Sister': Carrie Simon and the Founding of NFTS," in *Sisterhood: A Centennial History of Women of Reform Judaism*, ed. Carole B. Balin, Dana Herman, Jonathan D. Sarna, and Gary P. Zola (Cincinnati: Hebrew Union College Press, 2013), 23.

92. Sherry Blanton, "Lives of Quiet Affirmation: The Jewish Women of Early Anniston, Alabama," *Southern Jewish History* 2 (1999): 25–53.

93. "Rabbi Stern Signs Contract for Life," *Washington Herald*, March 27, 1913, 12.

94. Quoted in Nadell, " 'Synagog Shall Hear Call of Sister,' " 35.

95. Emma Lazarus, "The Jewish Problem," *Century Illustrated Magazine*, February 1883, 602ff.

96. Rosa Sonneschein, "Zionism in the Making," *Modern View* (St. Louis, 25th Anniverary Edition, 1925), 149–50.

97. Rosa Sonneschein, "The Zionist Congress," *American Jewess*, October 1897, 13–20; Rosa Sonneschein, "Anti-Semitism and Zionism," *American Jewess*, July 1897, 156–59; Rosa Sonneschein, "Zionism," *American Jewess*, September 1898, 5–9.

98. Quoted in Melvin I. Urofsky, *Louis D. Brandeis: A Life* (New York: Pantheon, 2009), 411.

99. Marvin Lowenthal, ed., *Henrietta Szold: Life and Letters* (New York: Viking, 1942), 37–38.

100. Jonathan D. Sarna, *JPS: The Americanization of Jewish Culture, 1888–1988* (Philadelphia: Jewish Publication Society, 1989), 47–94.

101. Quoted in Lowenthal, *Henrietta Szold*, 68.

102. Rosa Sonneschein, "Zionism," *American Jewess*, September 1898, 5.

103. Henrietta Szold, "Letter to Mrs. Julius Rosenwald, 17 January 1915," in *Four Centuries of Jewish Women's Spirituality: A Sourcebook*, ed. Ellen M. Umansky and Dianne Ashton, rev. ed. (Waltham, MA: Brandeis University Press, 2009), 166–67.

104. Erica B. Simmons, *Hadassah and the Zionist Project* (Lanham, MD: Rowman & Littlefield, 2006), 18–19.

105. Jewish Women's Archive, "Henrietta Szold Sends Nurses Rose Kaplan

and Rachel Landy to Palestine to Begin the Work of Hadassah," https://jwa.org/thisweek/jan/18/1913/henrietta-szold-sends-nurses-rose-kaplan-and-rachel-landy-to-palestine-to-begin.

106. Mary M. Cohen quoted in Eric L. Goldstein, *The Price of Whiteness: Jews, Race, and American Identity* (Princeton: Princeton University Press, 2006), 26.

107. Hannah Einstein, "Sisterhoods of Personal Service," *Jewish Encyclopedia* (New York: Funk & Wagnalls, 1901–6).

108. Lillian D. Wald, *The House on Henry Street* (New York: Henry Holt & Co., 1915), 4–7.

109. "Home for Jewish Mothers and Babies," *New York Times*, April 10, 1911, 6.

110. Perry, *Belle Moskowitz*, 53–54; "Mrs. Moskowitz, Smith Aide, Dies," *New York Times*, January 3, 1933, 1.

111. Julia Richman, "The Immigrant Child," *Journal of Education* 62, no. 4 (July 13, 1905): 106–7.

112. Meyer, *It's Been Fun*, 157–202.

113. Nathan, *Once Upon a Time and Today*, 110; Maud Nathan, "An Appeal to Christmas Shoppers," *New York Times*, November 15, 1903, 23.

114. Maud Nathan, "Some Positive Results of Woman Suffrage," *New York Times*, December 3, 1906, 8.

115. Annie Nathan Meyer, "Suffrage at Barnard: Are the Girls Really Interested in Votes for Women?" *New York Times*, December 24, 1910, 8; "Charges Head of Zoo Society Uses Post to Push Prejudice," Jewish Telegraphic Agency, May 2, 1935.

116. Nathan, *Once Upon a Time and Today*, 273–75.

117. Nathan, *Once Upon a Time and Today*, 102.

Chapter 3: "A new kind of Jewess"

1. Karen Pastorello, *A Power Among Them: Bessie Abramowitz Hillman and the Making of the Amalgamated Clothing Workers of America* (Urbana: University of Illinois Press, 2008).

2. Daniel Mendelsohn, *The Lost: A Search for Six of Six Million* (New York: HarperCollins, 2006), 162–63.

3. I. J. Singer, *Of a World That Is No More* (1970; rpt. Boston: Faber & Faber, 1987), 33–34. Jonathan Sarna discovered that the *Rod of Chastisement* is *Shevet Mussar*.

4. Rose Pines Cohen, Oral History by Marcie Cohen Ferris, Jewish Women's Archive, "Weaving Women's Words: Baltimore Stories" (April 24, 2001).

5. Quoted in Sadie Frowne, "An Immigrant Jewish Girl from Poland (1902)," in *The Jewish Americans: Three Centuries of Jewish Voices in America*, ed. Beth S. Wenger (New York: Doubleday, 2007), 144.

6. Mary Antin, *The Promised Land* (1912; rpt. Boston: Houghton Mifflin, 1969), 245–46, quoted in Barbara A. Schreier, *Becoming American Women: Clothing and the Jewish Immigrant Experience, 1880–1920* (Chicago: Chicago Historical Society, 1994), 59; Rose Cohen, *Out of the Shadow* (New York: George H. Doran, 1918), 154.

7. Antin, *Promised Land*, 187.

8. Quoted in Schreier, *Becoming American Women*, 104.

9. Theresa Malkiel, "The Housewife and the Eight-Hour Day" (1910), in *The Female Experience: An American Documentary*, ed. Gerda Lerner (Indianapolis: Bobbs-Merrill Educational, 1977), 136.

10. Isaac Metzker, ed., *A Bintel Brief: Sixty Years of Letters from the Lower East Side to the* Jewish Daily Forward (1971; rpt. New York: Schocken, 1990), 85–87; Irving Howe, *World of Our Fathers* (New York: Touchstone, 1976), 92.

11. Quoted in Gertrude Dubrovsky, "Growing up in Farmingdale," *American Jewish History* 71, no. 2 (December 1981): 242.

12. Kate Simon, *Bronx Primitive: Portraits in a Childhood* (1982; rpt. New York: Penguin, 1997), 90.

13. Hasia R. Diner, *Hungering for America: Italian, Irish, and Jewish Foodways in the Age of Migration* (Cambridge, MA: Harvard University Press, 2001), 183.

14. Quoted in Daniel Soyer, "The Voices of Jewish Immigrant Mothers in the YIVO American Jewish Autobiography Collection," *Journal of American Ethnic History* 17, no. 4 (Summer 1998): 92.

15. Sherwin B. Nuland, *Lost in America: A Journey with My Father* (New York: Knopf, 2003), 17–18.

16. Quoted in Susan A. Glenn, *Daughters of the Shtetl: Life and Labor in the Immigrant Generation* (Ithaca, NY: Cornell University Press, 1990), 75.

17. Anzia Yezierska, *Bread Givers* (1925; rpt. New York: Persea Books, 1975), 13–14.

18. Mark Schneyer, "Mothers and Children, Poverty and Morality: A Social Worker's Priorities, 1915," *Pennsylvania Magazine of History and Biography* 112, no. 2 (April 1988): 212; Bluma Goldstein, *Enforced Marginality: Jewish Narratives on Abandoned Wives* (Berkeley: University of California Press, 2007), 93.

19. Rose Schneiderman, "A Cap Maker's Story" (1905), in Lerner, *Female Experience*, 38–41.

20. Metzker, *Bintel Brief*, 152–53; Abraham Cahan, *Yekl: A Tale of the New York Ghetto* (New York: D. Appleton, 1896).

21. Claudia W. Strow and Brian K. Strow, "A History of Divorce and Remarriage in the United States," *Humanomics* 22, no. 4 (2006): 240.

22. Anna R. Igra, *Wives Without Husbands: Marriage, Desertion, and Welfare in New York, 1900–1935* (Chapel Hill: University of North Carolina Press, 2007), 59.

23. Robert A. Rockaway, *Words of the Uprooted: Jewish Immigrants in Early*

Twentieth-Century America (Ithaca, NY: Cornell University Press, 1998), 189.

24. Reena Sigman Friedman, " 'Send Me My Husband Who Is in New York City': Husband Desertion in the American Jewish Immigrant Community, 1900–1926," *Jewish Social Studies* 44, no. 1 (Winter 1982): 12–13.

25. Igra, *Wives Without Husbands*, 96–97.

26. Simon, *Bronx Primitive*, 123–26, 172; James McBride, *The Color of Water: A Black Man's Tribute to His White Mother* (1996; rpt. New York: Riverhead Books, 1997), 42; Ruth Rosen and Sue Davidson, eds., *The Maimie Papers* (New York: Feminist Press, 1977), 193.

27. Arthur A. Goren, "Mother Rosie Hertz, the Social Evil, and the New York Kehillah," *Michael: On the History of the Jews in the Disapora* 3 (1975): 189–90; Edward J. Bristow, *Prostitution and Prejudice: The Jewish Fight against White Slavery, 1870–1939* (1982; rpt. New York: Schocken, 1983), 158.

28. Metzker, *Bintel Brief*, 103–5.

29. Michael Gold, *Jews without Money* (1930; rpt. New York: Carroll & Graf, 1984), 31.

30. Rosen and Davidson, *Maimie Papers*, 4, 193–96.

31. Faith Rogow, *Gone to Another Meeting: The National Council of Jewish Women, 1893–1993* (Tuscaloosa: University of Alabama Press, 1993), 137; Polly Adler, *A House Is Not a Home* (New York: Rinehart, 1953), 4.

32. Frowne, "Immigrant Jewish Girl from Poland," 148.

33. Rosen and Davidson, *Maimie Papers*, 416.

34. Jenna Weissman Joselit, *Aspiring Women: A History of the Jewish Foundation for Education of Women* (New York: Jewish Foundation for Education of Women, 1996), 32.

35. Melissa R. Klapper, *Jewish Girls Coming of Age in America, 1860–1920* (New York: New York University Press, 2005), 65.

36. Simon, *Bronx Primitive*, 44; Pastorello, *Power among Them*, 42; Sydney Stahl Weinberg, *The World of Our Mothers: The Lives of Jewish Immigrant Women* (1988; rpt. New York: Schocken Books, 1990), 181.

37. Quoted in Weinberg, *World of Our Mothers*, 174–75.

38. Antin, *Promised Land*, 199–201.

39. Weinberg, *World of Our Mothers*, 175.

40. Quoted in *Clara Lemlich: A Strike Leader's Diary*, directed by Alex Szalat, written by Louisette Kahane (Brooklyn: Icarus Films, 2004).

41. Alfred Kazin, *A Walker in the City* (1951; rpt. New York: Harcourt, 1979), 67–68; Hilda Satt Polacheck, *I Came a Stranger: The Story of a Hull House Girl* (Urbana: University of Illinois Press, 1991), 57; quoted in Pastorello, *Power Among Them*, 17.

42. Hadassa Kosak, *Cultures of Opposition: Jewish Immigrant Workers, New York City, 1881–1905* (Albany: State University of New York Press, 2000), 67.

43. Karen Manners Smith, "New Paths to Power, 1890–1920," in *No Small*

Courage: A History of Women in the United States, ed. Nancy F. Cott (New York: Oxford University Press, 2000), 377.

44. Annie Polland, "Working for the Sabbath: Sabbath in the Jewish Immigrant Neighborhoods of New York," *Labor: Studies in the Working Class History of the Americas* 6, no. 1 (Spring 2009): 33–56.

45. Daniel E. Bender, " 'Too Much of Distasteful Masculinity': Historicizing Sexual Harassment in the Garment Sweatshop and Factory," *Journal of Women's History* 15, no. 4 (Winter 2004): 91–93.

46. Annelise Orleck, *Common Sense and a Little Fire: Women and Working-Class Politics in the United States, 1900–1965* (Chapel Hill: University of North Carolina Press, 1995), 72–74.

47. Dubrovsky, "Growing up in Farmingdale," 245.

48. "Rich Women and Poor Tailors Combine in Cause of Justice," *The World* (New York), October 27, 1898, 7.

49. Tony Michels, *A Fire in Their Hearts: Yiddish Socialists in New York* (Cambridge, MA: Harvard University Press, 2005), 88, 120–21.

50. Quoted in Steven Cassedy, *To the Other Shore: The Russian Jewish Intellectuals Who Came to America* (Princeton: Princeton University Press, 2014), 101.

51. Metzker, *Bintel Brief*, 11.

52. Metzker, *Bintel Brief*, 116–17, 121.

53. Quoted in Glenn, *Daughters of Shtetl*, 167.

54. Rose Schneiderman with Lucy Goldthwaite, *All for One* (New York: Paul S. Eriksson, 1967), 8.

55. David Von Drehle, *Triangle: The Fire That Changed America* (New York: Grove Press, 2003), 49.

56. "Waist Makers Quit at Philadelphia," *Atlanta Constitution*, December 5, 1909, D6; Howe, *World of Our Fathers*, 298–99.

57. "Miss Taft to Aid the Girl Strikers," *New York Times*, January 16, 1910, 1.

58. Quoted in Drehle, *Triangle*, 72.

59. Drehle, *Triangle*, 116–70.

60. Quoted in Howe, *World of Our Fathers*, 305; Joseph Berger, "A Century Later, the Roll of the Dead in a Factory Fire Now Has All 146 Names," *New York Times*, February 21, 2011, A13.

61. Quoted in Leon Stein, *The Triangle Fire* (1962; rpt. Ithaca, NY: ILR Press, 2001), 145–46.

62. Schneiderman with Goldthwaite, *All for One*, 100–1; "23 Die, 40 Hurt in Newark Fire," *New York Times*, November 27, 1910, 1ff.

63. "The Garment Strikes," *New York Times*, February 13, 1913, 12; Orleck, *Common Sense*, 53.

64. Quoted in Steven Fraser, *Labor Will Rule: Sidney Hillman and the Rise of American Labor* (New York: Free Press, 1991), 83; "Union Men Tell Healey Cops Are Brutal to Women Clothing Workers," *Chicago Day Book*, September 30, 1915.

65. Quoted in Paula E. Hyman, "Immigrant Women and Consumer Protest: The New York City Kosher Meat Boycott of 1902," *American Jewish History* 70, no. 1 (September 1980): 100; "Kosher Meat Riot in Boston," *Chicago Daily Tribune*, May 23, 1902, 11; "Mob Kosher Meat Shops," *Chicago Daily Tribune*, July 26, 1907, 2.

66. "Boycott Kosher Meat Markets," *Evening Statesman* (Walla Walla, WA), April 11, 1910, 1.

67. Dana Frank, "Housewives, Socialists, and the Politics of Food: The 1917 New York Cost-of-Living Protests," *Feminist Studies* 11, no. 2 (Summer 1985): 264.

68. "New Joan of Arc Leads Rent Strike," *New York Times*, December 27, 1907, 4; "Rent Strike in Chicago," *Washington (DC) Herald*, January 5, 1908.

69. J. H. Duckworth, "Tenants 'Strike' and Picket Flats," *Tacoma (WA) Times*, June 11, 1918, 1ff; F. H. Barkley, "Brownsville Brings Tenant Law up for Judgment," *New York Tribune*, June 23, 1918, 4.

70. Kate Simon, *A Wider World: Portraits in Adolescence* (New York: Harper & Row, 1986), 13.

71. Elinor Lerner, "Jewish Involvement in the New York City Woman Suffrage Movement," *American Jewish History* 70, no. 4 (June 1981): 456.

72. Rogow, *Gone to Another Meeting*, 79–80; Evelyn Salz, ed., *Selected Letters of Mary Antin* (Syracuse, NY: Syracuse University Press, 2000), xviii.

73. Pastorello, *Power among Them*, 42; Eileen L. McDonagh and H. Douglas Price, "Woman Suffrage in the Progressive Era: Patterns of Opposition and Support in Referenda Voting, 1910–1918," *American Political Science Review* 79, no. 2 (June 1985): 415–35.

74. Mary McCune, *"The Whole Wide World, Without Limits": International Relief, Gender Politics, and American Jewish Women, 1893–1930* (Detroit: Wayne State University Press, 2005), 71–72.

75. Belle Fligelman, "Mother Was Shocked," in *The American Jewish Woman: A Documentary History*, ed. Jacob Rader Marcus (New York: Ktav, 1981), 634.

76. Orleck, *Common Sense*, 96; McCune, *"Whole Wide World,"* 73–74.

77. Mollie Schepps, "Working Women for Suffrage," in *America's Working Women: A Documentary History, 1600 to the Present*, ed. Rosalyn Baxandall and Linda Gordon, rev. ed. (New York: Norton, 1995), 189–90.

78. Schneiderman with Goldthwaite, *All for One*, 121–22.

79. Quoted in Orleck, *Common Sense*, 99.

80. Seth Korelitz, "'A Magnificent Piece of Work': The Americanization Work of the National Council of Jewish Women," *American Jewish History* 83, no. 2 (June 1995): 177–203.

81. Linda Gordon, *Woman's Body, Woman's Right: Birth Control in America*, rev. ed. (New York: Penguin, 1990), 53.

82. Simon, *Bronx Primitive*, 68–70.

83. Margaret Sanger, *Margaret Sanger: An Autobiography* (1938; rpt. New York: Dover Publications, 1971), 89–92.

84. Morris H. Kahn, "A Municipal Birth Control Clinic," *New York Medical Journal*, April 28, 1917, in Margaret H. Sanger, *The Case for Birth Control* (New York, Modern Art Printing Co., 1917), 166–67.

85. Andrea Tone, "Contraceptive Consumers: Gender and the Political Economy of Birth Control in the 1930s," *Journal of Social History* 29, no. 3 (Spring 1996): 490–91. Melissa R. Klapper, *Ballots, Babies, and Banners of Peace: American Jewish Women's Activism, 1890–1940* (New York: New York University Press, 2013), 142.

86. Maud Nathan, *Once Upon a Time and Today* (New York: G. P. Putnam's Sons, 1933), 255.

87. "Emma Goldman and A. Berkman Behind the Bars," *New York Times*, June 16, 1917, 1.

88. Nathan, *Once Upon a Time and Today*, 253–57; Irwin Unger and Debi Unger, *The Guggenheims: A Family History* (New York: HarperCollins, 2005), 141.

89. Irma L. Lindheim, *Parallel Quest: A Search of a Person and a People* (New York: Thomas Yoseloff, 1962), 47–51.

Chapter 4: "Woman is looking around and ahead"

1. Carrie Simon quoted in Pamela S. Nadell, " 'The Synagog Shall Hear the Call of the Sister': Carrie Simon and the Founding of NFTS," in *Sisterhood: A Centennial History of Women of Reform Judaism*, ed. Carole B. Balin, Dana Herman, Jonathan D. Sarna, and Gary P. Zola (Cincinnati: Hebrew Union College Press, 2013), 35.

2. Gerda Lerner, *The Majority Finds Its Past: Placing Women in History* (Oxford: Oxford University Press, 1979), 49–50.

3. Rose Pines Cohen, oral history by Marcie Cohen Ferris, "Weaving Women's Words: Baltimore Stories" (April 24, 2001), Jewish Women's Archive; Paul Mendes-Flohr and Jehudah Reinharz, eds., *The Jew in the Modern World: A Documentary History*, 3rd rev. ed. (New York: Oxford University Press, 2011), 532; Lloyd P. Gartner, "The Midpassage of American Jewry," in *The American Jewish Experience*, ed. Jonathan D. Sarna, 2nd ed. (New York: Holmes & Meier, 1997), 264.

4. Deborah Dash Moore, *At Home in America: Second Generation New York Jews* (New York: Columbia University Press, 1981), 33.

5. Quoted in Moore, *At Home in America*, 38.

6. Samuel G. Freedman, *Who She Was: My Search for My Mother's Life* (New York: Simon & Schuster, 2005), 31–32.

7. Irving Cutler, *The Jews of Chicago: From Shtetl to Suburb* (Urbana: University of Illinois Press, 1996), 126–27.

8. Betty D. Greenberg and Althea O. Silverman, *The Jewish Home Beautiful* (New York: Women's League of the United Synagogue of America, 1941).

9. Peggy Dennis, *The Autobiography of an American Communist: A Personal View of a Political Life, 1925–1975* (Westport, CT: Lawrence Hill & Co., 1977), 20–21; Irma L. Lindheim, *Parallel Quest: A Search of a Person and a People* (New York: Thomas Yoseloff, 1962), 44–45.

10. Elsie Miller Legum, oral history by Elaine Eff, "Weaving Women's Words: Baltimore Stories" (April 19, 2001), Jewish Women's Archive.

11. Quoted in Constance Rosenblum, *Boulevard of Dreams: Heady Times, Heartbreak, and Hope Along the Grand Concourse in the Bronx* (New York: New York University Press, 2011), 56.

12. Alice Kessler-Harris, *Out to Work: A History of Wage-Earning Women in the United States* (New York: Oxford University Press, 1982), 122.

13. Emma Goldman, *Anarchism and Other Essays* (New York: Mother Earth Publishing Association, 1910), 234.

14. Quoted in Peter C. Engelman, *A History of the Birth Control Movement in America* (Santa Barbara, CA: Praeger, 2011), 143; Andrea Tone, "Contraceptive Consumers: Gender and the Political Economy of Birth Control in the 1930s," *Journal of Social History* 29, no. 3 (Spring 1996): 485.

15. Quoted in Tone, "Contraceptive Consumers," 485.

16. Susan Cotts Watkins and Angela D. Danzi, "Women's Gossip and Social Change: Childbirth and Fertility Control Among Italian and Jewish Women in the United States, 1920–1940," *Gender and Society* 9, no. 4 (August 1995): 479–82.

17. Michael Haines, "Fertility and Mortality in the United States," EH.Net-Economic History Services, https://eh.net/encyclopedia/fertility-and-mortality-in-the-united-states/; Sergio DellaPergola, "Patterns of American Jewish Fertility," *Demography* 17, no. 3 (August 1980): 263.

18. Ella Baker and Marvel Cooke, "The Bronx Slave Market," *Crisis*, November 1935, 330–31ff.

19. Ruth Glazer, "From the American Scene: The Jewish Delicatessen," *Commentary*, March 1946, 62; Donald Paneth, "From the American Scene: Bronx Housewife, The Life and Opinions of Mrs. Litofsky," *Commentary*, February 1951, 175.

20. Jenna Weissman Joselit, "Jewish in Dishes: Kashrut in the New World," in *The Americanization of the Jews*, ed. Robert M. Seltzer and Norman J. Cohen (New York: New York University Press, 1995), 250.

21. "Lane Bryant Dies: Founder of a Chain," *New York Times*, September 27, 1951, 31.

22. Van Buren Thorne, "'Twilight Sleep' Is Successful in 120 Cases Here," *New York Times*, August 30, 1914, SM8.

23. Paula S. Fass, *The Damned and the Beautiful: American Youth in the 1920's* (New York: Oxford University Press, 1977), 124.

24. Melissa R. Klapper, *Jewish Girls Coming of Age in America, 1860–1920* (New York: New York University Press, 2005), 91.

25. Kate Simon, *A Wider World: Portraits in an Adolescence* (New York: Harper & Row, 1986), 9; Freedman, *Who She Was*, 44, 61; Lois Gould, *Mommy Dressing: A Love Story, After a Fashion* (1998; rpt. New York: Anchor Books, 1999), 36.

26. Paneth, "From the American Scene: Bronx Housewife," 180.

27. Melissa J. Martens, " 'The Game of a Thousand Wonders': Mah Jongg in the American and Jewish Imagination," in *Mah Jongg: Crak, Bam, Dot*, ed. Patsy Tarr (New York: 2wice Arts Foundation, 2010); Elaine Schattner, "The Enduring Clicks of an Ancient Game," *New York Times*, February 13, 2009, CY5.

28. Ari Y. Kelman, *Station Identification: A Cultural History of Yiddish Radio in the United States* (Berkeley: University of California Press, 2009), 84–85.

29. Quoted in Michele Hilmes, *Radio Voices: American Broadcasting, 1922–1952* (Minneapolis: University of Minnesota Press, 1997), 1.

30. Glenn D. Smith, Jr., *"Something on My Own": Gertrude Berg and American Broadcasting, 1929–1956* (Syracuse, NY: Syracuse University Press, 2007), 37.

31. Quoted in Donald Weber, "Goldberg Variations: The Achivements of Gertrude Berg," in *Entertaining America: Jews, Movies, and Broadcasting*, ed. J. Hoberman and Jeffrey Shandler (Princeton: Princeton University Press, 2003), 119.

32. Patricia Erens, "The Flapper: Hollywood's First Liberated Woman," in *Dancing Fools and Weary Blues: The Great Escape of the Twenties*, ed. Lawrence R. Broer and John Daniel Walther (Bowling Green, OH: Bowling Green State University Popular Press, 1990), 131; Kate Simon, *Bronx Primitive: Portraits in a Childhood* (New York: Viking Press, 1982), 44–45.

33. Lila Corwin Berman, *Speaking of Jews: Rabbis, Intellectuals, and the Creation of an American Public Identity* (Berkeley: University of California Press, 2009), 53; Keren R. McGinity, *Still Jewish: A History of Women and Intermarriage in America* (New York: New York University Press, 2009), 64.

34. Berman, *Speaking of Jews*, 63; Rebecca E. Mack, *You Are a Jew and a Jew You Are!* (n.p: n.p., 1933), 33, 36.

35. McGinity, *Still Jewish*, xi, 91–92.

36. Freedman, *Who She Was*, 204–19.

37. Pew Research Center, *A Portrait of Jewish Americans* (Washington, DC: Pew Research Center, October 2013), 9; McGinity, *Still Jewish*, 101–5.

38. Israel Goldstein, *Jewish Justice and Conciliation: History of the Jewish Conciliation Board, 1930–1968, and a Review of Jewish Juridical Autonomy* (New York: Ktav, 1981), 88–89, 193–95.

39. Kessler-Harris, *Out to Work*, 249.

40. Theresa Wolfson, *The Woman Worker and the Trade Unions* (New York: International Publishers, 1926), 93, 205.

41. Simon, *Wider World*, 34.

42. Annelise Orleck, *Common Sense and a Little Fire: Women and Working-Class Politics in the United States, 1900–1965* (Chapel Hill: University of North Carolina Press, 1995), 172, 182–83.

43. Orleck, *Common Sense*, 169–71.

44. Orleck, *Common Sense*, 173; Wolfson, *Woman Worker and Trade Unions*, 32.

45. Margery Davies, "Woman's Place is at the Typewriter: The Feminization of the Clerical Labor Force," *Radical America* 3–4 (July–August 1974): 10.

46. Selma Litman, oral history by Marcie Cohen Ferris, "Weaving Women's Words: Baltimore Stories" (July 9, 2001), 9, Jewish Women's Archive.

47. Pamela S. Nadell, *Women Who Would Be Rabbis: A History of Women's Ordination, 1889–1985* (Boston: Beacon Press, 1998), 100–1.

48. Pauline Kronman, "Business Women Need Not Be Mannish," *American Hebrew*, November 5, 1926, 819; Libbian Benedict, "Jewish Women Headliners: Clarice M. Baright-Magistrate," *American Hebrew*, January 1, 1926; "Woman, Look After Your Home, Is Counsel of Mrs. Schweitzer," *Jewish Telegraphic Agency*, February 3, 1935; Schweitzer-Mauduit International, Inc. History, http://www.fundinguniverse.com/company-histories/schweitzer-mauduit-international-inc-history/.

49. Calvin Coolidge, "Address to the American Society of Newspaper Editors," January 17, 1925, http://www.presidency.ucsb.edu/ws/?pid=24180.

50. David B. Green, "The Jewish Inventor of the Bra," *Forward*, January 11, 2014.

51. Michael Kaminer, "As One Jewish Retail Empire Falls, Another Rises," *Forward*, December 26, 2013.

52. Litman oral history, 31–32.

53. Luba Bat, *Phoenix: Book One* (Mimeograph, Yad Vashem Library (85-0506F), n.d.), 43–44, 65–67.

54. Madeline R. Grumet, *Bitter Milk: Women and Teaching* (Amherst: University of Massachusetts Press, 1988), 34; Simon, *Bronx Primitive*, 48; quoted in Susan Dworkin, *Miss America, 1945: Bess Myerson and the Year That Changed Our Lives* (1987; rpt. New York: Newmarket Press, 2000), 28.

55. Ruth Jacknow Markowitz, *My Daughter, the Teacher: Jewish Teachers in the New York City Schools* (New Brunswick, NJ: Rutgers University Press, 1993), 20–21, 75–81, 86.

56. Markowitz, *My Daughter*, 132–35, 145; "Upholds Teacher Who Bore a Child," *New York Times*, November 15, 1913.

57. Nancy F. Cott, *The Grounding of Modern Feminism* (New Haven: Yale University Press, 1987), 182–83.

58. Rebecca Kobrin, "Teaching Profession," in *Jewish Women in America:*

An Historical Encyclopedia, ed. Paula E. Hyman and Deborah Dash Moore (New York: Routledge, 1997).

59. Stanley Rabinowitz, *The Assembly: A Century in the Life of the Adas Israel Hebrew Congregation of Washington, D.C.* (Hoboken, NJ: Ktav, 1993), 455–56.

60. Quoted in Nadell, " 'Synagog Shall Hear Call of Sister,' " 30.

61. Judith Kaplan Eisenstein, "No Thunder Sounded, No Lightning Struck," in *Eyewitnesses to American Jewish History: A History of American Jewry*, part 4: *The American Jew, 1915–1969*, ed. Azriel Eisenberg (New York: Union of American Hebrew Congregations, 1982), 30–32.

62. Paula E. Hyman, "The Introduction of Bat Mitzvah in Conservative Judaism in Postwar America," *YIVO Annual* 19 (1990): 135.

63. Judith Berlin Lieberman, "Judith Berlin Lieberman," in *Thirteen Americans: Their Spiritual Autobiographies*, ed. Louis Finkelstein (New York: Institute of Religious and Social Studies, 1953), 164.

64. Pines Cohen oral history.

65. Quoted in Nadell, *Women Who Would Be Rabbis*, 105.

66. Jenna Weissman Joselit, *New York's Jewish Jews: The Orthodox Community in the Interwar Years* (Bloomington: Indiana University Press, 1990), 119.

67. Lara Freidenfelds, *The Modern Period: Menstruation in Twentieth-Century America* (Baltimore: Johns Hopkins University Press, 2009), 15; quoted in Joselit, *New York's Jewish Jews*, 121.

68. Hannah G. Solomon, "Jewish Women Organize," in *The Jewish Americans: Three Centuries of Jewish Voices in America*, ed. Beth S. Wenger (New York: Doubleday, 2007), 153.

69. Quoted in Faith Rogow, *Gone to Another Meeting: The National Council of Jewish Women, 1893–1993* (Tuscaloosa: University of Alabama Press, 1993), 169; Maria Shriver and the Center for American Progress, *The Shriver Report: A Woman's Nation Pushes Back From the Brink* (Rosetta Books, January 2014), loc. 268 of 8217, Kindle.

70. Karen Pastorello, *A Power among Them: Bessie Abramowitz Hillman and the Making of the Amalgamated Clothing Workers of America* (Urbana: University of Illinois Press, 2008), 60.

71. Women of Reform Judaism, "Resolutions & Statements: By Year," https://wrj.org/resolutions-statements-year; Robyn Muncy, *Creating a Female Dominion in American Reform, 1890–1935* (New York: Oxford University Press, 1991), 104.

72. "Roosevelt Urged to Act for Jews," *New York Times*, May 19, 1939; Richard Breitman and Allan J. Lichtman, *FDR and the Jews* (Cambridge, MA: Belknap Press of Harvard University Press, 2013), 240–41.

73. Quoted in Mark A. Raider, *The Emergence of American Zionism* (New York: New York University Press, 1998), 16.

74. Mary McCune, "Formulating the 'Women's Interpretation of Zionism':

Hadassah Recruitment of Non-Zionist American Women, 1914–1930," in *American Jewish Women and the Zionist Enterprise*, ed. Shulamit Reinharz and Marc Raider (Waltham, MA: Brandeis University Press, 2005), xx, 89–111.

75. Mark A. Raider, "The Romance and the *Realpolitik* of Zionist Pioneering: The Case of the Pioneer Women's Organization," in Reinharz and Raider, *American Jewish Women*, 120.

76. Quoted in Erica B. Simmons, *Hadassah and the Zionist Project* (Lanham, MD: Rowman & Littlefield, 2006), 29; Irma Lindheim to Pearl Franklin, April 8, 1928, 6, RG 4, Folder 7, Hadassah Archives, American Jewish Historical Society.

77. "Hadassah Leaders Tell Aims to 1,500," *New York Times*, November 29, 1935.

78. Baila Round Shargel, "American Jewish Women in Palestine: Bessie Gotsfeld, Henrietta Szold, and the Zionist Enterprise," *American Jewish History* 90, no. 2 (June 2002): 141–61.

79. Rachel Rojanski, "At the Center or on the Fringes of the Public Arena: Ester Mintz-Aberson and the Status of Women in American Poalei Zion, 1905–35," *Journal of Israeli History: Politics, Society, Culture* 21, nos. 1–2 (June 2010): 27–53.

80. Pastorello, *Power among Them*, 240n12, quoted in Raider, "Romance and *Realpolitik* of Zionist Pioneering," 114.

81. Joseph B. Glass, "Settling the Old-New Homeland: The Decisions of American Jewish Women During the Interwar Years," in Reinharz and Raider, *American Jewish Women and Zionist Enterprise*, 192.

82. Golda Meir, "'They Couldn't Imagine an American Girl Would Do the Work' (Kibbutz Revivim, 1971)," in Reinharz and Raider, *American Jewish Women*, 325–26.

83. Quoted in Marie Syrkin, "Golda Meir and Other Americans," in Reinharz and Raider, *American Jewish Women*, 293.

84. Sarah Jane Deutsch, "From Ballots to Breadlines, 1920–1940," in *No Small Courage: A History of Women in the United States*, ed. Nancy F. Cott (New York: Oxford University Press, 2000), 456; quoted in Beth S. Wenger, *New York Jews and the Great Depression: Uncertain Promise* (New Haven: Yale University Press, 1996), 49–50.

85. Wenger, *New York Jews and Great Depression*, 119–21; quoted in Dworkin, *Miss America, 1945*, 15.

86. Faye Moskowitz, *A Leak in the Heart: Tales from a Woman's Life* (Boston: David R. Godine, 1985), 116–17.

87. Quoted in Wenger, *New York Jews and Great Depression*, 37.

88. Wenger, *New York Jews and Great Depression*, 63; Lucy S. Dawidowicz, *From That Place and Time: A Memoir, 1938–1947* (1989; rpt. New Brunswick, NJ: Rutgers University Press, 2008), 20, 23.

89. Wenger, *New York Jews and Great Depression*, 72–75; cf. Pines Cohen oral history, 41, and Franklin Delano Roosevelt, "Address of the President

to the Young Democratic Club of Maryland, Fifth Regiment Armory, Baltimore, MD, April 13, 1936," Speeches of President Franklin D. Roosevelt, 1933–1945, National Archives Catalog, https://catalog.archives.gov/id/197556.

90. Wenger, *New York Jews and Great Depression*, 75.

91. Kim Chernin, *In My Mother's House: A Daughter's Story* (1983; rpt. New York: Harper Colophon, 1984), 43, 90–91; "35,000 Jammed in Square: Views of the Red Rioting in Union Square Yesterday," *New York Times*, March 7, 1930.

92. Marjorie N. Feld, *Lillian Wald: A Biography* (Chapel Hill: University of North Carolina Press, 2008), 241n46.

93. Robert Shaffer, "Women and the Communist Party, USA, 1930–1940," *Socialist Review* 9 (May-June 1979): 73–118; Alice Kessler-Harris, *A Difficult Woman: The Challenging Life and Times of Lillian Hellman* (New York: Bloomsbury, 2012), 142.

94. Priscilla Murolo, "Communism in the United States," in *Jewish Women: A Comprehensive Historical Encyclopedia* (Jewish Women's Archive, 2009); Dennis, *Autobiography of an American Communist*, 125.

95. Anna Taffler, " 'I'm Going to Fight Like Hell': Anna Taffler and the Unemployed Councils of the 1930s," Geroge Mason University, History Matters, http://historymatters.gmu.edu/d/31/.

96. Quoted in Wenger, *New York Jews and Great Depression*, 114.

97. Annelise Orleck, " 'We Are That Mythical Thing Called the Public': Militant Housewives During the Great Depression," *Feminist Studies* 19, no. 1 (Spring 1993), 147–72.

98. Dawidowicz, *From That Place and Time*, 14.

99. Dawidowicz, *From That Place and Time*, 7.

100. Helen Jacobus Apte, *Heart of a Wife: The Diary of a Southern Jewish Woman*, ed. Marcus D. Rosenbaum (Wilmington, DE: Scholarly Resources, 1998), 18.

101. Apte, *Heart of a Wife*, 82.

102. Maud Nathan, *Once Upon a Time and Today* (New York: G. P. Putnam's Sons, 1933), 275; "Miss Perkins Gives Reply to 'Whispers,' " *New York Times*, April 5, 1936, 43; Glen Jeansonne, *Women of the Far Right: The Mothers' Movement and World War II* (Chicago: University of Chicago Press, 1996), 101–2.

103. Anonymous, "I Am a Jewess," *She*, November 1942, 19–22.

104. "Candid Survey of Anti-Jewish Prejudice," *She*, March 1943, 12–15ff.

105. "Four Deny Nazism Tainted Teaching," *New York Times*, June 1, 1935; Michael Greenberg and Seymour Zenchelsky, "Private Bias and Public Responsibility: Anti-Semitism at Rutgers in the 1920s and 1930s," *History of Education Quarterly* 33, no. 3 (Autumn 1993): 316–18.

106. Edna Ferber, *A Peculiar Treasure: An Autobiography* (1938; rpt. New York: Vintage, 2014), 371–72.

107. Sander L. Gilman, "The Jewish Nose: Are Jews White? Or, the History

of the Nose Job," in *The Other in Jewish Thought and History: Construc-tions of Jewish Culture and Identity*, ed. Laurence J. Silberstein and Robert L. Cohn (New York: New York University Press, 1994), 392–93.

108. Quotations from Melissa R. Klapper, *Ballots, Babies, and Banners of Peace: American Jewish Women's Activism, 1890–1940* (New York: New York University Press, 2013), 188; Feld, *Lillian Wald*, 179.

109. "100,000 March Here in 6-Hour Protest over Nazi Policies," *New York Times*, May 11, 1933.

110. "Wife of Rabbi Wise Joins Store Pickets," *New York Times*, December 24, 1935.

111. Mendes-Flohr and Reinharz, *Jew in Modern World*, 532.

112. Arthur Hertzberg, *A Jew in America: My Life and a People's Struggle for Identity* (New York: HarperSanFrancisco, 2002), 73; Rona Sheramy, " 'There Are Times When Silence Is a Sin': The Women's Division of the American Jewish Congress and the Anti-Nazi Boycott Movement," *American Jewish History* 89, no. 1 (March 2001): 105–21.

113. YIVO Institute for Jewish Research, "The Otto Frank File," https://yivo .org/Otto-Frank-File.

114. Ingeborg B. Weinberger, oral history by Jean Freedman, "Weaving Women's Words: Baltimore Stories" (May 20, 2001), Jewish Women's Archive.

115. Mitchell G. Ash, "Women Emigré Psychologists and Psychoanalysts in the United States," in *Between Sorrow and Strength: Women Refugees of the Nazi Period*, ed. Sibylle Quack (Washington, DC: German Historical Insti-tute, 1995), 251–54.

116. Atina Grossman, "New Women in Exile: German Women Doctors and the Emigration," in Quack, *Between Sorrow and Strength*, 215–38.

117. Shoshana Cardin, "Shoshana Cardin on Pearl Harbor," Jewish Women's Archive, http://jwa.org/media/shoshana-cardin-shares-memories-of-pearl -harbor.

118. Clementine Lazeron Kaufman, oral history by Jean Freedman, "Weav-ing Women's Words: Baltimore Stories" (March 16, 2002), Jewish Women's Archive; Mollie Weinstein Schaffer and Cyndee Schaffer, *Mollie's War: The Letters of a World War II WAC in Europe* (Jefferson, NC: McFarland, 2010), 162, 208.

119. Irwin Nadell, interview by author, March 16, 2014.

120. Robert W. Reichard, *One Soldier's Story* (2003), http://bobreichard .com/03chapter.html.

121. Phyllis K. Fisher, *Los Alamos Experience* (Tokyo: Japan Publications, 1985).

122. "Convention of Jewish Women's Organizations Discusses War Activi-ties," Jewish Telegraphic Agency, January 23, 1942.

123. "American Red Cross Praises Jewish Blood Donors; Red Cross Sabbath This Week-end," Jewish Telegraphic Agency, February 2, 1943.

124. Susan M. Hartmann, *The Home Front and Beyond: American Women in the 1940s* (Boston: Twayne, 1982), 77–78.

125. Hartmann, *Home Front*, 88; Liza Mundy, *Code Girls: The Untold Story of the American Women Code Breakers of World War II* (New York: Hachette, 2017), 13.

126. Quoted in Carole Bell Ford, *The Girls: Jewish Women of Brownsville, Brooklyn, 1940–1995* (Albany: State University of New York Press, 2000), 74.

127. Quoted in Emily Yellin, *Our Mothers' War: American Women at Home and at the Front During World War II* (New York: Free Press, 2004), 114.

128. Marian Gold Krugman, oral history interview, Women's Veteran Historical Project, Oral History Collection, University of North Carolina Greensboro, http://library.uncg.edu/dp/wv/results5.aspx?i=2734&s=5.

129. *Women in the Military: A Jewish Perspective* (Washington, DC: National Museum of American Jewish Military History, 1999).

130. Quoted in Bob Welch, *American Nightingale: The Story of Frances Slanger, Forgotten Heroine of Normandy* (New York: Atria Books, 2004), 196.

131. *Women in the Military*, 5, 29.

132. *Women in the Military*, 23.

133. Schaffer and Schaffer, *Mollie's War*, 93–94.

134. "Backer Says Jewish Life Will Be Restored in Europe; Calls on Jews Not to Despair," Jewish Telegraphic Agency, May 14, 1943.

135. "American Jewish Organizations Make Public Their Appeals to the Bermuda Parley," Jewish Telegraphic Agency, April 20, 1943; "American Jewish Conference: A Statement of the Organization of the Conference," American Jewish Archives, American Jewish Conference Nearprint.

136. "$300,000 Drive for Child Refugees Launched at Mizrachi Women's Conference," Jewish Telegraphic Agency, March 12, 1943; "Council of Jewish Women Asks Congress to Admit Child Refugees over Quota Limit," Jewish Telegraphic Agency, November 14, 1943.

137. R. Tourover to Gisela Warburg, October 29, 1942, Tourover to Warburg, December 6, 1942, and Hadassah Organization to Eliezer Kaplan, Jewish Agency, January 27, 1943, all in Hadassah Archives, American Jewish Historical Society, RG 7, Special Collections, Denise Tourover Papers, 1936–1981, Box 1, Folder 2, Teheran Children Series, October 23, 1942–February 18, 1943.

138. Ruth Gruber, *Haven: The Dramatic Story of 1000 World War II Refugees and How They Came to America* (New York: Three Rivers Press, 1983), 6–29.

139. "American Jewish Women Told of Their Obligations to Jews in Europe," Jewish Telegraphic Agency, October 12, 1942.

140. "Agency to Find Relatives in Liberated Europe Established in New York," Jewish Telegraphic Agency, August 9, 1944; "Representatives of Jewish Women's Organizations Participate in UNRRA Conference," Jewish Telegraphic Agency, October 22, 1944.

141. "Hadassah Convention Decides to Intensify Investigation of Arab-Jewish Problems," Jewish Telegraphic Agency, October 16, 1942; "American Jewish Women Dedicate Vocational School in Palestine to Ghetto Heroes," Jewish Telegraphic Agency, July 9, 1943.

Chapter 5: "Down from the pedestal
. . . up from the laundry room"

1. "Bronx Girl, 21, Wins 'Miss America' Title," *New York Times*, September 9, 1945; William R. Conklin, "Pair Silent to the End: Husband Is First to Die," *New York Times*, June 20, 1953; "Boxing Fan Wins $64,000 Decision," *New York Times*, December 7, 1955; "Nazi Victims Reunited," *New York Times*, March 14, 1961; Brock Milton, "Case of the Teenage Doll," *New York Times*, April 21, 1963; Irving Spiegel, "Women Endorsed as Reform Rabbis," *New York Times*, November 21, 1963.

2. Sylvia Barack Fishman, "The Changing American Jewish Family Faces the 1990s," in *The Jewish Family and Jewish Continuity*, ed. Steven Bayme and Gladys Rosen (Hoboken, NJ: Ktav, 1994), 6; Mimi Sheraton, *Eating My Words: An Appetite for Life* (New York: William Morrow, 2004), 37–38.

3. Jonathan D. Sarna, ed. *The American Jewish Experience*, 2nd ed. (New York: Holmes & Meier, 1997), 359; Sherry B. Ortner, *New Jersey Dreaming: Capital, Culture, and the Class of '58* (Durham, NC: Duke University Press, 2003), 51–56.

4. Barbara Winslow, "Women in Twentieth-Century America," in *Clio in the Classroom: A Guide for Teaching U.S. Women's History*, ed. Carol Berkin, Margaret Crocco, and Barbara Winslow (New York: Oxford University Press, 2009), 62; Erich Rosenthal, "Jewish Fertility in the United States," in *American Jewish Year Book* (Philadelphia: Jewish Publication Society of America, 1961), 62:3–27.

5. Lisa Ades, dir., *Miss America*, 2001, transcript, http://www.pbs.org/wgbh/amex/missamerica/filmmore/pt.html, accessed June 16, 2004.

6. Susan Dworkin, *Miss America, 1945: Bess Myerson and the Year That Changed Our Lives* (1987; rpt. New York: Newmarket Press, 2000); Anne Bernays and Justin Kaplan, *Back Then: Two Literary Lives in 1950s New York* (New York: William Morrow, 2002), 115.

7. Ortner, *New Jersey Dreaming*, 240.

8. Elaine Tyler May, *Homeward Bound: American Families in the Cold War Era* (New York: Basic Books, 1988), 78–80, 139–40.

9. Hasia R. Diner, Shira Kohn, and Rachel Kranson, eds., *A Jewish Feminine Mystique? Jewish Women in Postwar America* (New Brunswick, NJ: Rutgers University Press, 2010), 3.

10. Diana Bletter and Lori Grinker, *The Invisible Thread: A Portrait of Jewish American Women* (Philadelphia: Jewish Publication Society, 1989), 104–6;

Faye Moskowitz, *A Leak in the Heart* (Boston: David R. Godine, 1985), 82; Sheraton, *Eating My Words*, 38.

11. "Marriage Rates Reported Higher. Divorce Rates Lower for U.S. Jews," *Jewish Telegraphic Agency*, March 15, 1960; Dworkin, *Miss America, 1945*, 215; Samuel G. Freedman, *Who She Was: My Search for My Mother's Life* (New York: Simon & Schuster, 2005), 284.

12. Sheila Weller, *Girls Like Us: Carole King, Joni Mitchell, Carly Simon, and the Journey of a Generation* (New York: Atria Books, 2008), 46–47; Gerry Goffin and Carole King, "Will You Love Me Tomorrow?" Faber Music, 1961.

13. Grace Paley, *Just as I Thought* (New York: Farrar, Straus & Giroux, 1998), 13–20.

14. Sherri Chessen, "Rich Little Poor Girl," http://www.vfa.us/Sherri%20 Chessen.htm.

15. Rosemary Nossiff, *Before Roe: Abortion Policy in the States* (Philadelphia: Temple University Press, 2011), 92–93; Barbaralee D. Diamonstein, "We Have Had Abortions," *Ms.*, Spring 1972, 34–35.

16. "Orthodox Rabbis Say Jews Who Back Abortion Falsify Jewish Religion," *Jewish Telegraphic Agency*, January 29, 1976; Joe Winkler, "Pew: Jews Support Abortion Rights (Duh!)," *Jewish Telegraphic Agency*, July 29, 2013.

17. "Court Orders Jewish Couple to Surrender Adopted Catholic Child," *Jewish Telegraphic Agency*, February 16, 1956; John Wicklein, "Religious Rule on Adoption Bars Many Couples in State," *New York Times*, October 11, 1959.

18. Ann Fessler, *The Girls Who Went Away: The Hidden History of Women Who Surrendered Children for Adoption in the Decades before Roe v. Wade* (New York: Penguin, 2006), 127–32.

19. Keren R. McGinity, *Still Jewish: A History of Women and Intermarriage in America* (New York: New York University Press, 2009), 219.

20. Ortner, *New Jersey Dreaming*, 36–40.

21. "Nazi Victims Reunited"; Beth B. Cohen, *Case Closed: Holocaust Survivors in Postwar America* (New Brunswick, NJ: Rutgers University Press, 2007), 1.

22. Jeffrey Shandler, *While America Watches: Televising the Holocaust* (New York: Oxford University Press, 1999), 27–40.

23. Luba Bat, *Phoenix: Book One* (Mimeograph: Yad Vashem Library (85-0506F), n.d.), 18.

24. Luba Bat, interview by Cynthia Haft, Hebrew University of Jerusalem, Avraham Harman Institute of Contemporary Jewry, Jewish Survivors of the Holocaust—in the U.S., June 11, 1971.

25. Gerda Weissmann Klein, *All but My Life*, rev. ed. (New York: Hill and Wang, 1995); *One Survivor Remembers* acceptance speech, 68th Academy Awards, https://www.youtube.com/watch?v=5zn-fPM4KSo.

26. Eva Hoffman, *After Such Knowledge: Memory, History, and the Legacy of the Holocaust* (New York: Public Affairs, 2004).

27. William R. Conklin, "3 in Atom Spy Case Are Found Guilty; Maximum Is Death," *New York Times*, March 30, 1951; quoted in Ilene J. Philipson, *Ethel Rosenberg: Beyond the Myths* (New York: F. Watts, 1988), 2.

28. Rebecca T. Alpert, "Lesbianism," in *Jewish Women in America: An Historical Encyclopedia*, ed. Paula E. Hyman and Deborah Dash Moore (New York: Routledge, 1997).

29. Annelise Orleck, *Common Sense and a Little Fire: Women and Working-Class Politics in the United States, 1900–1965* (Chapel Hill: University of North Carolina Press, 1995), 137, 282–83, 310.

30. Clyde Kluckhohn, "The Complex Kinsey Study and What It Attempts to Do," *New York Times*, September 13, 1953; Jeffrey Shandler, "Gerry's Story: An Oral History," in *Twice Blessed: On Being Lesbian, Gay and Jewish*, ed. Christie Balka and Andy Rose (Boston: Beacon Press, 1989), 92–102.

31. Brenda Knight, *Women of the Beat Generation: The Writers, Artists, and Muses at the Heart of a Revolution* (Berkeley, CA: Conari Press, 1996), 145, 250–55.

32. Hettie Jones, *How I Became Hettie Jones* (New York: Dutton, 1990), 10.

33. Joyce Johnson, *Minor Characters: A Young Woman's Coming-of-Age in the Beat Orbit of Jack Kerouac* (1983; rpt. New York: Penguin Books, 1999), xiii; Wini Breines, "The 'Other' Fifties: Beats and Bad Girls," in *Not June Cleaver: Women and Gender in Postwar America, 1945–1960*, ed. Joanne Meyerowitz (Philadelphia: Temple University Press, 1994), 402.

34. Quoted in Deborah Dash Moore, "Hadassah," in *Jewish Women in America*, 1:579.

35. Rose Halprin, interview by John Wingate, *Nightbeat*, August 29, 1957, Hadassah Archives, American Jewish Historical Society, RG18-AudioRTR-B1-5, system number cjh_digitool1358864.

36. Faith Rogow, *Gone to Another Meeting: The National Council of Jewish Women, 1893–1993* (Tuscaloosa: University of Alabama Press, 1993), 185–87.

37. Raymond Mohl with Matilda "Bobbi" Graf and Shirley M. Zoloth, *South of the South: Jewish Activists and the Civil Rights Movement in Miami, 1945–1960* (Gainesville: University Press of Florida, 2004), 82–83.

38. Sylvie Murray, *The Progressive Housewife: Community Activism in Suburban Queens, 1945–1965* (Philadelphia: University of Pennsylvania Press, 2003), 6, 61–62; Betty Friedan, *It Changed My Life: Writings on the Women's Movement* (New York: Random House, 1978), 9.

39. Murray, *Progressive Housewife*, 77; Jones, *How I Became Hettie Jones*, 16.

40. Marge Piercy, *Parti-Colored Blocks for a Quilt* (Ann Arbor: University of Michigan Press, 1982), 122; Amy Swerdlow, *Women Strike for Peace: Traditional Motherhood and Radical Politics in the 1960s* (Chicago: University of Chicago Press, 1993), photo gallery.

41. Susan Strasser, *Never Done: A History of American Housework* (New York: Pantheon Books, 1982), 276.

42. Quoted in Gail Collins, *When Everything Changed: The Amazing Jour-*

ney of American Women from 1960 to the Present (New York: Little, Brown, 2009), 20.

43. Karen Pastorello, *A Power Among Them: Bessie Abramowitz Hillman and the Making of the Amalgamated Clothing Workers of America* (Urbana: University of Illinois Press, 2008), 164-174.

44. Elaine Reichek, "Untitled," in *Too Jewish? Challenging Traditional Identities*, ed. Norman Kleeblatt (New Brunswick, NJ; Rutgers University Press, 1996), 148; Carolyn G. Heilbrun, *Reinventing Womanhood* (New York: Norton, 1979), 21.

45. Daniel Horowitz, *Betty Friedan and the Making of the Feminine Mystique: The American Left, the Cold War, and Modern Feminism*, rev. ed. (Amherst: University of Massachusetts Press, 2000), 121–52.

46. Betty Friedan, *The Feminine Mystique* (New York: Norton, 1963); Friedan, *It Changed My Life*, 17–27; quoted in Ann Braude, ed., *Transforming the Faiths of Our Fathers: Women Who Changed American Religion* (New York: Palgrave Macmillan, 2004), 2.

47. Sonia Pressman Fuentes, *Eat First—You Don't Know What They'll Give You: The Adventures of an Immigrant Family and Their Feminist Daughter* (n.p.: XLibris, 1999); Sonia Fuentes to Jacqui Ceballos, April 14, 2013, forwarded to author, February 24, 2017.

48. Linda Charlton, "Women March Down Fifth in Equality Drive," *New York Times*, August 27, 1970; Friedan, *It Changed My Life*, 154.

49. Linda Buchwald, "How a Bat Mitzvah Helped Inspire a 'Good Girls Revolt,'" Jewish Telegraphic Agency, November 8, 2016.

50. Quoted in Pamela S. Nadell, "'Diamonds Are a Girl's Best Friend': Jewish Women and Baseball," in *Chasing Dreams: Baseball and Becoming Americans*, ed. Josh Perelman (Philadelphia: National Museum of American Jewish History, 2014), 162.

51. Bella Abzug with Mim Kelber, *Gender Gap: Bella Abzug's Guide to Political Power for American Women* (Boston: Houghton Mifflin, 1984), 158–61; quoted in Linda Gradstein, "In Jerusalem, a Feminist Call," *Washington Post*, December 10, 1988.

52. Quoted in Linda Hirshman, *Sisters in Law: How Sandra Day O'Connor and Ruth Bader Ginsburg Went to the Supreme Court and Changed the World* (New York: Harper, 2015), 16.

53. "Jane Eisner interviews Ruth Bader Ginsburg Transcript," *Forward*, February 5, 2018, https://forward.com/opinion/393687/jane-eisner-interviews-ruth-bader-ginsburg-transcript/; Anne Frank, *The Diary of a Young Girl: The Definitive Edition*, rev. ed. (New York: Doubleday, 1995), 318; Ira E. Stoll, "Ginsburg Blasts Harvard Law: Past, Present Deans Defend School," *Harvard Crimson*, July 23, 1993.

54. Robert Barnes, "Ginsburg Is Latest Justice to Reflect on Faith," *Washington Post*, January 15, 2008.

55. Susan Brownmiller, *Against Our Will: Men, Women, and Rape* (New

York: Simon & Schuster, 1975); Grace Lichtenstein, "Feminists Demand 'Liberation" in *Ladies' Home Journal* Sit-In," *New York Times*, March 19, 1970; "The Feminist Revolution: Susan Brownmiller," Jewish Women's Archive, https://jwa.org/feminism/brownmiller-susan.

56. Ruth Rosen, *The World Split Open: How the Modern Women's Movement Changed America* (New York: Viking, 2000), 160; Alix Kates Shulman, *A Marriage Agreement and Other Essays: Four Decades of Feminist Writing* (New York: Open Road Media, 2012); quoted in *Makers: Alix Kates Shulman*, https://www.makers.com/profiles/591f26af4d21a801db72e832; Alix Kates Shulman, "A Marriage Disagreement, or Marriage by Other Means," in *The Feminist Memoir Project: Voices from Women's Liberation*, ed. Rachel Blau DuPlessis and Ann Snitow (New York: Three Rivers Press, 1998), 284–303.

57. Alix Kates Shulman, interview by Bella Book, Jewish Women's Archive, https://jwa.org/blog/interview-with-alix-kates-shulman.

58. Gerda Lerner, *Fireweed: A Political Autobiography* (Philadelphia: Temple University Press, 2002), 134–47.

59. Gerda Lerner, "Women Among the Professors of History: The Story of a Process of Transformation," in *Voices of Women Historians: The Personal, the Political, the Professional*, ed. Eileen Boris and Nupur Chaudhuri (Bloomington: Indiana University Press, 1999), 1.

60. Marilyn Salzman Webb, "The Feminist," in *Generation on Fire: Voices of Protest from the 1960s, an Oral History*, ed. Jeff Kisseloff (Lexington: University Press of Kentucky, 2007), 167–82.

61. Debra L. Schultz, *Going South: Jewish Women in the Civil Rights Movement* (New York: New York University Press, 2001), 101, 179; Ellen K. Coughlin, "The Feminist Press's Chief Editor, Fund Raiser, and Cheerleader," *Chronicle of Higher Education*, November 14, 1990.

62. James A. Sleeper, "Introduction," in *The New Jews*, ed. James A. Sleeper and Alan L. Mintz (New York: Vintage Books, 1971), 16.

63. Alan Silverstein, "The Evolution of Ezrat Nashim," *Conservative Judaism* 30 (Fall 1975): 41–51.

64. "Ezrat Nashim's 'Jewish Women Call for Change,' March 14, 1972," Jewish Women's Archive, https://jwa.org/media/jewish-women-call-for-change.

65. Irving Spiegel, "Conservative Jews Vote for Women in Minyan," *New York Times*, September 11, 1973.

66. Ruth Abusch-Magder, "The First National Jewish Women's Conference: A Study of the Early Jewish Feminist Movement" (Senior Thesis, 1991), 13, American Jewish Historical Society, Ruth Abusch-Magder Papers, P-841; Rachel Adler, "The Jew Who Wasn't There: Halakhah and the Jewish Woman," in *On Being a Jewish Feminist: A Reader*, ed. Susannah Heschel (New York: Schocken, 1983), 12–18.

67. Pamela S. Nadell, *Women Who Would Be Rabbis: A History of Women's Ordination, 1889–1985* (Boston: Beacon Press, 1998).

68. Amy Stone, "The Jewish Establishment Is NOT an Equal Opportunity

Employer," *Lilith*, Fall/Winter 1977–1978; Sarah Blustain, "Rabbi Shlomo Carlebach's Shadow Side," *Lilith*, Spring 1998.

69. Pamela S. Nadell, "Yentl: From Yeshiva Boy to Syndrome," in *New Essays in American Jewish History*, ed. Pamela S. Nadell, Jonathan D. Sarna, and Lance J. Sussman (Cincinnati: American Jewish Archives, 2010), 467–83.

70. "Books That Made a Difference to Julia Roberts," *O Magazine*, February 2001, http://www.oprah.com/omagazine/books-that-made-a-difference-to-julia-roberts_1/all.

71. Marcia Freedman, *Exile in the Promised Land: A Memoir* (Ithaca, NY: Firebrand Books, 1990).

72. "Woman as Jew, Jew as Woman: An Urgent Inquiry," *Congress Monthly* 52, no. 2 (February/March 1985).

73. Luke 10:38–42; Babylonian Talmud Sotah 21b; Annette Daum, "Anti-Semitism in the Women's Movement," *Pioneer Woman* (September-October 1983): 11–13ff; Nancy Essex, "Intolerance: A Threat to the Women's Movement," *Sojourner: The Ohio State University Center for Women's Studies* 10, no. 7 March (1983): 1–4, http://hdl.handle.net/1811/76019; Caryn McTighe Musil, "Conference Report," *Feminist Studies* 10, no. 2 (Summer 1984): 353–57.

74. Friedan, *It Changed My Life*, 350.

75. Jocelyn Olcott, *International Women's Year: The Greatest Consciousness-Raising Event in History* (New York: Oxford University Press, 2017), 218.

76. Regina Schreiber, "Copenhagen: One Year Later," *Lilith*, 1981; Letty Cottin Pogrebin, "Anti-Semitism in the Women's Movement," *Ms.* (June 1982): 145–49; "1980 World Conference on Women: Copenhagen, July 14–30, 1980," Report of the World Conference of the United Nations Decade for Women: Equality, Development and Peace, held in Copenhagen July 14–30, 1980, A/CONF.94/35, para. 77, http://www.5wwc.org/conference_background/1980_WCW.html.

77. Rogow, *Gone to Another Meeting*, 176; Dov Waxman, *Trouble in the Tribe: The American Jewish Conflict over Israel* (Princeton: Princeton University Press, 2016), 32.

78. Sarah Bunin Benor, "The Changing Language of Reform Sisterhood Ladies, 1913–2012," in *Sisterhood: A Centennial History of Women of Reform Judaism*, ed. Carole B. Balin, Dana Herman, Jonathan D. Sarna, and Gary P. Zola (Cincinnati: Hebrew Union College Press, 2013), 314–37; quoted in Waxman, *Trouble in the Tribe*, 35–36.

79. Sharon Rose, "Zionism in the Middle East," in *The Jewish 1960s: An American Sourcebook*, ed. Michael E. Staub (Waltham, MA: Brandeis University Press), 180–83.

80. Quoted in Ezra Berkley Nepon, "New Jewish Agenda: A People's History, Jewish Feminist Task Force," https://newjewishagenda.net/about/national-taskforces/jewish-feminist-taskforce/.

81. Associated Press, "Natalie Portman Speaks Out After Snubbing an Israeli 'Nobel' Prize," April 21, 2018, https://www.usatoday.com/story/

life/people/2018/04/20/natalie-portman-speaks-out-after-snubbing-israeli
-nobel-prize/538504002/; Steven M. Cohen and Ari Y. Kelman, *Beyond Distancing: Young Adult American Jews and Their Alienation from Israel* (n.p.: Jewish Identity Project of Reboot, 2007).

82. Linda Maizels, "The Old Boys Club Is Keeping Women Out of Leadership Roles in the Jewish World," *Forward*, December 26, 2017; Larry Cohler-Esses, "The Gender Gap at Jewish Non-Profits Is Bad—and Getting Worse," *Forward*, December 11, 2017; Tamara Cohen, Jill Hammer, and Rona Shapiro, *Listen to Her Voice: The Ma'yan Report; Assessing the Experiences of Women in the Jewish Community and Their Relationship to Feminism* (New York: Ma'yan: Jewish Women's Project, 2005).

83. Rhonda Abrams, "One of My Donors Harassed Me. I Couldn't Afford to Stay Silent," Jewish Telegraphic Agency, December 21, 2017.

84. Debra Nussbaum Cohen, "Congressman Pressed on Agunah Issue," *Forward*, March 1, 2012; Nathan Guttman, "Is 'Chained' Wife Tamar Epstein's Remarriage Kosher—Even Without Orthodox Divorce?" *Forward*, December 2, 2015.

85. Ben Sales, "Orthodox Union's New Project Says Women Don't Need to Be Rabbis to Be Leaders," Jewish Telegraphic Agency, October 23, 2017.

86. Gradstein, "In Jerusalem, a Feminist Call."

87. Phyllis Chesler and Rivka Haut, eds., *Women of the Wall: Claiming Sacred Ground of Judaism's Holy Site* (Woodstock, VT: Jewish Lights, 2003), inter alia, xix, xx, 210, 219.

88. International Women's Strike US Platform, http://www.womenstrikeus .org/our-platform/; Emily Shire, "Does Feminism Have Room for Zionists?," *New York Times*, March 7, 2017; Collier Meyerson, "Can You Be a Zionist Feminist? Linda Sarsour Says No," *Nation*, March 13, 2017; Pew Research Foundation, "A Portrait of Jewish Americans" (2013), http://www.pewforum.org/ 2013/10/01/jewish-american-beliefs-attitudes-culture-survey/ "Caring about Israel" graph, 83.

89. Fishman, "Changing American Jewish Family," 3; Sylvia Barack Fishman and Steven M. Cohen, "Raising Jewish Children: Research and Indications for Intervention," Jewish People Policy Institute, http://jppi.org.il/ new/en/article/english-raising-jewish-children-research-and-indications -for-intervention/english-family-engagement-and-jewish-continuity -among-american-jews/english-findings/english-fewer-young-jews-are -married/#.Wmy3VqinGUk.

90. Marshall Sklare, *America's Jews* (New York: Random House, 1971), 83; Kassel Abelson and Elliot Dorff, "Mitzvah Children," Rabbinical Assembly Committee on Jewish Law and Standards (2007), https://www .rabbinicalassembly.org/sites/default/files/public/halakhah/teshuvot/ 20052010/mitzvah_children.pdf; I thank Alan Cooperman and Gregory Smith of the Pew Research Center for this data drawn from the "2013 Pew Research Center Survey of Jews"; "The National Jewish Population Sur-

vey, 2000–2001: Strength, Challenge, and Diversity in the American Jewish Population," United Jewish Communities Report, September 2003, rev. January 2004, 4, http://www.jewishdatabank.org/studies/downloadFile .cfm?FileID=1490; Sylvia Barack Fishman, "Public Jews and Private Acts: Family and Personal Choices in the Public Square and in the Private Realm," in *Jews and the American Public Square: Debating Religion and Republic*, ed. Alan Mittleman, Robert Licht, and Jonathan D. Sarna (Lanham, MD: Rowman & Littlefield, 2002), 266.

91. Jacob B. Ukeles, Ron Miller, and Pearl Beck, *Young Jewish Adults in the United States Today* (American Jewish Committee, 2006), 2, http://www .jewishdatabank.org/Studies/downloadFile.cfm?FileID=2940.

92. Stephanie Wellen Levine, *Mystics, Mavericks, and Merrymakers: An Intimate Journey among Hasidic Girls* (New York: New York University Press, 2003), 47; "A Portrait of American Orthodox Jews: A Further Analysis of the 2013 Survey of U.S. Jews," August 26, 2015, http://www.pewforum .org/2015/08/26/a-portrait-of-american-orthodox-jews/.

93. Bletter and Grinker, *Invisible Thread*, 187–88.

94. Betty Miller, oral history, September 8–9, 2008, Voices of the Vigil, Jewish Historical Society of Greater Washington, https://www.jhsgw.org/ exhibitions/online/voices/assets/file/Miller-Betty-OH.pdf.

95. Sheryl Sandberg to Kira Volvovsky, August 1981 and May 1983, Adele and Joel Sandberg papers (P-872), Box 1, Folder 3, pp. 2–3, American Jewish Historical Society; my email exchange with Kira Volvovsky, February 28–March 3, 2018.

96. Sophie Pinkham, "A Graphic Account of a Soviet Daughter," *Tablet*, March 23, 2017; Bletter and Grinker, *Invisible Thread*, 138–40.

97. Anya von Bremzen, *Mastering the Art of Soviet Cooking: A Memoir of Food and Longing* (New York: Crown, 2013), loc. 194 and 335 of 446, Kindle.

98. Madeleine Albright, *Madam Secretary: A Memoir* (New York: Hyperion, 2003), 302–3.

99. "Angela Buchdahl Named One of America's Most Influential Rabbis," April 16, 2011, Jewish Women's Archive, https://jwa.org/thisweek/ apr/16/2011/this-week-in-history-angela-buchdahl-named-one-of-america -s-50-most-influential; Joy Ladin, "What Was a Nice Jewish Girl Like Me Doing in a Man's Body?," *Lilith* (Winter 2009–10).

100. Ellen Wexler, "The New Year of the Woman," *Moment Magazine*, March 7, 2018.

101. Wendy Wasserstein, *Shiksa Goddess (Or, How I Spent My Forties): Essays* (New York: Vintage Books, 2002), ix.

INDEX

abolition, 41, 49, 50, 51
abortion, 150–51, 163, 222, 223–25, 239, 243
Abraham, covenant with God, 21
Abrahams, Kitty, 18
Abramowitz, Bessie (Bas-Sheva), 109–12, 128
  as garment worker, 113–14, 119, 130
  and labor movement, 136, 144–45, 175, 234–35
  marriage of, 144–45; *see also* Hillman, Bessie Abramowitz
Abzug, Bella, 233, 240, 245, 251, 255
Adams, Abigail, 27–28
Adams, John, 28
Addams, Jane, 62, 87, 154, 196
Adler, Pearl "Polly," 125–26, 132
Adler, Rachel, "The Jew Who Wasn't There," 246
African Americans:
  birth control clinics for, 153
  as household help, 163–64
  and Jim Crow, 211
Against Our Will: Men, Women, and Rape (Brownmiller), 241–42
Albright, Madeleine, 260
Alexander II, Tsar, assassination of, 55
All But My Life (Klein), 226
Alpert, Rebecca, 257
Amalgamated Clothing Workers of America, 134, 144–45, 175, 234
American, Sadie, 77

American Civil Liberties Union, 241
American Federation of Teachers, 181
American Hebrew, The, 177
American Israelite, The, 78–79
American Jewess, The, 61–64, 76–77, 79–80, 87, 88, 150
American Jewesses, 55–108
  activities outside the home, 59–61, 86–99, 101–7
  and charity movement, 89–92
  cookbooks and food, 69–70
  cultural activities, 70–72
  fundraising efforts of, 91–92, 93
  and Hadassah, *see* Hadassah
  influence of, 94, 107
  and Jewish definition, 86–87
  ladies' auxiliaries, 92–94
  marriage of, *see* marriage
  as mission workers, 90, 104
  Mothers in Israel, 64–65, 73, 74, 88–89
  moving across the country, 58–59
  and "new kind of Jewess," 55–56, 108, 109
  and religion, *see* religion
  sisterhoods, 89–94, 101–2, 105
  traditions of benevolence, 88–90
  women's associations, 86–94, 101
  workingwomen, 100, 103, 105–6
  as writers, 59–61, 71, 72, 76–77, 98
  and Zionism, 89, 95–97, 98–101
American Jewish Conference, 212

American Jewish Congress, 204, 250, 251
American Jewish Year Book, 89, 98
American Peace Society, 154
American Poalei Zion Party, 191, 203–4
American Revolution, 24–26
  charitable activities during, 24, 32
  deaths in, 26
  Jewish exile in, 24, 25, 26
  loyalty to the Crown in, 24, 25
  social life in, 26
  women as heads of household in, 25–26
American Union Against Militarism, 154
American Women, 235
Amos 'n' Andy, 169
anarchists, 135
Anne Frank: The Diary of a Young Girl
  (Frank), 226, 241
Anthony, Susan B., 61, 62, 80, 87
Antin, Fetchke (Frieda), 129
Antin, Israel, 113
Antin, Mary, 117, 129, 147, 161
  The Promised Land, 113
antisemitism, 199–205
  against children, 65, 201
  in Civil War, 43–45
  confrontation/defense against, 50–51,
    52–53, 83, 188, 203–4
  in Europe and Russia, 95, 96, 106–7, 110,
    154, 199–200, 204–5, 258–59
  and Henry Ford, 200
  and *Gentleman's Agreement,* 232–33
  in international conferences, 250–51, 252
  and Jewishness, 95, 203
  and Miss America, 219–20
  and Nazis, *see* Nazi Party
  restrictions on Jews, 44, 106–7, 159, 161,
    181, 200, 201, 206
  in social events, 202
  in the South, 200
  in U.S. politics, 193
  and white slavery, 84
  in women's movement, 107, 236–37, 251,
    255
  at work, 176, 180, 209–10
  and World War II, 209–10
  and Zionism, 95–96, 251–52
Apte, Day, 72
Apte, Helen Jacobus, 72–75, 86, 95, 166,
  200
Arab uprising (1936), 192
Arlington National Cemetery, 41
Asbury Park, New Jersey, 118
Asch, Sholem, *God of Vengeance,* 228

Ashkenazic Jews, 10, 56
Astaire, Fred, 170
"Aunt Babette's" Cook Book (Kramer),
  69–70
Auschwitz, 179, 225, 226
Australia, Hebrew schools in, 34
Austria-Hungary:
  Jewish immigration from, 56, 73
  and World War I, 107, 153
Azaria, Rachel, 253

Bacall, Lauren (Betty Perske), 203
Bachman, Hannah (Einstein), 101–2
Balfour Declaration, 156
Baltimore:
  Bureau for Contraceptive Advice, 152
  family economy in, 120
  garment industry in, 119, 131, 143
  German immigrants in, 70
  Hebrew schools in, 34
  Hutzler's in, 165
  night school in, 127
  Russian Jewish settlers in, 97–98, 112
Baltimore Hebrew College and Teachers
    Training School, 184
Bank of the United States, 193
Bara, Theda, 170
Baright, Clarice M., 177
bar mitzvah, 38–40, 182–83, 259
Barnard, Frederick A. P., 105
Barnard College, New York, 105, 106
Barry, Julia Wald, 80
Bass, Morris, 74
Bat, Luba, 179, 226
bat mitzvah, 39, 182–83, 246, 247, 259
Baum, Charlotte, xii
Beat Generation, 229–30
Beck, Evelyn Torton, *Nice Jewish Girls: A
    Lesbian Anthology,* 257
Belgium, and World War I, 107, 153
Ben-Zvi, Rahel Yanait, 191
Berg, Gertrude, 169–70
Bernays, Anne, 220
Bintel Brief (Bundle of Letters), 135
birth control, 15, 73–74, 85, 150–53, 157,
  162–63, 219, 222, 233, 243
Birthright, 261
B'nai B'rith, 82, 150, 187, 248
Bondi, August, 42
Booth, Heather, 243
Boston:
  garment workers in, 131, 143
  Jewish immigrants in, 112

kosher meat boycott in, 145
Mayyim Hayyim *mikveh* in, 249
social services in, 46
Boston Investigator, 50
Boston Women's Health Book Collective,
    Our Bodies, Our Selves, 243
Bradwell, Myra, 64
Brandeis, Louis D., 97, 189, 197
Brazil, Holy Inquisition in, 9
Brice, Fanny, 170, 203
Bridges, 257
Brill, Doris, 211
Britain:
    and American Revolution, 24–26
    and Balfour Declaration, 156
    immigration to Palestine restricted by,
        187, 212
    and War of 1812, 4
    and World War I, 107, 153
Brooklyn College, New York, 180
Brooks, Fanny, 58, 59
Brooks, Julius, 58
Brothers, Joyce Bauer, 217, 220–21, 234
Brownmiller, Susan, 240
    *Against Our Will: Men, Women, and
        Rape,* 241–42
Bryant, Lena Himmelstein, 165–66, 178
Buchdahl, Angela, 260
Bueno, Rachell and Joseph, 11
Butler, Benjamin F., 42–43
Byrne, Ethel, 152

Cable Act (1922), 84–85
California, mining camps in, 58
Carnegie, Hattie (Henrietta Köningeiser),
    178
Central Europe, Jewish immigration from,
    33, 55–56, 58
Charity Organization Societies, 89–90
Charleston:
    British occupation of (1778), 24–26
    Hebrew schools in, 34
    religious reforms in, 30, 37, 38
Chernin, Rose, 196, 227
Chicago:
    Columbian Exposition in, 60, 82, 85
    garment workers in, 114, 119, 130, 131,
        143, 144, 174
    German immigrants in, 70
    Jewish families in, 58, 70–71
    Jewish Ladies' Sewing Society, 82
    Lawndale suburb of, 159–60
    "new women" in, 62

Russian immigrants in, 113–14
social services in, 46
tenants' union in, 146
Chicago Woman's Club, 71, 80, 87
childbirth:
    birth control, *see* birth control
    birth rates, 73, 74, 81, 219
    dangers of, 5, 75–76
    in hospital, 75, 166
    infant mortality, 15, 75, 158
    infertility, 256
    midwives for, 75, 166
    obstetricians for, 166
    patterns of, 15
    and twilight sleep, 166
children, 14–15
    antisemitism against, 65, 201
    Baby Boom, 219
    confirmation of, 38–40
    delinquent, 90, 102
    education of, 14, 20, 28, 34–35, 65, 90,
        101, 104, 126, 158, 166–67
    infant deaths, 15, 75, 158
    Jewish law fulfilled by, 256
    Jewish refugees, 206–7, 213
    kindergartens, 87
    lack of, 256
    marriage prospects of, 23
    orphanages for, *see* orphanages
    parents' dreams for, 119, 128, 170, 193,
        198, 260
    raising, as mothers' most important job,
        166
    selling matches, 34
    starving, 116
    summer camps for, 134, 167, 184
    traditions passed to next generation,
        23, 26
    women nursing babies, 15
Christmas trees, 67
cigarettes, 168
Cincinnati:
    "queen city of the west," 39
    Sisterhood Sabbath in, 94
citizenship, 85, 102, 149
Civil Rights Act (1964), 187, 237
Civil War, U.S., 41–49
    absence of men during, 47–48
    aftermath of, 51–53
    antisemitism in, 43–45
    Confederacy in, 41–45, 48–49, 53
    death toll of, 82
    Emancipation Proclamation, 48–49

Civil War, U.S. (*continued*)
  espionage charges in, 43
  experiences in the North, 45–47, 48
  firing on Fort Sumter, 53
  honoring the dead, 52
  illiterate soldiers in, 43
  and Lost Cause, 52
  Loyal Leagues in, 49
  Needle Pickets in, 46–47
  popular opinion against, 48–49
  state secession in, 41
  surrender at Appomattox, 52, 53
  U.S. Sanitary Commission in, 46–47
  women's organizations in, 42–43, 47
  women widowed by, 76
Cleveland Jewish Orphan Asylum, 63
clothing:
  in eighteenth century, 10–11
  in nineteenth century, xi, 62, 113–14
  in seventeenth century, 10
  in twentieth century, 178
  see also garment industry
Cohen, Hettie, 229, 232
Cohen, Katherine M., 77
Cohen, Mary M., 77
Cohen, Miriam Moses, 41
Cohen, Moses J., 195–96
Cohen, Rose, 258, 261
Cohn, Fania, 174
Cold War, 218, 230, 233, 234
Collis, Charles T., 47
Collis, Septima Levy, 47
Columbian Exposition, Chicago, 60, 82, 85
Columbia University, 102, 104–5, 240, 241,
    242, 245
Columbus, Christopher, 4, 90
Committee for Protective Labor Legisla-
    tion, 234
common law of coverture, 11
Communist Party, 174, 196–99, 218, 259
  and Depression, 196–98
  and HUAC, 227–28, 231, 232, 233
  and red-diaper babies, 198
Comstock, Ada, 209–10
Comstock, Anthony, 73–74
Comstock Act (1873), 73, 135, 150, 152
Conservative Judaism, 17, 63
  bat mitzvah in, 182–83
  and family size, 256
  and feminism, 245, 246
  mixed seating in, 181–82
  sisterhoods, 94, 161, 182
  women rabbis in, 247, 249

consumer protections, 101
Consumers League, New York, 105–6
Coolidge, Calvin, 177
Corwin, Margaret, 202
Cosella Wayne (Wilburn), 72
cosmetics industry, 178
Costa, Isaac da, 25
Coughlin, Father Charles, 201, 204
Cowen, Elise, 229
Crosby, Bing, 169

D'Arwin (pseud.), 60, 71, 98
Daughters of Israel, 89
Daughters of the American Revolution, 154
Daughters of Zion, 99, 100
Dawidowicz, Lucy, 195, 199, 200, 252
"Day of Dead Soldiers, The" (Lazarus), 53
Deborah (prophetess and judge), 64
Deborah groups, 89
Declaration of Independence, 26, 49
Declaration of Mexico, 251
Delancey, Oliver, 13
Dennis, Peggy, 161, 197
Denver, National Jewish Hospital in, 63, 90
Der Fraynd (*The Friend*), 135
Der Tog, 135
Deutsch, Helene, *The Psychology of
    Women*, 206
Dewey, John, 195
Diamant, Anita, *The Red Tent*, 249
Die Deborah, 61
dietary laws, *see kashrut*
Dreier, Mary, 138
Dreyfus, Alfred, 96
Dubinsky, David, 175

Eastern Europe:
  Jewish immigrants from, 91, 108, 109,
    130, 158, 181
  Jewish women in America, 109–56
  World War I in, 97, 155
  and Zionism, 96
Eastern European Jewish women in Amer-
    ica, 109–56
  activism of, 147
  arrival in U.S., 55–56, 111–12
  assimilation, 112–14, 117–19, 147
  birth control 150–53
  dreams for their children, 119, 128
  earning money, 114, 115, 116, 119–21,
    129–47
  education, 126–29
  immigrant experiences, 108, 110–11

keeping house, 114–19
missing husbands, 117, 121–23
and pianos as symbol of assimilation, 118
sending money back home, 119
sexual abuse and prostitution, 124–26
vacations, 118–19
voting rights, 147–50, 156
and World War I, 153–56
and Zionism, 156
Edgeworth, Maria, 29
Education Act (1972), 239
Educational Alliance, New York, 103
Einstein, Hannah Bachman, 91, 101–2, 107
Einstein, William, 101
Eisenhower, Dwight D., 227
electricity, in the home, 81
Ellis Island, New York, 84, 109, 110, 112, 122
Elwell, Sue Levi, 257
Emancipation Proclamation, 48–49
Emergency Home Relief Bureau, 123
Emergency Quota Act (1921), 158
English language classes, 97, 103, 127
English-language immersion, 104
Enlightenment, 37
Equal Employment Opportunity Commission, 237
Equal Pay Act (1963), 237
Equal Rights Amendment, 186, 251
Esther, Queen, 80, 99
Europe:
    antisemitism in, 95, 96, 106–7, 110, 154, 199–200, 204–5
    Hitler's threat to, 203
    Jewishness in, 95
    Jewish refugees from, 33, 55–56, 58, 70, 204–7, 213–14, 237, 252
    Jews attempting to escape, 204, 212–13
    modernization in, 37, 38
    postwar aid to, 214–15
    as world in transition, 110–11
    World War I in, 97, 107, 153
Evans, Jane, 203, 217, 235
"Exodus, The" (Lazarus), 4
Ezekiel, Catherine, 41
Ezekiel, Moses, 41
Ezra, biblical, 96
Ezrat Nashim, 245–46, 248, 250

Faier, Gerry, 229
family:
    birth rates, 73, 74, 81, 219
    caregivers, 158
    gender divide in, 161–62

infant mortality, 15, 75, 158
and intermarriage, *see* marriage
nuclear, 218
size of, 14, 73, 74, 163, 196, 219; *see also* birth control
fascism, 197, 199
fashion industry, 178
FBI, 227, 231
Fechheimer, Emily (Seasongood), 39–40
Federation of American Zionists, 97, 99
Federation of Jewish Women's Organizations, 209
Feigenbaum, Benjamin, 138
Female Association for the Relief of Women and Children in Reduced Circumstances, Philadelphia, 32–33
Feminine Mystique, The (Friedan), 236–37
Feminist Press, 244
Ferber, Edna, 202–3
Finkbine, Sherri Chessen (Miss Sherri), 223, 224
First Zionist Congress (1897), 96
Fisher, Phyllis, 208–9
Fishman, Sylvia Barack, 256
Ford, Henry, 154
    The International Jew: The World's Foremost Problem, 200
Forward (Forverts), 135–36, 142, 149, 198
Fourteenth Amendment, 51
France:
    antisemitism in, 95, 96
    Dreyfus affair in, 96
    and World War I, 107, 153
Frank, Anne, 205, 226, 241
Frank, Edith, 205
Frank, Leo, 200
Frank, Margot, 205
Frank, Ray, 63, 98
Frankfurter, Felix, 241
Franks, Abigaill Levy, 12, 13, 14, 15, 18, 19, 20, 22–23, 26
Franks, David, 23, 26
Franks, Jacob, 12–13, 26
Franks, Moses, 14
Franks, Naphtali, 12, 13, 14, 15, 19, 22, 23
Franks, Phila (Delancey), 13, 18, 22–23, 172
Franks, Rachel (Solomon), 14
Franks, Rebecca, 26
Franks, Richa, 13, 18
Freedman, Marcia, 250
Friedan, Betty (Goldstein), 217, 232, 235, 238, 250, 251
    The Feminine Mystique, 236–37

garment industry, 113–14
 home workers in, 115, 119–20, 174
 improving working conditions in, 106
 mass production in, 130
 piecework, 131
 strikes in, 136–40, 143–45, 174
 sweatshops in, 114, 115, 119–20, 129–32
 unions in, 103, 134, 139–40, 143–44, 145, 173, 174, 234
Gentleman's Agreement (Hobson), 232–33
Germany:
 annexation of Austria by, 242
 antisemitism in, 95, 199
 economic boycott against, 204
 Jewish immigration from, 33, 56, 59, 70, 73, 74, 78, 237
 Kristallnacht, 199
 Nazi Party in, *see* Nazi Party
 Poland invaded by, 207, 212
 religious reforms in, 30
 and Soviet Union, 198
 submarine attacks by, 154
 and World War I, 107, 112, 153–54
 World War II surrender, 214
Ginsburg, Martin, 241
Ginsburg, Ruth Bader, xiv, 240–41
Ginzberg, Louis, 76
 Legends of the Jews, 98
God, Abraham's covenant with, 21
Godey's Lady's Book, 29–30
God of Vengeance (Asch), 228
Goldberg, Molly (fict.), 169–70
Goldman, Emma, 135, 155, 196
 Why and How the Poor Should Not Have Many Children, 152
Gomez, Amelia, 27
Gomez, David, 13
Gomez, Esther, 13
Gomez, Luis (Louis), 13
Gomez, Rebecca, 27
Gomez, Sarah, 27
Gomez family, 12, 23, 27
Good Housekeeping, 81
Gornish, Jean, 169
Gotsfeld, Bessie, 190
Gottheil, Emma, 99
Gottheil, Gustav, 99
Graf, Matilda "Bobbi," 231–32
Grant, Ulysses S., 44–45, 47, 53
Gratz, Barnard, 24
Gratz, Rachel, 24–25
Gratz, Rebecca, 31, 32–36, 37, 41, 50, 51, 67, 76, 89

Great Depression, 123, 163, 169, 190
 blame placed on Jews for, 201
 and Communism, 196–98
 stock market collapse and, 192–96
 unemployment in, 180, 206
Great War, *see* World War I
Greco, Charlie, 172, 173
Greenebaum, Henriette, 71
Greenebaum, Michael, 58, 61, 70
Greenebaum, Sarah Spiegel, 58, 61, 68, 70, 74, 81–82, 89
Griswold v. Connecticut, 150
Grobsmith, Lonia, 174
Groen, Ethel, 201
Grossinger, Malke and Asher, 118–19
Gruber, Ruth, 213–14

Hadassah, 179, 248
 and fundraising, 168, 190
 growth of, 187, 188, 252
 and Halprin, 230–31
 and Holocaust, 212, 215
 leadership skills developed in, 134, 148, 192
 and Lindheim, 86, 185, 191–92, 247
 and Palestine, 100, 212–13, 215
 and Szold, 97, 99–100, 185, 189, 192, 207, 213
 and World War II, 209, 212
 and Zionism, 99, 100–101, 148, 188–92, 230
Halprin, Rose, 204, 230–31
Hamlin, Caroline, *see* Spiegel, Caroline
Handler, Ruth, 217, 234
Hanukkah, Jewish dishes for, 19
Harper's New Monthly, 52
Hart, Esther, 25
Hart, Jacob, 2
Hart, Louisa B., 77
Hart, Schaffner, and Marx, 144
Harvard Law School, 240, 241
Hasidic Jews, 257–58, 261
Hatkin, Eleanor (Schulman), 172, 218, 220, 222
Hatkin, Rose, 160, 172
Hays, Abigail, 27–28
Hays, Gitlah, 22
Hays, Grace Mears Levy, 17
Hays, Hetty, 19
Hays, Josse, 21–22
health care:
 inadequate, 101
 for the poor, 102–3
 and women, 157–58, 187, 189, 248, 249, 261

Healy, Bernadine, 249
Hebrew Ladies' Benevolent Society, Quincy, 46
Hebrew language, 97
Hebrew Orphan Asylum, 121
Hebrew Sunday school, invention of (1838), 34
Hebrew Union College, 93, 185, 247
Hellman, Lillian, 197, 198
Hertzberg, Anna, 204–5
Herzig, Chaie, 251
Herzl, Theodore, 95, 96
Hillman, Bessie Abramowitz, 159, 257, 258, 261
    activism of, 144–45, 146, 148, 175, 186, 234–35
    see also Abramowitz, Bessie
Hillman, Sidney (Simcha "Shimkhe"), 144–45, 179, 234–35
Hitler, Adolf, 106, 170, 199, 203, 204, 207
Hobson, Laura Z., *Gentleman's Agreement*, 232–33
holidays:
    conception during, 74
    and Sabbath traditions, *see* Sabbath
    work forbidden during, 19
Holocaust, 188, 207, 212, 242, 244, 252, 260
    children to replace those lost in, 256
    second generation, 224, 226–27
Holocaust memory, 215, 226
Holocaust survivors, 224, 225–27, 259
homemaking:
    and business ventures, 16, 177–81, 206
    keeping kosher, *see kashrut*
    postwar, 218, 230–31
    school classes in, 91, 166–67
    as traditional focus of women, 50, 64–65, 69, 83, 97, 102, 114–19, 116, 163
    see also children; family; marriage
homosexuality, 228–29
Hoovervilles, 196
household goods:
    eighteenth century, 10–12
    ownership of, 11, 17, 32, 49–50
House Un-American Activities Committee (HUAC), 227, 231, 232, 233
Howe, Florence, 243–44
Hull House, Chicago, 87
Hungary, Jewish immigration from, 57, 260
Hungry Hearts (Yezierska), 195
Hunter College, New York, 129, 180, 195, 219

Hurst, Fannie, 209
Hyman, Paula, xii, 245

Ickes, Harold, 213–14
Illinois Industrial School for Girls, 87
industrialization, 101
industrial revolution, 130
industrial schools, 90, 127
influenza pandemic (1918), 112, 153
International Jew: The World's Foremost Problem, The (Ford), 200
International Ladies' Garment Workers' Union (ILGWU), 134, 137–38, 174
International Women's Decade, 250–51
International Women's Strike USA, 255
"In the Jewish Synagogue at Newport" (Lazarus), 5, 18
Isaacs, Jennet, 28
Israel:
    Arab-Israeli dialogue, 253
    expanding settlements in, 253
    feminists in, 250, 254–55, 256
    as Jewish homeland, 95, 96–97, 100, 215, 230, 252
    kibbutzim in, 192, 249–50
    Knesset, 250, 253
    new state of, 230, 231
    and Palestinian self-determination, 253
    return to, 95
    settlers in, 86
    Six-Day War (1967), 244, 252
    as socialist state, 191
    Western Wall in, 244, 255
    women in army, 249
    and Zionism, 86, 89, 95–99, 251
Israelitischer Frauen Verein, 89
Israel Women's Network, 250

Jacobs, Frances Wisebart, 90, 107
Jacobs, Rose, 215
Jane (abortion referral service), 243
Jastrow, Rachel Szold, 68, 70
Jazz Singer, The (movie), 170
Jewish Agency for Palestine, 213, 231
Jewish Arbitration Court, 173
Jewish community:
    and antisemitism, 43–45, 52–53, 106, 159, 181, 200, 201, 206
    children in, *see* children
    citizenship in, 37
    counterculture, 244–49
    defining Jews, *see* Jewishness
    diversity in, 9

Jewish community (*continued*)
  education in, 34, 101, 184
  foster homes in, 35
  ghettoes, 37, 114
  havurot in, 244–45
  immigrants in, 30–31, 33, 44, 56–57,
    70–71, 101
  mission schools, 83
  "new kind of Jewess" in, *see* "new kind
    of Jewess"
  orphanages in, *see* orphanages
  portrayal in literature, 29
  poverty in, *see* poverty
  proper Jewish homes in, 69
  public associations in, 31, 36, 71
  seventeenth century, 9–12
  shtetls, 257
  size of, 23
  social divide in, 31
  social mobility in, 159
  study circles, 83
  suburban, 219
  twenty-first century, 256–58
Jewish Cookery Book (Levy), 68–69
Jewish Denominational Congress, 82–83
Jewish Home Beautiful (Conservative
    Judaism), 94, 161
"Jewish Home Beautiful" pageants, 160
Jewish labor movement, 136–40
  old Jewish oath, 139
  and Triangle fire, 143
  and women's suffrage, 149
Jewish law:
  adaptations and changes in, 37, 117
  children required by, 256
  dietary laws, *see* kashrut
  divorce (*get*) in, 14, 122, 123, 222, 254
  on education, 128
  on female modesty, 257
  feminist challenges to, 245, 246, 247
  on marital relations, 15-16, 136, 185,
    276n37
  of *mikveh*, 15–16, 37, 181, 185
  moral laws, 38
Jewish men:
  action in American Revolution, 24
  assimilation of, 66, 206
  circumcision, 21
  Civil War soldiers, 52–53
  commercial activities of, 16, 26, 79
  and divorce, *see* marriage
  enabled by women, 66, 206, 236
  freedom to travel, 23

  and gender differences, 31, 129
  missing husbands, 117, 121–23, 225
  organizations excluding women, 245, 248
  protective of women, 42
  searching for a wife, 58
  skullcaps worn by, 38
  traditional roles of, 31, 35, 161–62
  unable to support wives, 33
  unfaithful, 60, 123
Jewish Messenger, The, 47, 60, 71, 98
Jewishness (Jewish identity), xiii, 66–67
  and antisemitism, 95, 203, 236–37
  and feminism, 107, 236–37, 256
  gender differences in responsibilities of, 86
  heritage of, 116, 161
  in mixed families, 172
  neighborhoods, 160–61
  racial definition of, 85–87, 95
  religious definition of, 86
  sharing biological ancestry, 85
  uniqueness of, 86, 261–62
Jewish New Year, 67
"Jewish Problem, The" (Lazarus), 95–96
Jewish Publication Society of America
    (JPS), 98, 99
Jewish Telegraphic Agency, 177
Jewish Woman in America, The (Baum,
    Hyman, Michel), xii
Jewish women:
  activities outside the home, 243–49
  aid to refugees, 205–7
  collective Jewish female past of, 262
  diversity of, 257, 260–61
  and feminism, 235–49
  sisterhoods, 235–36
  see also American Jewesses; Eastern
    European Jewish women in America
Jewish Women International, 248
Jewish Women's Congress, 61
"Jewish Women's Movement," 246
Jews:
  antisemitism against, *see* antisemitism
  assimilation of, 66, 67, 86, 91, 112–14,
    117–19, 126, 128, 135–36, 147, 202–3, 205
  blamed for death of Jesus, 43–44
  diaspora of, 4, 10, 45, 55, 109
  particularity of, *see* Jewishness
  population of, 57
  in urban tenements, 114–19
  in World War I, 153
Jochannah Lodge, 82, 89
Johnson, Joyce Glassman, 229–30
Johnson, Sonia, 251

Joint Emergency Committee for European Jewish Affairs, 212
Jolson, Al, 170
Jonas, Abraham, 46
Jonas, Annie (Wells), 46
Jones, LeRoi (later Amiri Baraka), 229
Josephson, Manuel, 16
Judah, Abigail, 12
Judaism:
   adapting, 37, 56
   conversion from other religions to, 41, 48, 78
   conversion to Christianity, 40
   fundamental tenets of, 20, 40
   gender discrimination in, 39
   modernization of, 36–40, 247
   mourning ritual (*kriah*), 79
   split of, 17–18
   studying, 83
   see also Jewish law

Kahn, Florence Prag, 233
Kahn, Morris, 151–52
Kaplan, Judith (Eisenstein), 182–83, 247
Kaplan, Mordecai, 182–83, 247
kashrut (kosher) dietary laws:
   keeping kosher, 19–20, 69, 70, 116–17, 161, 164, 219
   kosher meat boycott, 145–46
   kosher plates and utensils, 19–20
   and *"Trefa"* (unkosher foods), 70, 164
   Yes, I Keep Kosher, 94
Kennedy, Jacqueline, 259
Kennedy, John F., 234, 235, 259
Keren Hayesod Women's League, 99
Kerouac, Jack, 229
King, Carole, 217, 222–23
King James Bible, 34
Kinsey, Alfred, *Sexual Behavior in the Human Female*, 228–29
Klein, Gerda Weissman, 217, 225
   All But My Life, 226
Klosk, Louis, 194
Kohner, Hanna Bloch, 225
Kramer, Bertha F., *"Aunt Babette's" Cook Book*, 69–70
Kritzer, Eva, 210–11
Krugman, Marian Gold, 210
Ku Klux Klan, 232
Kussy, Sarah, 189

Labor Relations Board (LRB), 176
Ladies' Home Journal, 81, 241, 242

Lake Michigan, vacations at, 118
Lakeview Home, Staten Island, 103–4
Lane Bryant stores, 165–66
"Latch Keys for Women" (Sonneschein), 76–77
Lauder, Estée (Josephine Esther Mentzer), 178
Lazarus, Aaron, 28
Lazarus, Emma, 3–7, 50, 76, 88, 97, 108
   ancestors of, 56
   "The Day of Dead Soldiers," 53
   death of, 109
   "The Exodus," 4
   on immigration, 10, 31, 44
   "In the Jewish Synagogue at Newport," 5, 18
   "The Jewish Problem," 95–96
   legacy of, 6–7, 9, 104
   "The New Colossus," 3, 31
   and new Jewish immigrants, 55–56, 109
   and social divide, 31
   and Statue of Liberty, 3
   and Zionism, 95–96
Lazarus, Esther, 33
Lazarus, Josephine, 77
Lazarus, Rachel Mordecai, 28–29, 31, 40, 43, 75
League of Women Voters, 230
Lee, Robert E., 52, 53
Leeser, Isaac, 34, 37
Legends of the Jews (Ginzberg), 98
Leiserson's, 137–38
Lemlich, Clara (Shavelson), 130, 137–38, 140, 145, 148–49, 198–99
Lerner, Gerda Kronstein, 157, 235, 242–43
lesbianism, 228–29, 257, 261
Lesbian Rabbis: The First Generation (Alpert and Elwell, eds.), 257
Levine, Jacqueline, 250
Levy, Abigaill (Franks), 12
Levy, Esther, *Jewish Cookery Book*, 68–69
Levy, Grace Mears, 4
Levy, Michael, 14
Levy, Moses, 4
Levy, Rachel Phillips, 14
Levy, Rachel (Seixas), 4, 12
Levy, Septima (Collis), 47
Levy, Zipporah (Seixas), 13, 14
Levy-Franks family, 13
Lewisohn, Irene, 77
Life, 242
Lilienthal, Max, 39
Lilith, 248, 250, 251

Lincoln, Abraham, 45, 46, 47
    and Emancipation Proclamation, 48–49
Lindheim, Irma Levy, 86, 155, 161, 185,
    191–92, 247
Lindsay, John V., 240
"Lines on the Persecution of the Jews of
    Damascus" (Moïse), 44
Litman, Selma, 175–76, 254
Little League, 239, 243
Loehmann, Frieda, 178
Loehmann's, 178
Los Alamos, 209
Lost Cause, 52
Loyal Leagues, 49
Lubavitcher sect, 258
"lungers" (TB victims), 90
Lushan, Hannah, 225

Mack, Rebecca, 171, 173
magazines, in nineteenth century, 61, 81
Magdalen home for wayward girls, 125
mah-jongg, 168, 261
Maiden Form Brassiere Company, 178
Maloney, Helen Wise, 79, 80
Maloney, James, 79
Manischewitz, 169
marriage:
    age discrepancies in, 12–13, 16–17
    "A Marriage Agreement," 242
    annulment, 172–73
    average ages at, 13, 257
    avoidance of, 36, 256
    and birth control, 15, 150–53
    breakups of, 121–23
    changing ideas about, 77
    chuppah (canopy) for, 14
    companionate, 163
    and divorce, 14, 23, 60, 122, 123, 135–36,
        222, 245, 246, 254
    and duty, 77
    early years of, 73
    economic significance of, 13
    in eighteenth century, 12–16, 78
    and family, 14–15
    in Great Depression, 195–96
    as imperative for women, 64, 129, 220
    intermarriage, 22–23, 66, 78–80, 171–73,
        225
    Jewish traditions in, 13–14, 15–16, 276n37
    and jobs, 176, 180–81
    lesbian, 257
    and love, 77
    new bridal traditions in, 40
    in nineteenth century, 4–5, 78
    parental approval of, 13, 49
    postwar, 218
    preparations for, 73
    prospects for, 23
    purposes of, 13, 27
    time to marry, 57–58
    in wartime, 208, 222
    women's rights in, 238–39
marriage contract (*ketubah*), 13–14
Marx, Karl, 110, 111
Marx Brothers, 170
mass production, 130
Mattel Toy Company, 234
May Day parades, 134
McCarthy, Joseph, 227, 231, 232
McGinity, Keren, 171
Meir, Golda (Goldie Meyerson), 191, 192,
    204
Mercado, Judith, 9
Meyer, Annie Nathan, 79, 104–5, 106, 107,
    147
mezuzah, 69, 115, 219
Michel, Sonya, xii
mikveh (ritual bath), 15–16, 28, 37, 40, 181,
    185–86, 248
Miller, Betty, 259
Miller, Frieda, 228
Milwaukee, charitable activities in, 91–92
Mindell, Fania, 152
Minis, Abigail, 17, 23, 25, 27
Minis, Hannah, 17, 23
minyan (ten men required for prayer), 11,
    40, 183, 245, 246
Miss America, 157, 194, 219–20, 242
Mississippi Freedom Summer, 243–44
Mizrachi Organization of Religious Zion-
    ists, 190
Mizrachi Women's Organization of Amer-
    ica (AMIT), 190
Moïse, Abraham, 30
Moïse, Penina, 29–31, 34, 41, 76
    "Lines on the Persecution of the Jews of
        Damascus," 44
Moravia, Martha, 18
Mordecai, Emma, 43, 45, 51
Mordecai, Rachel (Lazarus), 28–29, 31, 40,
    43, 75
Morgenthau, Elinor, 213
Morgenthau, Henry, Jr., 201
Mormons, 251
Moses, Bessie, 152
Moses, Octavia Harby, 52

Moskowitz, Belle, 75–76, 88, 103–4, 107, 125
Moskowitz, Faye, 194
Mother Goose, 44
Mothers in Israel, 64–65, 73, 74, 88–89
Mothers of Sons Forum, 201
Mount Sinai, 39
movies, 170, 226, 232
Ms., 224, 239
mutual aid societies, 135
Myers, Rachel, 27–28
Myerson, Bella, 179, 194
Myerson, Bess, 194, 217, 219–20, 222

Nadel, Pearl, 208
Napoleon Bonaparte, 30
Nathan, Benjamin, 13, 14
Nathan, Frederick, 105
Nathan, Grace Mendes Seixas, 3–7, 29, 37
   deathbed of, 5
   descendents of, 14, 33
   fundraising by, 18
   legacy of, 6–7, 9, 55
   marriage to Simon, 12–16
   mother of, 12
Nathan, Leah, 14
Nathan, Maud, 88, 104, 105–7, 147, 154, 155, 201
Nathan, Simon, 4–5, 12–16, 24
National American Woman Suffrage Association, 77
National Association for the Advancement of Colored People (NAACP), 103, 164
National Council of Jewish Women, 63, 77, 83–85, 124, 230, 252
   and civil rights, 231
   and Equal Rights Amendment, 186
   founding of, 83
   and immigration issues, 84, 85, 93, 149, 204, 214
   leadership skills developed in, 134, 187
   mission of, 83, 84, 186, 248
   and Moskowitz, 103–4
   and Simon, 92–93
   and Solomon, 80, 83, 85, 148
   and woman suffrage, 147, 148
National Desertion Bureau, 123
National Federation of Temple Sisterhoods, 94, 182, 203, 235; *see also* Women of Reform Judaism
National Institutes of Health, 249
National Jewish Women's Organizations, 187

National League for Woman's Service, 155
National Organization for Women (NOW), 237
National Recovery Administration, 176
National Woman Suffrage Association, 87
National Women's Studies Association, 250
Nazi Party, 187, 188, 237
   attacks on Jews, 85, 190, 193, 199, 203–4
   concentration camps of, 179, 199, 205, 214, 219, 225, 226
   exterminating Jews as goal of, 212–14
   rescuing Jews from, 204, 213
   and Warsaw Ghetto Uprising, 215
Needle Pickets, 46–47
Netanyahu, Benjamin, 253
Neumark, Martha (Montor), 185
New Amsterdam:
   antisemitism in, 44
   immigrants to, 9–10
   see also New York
Newark, New Jersey:
   Bamberger's in, 165
   factory fire in, 143
   Hadassah in, 189
   Weequahic High School, 218–19, 225
"New Colossus, The" (Lazarus), 3, 31
New Deal, 176, 195
New Jewish Agenda, 253, 257
"new kind of Jewess," *see* Eastern European Jewish women in America
Newman, Pauline, 133, 137, 140, 145, 146, 149, 228, 257
New Orleans:
   Civil War in, 42, 43
   ladies' auxiliary in, 92
Newport, and Revolution, 24, 26
newspapers, foreign-language, 135–36
Newsweek, 238–39, 260
New York:
   Adoption Services, 224
   Ahios Mizrahi (Sisters of Mizrachi), 190
   B. Altman's in, 165
   British occupation of (1776), 24, 25, 26
   Cooper Union in, 138
   Federation of Sisterhoods, 101–2
   first confirmation in, 39
   first synagogue (1730) in, 11, 15
   garment industry in, 119–20, 131, 140–45, 174
   Great Hebrew Fair in (1895), 92
   Greenwich Village, 229–30
   Havurah, 245

New York (*continued*)
  Henry Street Settlement in, 76, 103, 154, 179
  immigrants to, 9–10, 159
  intermarriage in, 78
  Jewish Institute for Religion, 247
  Jewish Theological Seminary, 98, 247
  kosher meat boycott in, 145–46
  Lower East Side, 112, 127, 131, 136–37, 142, 146
  mikveh in, 16, 185
  Nurses Settlement in, 102–3
  prostitution in, 124, 126
  rent strikes in, 146
  social services in, 46, 91
  State Emigrant Refuge, Ward's Island, 55, 56, 108, 109, 273n1
  teachers in, 180–81
  Triangle fire in, 140–43
  union activities in, 234
  women's march for equality, 238
  women's suffrage in, 148
New York Consumers League, 105–6
New York Herald, The, 48
New York Medical Journal, 151
New York Society for the Suppression of Vice, 73–74
New York State:
  bungalow colonies (kuchalayns) in, 118–19, 168
  Catskills "Borscht Belt," 118–19
  Industrial Code, 143
  Widowed Mothers Pension Act (1915), 102
New York Times, The, 106, 246, 255
New York University, 177
New York World's Fair (1939), 160
Nice Jewish Girls: A Lesbian Anthology (Beck), 257
Nightingale, Florence, 5
  Notes on Nursing, 43
Nineteenth Amendment, 149–50, 157
Nixon, Richard M., 243
nuclear arms race, 233
Nuland, Sherwin, 119
Nunes, Ricke, 9

O Magazine, 249
One Survivor Remembers (film), 226
Orff, Annie Laurie Y., 61, 82
orphanages, 33, 34–35, 82, 102, 116, 121
Orthodox Judaism, 17, 63
  and bat mitzvah, 183
  and divorce, 254

  feminism in, 247, 250, 255, 261
  marriage in, 256–58
  and *mikveh,* 185
  sisterhoods, 94, 182
Other Things Being Equal (Wolf), 79
Ottoman Empire:
  immigrants from, 109
  and World War I, 107, 153
"Our Baltimore Letter" (Sulamith), 98
Our Bodies, Our Selves (Boston), 243
"Our St. Louis Letter" (D'Arwin), 60, 98
Owen, Robert, 49

Pale of Settlement, 109–10, 154
Palestine:
  and Balfour Declaration, 156
  British closing immigration to, 187, 212
  children and adolescents sent to, 207
  and Jewish homeland, *see* Israel
  self-determination for, 253
  women moving to, 191–92
  Women Worker's Council, 191
  and World War I, 107, 155
  Yishuv (Jewish community) in, 149–50, 188–92, 213
  and Zionism, 95–96, 98–100, 101
Palestine Liberation Organization (PLO), 253
Paley, Grace, 223, 224
Park Ridge School for Girls, 87–88
Passover:
  changes in observance of, 67, 118
  conception during, 74
  dietary laws for, 19, 69
  seder table for, 70
  traditions of, 160, 261
Peixotto, Simha, 77
Pember, Phoebe, 43, 45, 52, 179
Pene, Sarah, 171–72
pension law, 52
Perkins, Frances, 201
Pesotta, Rose, 175, 196
Phagan, Mary, 200
Pharaoh, Israelites persecuted by, 95–96
Philadelphia:
  American Sunday School Union in, 34, 44
  British occupation of, (1777), 24, 26
  charitable organizations in, 32–35, 47
  Congregation Keneseth Israel, 116
  Female Hebrew Benevolent Society, 33
  garment industry in, 119, 139, 143
  Jewish community in, 16, 112

Jewish Maternity Association in, 63
kosher meat boycott in, 145
mikveh in, 16
Mikveh Israel congregation in, 34
orphanages in, 33, 34–35
poor children peddling matches in, 34
social services in, 36, 46
strike in, 139
Phillips, Ellen, 77
Phillips, Eugenia Levy, 43, 52
Phillips, Rachel (Levy), 14
Phillips, Rebecca Machado, 14, 15, 18, 21, 32
Picon, Molly, *I Give You My Life,* 169
Pines, Rose (Cohen), 111, 112, 120, 126, 129, 158, 165, 183–84, 195–96
Pinto, Rachel, 18–19, 25
Pinzer, Maimie, 124, 125, 126
Pioneers (literary/culture club), 59, 87
Pioneer Women (today Naamat U.S.A.), 191, 209, 215
Planned Parenthood, 152
Poland:
    antisemitism in, 199
    German invasion of, 207, 212
    immigrants from, 56, 109, 212
    immigration quotas, 158
    Warsaw Ghetto Uprising, 215
    and World War I, 112
polio vaccine, 167
Pool, Tamar de Sola, 213
Popular Front, 197
Portman, Natalie, 253–54
Portugal, Jews driven from, 4
poverty, 33–35
    and charity, 32, 33, 82
    and health care, 102–3
    and labor movement, 134
    and left-wing politics, 134
    and school, 128–29
    in urban tenements, 115–16
    war on, 91
    welfare system, 52
    women in straightened circumstances, 18, 32, 33, 72, 81–82
Povich, Lynn, 239, 246
Presidential Commission on the Status of Women, 234, 235
Pressler, Sylvia, 239
Pressman, Sonia, 235, 237
Priesand, Sally, 247
Prince of the House of David, The (Ingraham), 44
Progressive Era (1890–1920), 101–7, 143

Promised Land, The (Antin), 113
Protestant confirmation rites, 38–39
Protestant Sunday School, 34
Psalm 78, 12
Psychology of Women, The (Deutsch), 206
public housing, 199
Public Press Congress, Women's Auxiliary, 60

Quaker women:
    conversion to Judaism, 41
    never wed, 36

rabbis:
    on children required by Jewish law, 256
    and confirmation, 39
    first ordained in U.S., 37
    gay or lesbian, 257
    lay ministers, 37
    on marriage as duty, 77
    men only as, 183, 185
    new rituals written by, 248
    on radio programs, 169
    wives of, 65
    women as, 63, 82–83, 94, 181, 235, 245, 246–48, 250, 254, 255, 260, 261
Rabin, Leah, 251
radio broadcasts, 168–70
Raphall, Morris, 40
rationalism, 50
Razovsky, Cecilia, 204, 206
Reconstructionist movement, 247
Red Cross, 209
Red Scare (1917–20), 196
Redstockings, 223
Red Tent, The (Diamant), 249
Reformed Society of Israelites, Charleston, 30, 37
Reform Judaism:
    and changing traditions, 63, 66–67, 70, 181, 183, 246
    formation, 17–18, 30, 37–38, 58
    and immigration, 30
    and Israel, 252
    and social reform, 83
    and Sonneschein, 59–60, 63
    and woman suffrage, 148
    and women's roles, 60, 83, 93–94, 182–83, 235, 245–47
    and Zionism, 99–100
religion:
    atheism, 50
    bibles, 34, 40, 43

religion (*continued*)
  changes in, 30, 36–40, 50, 63, 66–68, 246
  Christian women's organizations, 88–89
  confirmation rites, 38–39, 41, 63
  conversions, 40, 41, 48, 78
  different degrees of observance in,
    66–67
  in eighteenth century, 11, 15, 17–21
  as focus of women's lives, 36
  in the home, 11
  interaction with Christians, 20–21
  intermarriage, 22–23, 66, 78–80, 171–73,
    225
  Jewishness defined by, 86
  Judaism, *see* Judaism
  ladies' auxiliaries, 92–94
  lay ministers, 37
  minyan required for prayer, 11, 40, 183,
    245, 246
  missionary societies, 88
  modernization in, 36–40
  New Testament, 67
  in nineteenth century, 36–40, 49–50
  in public schools, 65
  rabbis, *see* rabbis
  rationalism, 50
  rhythms and cycles of, 17
  Second Great Awakening, 36
  separation of church and state, 37
  in seventeenth century, 10
  Sh'ma (central prayer), 4
  Sunday schools, 34, 67
  in wartime, 211–12
  women as agents of change in, 21–22,
    49–50
  women's ordination, 94, 98, 185, 245
  women's roles in, 18, 27–28, 36, 38–41,
    60, 63, 66–67, 83, 92–94, 181–86, 245
rent strikes, 146–47, 194, 198, 199
Response, 246
Rice, Abraham, 37
Richman, Julia, 76, 104, 107, 126
Richmond, Civil War in, 45, 51
Roberts, Julia, 249
Rod of Chastisement, The, 111
Rogers, Ginger, 170
Roosevelt, Edith, 75
Roosevelt, Eleanor, 176, 207
Roosevelt, Franklin Delano, 121, 169, 187,
  196, 200–201, 213, 214
Roosevelt, Theodore, 147
Rose, Ernestine Potowski, 49–51, 148
Rose, Sharon, 253

Rose, William, 49
Rosenberg, Anna, 176
Rosenberg, Ethel Greenglass, 217, 227–28
Rosenberg, Julius, 227–28
Rosenfeld, Morris, 142
Rosenfeld sisters, typewriting business, 62
Rosenthal, Ida, 178
Rosh Hashanah, 67
Rosie the Riveter, 209
Rubenstein, Selma, 172, 173
Rubinstein, Helena (Chaja), 172, 178
Rush, Dr. Benjamin, 14, 21
Russia:
  between 1922 and 1991, *see* Soviet Union
  antisemitism in, 110, 154, 258–59
  Bolsheviks in, 197
  conscription in, 154, 155
  immigration quotas, 158
  Jewish immigrants from, 55–56, 78, 90,
    97–98, 101, 109–10, 113–14, 153–54,
    258–59
  Jewish life in, 111
  Pale of Settlement in, 109–10, 154
  pogroms in, 96, 110, 153, 154, 242
  revolution in, 153
  and World War I, 107, 112, 153–54
Rutgers University, 202, 241

Sabbath:
  candles for, 11, 115, 117, 120, 160, 276n37
  sermons in English, 37
  Sisterhood Sabbath, 94
  special foods for, 69
  traditions of, 30, 40, 67, 69, 73, 117, 118,
    120, 261, 275–76n37
  work ceased for, 17, 19
  working on, 131–32
Sachs, Jules, 208
Sachs, Sadie, 151
Sadat, Jihan, 251
St. James Episcopal Church, Wilmington,
  North Carolina, 40
St. Louis:
  Congregation Shaare Emeth in, 59
  social season in, 71
  Sonneschein family in, 59–61
  World's Fair Board of Lady Managers, 61
Salome of the Tenements (Yezierska), 195
Salomon, Haym, 14
Salzburger family, 20
Salzburg Lutherans, 44
Salzman, Marilyn (Webb), 240, 243
Sampter, Jessie, 192

Samuel, Judah, 10–11
Samuel, Rachel Hendricks, 10–11
Samuel, Rebecca, 19
Sandberg, Sheryl, 259
Sanger, Margaret Higgins, 150, 151
   What Every Girl Should Know, 152
Sarah (biblical matriarch), 69
Sarsour, Linda, 255–56
Savannah:
   British occupation of (1778), 24, 25
   Jewish children killed in, 26
   Salzburg Lutherans in, 44
Schaar, Sophie (Szold), 57
Scheier, Mildred, 212
Schiff, Jacob, 103
Schneiderman, Rose, 121, 140, 142, 143,
   145, 149, 154, 176, 228
Schreiber, Regina, 251
Schulman, Eleanor Hatkin, 172, 218, 220,
   222
Schulman, Lenny, 172
Schweitzer, Rebecca, 177
Schwesterbund (sisterhood), 93
Schwimmer, Rosika, 154
scientific charity movement, 89–92
Seaver, Horace, 50–51
Second Great Awakening, 36
Second National Woman's Rights Conven-
   tion (1851), 49
Second World Zionist Congress (1898), 99
Seixas, Gershom Mendes, 37
Seixas, Isaac Mendes, 4
Seixas, Jochebed, 12
Seixas, Rachel Levy, 4, 12
Seixas, Zipporah Levy, 13, 14
Seligman, Joseph and Babet, 96
Selma, ladies' auxiliary in, 92
Seltzer, Minnie, 127, 128–29
Seneca Falls, New York, Woman's Rights
   movement in (1848), 49, 149, 185
Sephardic Judaism, 10, 56
Settlement Cook Book (Milwaukee Settle-
   ment), 92
settlement houses, 87, 90–92, 102–3, 115,
   154
sexism, 175
Sexual Behavior in the Human Female
   (Kinsey), 228–29
sexual harassment, 132–33, 178–79, 239, 254
Shavuot:
   confirmation, 39
   Jewish dishes for, 19
She, 201–2

Shearith Israel, New York, 15, 18, 20,
   21–22, 27–28, 33
Sheftall, Benjamin, 20–21, 25, 44
Sheftall, Frances, 17, 25–26
Sheftall, Perla, 20–21, 25, 44
sheitel, xi, 112–13
Sheraton, Mimi Solomon, 218, 220, 221, 222
Ship Island prison, 43
Shire, Emily, 255, 256
Shirelles, 217, 222
Shirtwaist Makers Union, 142
Sh'ma (central prayer), 34
Shulman, Alix Kates, 240, 242
Simon, Abram, 93
Simon, Carrie Obendorfer, 92–94, 250
Simon, Kate (Kaila Grobsmith), 117, 124,
   126–27, 128, 147, 151, 167, 170, 174,
   175, 179
Sinclair, Jo, *Wasteland,* 228
Singer, Bathsheba, 110–11
Singer, Isaac Bashevis, 248
Singer, Israel Joshua, 110
Sioux City, Jewish immigrants in, 112
Sisterhoods of Personal Service, 89–92,
   101
Sklare, Marshall, 256
Slanger, Frances, 211
Slaton, John, 200
slaves:
   abolition of slavery, 41, 49, 50, 51
   and Fourteenth Amendment, 51
   ownership of, 12, 17, 41, 42, 51
   white slavery, 84, 101
Smith, Al, 104
socialism, 134, 135–36, 161, 196
   and Zionism, 190–91
Socialist Party, 137, 149, 155
social reform, 49, 101–7
social services, 36, 103
social welfare system, 52, 81, 92, 99, 100
Society for the Colonisation and Improvement of Eastern European Jews, 96
Solomon, Clara, 42, 45–46, 52
Solomon, Hannah Greenebaum, 71–72, 74,
   78, 86
   and Jewish Women's Congress, 82–83
   and National Council of Jewish Women,
   80, 83, 85
   public service activities of, 61, 80–81,
   87–88, 107
   and tradition, 67, 68, 72
   on women's suffrage, 148
Solomon ibn Gabirol, 6

Solomon, Miriam, 218
Sonneschein, Rosa Fassel, 57, 59–64, 67, 71,
    81, 82, 91, 98, 122
  and *American Jewess,* 61–64, 76–77, 80,
    87, 88
  on Jewish definition, 86, 95
  and Pioneers, 59, 87
  and women's equality, 60, 63, 246
  and Zionism, 96
Sonneschein, Solomon Hirsch, 57, 66
Soviet Union:
  before 1922 and after 1991, *see* Russia
  and Cold War, 218, 234
  and Germany, 198
  Jewish immigrants from, 258–60
  Jews in, 244, 259–60
Spain, Jews driven from, 4, 10, 109
Spiegel, Caroline Hamlin, 41, 47–48, 52,
    68, 72, 78
Spiegel, Marcus, 41, 47–48, 68, 78
Spinoza, Baruch (Benedict de), 6
Stalin, Joseph, 258–59
Stanton, Elizabeth Cady, 87
Statue of Liberty, 3, 111
Stein, Mrs. Aaron, 146–47
Steinberg, Pauline, 177
Steinem, Gloria, 224, 251
Still, Margaret, 22
stock market crash (1929), 192–96
Stokes, Rose Pastor, 139, 197
Story, Alfred T., *Woman in the Talmud,* 77
Strauss, Roberta, 232
Streisand, Barbra, 248–49
Stuyvesant, Peter, 44
Sukkot:
  etrog (citron) used during, 12
  settlement house activities, 91
Sulamith (pen name), 98
Sunday, as day of rest, 69, 83
synagogue:
  changes in, 36–40, 66
  disputes in, 21–22, 27
  in eighteenth century, 11, 15, 17–19
  and feminists, 243–49
  gay and lesbian, 257
  genders separated in congregation, 18,
    21, 27–28, 36, 63, 182, 183, 233, 245, 255
  gifts to, 18–19
  ladies' auxiliaries, 92–94
  ladies' temple societies, 93–94
  mixed seating in, 38, 181–82
  music in, 30, 38, 93
  in nineteenth century, 36–40, 56

  parnassim in, 18, 19, 22
  prayer shawls in, 246, 255, 261
  rabbis in, *see* rabbis
  sermons in English, 37
  shammash position in, 27–28
  sisterhoods, 89–92, 94, 101–2, 105, 182,
    230, 235–36
  and Temple, 66–67
  in twentieth century, 182–83
  women's place in, 150, 183, 245–49, 254,
    255
Szold, Benjamin, 57, 67
Szold, Henrietta, 36, 65, 70, 71, 76, 127,
    128, 247
  and Hadassah, 97, 99–100, 185, 189, 192,
    207, 213
  move to Jerusalem, 99, 191, 192
  and women's suffrage, 149
  and Zionism, 98–100, 188
Szold, Sophie Schaar, 57, 65, 68

Taft, Helen, 139
Taft, William Howard, 127, 139
Talmud Torah (school), 183–84
tango teas, 103–4
television, 169, 170, 218, 222
Temple Emanu-El, New York, 91, 92, 99,
    101
thalidomide, 223
Tipat Halav (Drop of Milk) pasteurized
    milk distribution program, 189
Torah scroll, 11, 18, 39, 49, 183, 246, 255
totalitarianism, 203
Tourover, Denise, 213
Triangle Waist Company, 137, 138, 140–43,
    149
Trump, Donald, 255, 256
tuberculosis, 119
Tucker, Sophie "The Last of the Red Hot
    Mamas," 170

unionization:
  and Communist Party, 174
  in garment industry, 103, 134, 139–40,
    143–44, 145, 173, 174, 234
  immigrant Jews and, 134–36, 143–44
  and industrial feminism, 137, 140
  men in control of, 174–75, 235
  of teachers, 181
  and women's movement, 139–40
Union of Orthodox Jewish Congregations
    of America, 94
Unitarianism, 66, 172

United Garment Workers union, 144
United Hebrew Charities, 121
United Hebrew Trades, 134
United Nations:
    antisemitic activities in, 251
    founding of, 231
    International Women's Decade, 250–51
United Order of True Sisters Jochannah
    Lodge, 82, 89
United States:
    antisemitism in, 96
    finding jobs in, 205–6
    immigration quotas in, 112, 156, 158,
        187, 212
    internal migration in, 159–61
    obstacles to immigration to, 204–5
    populism in, 193
    segregation in, 211
    ships' tickets for, 111–12, 119
    and World War I, 107
    Zionism in, 97–101
Uprising of the Twenty Thousand (1909),
    137, 143, 198
urbanization, 101, 103
U.S. Armed Forces, 155, 210
U.S. Industrial Commission, 136
U.S. Sanitary Commission, 46–47
U.S. Supreme Court, 64, 150, 239, 241, 243

"Vacation House, The" (Yezierska), 90
Victoria, queen of England, 64–65
Vietnam War, 240
vocational training, 87, 103, 166–67, 190
    civil service exams, 176
    commercial classes, 175–76
    industrial schools, 90, 127
Vogue, 178
Volunteer Corps of Friendly Visitors, 89
Volvovsky, Kira, 259
voting rights:
    and Fourteenth Amendment, 51
    and Nineteenth Amendment, 149–50, 157
    and political activity, 186
    of women, 50, 85, 87, 105, 106, 147–50

Wage Earners' League for Woman Suf-
    frage, 148–49
Wald, Julia (Barry), 79, 80
Wald, Lillian, 76, 77, 79, 102–3, 107, 128,
    154, 179, 196
Warburg, Gisela, 213
Ward's Island, New York, 55, 56, 108, 109,
    273n1

War of 1812, 4
Washington:
    Adas Israel congregation in, 182
    government workers in, 176
    Hebrew Congregation in, 92
    Hebrew Ladies' Auxiliary in, 93
Washington, George, 32
Washington, Martha, 89
Wasserstein, Wendy, 262
Wasteland (Sinclair), 228
weddings, *see* marriage
Weinberger, Ingeborg Cohn, 205, 206
Weinstein, Mollie, 208, 211, 212
Weis, Judith, 239
weiss, ruth, 229
welfare system, 52, 89
What Every Girl Should Know (Sanger),
    152
*What Every Woman Should Know About
    Citizenship* (NCJW), 149
white slavery, 84, 101, 112, 124
Who's Who in American Jewry, 176–77
*Why and How the Poor Should Not Have
    Many Children* (Goldman), 152
Wilburn, Cora, *Cosella Wayne*, 72
Willard, Frances E., 62, 88
Wilson, Woodrow, 107, 148
Winfrey, Oprah, 249
Wise, Isaac Mayer, 37, 38, 39, 61, 79, 80
Wise, Louise Waterman, 204
Wise, Stephen S., 204
Wolf, Emma, *Other Things Being Equal*,
    79
Wolfson, Theresa, 175
Woman in the Talmud (Story), 77
Woman's Christian Temperance Union,
    62, 88
Woman's Journal, 77
Woman's Loyal National League, 49
Woman Suffrage Party of New York, 147
Woman Voter, The, 147
women:
    abandoned, 33, 35, 102, 122, 123, 124
    and abortion, 150–51, 163, 222, 223–25,
        239, 243
    in abusive relationships, 88
    activism of, 31–35, 47, 50–51, 62, 82–83,
        87–99, 101–7, 137–40, 142–47, 175, 181,
        186–92, 198–99, 230–33, 236–49
    and American Revolution, 24–26
    aspirations of, 6, 66
    and birth control, *see* birth control
    "bra-burners," 242

women (*continued*)
business activities of, 16–17, 27, 52, 61, 62, 64, 72, 162, 173–81, 206, 234
charitable activities of, 65, 68, 81–82, 89–94
and citizenship, 84–85
city life of, 76
civil rights of, 49, 50–51, 74, 88, 101, 105–6, 139, 149, 185, 231
in Civil War, 41–47, 76
clothing of, *see* clothing
consciousness-raising by, 239, 250
consumer protests, 145–47, 199
and domestic violence, 239, 251, 261
and duty, 77
education of, 29, 33, 76, 91, 97, 101, 102, 104–5, 110, 126–29, 136, 174–75, 184, 190, 195, 220–21, 256, 257
equality sought by, 62–63, 235–40, 245–46
fallen, 87
feminists, 6, 107, 137, 140, 158, 191, 233–56
and gender differences, 31
handling finances, 117–18
having it all, 181
as heads of household, 17, 25–26, 47–48, 82
and health care, 157–58, 187, 189, 248, 249, 261
in history, xii, 5–6
home and family as focus of, *see* homemaking
international problems facing, 250–51
international women's movement, 107
Jewish, *see* American Jewesses; Eastern European Jewish women in America; Jewish women
and labor-saving devices, 81
leadership roles of, 63, 82–83, 85, 86, 87, 94, 134, 221, 243
legacy of, 35
leisure activities of, 168–70
lesbians, 228–29, 257, 261
letters written by, 13, 29–31, 51–52
life expectancy of, 81, 233
literary societies, 59, 97, 99
living on their own, 230
and marriage, *see* marriage
men enabled by, 66, 206, 236
modern age for, 157–58
mothers' pensions, 102
music written by, 30
never married, 36
new paths open for, 28–29, 31–33, 34, 35, 36–40, 63, 76, 81, 85, 86–89

in nineteenth century, 31–35, 49–51, 55–108
nonsectarian associations, 89
nurses, 45, 76, 102, 179, 188–89, 211
nursing babies, 15
outliving men, 16–17
paid employment of, 43, 132
personal fulfillment sought by, 62
and politics, 186–92, 196–99, 203, 230–33, 261
and poverty, 18, 32, 33, 72, 81–82
property rights of, 11, 17, 32, 49–50
and prostitution, 42, 84, 87, 88, 124–26, 135
in public service, 81, 83, 87–89
public speakers, 134–35
and rape, 239, 241–42, 248
receiving visitors at home, 71
and religion, *see* religion
reproductive rights of, 248
running for public office, 261
servants and employees of, 65, 68, 69
sexual abuse of, 124–26, 261
sexual double standard for, 222–23, 224
sexual harassment of, 132–33, 178–79, 239, 254
and sexuality, 162, 228–29
and *sheitel* (wig), xi, 112–13, 257
shopping, 164–65
sisterhoods, 89–94, 101–2, 105, 235–36
social activities of, 59, 67, 68–72, 133, 186
stereotypes of, 79
suffragists, 50, 62, 76, 77, 85, 87, 105, 106, 139, 147–50, 154, 157
in sweatshops, 105–6, 114, 115
taking in boarders, 120–21, 195
taking in washing, 116
as teachers, 28–29, 35, 97, 167, 179–81
traditional roles of, 12, 31, 35, 64, 69, 86, 116, 235
unemployment of, 193, 195
unmarried, 76–77, 196
unwed mothers, 103–4
virginity of, 222
volunteer activities of, 168
wealth of, 64, 72
wet nurses, 15
in white slavery, 84, 101, 112, 124
widowed, 17, 18, 33, 52, 63, 76, 82, 102, 116
women's magazines, 61–64
at work, 43, 62–63, 72, 101, 106, 114, 119–20, 127, 129–47, 162, 173–81, 195, 209–10, 225
working-class, at dance halls, 103–4, 125
and World War I, 107, 154, 155–56, 173, 203

and World War II, 207–15
as writers, 29–31, 52, 59–61, 71, 72, 76–77, 98
Women of Reform Judaism, 94; *see also* National Federation of Temple Sisterhoods
Women's Army Corps, 178, 210–11
women's club movement, 87–89
Women's Friends of Soviet Russia, 197
Women's History Month, 235, 243
Women's International League for Peace and Freedom, 203
Women's League for Conservative Judaism, 94
women's liberation movement, 107, 237–43, 250–51, 255–56
Women's March (2017), 256
Women's Strike for Equality, 237–38
Women's Trade Union League, 138, 139, 140, 154
Women Strike for Peace, 233, 240
Women's Zionist Organization of America (Hadassah), 97, 99
working conditions:
  antisemitism, 176, 180, 202, 209–10
  closed shop, 139–40
  in the Depression, 193–95
  discrimination, 187, 234, 235, 237–38, 239, 241
  glass ceiling, 176, 234, 254
  home businesses, 177, 191
  improving, 101, 103, 105–6, 140
  jobs opening for women, 238–39
  labor movement, 133–36
  minimum wage, 106, 136
  and strikes, 133–40, 143–45, 174, 234
  sweatshops, 105–6, 114, 115
  and Triangle fire, 141–42, 143
  unequal pay, 138
  worker efficiency, 130
Workingwomen's Society (Arbeterin Fareyn), 135
Workmen's Circle (Arbeter Ring), 134–35, 148, 149
Works Progress Administration, 195
World of Our Fathers (Howe), 236
World's Fair (St. Louis) Board of Lady Managers, 61
World War I, 97, 100, 125–26, 153–56, 166
  Allies vs. Central Powers in, 107, 153
  barbarism in, 153, 203
  as Great War, 107–8, 112
  Jews uprooted in, 153

and rent strikes, 146–47
and rising food prices, 146
women's march for peace in, 154, 203
women's wartime activities, 107, 154–56, 173
World War II, 207–15
  atomic bombs dropped in, 209
  end of, 218, 219
  Holocaust in, 188, 207, 212
  isolationists in, 201
  Pearl Harbor, 207
  postwar roles for women, 214–15, 217–21
  Victory Gardens in, 209
  war bonds, 209
  women in military, 210–12
World Zionist Congress, 190
World Zionist Organization, 100

Yentl (movie), 248–49
Yes, I Keep Kosher (Orthodox Women's Branch), 94
Yezierska, Anzia, 90, 121, 195
Yiddish, 56, 84, 100, 112, 126, 133, 134, 135, 138, 152, 268n12
Yiddish films, 170
Yiddish prayers, *techines* (books of), 40
Yiddish press, 155
Yiddish radio programs, 169
Yidish Froyen Program (Jewish Women's Program), 169
Yom Kippur, 22, 63, 67, 212
Young Jew, The (American Sunday School Union), 44
Young Men's Hebrew Associations, 71
Young Women's Christian Association, 88
Young Women's Hebrew Association, 89
Youth Aliyah, 190, 207, 213

Zametkin, Adella Kean, 135, 149, 232
Ziegfeld Follies, 170
Zionism, 89, 118, 156, 197, 229, 261
  and antisemitism, 95–96, 251–52
  divided opinions about, 96, 195, 252
  and feminists, 255
  and Hadassah, 86, 97, 99, 100–101, 148, 188–92, 230
  post-World War II, 215
  purpose of, 95, 97
  and socialism, 190–91
  and Szold, 98–100, 188
"Zionism as racism," 251
Zionist Organization of America, 188, 189, 190